토익 급상승

퍼펙트 600제

제 ❶ 라운드 · 문제집

新 이지투 토익 급상승 퍼펙트 600제 제❶라운드

저 자 오해원, 박은주, 최석원 외 3인
발행인 고본화
발 행 반석출판사
2016년 6월 15일 초판 1쇄 인쇄
2016년 6월 20일 초판 1쇄 발행
홈페이지 www.bansok.co.kr
이메일 bansok@bansok.co.kr
블로그 blog.naver.com/bansokbooks

157-779 서울시 강서구 양천로 583번지 B동 904호
(서울시 강서구 염창동 240-21번지 우림블루나인 비즈니스센터 B동 904호)
대표전화 02) 2093-3399 **팩 스** 02) 2093-3393
출 판 부 02) 2093-3395 **영업부** 02) 2093-3396
등록번호 제315-2008-000033호

ISBN 978-89-7172-804-8 (13740)

■ 교재 관련 문의: bansok@bansok.co.kr을 이용해 주시기 바랍니다.
■ 이 책에 게재된 내용의 일부 또는 전체를 무단으로 복제 및 발췌하는 것을 금합니다.
■ 파본 및 잘못된 제품은 구입처에서 교환해 드립니다.

퍼펙트 600제

제**1**라운드 · 문제집

Bansok

머리말

잠을 자는 이는 꿈을 꾸고, 깨어 있는 이는 꿈을 이룬다

먼저 이 책을 구입한 여러분께 무한한 감사를 드립니다. 시험영어인 토익에 대한 개인적인 생각과 저만이 만들어낸 여러 토익 공식들을 담은 이 한 권의 책을 소개해드립니다. 반석출판사의 토익 야심작 '토익 급상승' 시리즈 중 2016년 5월부터 새롭게 시작되는 新토익시험의 출제경향에 맞춘 〈新 이지투 토익 급상승 퍼펙트 600제 제❶라운드〉의 저자로 여러분을 만나 뵙게 되어 영광입니다. 더불어 이 책이 완벽한 新토익시험 대비 수험서로써 여러분의 토익 고득점을 향한 여정을 함께할 최선의 선택이 될 것임을 자신하기 때문에 저자로서의 자부심을 느껴봅니다.

학원 현장에서 대구 최다·최고의 실전반 Oz Toeic 수강생들을 만나오면서, 혹은 온라인상의 토익 카페들에서 운영자로 활동하며 토익 수험생의 궁금점 및 애로사항을 들어오면서, 대부분의 학생들이 공통적으로 어려워하는 부분들을 찾아내려 노력하였고 그에 대한 결실을 이렇게 한 권의 책에 담아냈습니다. 한 문제 한 문제마다 저자진의 혼(魂)을 실어 3세트의 알찬 新토익 모의고사를 탄생시켰습니다.

오늘 하루도 목표하는 바를 달성하기 위해 한 걸음 한 걸음 더디지만 성실하게 나아가는 여러분께 격려의 박수를 보내드리며, 하나의 고지를 점령하기까지 지금의 의지를 잊지 마시기 바랍니다.

본 교재를 베개 삼아 꿈을 꾸는 수단으로 만들지, 목표한 토익 점수의 꿈을 전해주는 메신저로 만들지, 그 선택은 여러분의 몫으로 돌리겠습니다.

감사합니다.

저자 대표 오해원 드림

목차

이 책의 특징 및 활용 방법

1. 5월 29일부터 시행되는 新토익, 무엇이 어떻게 달라지는지 완벽 분석!

2. 新토익 예상 출제경향과 난이도를 반영한 LC + RC 실전문제 3회분(600제) 제공!

3. 전체 문제에 대한 해석과 꼼꼼한 해설 제공으로 새로운 유형은 물론 기존 유형의 문제까지 완전 정복!

4. 실제 토익시험과 똑같은 방식으로 미국, 영국, 캐나다, 호주 성우들이 녹음한 mp3 (CD)와 스크립트 제공 + 복습용 문제별 mp3 홈페이지(http://bansok.co.kr) 제공!

5. RC 주요 문제에 대한 음성강의 제공!

新토익이 도입되면서 많은 수험생들이 기존의 토익에 비해 무엇이 얼마나 바뀔지, 또 얼마나 어려워질지, 新토익을 어떻게 준비해야 할지 등에 대해 걱정하고 있습니다. 〈新 이지투 토익 급상승 퍼펙트 600제 제❶라운드〉는 이러한 고민을 날려줄 것입니다. 新토익 출제경향을 예측하고 면밀히 분석한 이 책은 新토익 실전문제 3회분(LC + RC)을 제공합니다. 또한 전체 문제에 대한 꼼꼼한 해석과 해설로 수험생들의 新토익에 대한 실전 적응력을 높여줄 것입니다. 실제 토익과 똑같이 미국, 영국, 캐나다, 호주 성우들이 녹음한 문제 음원과 RC 주요 문제에 대한 음성강의를 CD로 제공합니다. 복습하기에 용이하도록 문제별로 분할된 음원은 반석출판사 홈페이지(http://bansok.co.kr)에서 무료로 다운받을 수 있습니다.

*음성 해설강의(차형석 선생님): 한국외국어대학교를 졸업하고 미국 필라델피아 Drexel LeBow MBA스쿨에서 경영학을 공부했습니다. 현재는 '영어 전도사'로서 살아 있는 영어를 강의(토익, 텝스, 비즈니스영어)하며 번역활동을 겸하고 있습니다.(instagram.com/heungsok)

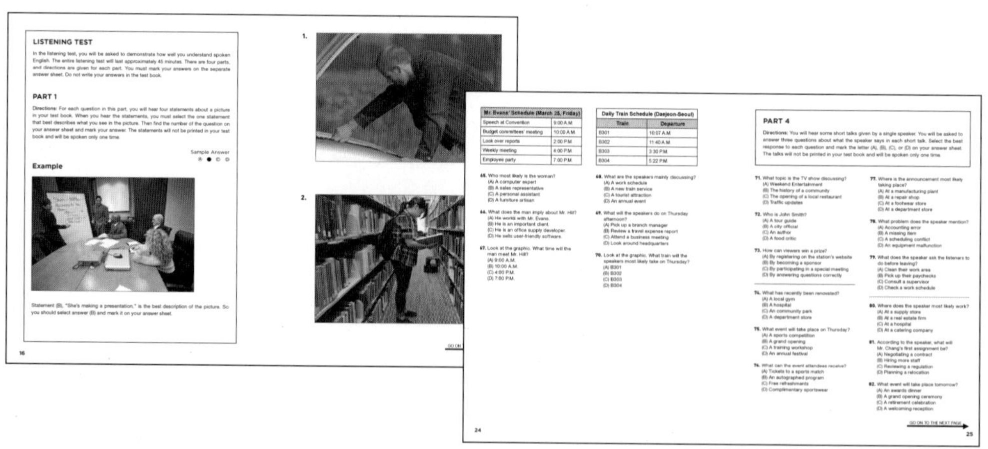

❯ 실제 고사장과 비슷한 환경에서 제한시간 LC 45분 / RC 75분 내에 실전문제를 풀어보세요.

저자 소개

오해원 (ohtoeic@daum.net) 이지투어학원 중앙로캠퍼스

2002년 토익강의에 첫 발을 내딛은 오해원 선생님은 그만의 독특한 토익강의 기법과 스파르타식 Oz 스터디 그룹의 운영을 통해 스타강사로 발돋움하였고 21권의 토익수험서를 출간하였습니다. 온라인 서점인 알라딘이 선정한 전국 영어 명강사 12인에 선발되기도 하였습니다. YBM어학원 대구 동성로센터에서 토익강의를 하였으며, 현재 대구 이지투어학원 1, 2호점을 운영하고 있고 경북 구미에 3호점을 개원할 예정입니다.

박은주 (siwon80@daum.net) 경운대학교_기출응용문제 출제 담당

고려대학교 교육대학원에서 영어교육을 전공하였습니다. YBM어학원 신촌센터, 연세대에서 토익강의를 하였습니다. 현재 경운대학교에서 토익강의를 진행하면서 토익교육 전문회사인 TOEICCOMPANY 대표를 역임하고 있습니다. 2005년부터 12년 연속 990점 만점을 받아오고 있습니다.

최석원 (choosemeb@nate.com) 이지투어학원 중앙로캠퍼스_기출응용문제 출제 담당

이지투어학원 2호점인 중앙로캠퍼스에서 토익 대표강사로 활동하고 있습니다. 알기 쉽고 흥미를 유발시키는 기초토익강좌와 심도 있는 실전토익강좌를 진행하고 있습니다. 저서로 반석출판사의 〈토익 급상승 1560제 2라운드〉, 〈토익 급상승 1560제 3라운드〉가 있습니다.

김철홍 (eager74@daum.net) YBM어학원 동성로센터_기출응용문제 분석 담당

금오공대 외국어교육원에서 토익강의를 하였으며 교육원 역대 최다 수강생을 기록하였습니다. 대구 경북 소재 다수의 대학에서 토익강의를 하였고, 현재 YBM어학원 대구 동성로센터에서 매출 2위를 달리고 있는 스타강사입니다.

Jamie 이지투어학원 동성로캠퍼스_기출응용문제 교정 담당

이지투어학원 1호점인 동성로캠퍼스에서 '독종토익'의 LC 대표강사로 활동하고 있습니다. 본 교재의 LC파트 문제 및 해석 검정작업을 수행하였고, 최종 원고에 대한 철저한 교정작업을 수행하였습니다. 저서로 반석출판사의 〈토익 급상승 1560제 3라운드〉가 있습니다.

심미현 이지투어학원 동성로캠퍼스_기출응용문제 교정 담당

이지투어학원 1호점인 동성로캠퍼스에서 '독종토익'의 RC 대표강사로 활동하고 있습니다. 본 교재의 RC파트 문제 및 해석 검정작업을 수행하였고, 수차례 기출문제의 베타테스트를 거치면서 교재의 완성도를 높이는 작업을 수행하였습니다. 저서로 반석출판사의 〈토익 급상승 1560제 3라운드〉가 있습니다.

新토익이란?

1. 기존 TOEIC vs 신 TOEIC

구성	PART	내용		기존 문항 수		새로운 문항 수	시간	배점
LC	1	사진 묘사		10문항		6문항	45분	495점
	2	짧은 질문에 대한 응답		30문항		25문항		
	3	짧은 2~3인 대화		30문항		39문항		
	4	짧은 1인 담화		30문항		30문항		
RC	5	단문 빈칸 채우기(문법/어휘)		40문항	⇒	30문항	75분	495점
	6	장문 빈칸 채우기(문법/어휘)		12문항		16문항		
	7	독해	단일지문: 지문 1개에 2~4개의 문제풀이	28문항		29문항		
			다중지문: 지문 2~3개에 5개의 문제풀이	2중지문 20문항		2중지문 10문항		
						3중지문 15문항		
				200문항		200문항	120분	990점

2016년 5월 29일부터 시행되는 新토익시험은 기존의 토익시험에 비해 기본적인 시험의 틀이 위의 표와 같이 바뀌게 되었다. 총 990점 만점에 시험을 치르는 시간은 120분으로 변화가 없지만, 파트별로 문항 수가 조절되었다. 일반적으로 평이한 파트로 분류되는 Part 1, 2, 5의 문항 수가 줄어든 반면, 난이도가 높은 Part 3, 6, 7의 문항 수가 늘어나게 되면서 시험의 난이도는 전반적으로 상승하였다.

토익시험을 출제하는 ETS에서는 동일한 난이도로 설정하였다고 하지만 문제의 난이도는 차치하고, 어려운 파트의 문항 수가 늘어난 자체만 하더라도 新토익시험의 난이도는 높아졌다고 볼 수 있다.

2. 新토익에서 크게 변한 파트

1) Part 3, 4

우선 LC Part 3에서 큰 변화가 생겼다. 2명의 대화를 듣고 3문제를 풀이하는 방식에서 2명뿐 아니라 **3명의 대화를 듣고 풀이해야 하는 문제**가 새롭게 만들어졌다. 또한 문제에 **그래프나 도표가 첨부**되어 대화를 듣는 동시에 참조자료를 보면서 풀어야 하는 문제가 2~3문제가량 추가되었다.

예 1

Daily Train Schedule (Daejeon-Seoul)

Train	Departure
B301	10:07 A.M.
B302	11:40 A.M.
B303	3:30 P.M.
B304	5:22 P.M.

68. What are the speakers mainly discussing?
(A) A work schedule
(B) A new train service
(C) A tourist attraction
(D) An annual event

69. Why does the woman say, "I promise"?
(A) She wants a quick response.
(B) She will get the goods shipped.
(C) She should explain her problem.
(D) She supports the man's stance.

70. Look at the graphic. What train will the speakers most likely take on Thursday?
(A) B301
(B) B302
(C) B303
(D) B304

69번과 같이 **짧은 구어체 문장의 올바른 의미를 찾는 문제**도 새로운 유형의 문제이며 1~2문제가량 출제된다. 70번 문제는 대화를 들으면서 **그래프를 보고 문제를 풀어야 하는 상황**이다. 2문제가 출제된다.

Part 4도 기존 시험의 틀은 유지하되 Part 3와 마찬가지로 **그래프나 도표가 첨부**되어 1인의 담화를 듣는 동시에 참조자료를 보면서 풀어야 하는 문제가 3문제 추가되었다.

2) Part 6

기존 시험의 틀은 유지하되 각 지문당 **적절한 문장 집어넣기 문제가 1문제 추가**되었다.

예 2

Geneva Networking
3030-2nd Ave. S.W.
Calgary AB T2N 5N7

Ms. Geneva Elrond
Investment Properties Company
Toronto, ON M7Y 2C5

Dear Elrond,

This is to inform you that your application for our company has finally been approved. As mentioned in the ------ description and during the interview, you will assume all duties that
139.
the retiring manager has been in charge of.

During the first 5 months of employment, you will go through the orientation session by Britny Spears, whom you ------ during your interview.
140.
Should you ------ our offer, you will start to work on September 3rd.
141.

142.

Sincerely,

Richard Aragon
Personnel director

---

139. (A) hire
(B) appointment
(C) career
(D) job

140. (A) will meet
(B) meet
(C) met
(D) will have met

141. (A) acknowledge
(B) reply
(C) accept
(D) record

142. (A) Please notify us whether you will accept our offer no later than August 31.
(B) You are cordially invited to attend the upcoming retirement party.
(C) You are advised to submit your application form by August 31.
(D) You will soon be informed of when you will be interviewed.

기존 토익시험에서는 장문의 글 하나에 문법과 어휘 문제가 총 3문제 출제되었지만, 新토익에서는 문법 및 어휘 3문제와 아울러 **문맥에 맞는 문장을 집어넣는 문제가 1문제 추가**로 출제된다. 전문을 읽으면서 글의 맥락을 파악해야 되기 때문에 시간이 많이 소요되는 고난도 문제다.

3) Part 7

지문 양식에 채팅창과 같은 **메신저 지문이 추가**되었다. 또한 3개의 지문을 읽고 5개의 질문에 답하는 문제가 총 **15문제 추가**되었다. 마지막으로 지문 흐름상 주어진 문장을 삽입할 적절한 위치를 묻는 **문장 삽입 문제가 1~2문제**가량 추가되었다.

Economic Board's Outlook

May 10 - Mexico City Economic Board has announced its latest Regional Work Forecast. The report contains details on the fastest growing industries, occupations and declining ones. —[1]— The report is released biannually, in May and October, to ensure that the information reflects the existing work market in Mexico City and the nearby areas.

—[2]— Apparently, the greatest job growth is expected for surgeons, dentists, nursing resources, and health-care providers over the following two quarters. Each of these categories is expected to grow more than 5 percent this year. Moderate growth is anticipated for almost all positions in the accommodation sector since the tourism and hospitality industry continues to grow and holiday season starts. —[3]—

For the full report, visit www.mexicicity.go.or/economic_board, where you can read projections for more than ten industries. —[4]—

168. What's discussed in the report?
(A) Increase in local salaries
(B) Workplace safety concerns
(C) Future jobs in Mexico City and the surrounding areas
(D) Changes in manufacturers' strategy

169. How often is the report published?
(A) Every quarter
(B) Every year
(C) Once a month
(D) Twice a year

170. The word "over" in paragraph 2, line 2, is closest in meaning to
(A) beyond
(B) near
(C) during
(D) above

171. In which of the positions marked [1], [2], [3] and [4] does the following sentence best belong?

"On the other hand, positions in manufacturing are expected to decline by 9 percent as domestic sales of IT items are continually decreasing."

(A) [1]
(B) [2]
(C) [3]
(D) [4]

3. 新토익에 대한 수험생의 대비 방안

대박 어려워진 新토익

1995년부터 토익시험을 거쳐온 토익강사로서 이번에 새롭게 바뀌는 新토익에 대한 총평을 해보자면 한마디로 "대박 어려워졌다"이다. RC의 경우 읽어야 할 어휘 개수만 따져보더라도 20년 전에 비해 두 배에 달한다. 즉 이전 시험에 비해 동일한 시간에 읽어야 할 분량이 현격히 늘었다는 말이다. 토익시험을 치러본 수험생이라면 토익이 얼마나 시간이 부족한 시험인지 알 수 있을 것이다. 2006년 5월에 한 차례 변화를 겪으면서 읽어야 할 분량이 대거 늘어났는데, 2016년 5월의 새로운 토익시험에서도 마찬가지 현상이 나타났다. 비단 RC뿐 아니라 LC에서도 들어야 할 분량이 훨씬 늘어났으며 문제의 길이도 늘어났다.

독해력이 고득점의 관건

이로 인하여 토익수험생이 준비해야 할 부분도 그에 비례하여 늘어났다. LC 파트건 RC 파트건 관계없이 新토익 대비책으로 가장 필요한 것은 두말할 것 없이 바로 **독해력**이다. 그것도 늘어난 분량에 맞춰 주어진 시간 내에 모든 문제를 풀이할 수 있는 속독력이 겸비된 독해력이 필요하다. LC에서도 길어진 대화 및 담화를 들으면서 동시에 그래프를 읽어내기 위해서는 독해력이 필요하다. RC Part 6에서도 장문의 글 맥락에 맞는 적절한 문장을 집어넣는 문제는 반드시 지문을 모두 읽어야 풀 수 있는 독해 문제에 해당된다. 또한 Part 7에 무려 3개의 지문을 읽고 5문제를 푸는 부분이 생기면서, 빠르면서도 정확한 정보를 캐치해낼 수 있는 독해력이 고득점의 관건이 된다. 따라서 新토익을 준비하는 수험생들은 기본적으로 독해 공부 비중을 현격히 늘려야 한다. 또한 새로운 토익시험을 치르기 전에 시중에 판매되는 新토익 유형으로 만들어진 전 파트 모의고사를 3회 이상 치러보면서 시간 안배에 대한 훈련을 무엇보다도 충실히 해야 한다.

LC: 대화의 흐름 파악

듣기의 경우 도표나 그래프를 읽으면서 풀어야 하는 문제가 새로운 유형이긴 하나 문제 자체의 난이도가 높진 않다. 계산이 필요한 문제라기보다 언급된 정보를 끼워맞추기 식으로 푸는 유형의 문제이다. 모의고사 3회 정도면 쉽게 적응 가능하다. 오히려 구어체로 표현된 부분을 적절한 문장으로 재표현해야 하는 新유형 문제가 어렵다. 단편적인 어구 몇 개로 풀 수 있는 게 아니라 대화의 흐름을 제대로 파악해서 풀어야 하는 까다로운 문제이기 때문에 이 유형에 대한 많은 연습이 필요하다.

읽기의 경우 Part 5 30문제는 12분 내로, Part 6 16문제는 10분 내로 풀 수 있어야 Part 7 54문제를 위한 53분의 풀이시간을 확보할 수 있다. 대개 토익시험장에서 오전 10시 20분에 토익시험이 시작되기 때문에 11시 17분에 Part 5 문제풀이가 끝나고 11시 27분에 Part 6가 마무리되면, 12시 20분까지 Part 7 독해문제를 풀 수 있는 무난한 시간 안배라 볼 수 있다.

그러나 앞서 언급한 新토익에 대한 한 마디 "대박 어려워졌다"에 대해 수험생이 겁먹을 필요는 없다. 내가 어려워진 만큼 남도 어려워졌음에 틀림없다. 토익시험의 성적은 상대평가시스템이다. 나 자신이 새로운 유형의 토익문제에 대한 적응을 마치고 모의고사를 통해 시간 안배 연습을 해둠으로써 모두가 어려워진 시험에서 오히려 대박 점수를 꿈꿀 수 있는 것이다.

오해원 대구 이지투어학원 토익강사

2002년부터 토익강의를 시작하여 대구 경북지역 어학원 및 대학에서 강의 중
2007년부터 2014년까지 대구 동성로 지역 어학 강의 매출 1위
新 이지투 토익 급상승 퍼펙트 600제 시리즈(반석출판사)를 포함 21권의 토익교재 저자

[점수 그래프]

LC Score

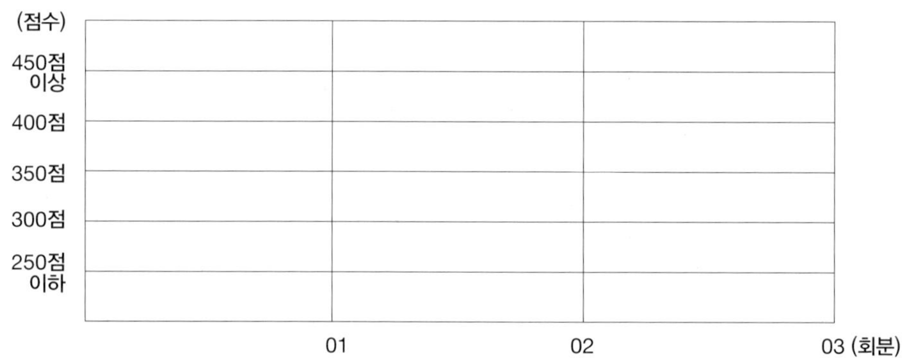

RC Score

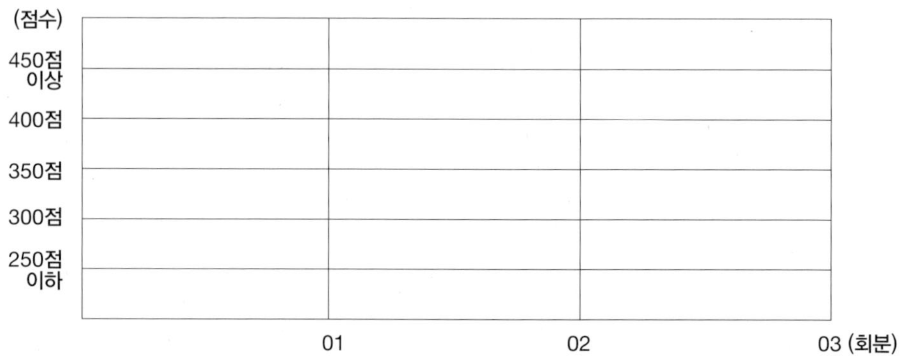

ACTUAL TEST

01

LISTENING TEST

In the listening test, you will be asked to demonstrate how well you understand spoken English. The entire listening test will last approximately 45 minutes. There are four parts, and directions are given for each part. You must mark your answers on the separate answer sheet. Do not write your answers in the test book.

PART 1

Directions: For each question in this part, you will hear four statements about a picture in your test book. When you hear the statements, you must select the one statement that best describes what you see in the picture. Then find the number of the question on your answer sheet and mark your answer. The statements will not be printed in your test book and will be spoken only one time.

Sample Answer
Ⓐ ● Ⓒ Ⓓ

Example

Statement (B), "She's making a presentation," is the best description of the picture. So you should select answer (B) and mark it on your answer sheet.

1.

2.

GO ON TO THE NEXT PAGE

3.

4.

5.

6.

GO ON TO THE NEXT PAGE

PART 2

7. Mark your answer on your answer sheet.

8. Mark your answer on your answer sheet.

9. Mark your answer on your answer sheet.

10. Mark your answer on your answer sheet.

11. Mark your answer on your answer sheet.

12. Mark your answer on your answer sheet.

13. Mark your answer on your answer sheet.

14. Mark your answer on your answer sheet.

15. Mark your answer on your answer sheet.

16. Mark your answer on your answer sheet.

17. Mark your answer on your answer sheet.

18. Mark your answer on your answer sheet.

19. Mark your answer on your answer sheet.

20. Mark your answer on your answer sheet.

21. Mark your answer on your answer sheet.

22. Mark your answer on your answer sheet.

23. Mark your answer on your answer sheet.

24. Mark your answer on your answer sheet.

25. Mark your answer on your answer sheet.

26. Mark your answer on your answer sheet.

27. Mark your answer on your answer sheet.

28. Mark your answer on your answer sheet.

29. Mark your answer on your answer sheet.

30. Mark your answer on your answer sheet.

31. Mark your answer on your answer sheet.

PART 3

Directions: You will hear some conversations between two or more people. You will be asked to answer three questions about what the speakers say in each conversation. Select the best response to each question and mark the letter (A), (B), (C), or (D) on your answer sheet. The conversations will not be printed in your test book and will be spoken only one time.

32. Where most likely are the speakers?
(A) At a bakery
(B) At a flower shop
(C) At a concert hall
(D) At a party supply store

33. Why does the man apologize?
(A) A product has sold out.
(B) A reservation wasn't correct.
(C) An order was sent to the wrong address.
(D) A bill was not accurate.

34. What does the man suggest?
(A) Contacting another shop
(B) Requesting a replacement
(C) Placing an order
(D) Cancelling an event

35. Why is the man at the woman's office?
(A) To do some cleaning
(B) To make a repair
(C) To bring a package
(D) To ask about holidays

36. Why is the woman surprised by the man's visit?
(A) She canceled a delivery of shipments.
(B) She just saw the man last week.
(C) She was expecting someone else.
(D) She didn't receive notification.

37. What does the man offer to do?
(A) Send another employee
(B) Refund an item
(C) Provide a complimentary delivery
(D) Revise an estimate

38. What does the man ask the woman about?
(A) Rescheduling a calendar
(B) Visiting a local museum
(C) Extending a reservation
(D) Placing a phone call

39. What does the woman offer to do?
(A) Remove a charge from a credit card
(B) Book a sightseeing tour
(C) Contact with a director
(D) Apply a discounted rate

40. What does the man say he plans to do?
(A) Meet a brother
(B) Register a complaint
(C) Participating in a meeting
(D) Rent a vehicle

41. Where are the speakers?
(A) At a library
(B) At a newspaper company
(C) At a publishing company
(D) At a print shop

42. What problem does the woman mention?
(A) A book is out of stock.
(B) A newspaper delivery is late.
(C) A facility is under renovation.
(D) A printer is not working.

43. What does the woman suggest the man do?
(A) Cancel a subscription
(B) Call technical support
(C) Come back later
(D) Visit another branch

GO ON TO THE NEXT PAGE

44. Why is the man calling?
(A) To obtain a report
(B) To pay an invoice
(C) To sigh up for an event
(D) To order some software

45. According to the woman, what does the man have to do?
(A) Make an appointment
(B) Complete a task online
(C) Submit a proposal
(D) Approve an expense

46. What does the woman request?
(A) Some contact information
(B) Presentation slides
(C) Details from a bill
(D) Proof of employment

47. Why is the woman calling?
(A) To get driving directions
(B) To ask about a missing item
(C) To arrange a meeting
(D) To discuss a contract

48. What does the man offer to do?
(A) Order a chair
(B) Call a client
(C) Obtain a report
(D) Scan some documents

49. What information does the woman ask for?
(A) Some sales figures
(B) A phone number
(C) A street name
(D) Some project dates

50. What is the topic of the workshop?
(A) Recruiting training expert
(B) Developing presentation skills
(C) Writing resumes
(D) Taking an annual inventory

51. What does the man find challenging?
(A) Leading small-group activities
(B) Obtaining letters of reference
(C) Learning new computer programs
(D) Interviewing for a position

52. What does the woman say will happen next week?
(A) Some jobs will be posted online.
(B) A follow-up survey will be distributed.
(C) Another workshop will be held.
(D) An instruction manual will be published.

53. What kind of event is being discussed?
(A) A company's founding anniversary
(B) A store opening
(C) An executive's promotion
(D) A laser display

54. What do the men imply about the company?
(A) The work is rewarding.
(B) It leads the laser show industry.
(C) It offers affordable benefits.
(D) All of its items are not cheap.

55. According to the woman, what is the company giving staff members?
(A) Complimentary furniture
(B) Cash refund
(C) Merchandise discounts
(D) Extra holidays

56. What aspect of a charity event are the speakers discussing?
(A) Booking a room
(B) Contacting a caterer
(C) Providing entertainment
(D) Recruiting volunteers

57. What concern does the man have?
(A) Funding is limited.
(B) Invitations have not been sent.
(C) The weather condition is bad.
(D) A meeting room is too crowded.

58. What does the man say he will do?
(A) Advertise on the website
(B) Consult with a supervisor
(C) Cancel an event
(D) Meet a decorator

59. What are the speakers talking about?
(A) A procedure for delivery
(B) Missing items
(C) A delayed order
(D) Wrong client information

60. What does the man imply about the supplies?
(A) They should be heavily discounted.
(B) They will be picked up at the warehouse.
(C) They must be repaired as soon as possible.
(D) They are necessary for his business.

61. Why does the woman say, "I promise"?
(A) She wants a quick response.
(B) She will get the goods shipped.
(C) She should explain her problem.
(D) She supports the man's stance.

62. What are the speakers talking about?
(A) Training for job applicants
(B) A marketing event
(C) The prices of cars
(D) The organization of new teams

63. What will the company do in March?
(A) Increase staff
(B) Release new products
(C) Give training to staff
(D) Reward employees

64. What does the woman imply about the interviews?
(A) They will be attended by team managers.
(B) They are conducted once a week.
(C) They will be rescheduled for next week.
(D) They will be held at a car showroom.

GO ON TO THE NEXT PAGE

Mr. Evans' Schedule (March 25, Friday)	
Speech at Convention	9:00 A.M.
Budget committees' meeting	10:00 A.M.
Look over reports	2:00 P.M.
Weekly meeting	4:00 P.M.
Employee party	7:00 P.M.

Daily Train Schedule (Daejeon-Seoul)	
Train	Departure
B301	10:07 A.M.
B302	11:40 A.M.
B303	3:30 P.M.
B304	5:22 P.M.

65. Who most likely is the woman?
(A) A computer expert
(B) A sales representative
(C) A personal assistant
(D) A furniture artisan

66. What does the man imply about Mr. Hill?
(A) He works with Mr. Evans.
(B) He is an important client.
(C) He is an office supply developer.
(D) He sells user-friendly software.

67. Look at the graphic. What time will the man meet Mr. Hill?
(A) 9:00 A.M.
(B) 10:00 A.M.
(C) 4:00 P.M.
(D) 7:00 P.M.

68. What are the speakers mainly discussing?
(A) A work schedule
(B) A new train service
(C) A tourist attraction
(D) An annual event

69. What will the speakers do on Thursday afternoon?
(A) Pick up a branch manager
(B) Review a travel expense report
(C) Attend a business meeting
(D) Look around headquarters

70. Look at the graphic. What train will the speakers most likely take on Thursday?
(A) B301
(B) B302
(C) B303
(D) B304

PART 4

Directions: You will hear some short talks given by a single speaker. You will be asked to answer three questions about what the speaker says in each short talk. Select the best response to each question and mark the letter (A), (B), (C), or (D) on your answer sheet. The talks will not be printed in your test book and will be spoken only one time.

71. What topic is the TV show discussing?
(A) Weekend Entertainment
(B) The history of a community
(C) The opening of a local restaurant
(D) Traffic updates

72. Who is John Smith?
(A) A tour guide
(B) A city official
(C) An author
(D) A food critic

73. How can viewers win a prize?
(A) By registering on the station's website
(B) By becoming a sponsor
(C) By participating in a special meeting
(D) By answering questions correctly

74. What has recently been renovated?
(A) A local gym
(B) A hospital
(C) An community park
(D) A department store

75. What event will take place on Thursday?
(A) A sports competition
(B) A grand opening
(C) A training workshop
(D) An annual festival

76. What can the event attendees receive?
(A) Tickets to a sports match
(B) An autographed program
(C) Free refreshments
(D) Complimentary sportswear

77. Where is the announcement most likely taking place?
(A) At a manufacturing plant
(B) At a repair shop
(C) At a footwear store
(D) At a department store

78. What problem does the speaker mention?
(A) Accounting error
(B) A missing item
(C) A scheduling conflict
(D) An equipment malfunction

79. What does the speaker ask the listeners to do before leaving?
(A) Clean their work area
(B) Pick up their paychecks
(C) Consult a supervisor
(D) Check a work schedule

80. Where does the speaker most likely work?
(A) At a supply store
(B) At a real estate firm
(C) At a hospital
(D) At a catering company

81. According to the speaker, what will Mr. Chang's first assignment be?
(A) Negotiating a contract
(B) Hiring more staff
(C) Reviewing a regulation
(D) Planning a relocation

82. What event will take place tomorrow?
(A) An awards dinner
(B) A grand opening ceremony
(C) A retirement celebration
(D) A welcoming reception

GO ON TO THE NEXT PAGE

83. Why is the speaker moving to Seoul?
(A) To live near her family
(B) To teach at a school
(C) To study Korean
(D) To start a real estate business

84. What does the man mean when he says, "I'm really glad about that"?
(A) He can live with his family.
(B) He found the place he was looking for.
(C) He doesn't have to move.
(D) He can advertise a property.

85. What additional information does the speaker want to know?
(A) What parking options are available
(B) Whether residents are allowed to have pets
(C) The amount of the security deposit
(D) Where the nearest supermarket is

---

86. Where is the announcement being made?
(A) At a butcher shop
(B) At a sporting goods store
(C) At a fitness center
(D) At a post office

87. What problem does the speaker mention?
(A) A pipe needs to be fixed.
(B) A shipment was sent to a wrong address.
(C) An office is not for sale.
(D) A schedule is incorrect.

88. Why are the listeners asked to visit the website?
(A) To find other branch locations
(B) To learn when a facility will reopen
(C) To sign up for a mailing list
(D) To provide a review on a service

89. What does the speaker mention about World Smith, Inc.?
(A) It has experienced problems with leadership.
(B) Its new product will be launched soon.
(C) It sells products made by Neo International.
(D) It has tried to expand overseas.

90. What does the man mean when he says, "it won't happen"?
(A) He doesn't agree with a proposal.
(B) He is reporting on a plan's failure.
(C) He doesn't support a policy.
(D) He thinks a product will be unpopular.

91. What is indicated about Neo International?
(A) It changed its product price.
(B) It opened other branches.
(C) Its CFO left the company.
(D) It received investment funds.

Category	Prize
Grand Prize	**3D TV**
Gold Prize	**Vacuum Cleaner**
Sliver Prize	**Blender**
Bronze Prize	**Two Movie tickets**

92. What is being advertised?
(A) A local workshop
(B) A sports competition
(C) An art gallery
(D) A community event

93. According to the advertisement, what can visitors do at the event?
(A) Attend a debate
(B) Sample international cuisine
(C) Watch live performers
(D) Meet a famous writer

94. Look at the graphic. How many people will receive a blender?
(A) One
(B) Three
(C) Ten
(D) Twenty

Representative	Product Line
Chris	Desktop
Green	Mobile Phone
Max	Tablet Computer
Brian	Laptop

Schedule	
Demonstration 1	9:00-9:40
Demonstration 2	9:40-10:40
Morning Break	10:40-11:00
Demonstration 3	11:00-11:50
Demonstration 4	11:50-12:10

95. Why is the speaker calling?
(A) To follow up on a business proposal
(B) To announce an ongoing renovation
(C) To request some product samples
(D) To thank a customer for reporting a problem

96. What happened on March 25?
(A) A new electronic line was launched.
(B) A computer products store was opened.
(C) A product demonstration took place.
(D) A tablet computer workshop was held.

97. Look at the graphic. Who will be talking to Ms. Yang?
(A) Chris
(B) Green
(C) Max
(D) Brian

98. Who is Selina Blond?
(A) A business owner
(B) An government official
(C) A show host
(D) A famous author

99. What will Ms. Blond give a demonstration about?
(A) Managing hotels for a long time
(B) Keeping in shape
(C) Writing a cook book
(D) Making use of healthful ingredients

100. Look at the graphic. How long will Ms. Blond's demonstration last?
(A) 20 minutes
(B) 40 minutes
(C) 50 minutes
(D) 60 minutes

GO ON TO THE NEXT PAGE

READING TEST

In the Reading test, you will read a variety of texts and answer several different types of reading comprehension questions. The entire Reading test will last 75 minutes. There are three parts, and directions are given for each part. You are encouraged to answer as many questions as possible within the time allowed.

You must mark answers on the separate answer sheet. Do not write your answer in your test book.

PART 5

Directions: A word or phrase is missing in each of the sentences below. Four answer choices are given below each sentence. Select the best answer to complete the sentence. Then mark the letter (A), (B), (C), or (D) on your answer sheet.

101. If approved by the private investors, the ------- of the Proton Appliance Facility to Birmingham will take place in May.
(A) relocated
(B) relocates
(C) relocation
(D) relocate

102. Ms. Green has served at Lemona Cecome Company ------- more than five years.
(A) for
(B) from
(C) after
(D) beside

103. Mr. Choi should look over the proposal at least two days before ------- is due to the client.
(A) its
(B) itself
(C) its own
(D) it

104. Kovoelo Construction is going to agree to ------- all the materials needed for the Washington Community's expansion project.
(A) widen
(B) begin
(C) supply
(D) ignore

105. As originally scheduled, some survey technicians ------- mapping the property lines at North Lincoln Avenue last Tuesday.
(A) will finish
(B) in finishing
(C) finishes
(D) finished

106. The university's football game was canceled ------- the unexpected rain, which left the playing fields unusable.
(A) until
(B) whenever
(C) because of
(D) just as

107. Samdong Bread has ------- agreed to donate one tray of snacks every week for the city's volunteer activity.
(A) generous
(B) generosity
(C) generously
(D) more generous

108. Skytech Telecom will be closed for a week ------- a new security system is installed.
(A) while
(B) against
(C) during
(D) that

109. If you register now, you can receive a free catalog with ------- information about Hamnar Motors cars.
(A) detail
(B) detailer
(C) detailed
(D) details

110. The organizer wants to review a ------- of last Thursday's meeting with American Bank.
(A) transaction
(B) capability
(C) requirement
(D) summary

111. In compliance with the delivery policy, Kao Corporation's beverages are packaged in glass bottles to preserve ------- flavor and nutritional content.
(A) their
(B) them
(C) theirs
(D) themselves

112. Mark Hunter, CEO of Kyunghee Aluminum Co., is ------- awaiting earnings reports from all departments.
(A) accurately
(B) comparably
(C) eagerly
(D) greatly

113. After carefully considering options, Ehdores Plastics plans to increase overall production levels by ------- its assembly-line process.
(A) updated
(B) updates
(C) updating
(D) to update

114. Chef Rangsh, who likes to receive feedback from customers, always changes the restaurant's menu throughout the year to feature ------- fruits and vegetables.
(A) internal
(B) seasonal
(C) resulting
(D) wasteful

115. According to ------- publicist, Mr. Steve has been selected to build a new bridge in the city.
(A) he
(B) his
(C) him
(D) himself

116. Some research indicates that physicians can ------- reduce healing time for patients by using Stingheal's new surgical laser.
(A) significant
(B) most significant
(C) significance
(D) significantly

117. Partnered with the local government, the Cerena National Museum contains one of the most ------- significant collection of ancient art in the world.
(A) preventively
(B) gratefully
(C) historically
(D) excitedly

118. ------- impresses shareholders the most is that the Ronson King Corporation has enhanced nationwide recognition of its brand this year.
(A) Which
(B) What
(C) Nothing
(D) Neither

119. ------- 50 percent of executive officers held senior-level positions in related fields before they were promoted to top management.
(A) About
(B) Ever
(C) By
(D) Even if

120. An article in the latest edition of High Developments Today covers a lot of great ideas for ------- grant writing.
(A) successful
(B) supposed
(C) previous
(D) numerous

GO ON TO THE NEXT PAGE

121. The Metropolitan Transportation Authority will investigate the ------- of the planned road maintenance on local communities.
(A) service
(B) cause
(C) impact
(D) opinion

122. The renovation of the Heven Gow Building ------- the temporary closing of Dal-sung Avenue.
(A) necessarily
(B) necessary
(C) necessitates
(D) necessitate

123. ------- the terms and conditions of the acquisition had an oral agreement at the meeting, they still must be formally approved.
(A) Rather than
(B) In spite of
(C) Regarding
(D) Even though

124. Renowned fashion designer Tomas Geller developed new tailoring skills by making clothes for ------- members of his family.
(A) anyones
(B) others
(C) several
(D) each

125. Security guards at the company can be reached 24 hours a day ------- Manhattan National Bank's online chat service.
(A) through
(B) including
(C) between
(D) such as

126. Fierce Vrosnan was chosen for the managerial position of the new research team now that his background was very -------.
(A) qualified
(B) pleased
(C) knowledgeable
(D) impressive

127. Next week, a ------- of all sales at Yogoyo Book Store will be given to local orphanages.
(A) rank
(B) quality
(C) team
(D) portion

128. Avoid traffic congestion on the Ereetian Bridge tonight while construction workers ------- the resurfacing project.
(A) complete
(B) completing
(C) are completed
(D) to be completing

129. Please take a moment to ------- your decision before you cancel your subscription to Worldwide Network Times.
(A) reconsider
(B) suppose
(C) remind
(D) apply

130. The ventilation systems at the Feders operations were modified last year ------- comply with new standards.
(A) leading to
(B) in order to
(C) due to
(D) in addition to

PART 6

Directions: Read the texts that follow. A word, phrase, or sentence is missing in parts of each text. Four answer choices for each question are given below the text. Select the best answer to complete the text. Then mark the letter (A), (B), (C), or (D) on your answer sheet.

Questions 131-134 refer to the following article.

Eric Jackson Comes to the Reading Pleasure Bookstore

New York(March 25) – New York Voice book reviewer Clark Kent will ------ Eric Jackson at the
131.
Reading Pleasure Bookstore on March 27 at 10 A.M. After their discussion, Mr. Jackson will

read from his latest book of travel essays, Snow in Alaska. He will ------ sign copies for those in
132.

attendance. ------
133.

Mr. Jackson is the writer of the award-winning travel novel Leave Suddenly and several

collections of travel essays. His body of work has been named "a remarkable ------" by the
134.

critics of the New Revolution of Journey Literature.

If you need details about the event, you can visit our website at www.readingpleasure.com or

call the bookstore at (473) 293-5839 to learn more.

131. (A) recommend
(B) invite
(C) replace
(D) interview

132. (A) today
(B) ahead
(C) also
(D) rather

133. (A) His book has sold more than double unlike most reviewers expected.
(B) Every session including lunch break and talks with the author will last until 5 P.M.
(C) He was born and grew up in New York City.
(D) The publishing company has earned significant revenue through sales from his book.

134. (A) achiever
(B) achieved
(C) achievable
(D) achievement

GO ON TO THE NEXT PAGE

From: Remington Steel

To: Long-term employees

Cc: Taylor Momson

Subject: Service Anniversary

Date: October 10

Attachment: Gift list

Dear Employees;

Congratulations! I am pleased to commend you on your service to Jeepson Advertising Company. Our long-term professionals ------ greatly to our success.
135.

------, it is due to your exceptional contribution to Jeepson that we have been widely recognized
136.
as one of the best companies to act in the country. Therefore, ------
137.

Please ------ Taylor Momson of your selection from the attached list by November 11.
138.

With sincere gratitude,

Remington Steel

Chief Executive Officer

135. (A) contributing
(B) contribute
(C) was contributing
(D) are contributed

136. (A) On the contrary
(B) By comparison
(C) In fact
(D) However

137. (A) Most of our workers should focus their attention to sales increases.
(B) The management has offered every worker many opportunities to raise the awareness of our company.
(C) We will financially suffer from economic recession because of unexpected sales decrease.
(D) The board members are pleased to award you with a gift in appreciation of your valuable devotion.

138. (A) announce
(B) notify
(C) learn
(D) recommend

Geneva Networking

3030-2nd Ave. S.W.

Calgary AB T2N 5N7

Ms. Geneva Elrond

Investment Properties Company

Toronto, ON M7Y 2C5

Dear Elrond,

This is to inform you that your application for our company has finally been approved. As mentioned in the ------ description and during the interview, you will assume all duties that the
139.
retiring manager has been in charge of.

During the first 5 months of employment, you will go through the orientation session by Britny Spears, whom you ------ during your interview.
140.

Should you ------ our offer, you will start to work on September 3rd. ------
141. **142.**

Sincerely,

Richard Aragon

Personnel director

---

139. (A) hire
(B) appointment
(C) career
(D) job

140. (A) will meet
(B) meet
(C) met
(D) will have met

141. (A) acknowledge
(B) reply
(C) accept
(D) record

142. (A) Please notify us whether you will accept our offer no later than August 31.
(B) You are cordially invited to attend the upcoming retirement party.
(C) You are advised to submit your application form by August 31.
(D) You will soon be informed of when you will be interviewed.

GO ON TO THE NEXT PAGE

To: Ian Holmes

From: Peter Jackson

Date: May 15, 2016

Subject: Next meeting

Dear Mr. Ian Holmes,

Hi, Mr. Holmes. I have great news that our presentation delivered last week was a ------. Kintex
143.
Inc. was completely satisfied with our work, and ------ to work with us for their next construction
144.
campaign. They want to meet with us later this month to begin finalizing the deal. ------ There
145.
are a few changes that I think we need to make before we show ------ the contract.
146.

Respond to my e-mail as soon as possible please.

Sincerely,

Peter Jackson

---

143. (A) depression
(B) success
(C) disruption
(D) mistake

144. (A) like
(B) will like
(C) is liking
(D) would like

145. (A) We can make sure that our partner will request us to make second presentation.
(B) We had a somewhat difficult time finishing it before the deadline.
(C) It is expected to give a substantial effect on our financial situation sooner or later.
(D) Why don't we meet sometime next week and go over the contract and other details?

146. (A) him
(B) you
(C) her
(D) them

PART 7

Directions: In this part you will read a selection of texts, such as magazine and newpaper articles, e-mails, and instant messages. Each text or st of texts is followed by several questions. Select the best answer to complete the text. Then mark the letter (A), (B), (C), or (D) on your answer sheet.

Questions 147-148 refer to the following text message.

From: Eplus Telecom
Date: Sep 3
Subject: Payment due

Your monthly bill of $ 55.50 will be automatically charged to your credit card ending in 0304 today, September 3rd. If you need to change your due date or method of payment, you are advised to visit us online, www.eplustelecom.com. You received this automatical message since you agreed to receive text reminders. To unsubscribe, send us your message with the word "stop."

Thank you for your patronage.

147. Why is the text message written?
(A) To issue a reminder
(B) To attract a new customer
(C) To confirm a late payment
(D) To schedule a meeting date

148. What can a customer do on the web page?
(A) Unsubscribe from a charge program
(B) Agree to receive a new credit card
(C) Change a payment schedule
(D) Deny receiving messages

GO ON TO THE NEXT PAGE

Carson Entertainment

Will your office host a party? We have an answer.

The Carson Entertainment offers special dishes for any kind of events, ranging from a simple casual dinner to an official one. We specialize in Chinese, Mexican, and Indian cuisines with an emphasis on hot spicy dishes, and our desserts are known as the best in our city.

Please check out our complete menu on our website or visit our shop personally at 31 Wellington Street to consult with one of our service representatives and taste dishes of your choice for free.

You can surely learn why we are rated as the best from local business owners for a special business occasion.

www.carsonentertainment.com

149. What kind of business does Carson Entertainment do?
(A) A movie production
(B) A kitchen supply store
(C) A web design
(D) A food preparation service

150. What does the company offer at no cost?
(A) Sample movies
(B) Product samples
(C) Express shipping
(D) Marketing consulting

Bom Bom Cafe

open 8 A.M. to 2 P.M. everyday except Sunday

Two Eggs boiled or baked ....$ 4.50

Blueberry waffle
Baked waffle, fresh Blueberries and whipped cream ....$ 4.50

Pancake set
Potato chips or strawberries for $ 1 more ....$ 4.50

Bom Bom Omelet special
Made with three eggs, grilled garlics, and sliced tomato, served with toast.
Get bacon for $ 1 more ....$ 5.25

Sausage special
Three eggs baked, chopped sausages, toast and fried carrots ....$ 5.75

Early Bird special
One baked pancake, two eggs, fried chicken, and fresh tomato
Get bacon for $ 1 more .... $ 5.75

Celebrating 5 years of serving our famous pork sausages!

151. What is suggested about the Bom Bom Cafe?
(A) It is a new dining place.
(B) It is closed in the evening.
(C) It sells a variety of vegetables and fruits.
(D) It sells products at a low cost.

152. To what item can a customer add fruit for an additional cost?
(A) The Pancake Set
(B) The Sausage Special
(C) The Blueberry Waffle
(D) The Early Bird Special

153. What food do all the specials have in common?
(A) Tomato
(B) Potato
(C) Toast
(D) Egg

GO ON TO THE NEXT PAGE

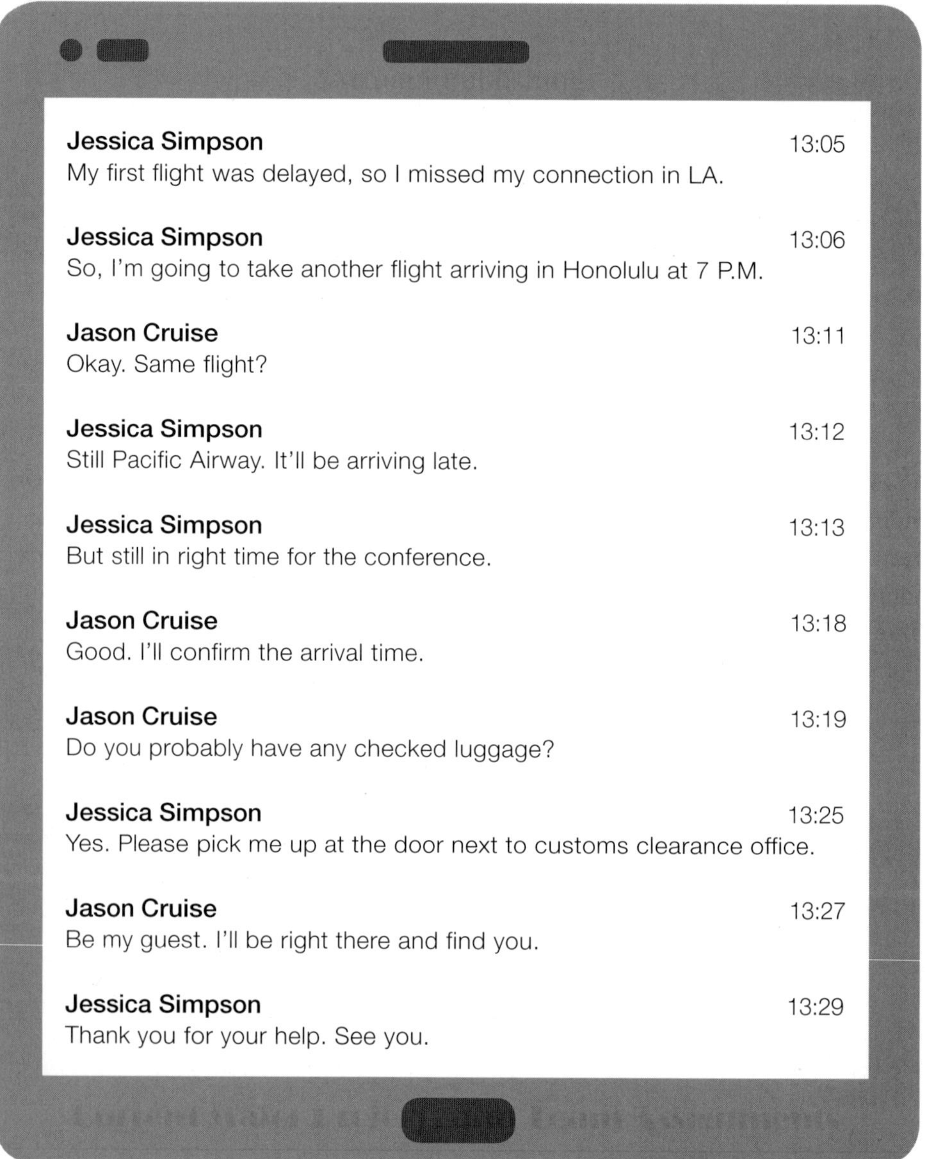

154. What is indicated about Ms. Simpson?
(A) She has once been to LA.
(B) She in on a business trip.
(C) She works for Pacific Airways.
(D) She is currently working in Honolulu.

155. At 13:27, what does Mr. Cruise mean when he writes, "Be my guest"?
(A) He has confirmed her arrival time.
(B) He agrees to wait near the customs area.
(C) He thinks his guest might be unable to pass throughout customs.
(D) He will meet the customs office manager.

http://www.theoneairline.co.oz			
HOME	RESERVATION	**Baggage Transport**	Reviews

Easy Transport

We are pleased to provide convenient baggage transport for passengers using The One Airline. We will pick up and drop off your baggage at any place within Australia. You can easily sign up for Easy Transport when purchasing your ticket at ticketing booths up to 24 hours before your departure.

Service costs are dependant upon the number and size of your baggage.

Starting on 3 September, Easy Transport will expand abroad. Customers will soon check for a complete list of international cities providing this service.

156. What is being advertised on the information?
(A) An changed flight schedule
(B) An expanded ticketing booths
(C) A luggage handling service
(D) An improved passenger claim system

157. What is true about Easy Transport?
(A) It requires advance registration.
(B) It will operate on 3 Sep.
(C) It is available internationally.
(D) Customers can use it free for charge in Australia.

GO ON TO THE NEXT PAGE

EZ PROPERTY

10 Pitt Street, Hong Kong 43025

17 December

Dear Zenith Tower Residents,

The monthly community gathering will be held in our 3rd floor community center on Friday, 18 December, at 10 A.M. We will welcome the newest members of our community who have moved in over the last month. After brief introductions, we will talk about the upcoming renovation work on the parking area and the fitness center, both scheduled next month. We will also review the proposed plan to expand the Zenith Tower. We will discuss how the closure of the community center and the slight rise in a rent will affect Zenith Tower residents.

If you cannot attend but have questions or concerns that you might have, please contact me at mao0903@rocketmail.com or stop by the managerial office from 9 A.M. to 8 P.M., Monday to Friday.

Sincerely

Mao Chuddung

Mao Chuddung

General manager

158. What is indicated about EZ Property?
(A) It provides high-cost residence.
(B) It regularly holds meetings for residents.
(C) It recently renovated the tower complex.
(D) It has commercial area for rent.

159. What will happen next month?
(A) Maintenance work will begin.
(B) Residence fees will rise slightly.
(C) A general manager will deliver his private speech.
(D) A tower complex will be enlarged.

160. According to the letter, why might residents be concerned?
(A) The fitness center will close for two months.
(B) The gathering date will be changed.
(C) They may have limited views of the city.
(D) They may lose access to some facilities.

http://www.hilton.edu			
Direction	**Home**	**Contact Us**	**Faculty**

Faculty Profile

London Campus

Dr. Antonio Najar

Business Management

bajar@hilton.edu

Dr. Antonio Najar graduated from Mohito University located in Chelsea with the dual degrees in business management and English history. He embarked on his academic career as an educator when, as the graduate student in Cambridge University located in Manchester, he led Business introductory courses, tutoring the students. After receiving his degree in Business Management from Cambridge University, he arrived at the London Campus of Hilton University as business faculty member. He is the main author of "Why Your Business Always Failed (published by Hilton University Press)." He is also serving on the Big Ben Business Council as counselor. Dr. Najar left Hilton University and currently conducts a range of international business seminars at Europe Business Association at Frankfurt, German.

161. What is the purpose of the information?
(A) To publicize a business seminar
(B) To describe facts about an employee
(C) To invite business faculty members to purchase a book
(D) To offer details for a job application

162. Where did Professor Najar start his teaching career?
(A) In Chelsea
(B) In London
(C) In Manchester
(D) In Frankfurt

163. What is suggested about Professor Najar?
(A) He is a professor of English history at the moment.
(B) He used to work for the Big Ben Business Council.
(C) He is working temporarily in German.
(D) He owns a publishing company.

GO ON TO THE NEXT PAGE

To: Undisclosed recipients   **From:** andyoh@gimusicconcert.org

Date: September 3   **Subject:** Great Island Music Concert

Attachment: volunteer confirmation form

Hello, Honolulu Music Fans!

Many of the volunteers have contacted me to express their interest in assistance again at the Great Island Music Concert. Enjoying a variety of fantastic performances for three whole days is surely a perfect way to spend this weekend in Hawaii. As always, concert volunteers will receive free meal coupons and passes in exchange for your volunteer work.

In anticipation of a larger crowd this year, preparations have been already made. In fact, we have already sold far more advance tickets than last year.

Every returning volunteer should participate in the orientation session scheduled for the evening of September 10. You should send the attached volunteer confirmation form back to me no later than September 9, indicating your volunteer job in which you want to participate and your three top choices in regard to a work team. Like last year's structure, the principal teams will be in charge of staffing the information and help desk, coordinating food stands, managing the stage set up and breakdown, and assisting with car parking control. Unfortunately, we cannot guarantee everyone's first assignment choice but will do our best to accommodate it.

Thank you – I'll soon contact you with more instructions. I'm looking forward to meeting all of you again this year!

Andy Oh

164. What is NOT true about the e-mail recipients?
(A) They are musicians who will perform at the concert.
(B) They attended the concert last year for free.
(C) They have met Andy Oh before.
(D) They are familiar with jobs at a large public event.

165. How will this year's Great Island Music Concert be different from last year?
(A) It will take place indoors.
(B) It will be held for three days.
(C) It will be attended by more people.
(D) It will be less expensive to attend.

166. What information is required on the volunteer confirmation form?
(A) The number of passes requested
(B) Meal preferences
(C) Personal banking information
(D) Desired team assignments

167. What volunteers' task is mentioned?
(A) Cooking food
(B) Setting up performance equipment
(C) Advertising the concert
(D) Arranging accomodations for performers

Economic Board's Outlook

May 10 - Mexico City Economic Board has announced its latest Regional Work Forecast. The report contains details on the fastest growing industries, occupations and declining ones. —[1]— The report is released biannually, in May and October, to ensure that the information reflects the existing work market in Mexico City and the nearby areas.

—[2]— Apparently, the greatest job growth is expected for surgeons, dentists, nursing resources, and health-care providers over the following two quarters. Each of these categories is expected to grow more than 5 percent this year. Moderate growth is anticipated for almost all positions in the accommodation sector since the tourism and hospitality industry continues to grow and holiday season starts. —[3]—

For the full report, visit www.mexicicity.go.or/economic_board, where you can read projections for more than ten industries. —[4]—

168. What's discussed in the report?
(A) Increase in local salaries
(B) Workplace safety concerns
(C) Future jobs in Mexico City and the surrounding areas
(D) Changes in manufacturers' strategy

169. How often is the report published?
(A) Every quarter
(B) Every year
(C) Once a month
(D) Twice a year

170. The word "over" in paragraph 2, line 2, is closest in meaning to
(A) beyond
(B) near
(C) during
(D) above

171. In which of the positions marked [1], [2], [3] and [4] does the following sentence best belong?

"On the other hand, positions in manufacturing are expected to decline by 9 percent as domestic sales of IT items are continually decreasing."

(A) [1]
(B) [2]
(C) [3]
(D) [4]

GO ON TO THE NEXT PAGE

To: Mark Jordan <markjordan@rocketmail.com>
From: Chris Brown <chris1980@navel.com>
Date: March 5
Subject: Delivery issue

Dear, Mr. Jordan

Thank you for bringing to our attention the inaccuracy in the order that you recently placed with us at Adidas Sports Gear. You mentioned that the roughly 400 women's clothing products you had ordered didn't arrive.

Unfortunately, a system error did happen early in the evening of March 1. This failure caused not only our website's malfunction for a while but also some deletion of orders placed on that day. After all, our company couldn't receive your order while our billing department could.

We recognize that you must have felt disappointed when you were charged for the order you didn't receive. We also know that you are a new customer and don't want you to leave us for another deal. As a result, to make up for the problem, we will send all missing items by overnight delivery free of charge. In order to compensate you for the unpleasant experience, you will receive an unlimited gift voucher valid for any future order. In addition, you will receive a 30% extra discount on any order you will place within 2 months.

We apologize for the inconvenience this may have caused and wish you will be satisfied with our sincere reaction. Please feel free to contact me if you have any questions. Thanks.

Sincerely,

Chris Brown
Chris Brown
Customer Service manager

172. Why did Mr. Brown send the e-mail?
(A) To offer an apology
(B) To submit a complaint form
(C) To prompt the recipient to send the
order again
(D) To accept a candidate's application

173. What is indicated about Mr. Jordan?
(A) He works at a sports gear company.
(B) He placed an order on March 1.
(C) He prefers to buy sports products
online.
(D) He will pay off his bill as soon as he
receives the new shipment.

174. The word "recognize" in paragraph 3,
line 1 is closest in meaning to
(A) remember
(B) agree with
(C) approve of
(D) acknowledge

175. What does Mr. Chris NOT provide to
Mr. Jordan?
(A) A partial refund on the existing order
(B) A limited reduction on the future order
(C) A deduction on another purchase
(D) Expedited shipping on items already
purchased

GO ON TO THE NEXT PAGE

Free Lectures Series
Sponsored by Kansas University General Hospital (KUGH)

KUGH is pleased to announce its Autumn lecture series for local clinic professionals. The series provides the opportunity to meet some of the health care-related leading figures who manage medical systems. All lectures are conveniently held at Kansas University Lecture Campus and are available on a first-come, first-served basis. Sessions are open an hour before the lecture begins.

Wednesday, 1 September, 6:00 P.M., Room 21
Speaker: Jake Mercedes, Jake's Medical Clinics
Medical Time Management – Find out how to use your medical time effectively.

Wednesday, 8 September, 6:00 P.M., Room 19
Speaker: Nancy Orlando, Orlando Health-Care Center
Effective Communication - Enjoy simple techniques to make your connection with your administrative staff more effective.

Saturday, 11 September, 9:00 A.M., Room 19
Speaker: Mora Kano, Digital Medical Records
Data Management - Get information on patient record guidelines and data security.

Monday, 13 September, 5:30 P.M., Room 34
Speaker: Sul Hyun, Kansas Insurance Association
Finance Management - Learn how new invoicing practices can prompt patients and insurance firms to make timely payments.

Please contact Gary Lesmore at gary09@netian.com for further details.

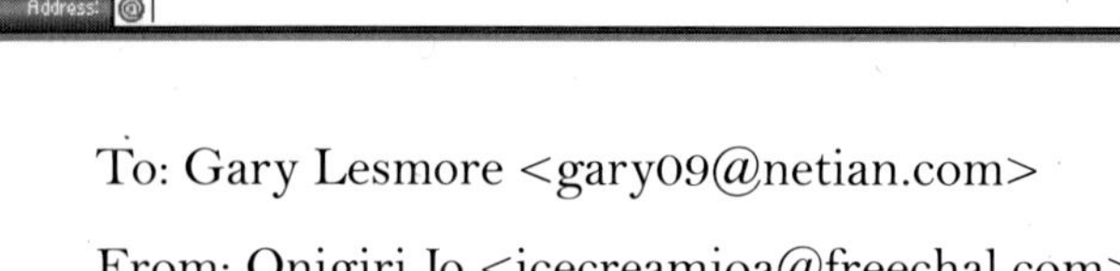

To: Gary Lesmore <gary09@netian.com>

From: Onigiri Jo <icecreamjoa@freechal.com>

Subject: Lecture Schedule

Date: 12 September

Dear Mr. Lesmore,

I received your brochure about the Autumn lecture series. I was looking forward to the presentation from a representative of Digital Medical Records, because I recently installed licensed software and am not good at using it. However, when I went to the School of Public Health yesterday morning, no one was in room 19. I inquired at the front desk, but the security guard did not have any information about the lecture. If this lecture has been rescheduled, please let me know when and where it will be.

Sincerely,

Onigiri Jo

176. In the brochure, the word "figures" in paragraph 1, line 3, is closest in meaning to
(A) numbers
(B) people
(C) information
(D) studies

177. What is mentioned about the lectures?
(A) They are limited to groups of 50 attendees.
(B) They will be held at Kansas University Hospital.
(C) They will be followed by a question-and-answer session.
(D) They are intended for those who manage medical offices.

178. What will be discussed at the lecture on September 13?
(A) How to work together efficiently
(B) How to keep patients' health records
(C) How to ensure that bills are paid shortly
(D) How to communicate effectively with patients

179. Whose lecture does Mr. Onigiri Jo wish to attend?
(A) Ms. Mercedes'
(B) Mr. Orlando's
(C) Ms. Kano's
(D) Mr. Oh's

180. Why did Mr. Onigiri Jo write the e-mail?
(A) To request an update
(B) To register for a lecture
(C) To join a mailing list
(D) To change his work schedule

GO ON TO THE NEXT PAGE

http://www.ozcastle.com/intro

Welcome to Oz Castle

Intro	**Tours**	**Reservations**	**Contact**	**Reviews**

Oz castle is a luxurious and fancy hotel built near the most famous lake, Hoam Quiem in Hanoi, Vietnam. It is located at the end of Hoam Quiem Avenue, a quiet street. We provide 30 spacious rooms with outdoor coffee lounge and wireless Internet access.

Visit us for a relaxing holiday or for adventure tour. The hotel is conveniently located midway between downtown and the Pacific coast, providing complimentary shuttles to gorgeous beaches in Ha Long Bay and to the popular shopping district in Hanoi. Hotel guides are also available for casual walk through the jungle on the hotel ground or for excursion to untouched lands.

Please contact us for an exact room charge, as prices are considerably lower during the monsoon season.

http://www.ozcastle.com/reviews

Welcome to Oz Castle

Intro	**Tours**	**Reservations**	**Contact**	**Reviews**

I usually compare various accommodations online before reserving a hotel room but not this time. I received a free coupon for Oz Castle from the Ghana Car Rental Service, and I decided to try it. Because I have already read some testimonials from online social clubs, I know that I was not the only one who appreciated Oz Castle. It has received high ratings from major tour websites.

My stay at Oz Castle was fantastic and I believe anyone seeking peaceful vacation place should consider Oz Castle seriously. The room was very cozy and comfortable. The freshly prepared meals made me taste home-cooked Vietnamese Cuisine for the first time. Also, I thoroughly enjoyed my relaxing day trip to Ha Long Bay.

That the street where the hotel is located is covered with a dusty dirt road with some deep holes is my only negative comment. This was still not a serious problem because there was not much traffic on the road.

Thanks

Lisa White

181. What is indicated about Oz Castle?
(A) It provides a variety of rooms in size.
(B) Its prices vary seasonally.
(C) It is operated by the Vietnamese government.
(D) It is open 24 hours 365 days.

182. What is NOT offered at Oz Castle?
(A) Outdoor seating area
(B) Internet access
(C) Free room upgrade
(D) Home cooked meals

183. What does Ms. Lisa White mention in her review?
(A) She disagrees with online testimonials.
(B) She usually stays with relatives at Vietnam.
(C) She discovered Oz Castle through a website.
(D) She recommends Oz Castle to others.

184. What outdoor activity does Ms. Lisa White indicate that she participated in?
(A) Walk in the jungle
(B) Shopping in Hanoi
(C) Visiting a beach
(D) Exploring an untouched land

185. What is implied about Hoam quiem Avenue?
(A) It is unpaved.
(B) It is hard to find.
(C) It is near a beach.
(D) It is crowded during a night time.

GO ON TO THE NEXT PAGE

Oz Katok

Takoyaki   16:35
Mr. Jonathan, can I confirm the meeting time with Mr. Haywood?

Jonathan   16:40
Yes, wait a second.

Jonathan   16:41
Mr. Haywood will meet the legal team member at 8:30 as scheduled. Still OK?

Takoyaki   16:43
I'm sorry but I can't. I was called from the board. I have to attend the emergency meeting with a subcontractor early Thursday morning.

Jonathan   16:44
Sorry to hear that. You need the meeting schedule changed to more convenient time.

Takoyaki   16:45
Of course, I want to ask to postpone that meeting to Monday morning next week.

Jonathan   16:46
Well, let me check Mr. Oh's schedule first.

Jonathan   16:48
Fortunately, he has no schedule on that time. I'll let him know the changed meeting time with you.

Takoyaki   16:49
Thank you. Please send Mr. Oh my sorry for an unexpected scheduling change.

From: andrewjonathan@ez2group.com   To: haywood@ez2group.com
Date: 4 Sep   Subject: Daily Update
Attachment: Copy of e-mail

Dear Mr. Oh,

I'm attaching some quick updates regarding your schedule this week. First, the legal supervisor has asked if the meeting scheduling may be changed. —[1]— I can fill that time slot with Charles Duff, photographer whom you want to meet for an interview. You mentioned you wanted to meet him and check out his potential work on Calgary project. —[2]—

Additionally, Oltega Gonzales from the financial committee has confirmed that he will be joining the meeting on Friday to attend the video conference. —[3]— I have already reserved the multimedia conference hall.

Finally, because you'll be out of town this afternoon, I am sending a copy of the e-mail from Omega City Hotel that confirms the reservation. —[4]— I guess that you already have the air tickets and a detailed itinerary. Let me know if you don't and I will send them electronically.

Sincerely,

Andrew Jonathan

The EZ2 Group-Haywood Oh's schedule- 3-7 September

Monday	Tuesday	Wednesday	Thursday	Friday
9:00 A.M. marketing meeting 1:15 P.M. lunch with Jaydong Kim 4:00 P.M. executive staff board meeting meeting	8:45 A.M. review budgets with department managers 2:40 P.M train departs for Brisbane, arrival 4:45	9:15 A.M. meeting with Brisbane office team to plan upcoming advertising campaign 1:00 P.M. return to Gold Coast arrival 2:05 5:30 P.M. prepare for quarterly board meeting	8:30 A.M. meet with Mimi Takoyaki (Legal team) 1:45 P.M. meet with Martha Stone with her revisions 4:30 P.M. monthly board meeting 5:30 P.M. Seoul office conference call	8:00 A.M. New York office conference call 10:00 A.M. meet with IT to go over website 2:00 P.M. meet to review video campaign

186. What is indicated about the EZ2 Group?
(A) It opened within a year.
(B) It has offices in several cities.
(C) It has more than 50 staff members.
(D) It is the largest marketing company in the country.

187. What electronic file is sent with the e-mail?
(A) Train tickets
(B) Digital photographs
(C) A hotel confirmation
(D) A boarding meeting itinerary

188. When will probably Mr. Oh meet the legal team member?
(A) Sep 3
(B) Sep 6
(C) Sep 10
(D) Oct 6

189. When will Mr. Oh and Mr. Gonzales meet?
(A) 9:15 A.M. Wednesday
(B) 8:00 A.M. Friday
(C) 2:00 P.M. Friday
(D) 5:30 P.M. Thursday

190. In which of the positions marked [1], [2], [3] and [4] does the following sentence best belong?

"Please let me know whether I should call him for an interview arrangement."

(A) [1]
(B) [2]
(C) [3]
(D) [4]

GO ON TO THE NEXT PAGE ▶

Armani Publishing
335 George Street
Dallas, Houston 10034

April 27
Laura Johns
31 Elizabeth Avenue
Arizona, Nevada 30453

Dear Ms. Johns

We welcome you to work as a new contributor to Armani Travel Guides Services and as a contracted writer. For reimbursement of all expenses, you are required to submit a form of proof for services that have been previously approved by the project's writing editor. It is necessary that a submitted invoice include your contact number, the number of your project, and your supervisor's name. Please send it to me and it will be forwarded to our payroll department. Please contact Mr. Trump for detailed instructions on the invoice for your photographs. The photography department will show you its own template for their invoice that I suspect you will receive soon.

Sincerely

Mike Tyson

Armani PUBLISHING
Current Major Projects and Team Assignments

Project names / Key assignments	Holiday Series	Armani Travel Guides Series	** Downtown Series
Writing Editor	Julia Ridell	Isabel Tompson	Eric Kim
Article and Photography Editor	Benjamin Franklin	Eaton Jackson	Benjamin Franklin
Administrative Assistant	Kate Homes	Ray Williams	Mike Tyson

** Detailed instructions will soon be sent to you by e-mail.

From: sakurai5@armanipublishing.com
To: erickim@armanipublishing.com
Date: 2 May
Subject: More detailed instructions
Attachment: Copy of job duties

Dear Mr. Kim

Please note that your new team member, Ms. Laura Johns will shortly join your project team, which will free up Ms. Franklin so that she can dedicate more attention to her other team assignment, Holiday Photography. It also involves the upcoming release of another issue. In case that as a team leader, you want to receive more detailed job duties for your new member, I am enclosing them with this e-mail. They will surely help you oversee your team members effectively.

Sincerely,

Sakurai Oh
HR director Armani Publishing

191. What does the letter explain?
(A) How to obtain payments
(B) How to submit travel articles
(C) How to get writing assignments
(D) How to apply for project opening positions

192. What is NOT true about Mr. Tyson and Ms. Johns?
(A) Mr. Tyson accepts invoices for written work.
(B) Mr. Tyson oversees travel photographs projects.
(C) Ms. Johns has completed work for Armani Publishing for the first time.
(D) Ms. Johns took photographs for an article she wrote.

193. In the letter, the word "suspect" in line 8 is closest in meaning to
(A) believe
(B) hope
(C) distrust
(D) accuse

194. What is the most likely true about Ms. Ridell?
(A) She serves as a new chief editor at Armani Publishing.
(B) She has worked together with Ms. Jackson.
(C) She preapproved Ms. Johns' contract.
(D) She oversees Kate Homes' tasks.

195. What change will happen to the project assignments?
(A) The team assigned to the Holiday Series will no longer be needed.
(B) A fourth project team is being created.
(C) Mr. Kim will be leaving to work at another company.
(D) A new article and photography editor will be added to a team.

GO ON TO THE NEXT PAGE

Asian Doctor Council Workshop

The Asian Doctor Council invites you to submit an abstract of no more than 1,000 words for the ninth annual health workshop which will be held in Bangkok, Thailand 4 to 10 November. The conference gathers Asian surgeons and physicians from a range of health care and medical sectors.

This year's theme is "Outreach: Expanding medical services, Increasing public awareness." Outreach includes all kinds of medical activities and distribution of medical services and products. Every aspect of the topic will be considered. In the mean time, the workshop discusses all efforts that look into the application of new technologies to medical care, medical equipment and the delivery of medical services. Each presentation must not exceed 40 minutes. One entry of presenter or group of presenters is allowed.

Each of the presenters should prepare his or her own travel and accommodation for the workshop. A complete list of hotels offering discounted prices for the participants is available on our website, www.asiandoctorcouncil. com/workshop. Registration forms can be available on the site. Limited fund support for the nonprofit organization is available. Qualified applicants should fill out the application form and send it from 24 October to 7 November. Please don't forget to include the name of a presenter and e-mail address in it.

Name: Alfred Kline **E-mail address:** alfredkline@ez.net
Presentation Title: A Rewarding Connection Between Outreach and Social Media

Abstract:
Our presentation will address the use of mobile phone messaging as a means to raise awareness about medical services among the public who are nor familiar with them. My employer, which is the Bangkok Medical Clinic, a non-profit organization in Bangkok, Thailand, needed to advertise a new medical service. Then, it focused on the mobile phone. The effort, which was undertaken four years ago by our technology team in cooperation with an award-winning advertising firm, led to significant demand for the new service, and furthermore attracted more traffic to our clinic as well as website. The session will describe the obstacles that we had to overcome in implementing the unique strategy, the results of improved doctor-patient relationships, and every aspect of text messaging to communicate conveniently with patients.

Asian Doctor Council Workshop Series

Asian Doctor Council is pleased to announce its winter workshop for the ninth annual health workshop for health care professionals. It offers the opportunity to learn from a variety of leaders in our field who supervise medical practices and health-care systems. Seating for all presentations is available through our online reservation. All participants can attend each presentation 20 minutes ahead of each lecture.

Monday, 4 November, 3:00 P.M., Diamond Hall
Speaker: Gary Nelson, Singapore General Hospital
Medical Advancements – Find out how asian medical technology has advanced and how many patients seek medical tour of medical technology-advanced countries.

Wednesday 6 November, 6:00 P.M., Gold Hall
Speaker: Jessica Johnson, Johnson's Health-Care Consulting
Effective Communication - Learn simple techniques to help you connect effectively with your medical staff.

Sunday, 10 November, 11:00 A.M., Diamond Hall
Speaker: Alfred Kline, Bangkok Medical Clinic
Mobile Medical Service - Get an overview of the convenient mobile messaging service for patients.

Please contact Andy Oh at **andyoh@asiandoctorcouncil.net** for additional information.

196. What is NOT indicated about Asian Doctor Council?
(A) It will not accept abstracts submitted on 10 November.
(B) It has organized workshops over the past years.
(C) It will allow more than one submission from a group.
(D) It will encourage Asian doctors to participate.

197. According to the notice, why should participants visit the website?
(A) To find reduced rates on accommodations
(B) To look at an example of interactive discussion
(C) To check out a complete conference agenda
(D) To learn more about how to write an abstract

198. What is suggested about Bangkok Medical Clinic?
(A) It has won numerous awards.
(B) Its outreach initiative was successful.
(C) It has recently updated its website.
(D) It is one of the best-known medical centers in Thailand.

199. What is suggested about the morning presentation?
(A) It will describe the effective communication with medical staff.
(B) It will be held in Diamond Hall on the first day of workshop series.
(C) It will address to participants how to increase the number of patients.
(D) It will last more than 40 minutes.

200. What is most likely true about Mr. Kline?
(A) He joined Bangkok Medical Clinic 3 years ago.
(B) He won an award for his innovative advertisements.
(C) He qualifies for financial aid offered by conference organizers.
(D) He suggested the idea to use mobile phone messaging for the first time.

[점수 그래프]

LC Score

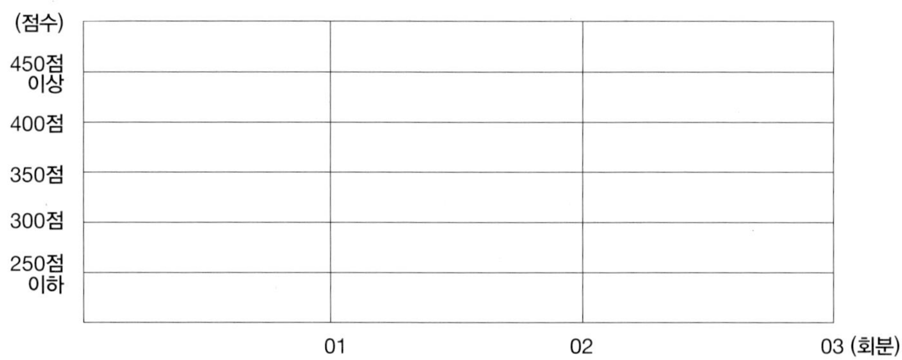

RC Score

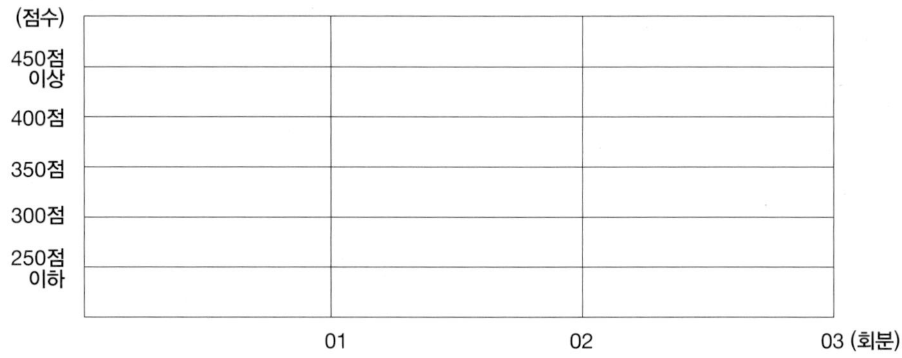

ACTUAL TEST

02

LISTENING TEST

In the listening test, you will be asked to demonstrate how well you understand spoken English. The entire listening test will last approximately 45 minutes. There are four parts, and directions are given for each part. You must mark your answers on the separate answer sheet. Do not write your answers in the test book.

PART 1

Directions: For each question in this part, you will hear four statements about a picture in your test book. When you hear the statements, you must select the one statement that best describes what you see in the picture. Then find the number of the question on your answer sheet and mark your answer. The statements will not be printed in your test book and will be spoken only one time.

Sample Answer

Example

Statement (B), "She's making a presentation," is the best description of the picture. So you should select answer (B) and mark it on your answer sheet.

1.

2.

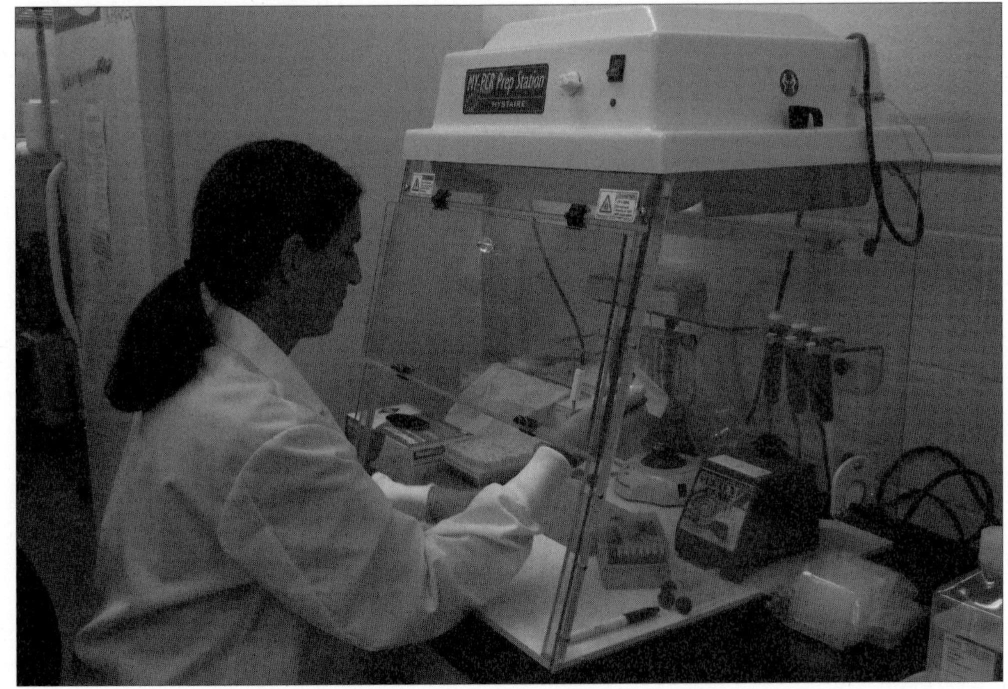

GO ON TO THE NEXT PAGE →

3.

4.

5.

6.

GO ON TO THE NEXT PAGE

PART 2

Directions: You will hear a question or statement and three responses spoken in English. They will not be printed in your text book and will be spoken only one time. Select the best response to the question or statement and mark the letter (A), (B), or (C) on your answer sheet.

7. Mark your answer on your answer sheet.

8. Mark your answer on your answer sheet.

9. Mark your answer on your answer sheet.

10. Mark your answer on your answer sheet.

11. Mark your answer on your answer sheet.

12. Mark your answer on your answer sheet.

13. Mark your answer on your answer sheet.

14. Mark your answer on your answer sheet.

15. Mark your answer on your answer sheet.

16. Mark your answer on your answer sheet.

17. Mark your answer on your answer sheet.

18. Mark your answer on your answer sheet.

19. Mark your answer on your answer sheet.

20. Mark your answer on your answer sheet.

21. Mark your answer on your answer sheet.

22. Mark your answer on your answer sheet.

23. Mark your answer on your answer sheet.

24. Mark your answer on your answer sheet.

25. Mark your answer on your answer sheet.

26. Mark your answer on your answer sheet.

27. Mark your answer on your answer sheet.

28. Mark your answer on your answer sheet.

29. Mark your answer on your answer sheet.

30. Mark your answer on your answer sheet.

31. Mark your answer on your answer sheet.

PART 3

Directions: You will hear some conversations between two or more people. You will be asked to answer three questions about what the speakers say in each conversation. Select the best response to each question and mark the letter (A), (B), (C), or (D) on your answer sheet. The conversations will not be printed in your test book and will be spoken only one time.

32. What is the conversation mainly about?
(A) Reserving a meeting
(B) Renovating an office
(C) Stopping mail delivery
(D) Finding a lost product

33. Why does the woman decline the man's suggestion?
(A) She has already received an item.
(B) She will be out of the country.
(C) The room is quite small.
(D) The price for service is too high.

34. What will the woman most likely tell the man next?
(A) Her office expansion project
(B) Her temporary address
(C) The purpose of her speech
(D) The date of her return

35. Where does the man most likely work?
(A) At a technical school
(B) At a clothing factory
(C) At a watch repair store
(D) At a flower shop

36. What does the man show the woman?
(A) A piece of machinery
(B) A list of courses
(C) Items in a display case
(D) A product catalog

37. What does the man offer the woman?
(A) A discounted price
(B) A later appointment
(C) A business recommendation
(D) A training session

38. In what department does the man most likely work?
(A) Personnel
(B) Accounting
(C) Technical Support
(D) Product Development

39. What does the woman give the man?
(A) A new employee directory
(B) A job application form
(C) A training schedule
(D) Survey findings

40. What does the woman suggest the man do?
(A) Book a conference room
(B) Go over plans with a colleague
(C) Delay a workshop
(D) Develop a software program

41. What is the man interested in purchasing?
(A) Computer program
(B) Office furniture
(C) Spring clothing collection
(D) Advertising space

42. Why does the woman direct the man to a website?
(A) To read a review from customers
(B) To purchase a store credit card
(C) To try a new viewing feature
(D) To enter a serial number

43. What additional information does the man ask for?
(A) Warranty terms
(B) A free delivery service
(C) Available sizes
(D) Product measurements

GO ON TO THE NEXT PAGE ▶

44. What are the speakers discussing?
(A) A piece of equipment
(B) A work list
(C) A power failure
(D) A customer review

45. What has the woman noticed?
(A) An item was missing.
(B) An order was placed.
(C) A colleague is away.
(D) A warning light is on.

46. What does the woman ask the man to do?
(A) Contact a factory manager
(B) Provide an up-to-date recipe
(C) Turn on a machine
(D) Prepare for a customer order

---

47. What position is the man inquiring about?
(A) A magazine writer
(B) A graphic designer
(C) A sales clerk
(D) A computer programmer

48. What job qualification does the woman mention?
(A) Recommendation from past employers
(B) A portfolio of art samples
(C) Knowledge of special software
(D) A certificate from a design academy

49. What does the woman say will happen next week?
(A) Excellent candidates will be interviewed.
(B) Computer programs will be upgraded.
(C) A new office branch will be open.
(D) A recruiting manager will lead an orientation session.

50. What problem does the woman mention?
(A) She has many assignments.
(B) A fee is too high.
(C) A fitness center is closing.
(D) A building is under renovation.

51. What does the man say about the running track?
(A) It will not be open this month.
(B) It has running instructors available.
(C) It was recently renovated.
(D) It is not used a lot in the morning.

52. How can a woman obtain a discount?
(A) By showing a proof of employment
(B) By providing a friend's name
(C) By using a facility on weekends only
(D) By paying in cash

---

53. What does the woman say she did in university?
(A) She led a band.
(B) She created a web page.
(C) She played in a musical group.
(D) She taught guitar.

54. What is available on the store website?
(A) Complimentary instruments
(B) Instruction videos
(C) Comments from musicians
(D) A list of local festivals

55. What does the woman imply when she says, "Oh, that would be helpful"?
(A) An e-mail address is not needed.
(B) A lesson seems competitively prices.
(C) An instrument was already tuned.
(D) She can join a mailing list.

56. What is the woman preparing to do?
(A) Visit a customer
(B) Give a presentation
(C) Hire a new department manager
(D) Correct a pricing policy

57. Why is the woman's work taking extra time to finish?
(A) Some resumes have not been sent.
(B) A computer is outdated.
(C) A colleague is away on holiday.
(D) Some data are incorrect.

58. What does the man say he will do?
(A) Schedule a meeting
(B) Prepare a job description
(C) Add another person to a project
(D) Contact department head

---

59. Where does the woman most likely work?
(A) At a restaurant
(B) At a ticket office
(C) At a bank
(D) At a hotel

60. Why does Jack say, "I don't buy it"?
(A) He has no intention to purchase the product.
(B) He is not excited about the conference.
(C) He didn't hear about the reschedule.
(D) He feels disappointed.

61. What do the men imply about the conference?
(A) It changes dates on short notice.
(B) It is held every year.
(C) It is exclusively for overseas buyers.
(D) There is no fee to participate in the conference.

62. What is the conversation mainly about?
(A) Enlarging office space
(B) Moving into an international market
(C) Increasing staff numbers
(D) Changing company leadership

63. Why does the woman say, "It's so amazing"?
(A) She doesn't agree.
(B) She needs an explanation.
(C) She feels bored.
(D) She is happily surprised.

64. What do the men imply about the company?
(A) It was recently renovated.
(B) It is planning to increase benefits.
(C) It is in a good financial condition.
(D) It has branches overseas.

GO ON TO THE NEXT PAGE

Desk and Chair Set	Price
Model A	$ 795
Model B	$ 695
Model C	$ 595
Model D	$ 495

Schedule	
Workshop	Time
Sales Figures	9:30-10:30 A.M.
Team Project	10:40-11:40 A.M.
LUNCH	11:40 A.M.-12:40 P.M.
Market Share	12:40-1:40 P.M.
Q&A Session	1:40-2:40 P.M.

65. What does the woman ask the man to do?
(A) Order some supplies
(B) Find a new supplier
(C) Repair a desk
(D) Contact a job applicant

66. What problem does the man mention?
(A) An instructor will leave the company.
(B) Prices for supplies have increased.
(C) Some desk models have been discontinued.
(D) A division budget has been decreased.

67. Look at the graphic. What model will the man order?
(A) Model A
(B) Model B
(C) Model C
(D) Model D

68. Where most likely is the conversation taking place?
(A) At a department store
(B) At a company office
(C) At a fitness center
(D) At a public library

69. What does the woman plan to do?
(A) Give a presentation
(B) Rent a larger meeting room
(C) Post a video on the website
(D) Look over a sales proposal

70. Look at the graphic. According to the speaker, which workshop will now be held third?
(A) Sales Figures
(B) Team Project
(C) Market Share
(D) Q&A Session

PART 4

Directions: You will hear some short talks given by a single speaker. You will be asked to answer three questions about what the speaker says in each short talk. Select the best response to each question and mark the letter (A), (B), (C), or (D) on your answer sheet. The talks will not be printed in your test book and will be spoken only one time.

71. Who most likely is the speaker?
(A) A house cleaner
(B) A patient
(C) A tenant
(D) A carpenter

72. What is the purpose of the call?
(A) To give an advice
(B) To report a problem
(C) To reschedule an appointment
(D) To settle a bill

73. What does the caller request?
(A) A reference letter
(B) A heavy discount
(C) A product catalogue
(D) A return call

74. What is being advertised?
(A) A musical
(B) A Italian restaurant
(C) A computer store
(D) A monthly publication

75. What will a new customer receive for a limited time?
(A) Free vouchers for the restaurant
(B) Invitations to the workshop
(C) Entry tickets to a museum
(D) Souvenir mugs

76. What are the listeners asked to do on the website?
(A) Use a promotional code
(B) Look at some pictures
(C) Enter a contest
(D) Join a mailing list

77. What is the purpose of the event?
(A) To honor new graduates
(B) To purchase a building
(C) To celebrate a manager's retirement
(D) To raise funds for charity activities

78. What does the video depict?
(A) A new manager
(B) The company's history
(C) The town's landmarks
(D) A training session

79. What will take place after the meal?
(A) A museum tour
(B) A dance party
(C) A graduate's speech
(D) A group discussion

80. What is the subject of the workshop?
(A) Safety procedure
(B) Business presentations
(C) Marketing strategies
(D) Career changes

81. What does the speaker recommend?
(A) Getting along with other professionals
(B) Achieving goals by deadlines
(C) Looking for business trends online
(D) Practicing reading before presentation

82. What will listeners probably do next?
(A) Have a meal
(B) Work in small teams
(C) Watch videos
(D) Provide reviews

GO ON TO THE NEXT PAGE

83. What are listeners asked to provide?
(A) A feedback
(B) A vacation schedule
(C) An employee contract
(D) A form of identification

84. What special feature is mentioned about a new digital key?
(A) It can be easily exchanged.
(B) It can be used for the new buildings.
(C) It can monitor who enters a building.
(D) It can work with a previous lock.

85. What does the speaker mean when she says. "Make sure to pick it up"?
(A) Employees should go on the website.
(B) Employees should find their ID.
(C) Employees should read a document.
(D) Employees should buy some cards.

---

86. What is the purpose of the broadcast?
(A) To talk about the closure of the company
(B) To announce a business merger
(C) To discuss the latest items
(D) To report a change in policies

87. What type of business is Weston Apparel?
(A) A building company
(B) An advertising company
(C) An interior design firm
(D) A clothing company

88. What does the speaker encourage the listeners to do?
(A) Listen to an interview
(B) Visit a store
(C) Apply for a job opportunity
(D) Enter a competition

89. What bothers the woman about Seoul Advertising Agency?
(A) Their intention to extend deadlines
(B) Their mistakes with bills
(C) Their plan to renew a contract
(D) Their focus on increasing prices

90. What does the woman mean when she says, "Here's the thing"?
(A) She will give a demonstration of a product.
(B) She has forgotten a password.
(C) She has found the item she was seeking.
(D) She will talk about the important thing.

91. What are the listeners asked to look at?
(A) A design specification
(B) A business contract
(C) An advertising estimate
(D) A budget for the previous year

Program	
Presenter	Time
Ms. Keith	*1:00-1:40*
Mr. Gurida	*1:50-2:30*
BREAK	*2:40-3:00*
Mr. Chris	*3:00-3:40*
Ms. Green	*3:50-4:30*

92. Where most likely is the speaker?
(A) At an electronics store
(B) At a concert hall
(C) At an opening ceremony
(D) At a training workshop

93. What are listeners asked to do?
(A) Stay silent during the break
(B) Carry their valuables with them
(C) Return any borrowed devices
(D) Share printed sheet with others

94. Look at the graphic. Who will be the second presenter?
(A) Ms. Keith
(B) Mr. Gurida
(C) Mr. Chris
(D) Ms. Green

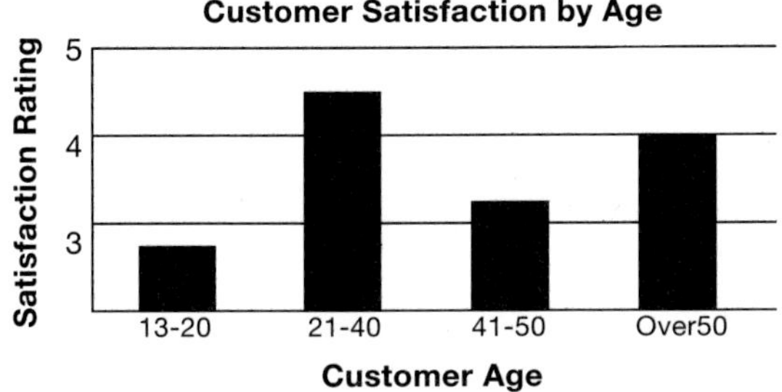

To buy:	
· **Blue Paper**	- *$ 80 full-price*
· **Red Paper**	- *$ 53 ON SALE*
· **Yellow Paper**	- *$ 45 ON SALE*
· **Orange Paper**	- *$ 68 full-price*

95. What does the speaker say she was wrong about?
(A) Online sales figures
(B) A website malfunctioning
(C) The availability of a product
(D) The cost of advertising

96. What does the speaker say is a popular website feature?
(A) Electronic billing
(B) Customer comments
(C) Free shipping
(D) E-mail notifications

97. Look at the graphic. What age group does the speaker ask Chang to look into?
(A) 13-20
(B) 21-40
(C) 41-50
(D) Over 50

98. Where is the woman calling from?
(A) An office building
(B) A supply store
(C) A bike store
(D) An advertising company

99. Look at the graphic. What price is now incorrect?
(A) $ 80
(B) $ 53
(C) $ 45
(D) $ 68

100. What most likely will happen on Tuesday?
(A) Employee training sessions will start.
(B) New equipment will be placed.
(C) A renovation will be complete.
(D) A project deadline will be extended.

READING TEST

In the Reading test, you will read a variety of texts and answer several different types of reading comprehension questions. The entire Reading test will last 75 minutes. There are three parts, and directions are given for each part. You are encouraged to answer as many questions as possible within the time allowed.

You must mark answers on the separate answer sheet. Do not write your answer in your test book.

PART 5

Directions: A word or phrase is missing in each of the sentences below. Four answer choices are given below each sentence. Select the best answer to complete the sentence. Then mark the letter (A), (B), (C), or (D) on your answer sheet.

101. You will be contacted by Mr. Albert to make an appointment for your baggage -------.
(A) deliver
(B) delivers
(C) delivered
(D) delivery

102. Ms. Rosemary suggested that she becomes quite ------- in the position of personnel director.
(A) interested
(B) interesting
(C) interests
(D) interest

103. Real estate veterans help multinational corporate clients stay within ------- budgets when renting the right office space for up to 5000 workers.
(A) their
(B) them
(C) they
(D) themselves

104. This coming Friday, Vanessa's Customized Shoes will be ------- a 30 percent off to all regular customers.
(A) notifying
(B) offering
(C) performing
(D) joining

105. Mr. Ohbama expects that Aepple's latest laptop will be a great ------- in the retail industry.
(A) to succeed
(B) success
(C) successfully
(D) succeeding

106. We apologize for the mistake in the fee charged for your furniture repair, ------- a new invoice has been enclosed with this memo.
(A) and
(B) nor
(C) yet
(D) or

107. All desserts at the Billy's Cafe are ------- prepared by a well-known patisserie Sophia Lucy.
(A) expert
(B) expertly
(C) expertise
(D) experts

108. Mr. Evan suggested in his financial analysis that gas -------, which have been steady for a while, will likely rise next month.
(A) price
(B) prices
(C) pricing
(D) priced

109. Audience members who want to leave the concert hall are requested to exit ------- in order not to interrupt the ongoing performance.
(A) quiet
(B) quietly
(C) quieter
(D) quietness

110. Among the ------- charms of Stella Star Hotel is its scenic view of the Pacific ocean.
(A) many
(B) much
(C) more
(D) most

111. The head patisserie chef in Paris Hidden Diamond has planned to add a much broader ------- to the menu.
(A) supply
(B) distribution
(C) excursion
(D) variety

112. In observance of new company policy, any frozen fruit left in the refrigerator that are not ------- within a day will be discarded.
(A) claim
(B) claims
(C) claimed
(D) claiming

113. Adelle System yesterday unveiled a miniature USB port one-quarter the size of last season's model, making it easily the ------- device on the market.
(A) brightest
(B) widest
(C) weakest
(D) smallest

114. The opening of the new resting place on National Road 45th was postponed because the initial food shipment did not ------- on time.
(A) arrive
(B) arrival
(C) arrived
(D) arriving

115. Dr. Helen was selected to reorganize Winnie Pharmaceutical company's vitamin pill development process in an ------- to boost its effectiveness.
(A) item
(B) issue
(C) advice
(D) effort

116. The LA Community College's proposal to attract more foreign students to its language immersion course will be ------- later this week.
(A) reminded
(B) reduced
(C) finalized
(D) confused

117. Customers ------- return to Perfect Wireless Broadband due to its low fees and outstanding customer service.
(A) greatly
(B) moderately
(C) mutually
(D) frequently

118. Speedy Motors executives cited poor sales as the reason for the decision ------- the 502 Alvin sports utility vehicle line.
(A) have discontinued
(B) was discontinuing
(C) will discontinue
(D) to discontinue

119. Before she came to Singapore, Ms. Catherine worked ------- a curator in a France art museum.
(A) up
(B) to
(C) from
(D) as

120. If ------- has completed the top agenda items, please let Cindy Naomi in personnel division know.
(A) himself
(B) other
(C) anyone
(D) yourself

GO ON TO THE NEXT PAGE ▶

121. Edith Sports Complex's cooling system ------- by the government's building-safety department.
(A) inspection
(B) is being inspected
(C) were inspecting
(D) inspector

122. New interns are encouraged to go over the employee handbook ------- prior to contacting human resources representatives with any questions.
(A) thoroughly
(B) incidentally
(C) relatively
(D) previously

123. Free Breeze Magazine has been a top choice in national commercial advertising ------- it was named corporate magazine of the year.
(A) instead
(B) while
(C) however
(D) since

124. Bianca Catering's menu items can differ widely from those provided online depending ------- the availability of staple ingredients in cooking.
(A) there
(B) upon
(C) entirely
(D) with

125. Every telephone call received ------- 6:00 P.M. will be returned by Ms. Isabel the following morning sharply at 9 A.M.
(A) except
(B) during
(C) between
(D) after

126. In ------- of your continued business with us, we would like to invite you and your family members or friends to an exclusive dinner at the Comfort First Hotel.
(A) comment
(B) response
(C) appreciation
(D) description

127. Nonmembers can take part in the Songwriting & Producing seminar ------- they enroll in advance.
(A) so far
(B) so that
(C) as though
(D) as long as

128. Because the new copy machine is very -------, it requires at least three workers to carry it.
(A) careful
(B) heavy
(C) busy
(D) remote

129. Light colored window shades will be removed in all company buildings ------- the next five days.
(A) about
(B) along
(C) over
(D) toward

130. For ------- in the customer satisfaction survey, regulars will receive a complimentary voucher valid for use on one medium-sized coffee.
(A) participate
(B) participates
(C) participating
(D) participated

PART 6

Directions: Read the texts that follow. A word, phrase, or sentence is missing in parts of each text. Four answer choices for each question are given below the text. Select the best answer to complete the text. Then mark the letter (A), (B), (C), or (D) on your answer sheet.

Questions 131-134 refer to the following notice.

To all assembly line workers,

As you probably know, we have some final pending decisions about the installation of panels to car doors. ------, this process is completed by hand.
       131.

As of June 10, it will be substituted for automatic robots. ------ will tightly fasten side panels to
                                                             132.
the outside of each vehicle's doors.

In addition, the interior panels are no longer made up of a single piece, but of ------ parts.
                                                                                133.

Training sessions for assembly line workers will be scheduled shortly. ------
                                                                      134.

131. (A) At present
(B) To illustrate
(C) Even so
(D) In conclusion

132. (A) It
(B) You
(C) They
(D) What

133. (A) multiple
(B) genuine
(C) new
(D) sincere

134. (A) You will find the exact time schedule and place on the company's website.
(B) Robots are used to dig a long tunnel.
(C) Night shift workers should follow safety regulations.
(D) Discount train tickets are available for those who are under 25.

GO ON TO THE NEXT PAGE ➤

To: All employees

The Beyond the Rainbow Ltd.'s board of directors is ------ to mention that chief financial officer
135.
Lois Cho Shang has been chosen as interim president of the organization shortly after the
resignation of Violet Lucy.

The board and staff fully appreciate Ms. Lucy's dedication to our mission during the last
ten years and wish her the best luck in her future endeavors. In the meantime, a personnel
committee searching for a new permanent president has been formed. Ms. Shang will resume
her duties as C.F.O ------ a new president is named.
136.

Please feel free to contact me if you have any questions or concerns as we ------ transitions in
137.
leadership here at Beyond the Rainbow Ltd. ------
138.

Sincerely,

Julie Kim, Communications Director

135. (A) pleased
(B) pleasing
(C) pleasant
(D) pleasure

136. (A) so
(B) when
(C) because
(D) although

137. (A) question
(B) reconsider
(C) undergo
(D) avoid

138. (A) Colorful rainbow is hanging in the
mountain.
(B) More time will be needed to complete
the interim financial report.
(C) You can reach me at my extension
4885 during office hours.
(D) Courtesy buses to and from the
airport stop running.

Florence Convention Center

Exhibitor Access

Deliverers carrying supplies to the Florence Convention Center's exhibition hall should use the Emerson Street entrance to the parking garage. Clearance at this entry is 2.5 meters. Any vehicles that exceed this ------ must make deliveries through the west gate of the building.
139.

Please plan ------ to avoid the need to refurbish your company display booth.
140.

Vendors who require the use of the west gate while the event is under way could ------ significant wait times. ------
141.
142.

139. (A) target
(B) height
(C) goal
(D) weight

140. (A) around
(B) again
(C) ahead
(D) near

141. (A) face
(B) facing
(C) to face
(D) faces

142. (A) Business hours are Monday through Friday.
(B) This exhibition event will continue until the end of this month.
(C) They expect approximately half an hour of mean waiting time.
(D) Light refreshment was served and raffle tickets were distributed.

GO ON TO THE NEXT PAGE

From: Naomi Irene <airene@pellcraft.com>

To: Sophia Isabel <sisabel@pellcraft.com>

Date: August 24

Re: Your suggestion

Dear Sophia,

Lately, you suggested that we recycle the wood shavings ------ when we manufacture our
143.
chopsticks by selling the material as bedding for farm animals.

This idea has been reviewed and found to be ------. Thus, a plan to package this sawdust and
144.
sell it to farm owners will be implemented two to three months from today. ------ recycling
145.
process will result in greater profits for our company, and potential benefits for our environment.
Also, additional incentives will be rewarded to all workers. ------
146.

Please accept our congratulations and gratitude for your recommendation.

Sincerely,

Naomi Irene

President

Pellcraft Chopsticks Makers

---

143. (A) are produced
(B) to produce
(C) producing
(D) produced

144. (A) adapted
(B) compliant
(C) sincere
(D) practical

145. (A) This
(B) His
(C) Then
(D) Her

146. (A) Salary will be commensurate with
your previous work experience.
(B) Various farm animals in factory
farming will be treated better.
(C) Recycling to protect polar regions is
essential.
(D) All employees will get this extra
allowance in their next paycheck.

PART 7

Directions: In this part you will read a selection of texts, such as magazine and newpaper articles, e-mails, and instant messages. Each text or st of texts is followed by several questions. Select the best answer to complete the text. Then mark the letter (A), (B), (C), or (D) on your answer sheet.

Questions 147-148 refer to the following information.

You have purchased an At the Corner black leather jacket from Golden Breeze Department. All of our products are imported from Naples, Italy. They are woven from 100% dark leather that has been dyed by hand using a process which is gentle on the leather and not harmful to the environment.

Variations in color and marking result naturally from the process of hand-dyeing. These variations make each leather products some unique works of art. Dry-cleaning is highly recommended to reduce a wear and tear and to keep their shape.

147. Where would this information most likely be found?
(A) In a brochure about traveling to Italy
(B) In a magazine about silk merchandise
(C) On a bottle of hair dye
(D) On a tag included with leather products

148. What is mentioned about At the Corner products?
(A) They are sold mainly in Naples.
(B) They are made from a selection of materials.
(C) They may have uneven coloration.
(D) They can be easily washed by washing machine.

The Mega Sale Market always welcomes your feedback! If you have a comment, concern, or suggestion, please fill out this comment card and place it in the mailbox. Postage is unnecessary.

Name: Amy Dustin

Suggestion:
You have a talented team who put much effort on developing effective marketing strategies to appeal to customers. And therefore I enjoy shopping in your store. It would be great if you could make your shop freely accessible online. I work in a hospital as a nurse and I often work a night shift. Your normal business hours are 10 to 10 so it is sometimes hard for me to buy the necessary things in your shop after work.

The Star Super Store already opened a premium online shopping mall. If you start doing this as well, I'll be much more likely to be your regulars in the new year. Thanks!

149. What can be inferred about Ms. Dustin?
(A) She is a Mega Sale Market customer.
(B) She wants to apply for an opening in a hospital.
(C) She plans to upgrade her desktop computer.
(D) She usually works at home.

150. What does Ms. Dustin suggest that the Mega Sale Market should do?
(A) Hire more experienced sales clerks
(B) Open an online store
(C) Include news from the Star Super Store
(D) Sell the newspaper at the market

151. What is mentioned in this form?
(A) Star Super Store closes at 10.
(B) Dustin plans to retire within six months but nothing is sure yet.
(C) Amy wasn't able to shop at Mega Sale Market after work during night shift.
(D) Mega Sale Market has operated its online shopping mall for quite a long time.

Winnie
Rachel, are you busy this afternoon?   11:20

Rachel
Yes, a little bit. Why do you ask?   11:21

Winnie
I want you to check my sales report for any spelling
errors before the presentation.   11:23

Rachel
Hmm. I have work to do now. But I will have some time
after lunch around 2.   11:24
Is that okay for you?   11:25

Winnie
You bet!   11:26
Thank you for your help. Come and meet me at my
office at 2.   11:27

152. What is suggested about Mr. Winnie?
(A) He has met Ms. Rachel before to
   confirm the time and date.
(B) He prepares for some documents.
(C) He cancelled his lunch appointment
   with his client.
(D) He will meet Rachel in her room at 2.

153. At 11:26, what does Mr. Winnie mean
when he writes, "You bet"?
(A) He agrees to have lunch with Rachel.
(B) He knows he made a mistake on his
   sales report.
(C) He is certain that he can complete
   the sales report.
(D) He has confirmed he can meet her as
   mentioned above.

GO ON TO THE NEXT PAGE

April 24
Amanda Rosemary
Fantastic Parade Band
2580 Glasgow Point Blvd
Fayetteville, Arkansas 790310

Dear Ms. Rosemary,

Congratulations! Your parade band has been chosen to perform in the Fayetteville Spring March. The parade will begin at 1:00 P.M on Sunday, May 5. Please tell your musicians to arrive at the city hall no later than 12:00 P.M. Performers will gather near the main entrance of the city hall to start and then head west on Fayetteville Parkway, past the national museum, and toward the Memphis and Arkansas Bridge. The marching will end at Bluestone Park, where shuttle buses back to the city hall will be available.

We look forward to seeing you there!

Sincerely,

Bianca Cecil
Bianca Cecil
Event Coordinator

154. Who most likely is Ms. Rosemary?
(A) A bandleader
(B) A bus conductor
(C) A city hall official
(D) A parade organizer

155. Where will the parade begin?
(A) At the convention center
(B) Under the Memphis and Arkansas Bridge
(C) In Bluestone Park
(D) At the city hall

Weekly Movie News

Invisible Invader is a new horror film with an award-winning cast star Sam Albert in the leading role of Dean Winchester, a priest who exorcised evil spirit from beautiful young girls. Directed by Baxter Farrell, this highly thrilling movie presents nonstop action from start to finish and is certain to be a box-office hit. Look for it in theaters on Thursday, January 24.

156. Who is Sam Albert?
(A) A movie director
(B) A priest
(C) An actor
(D) An awarding winning writer

157. According to the article, what will occur on January 24?
(A) A movie script will be finalized.
(B) A movie will be released.
(C) A non-stop flight will be available.
(D) An award will be granted.

GO ON TO THE NEXT PAGE

Language Immersion Program
The fun classes for shy people
The 5th anniversary is coming
Monday July 1
20% off your registration fees
Enjoy refreshment, prize drawings, and games
Bring the whole family

At Language Immersion Program, we meet all your needs. Help make you fluent in at least one language from English and Spanish to Korean and Chinese. And now you can enroll in more than 30 institutes across the country.

Visit LIP.com to print out a coupon. You must present it to the receptionist to receive a discount. Previously or currently attended classes are ineligible. The coupon is valid until July 25 only.

158. What is being promoted?
(A) Sales on online games
(B) A discount sales on language learning class
(C) Tickets to fly to England, Spain, or Korea
(D) A store's grand opening celebration

159. What is indicated about Language Immersion Program?
(A) It has multiple locations.
(B) It organizes sports games.
(C) It sells an array of refreshments.
(D) It recruits language teachers.

160. How can customers get the 20% savings on classes?
(A) By entering a game contest
(B) By registering for a class well in advance
(C) By spending $ 30
(D) By showing a coupon

From: cards@teagarden.co.uk	**To:** hdaria@cardiff-office.co.uk
Subject: Your cards	**Date:** 10 March

Dear customer,

Thank you for signing up for the Tea Garden's silver membership, the TG Silver.

Your membership card will be sent to you within a week at the following address.

Helen Daria

33 Ocean-view Road

Cardiff OF 10 3NP

If the address listed above is not correct, please access profile at www.teagarden.co.uk as soon as possible and make the necessary changes.

Your TG Silver membership allows you to take advantage of discount offer on domestic and international tea. There are also hundreds of china teapots to choose from, and more are added each year, so you're sure to find your favorites.

If you want to buy herbal teas before your card arrives, simply mention your membership number (TG-800109) when you make a purchase.

Visit the website to start taking advantage of all your membership has to offer!

Sincerely yours,

The Tea Garden members

161. What is the main purpose of the e-mail?
(A) To respond to a customer complaint
(B) To export organically grown herbs
(C) To confirm a registration
(D) To notify card holders of a new company policy

162. What is mentioned as something that Ms. Daria can do on the website?
(A) Recommend herbal tea
(B) Make a list of her favorite items
(C) Go over customers' comment on herbal teas
(D) Update her contact information

163. What is mentioned about the membership number?
(A) It is valid exclusively for herbal tea within the United Kingdom.
(B) It can be used by Ms. Daria's family.
(C) It is valid only for one year.
(D) It can be used at once.

GO ON TO THE NEXT PAGE ▶

Cordelia Glassware Manufacturer
7000 Fifth Street Avenue
Belgium, 82479

Mr. Adolph Corby
925 State of Montana
Suite A building 3542

Dear, Mr. Corby

We regret to notify you that the following item you ordered on June 7 is currently not in stock and moreover is no longer being manufactured. —[1]—
Item #201 glassware (2L), Qty: 5, $ 12.50/each —[2]—
Item #202 glassware (2L), $ 13.00/each —[3]—
The only difference between the new glassware and the old one is that the new one is made of even thicker glass. If you would like us to change your original order to include the new glassware item number 202, please contact us at 801-352-9256. All other products listed in your initial order are available and therefore will be delivered as scheduled. —[4]—

Thank you for your business.

Connie Dollis
Customer Service Specialist, Cordelia Glassware Manufacturer

164. What is the problem in Mr. Corby's order?
(A) His delivery information is incorrect.
(B) His payment has not been received in full.
(C) Some items have been delivered in damaged condition while in transit.
(D) A product he ordered is unavailable.

165. According to the letter, why should Mr. Corby call the company?
(A) To ask for an updated product catalog
(B) To approve a change to his order
(C) To receive a refund
(D) To make a delivery of glassware

166. What is suggested about Cordelia Glassware Manufacturer?
(A) The company has a discontinued model.
(B) It has sent wrong glassware to Adolph Corby.
(C) All orders are processed automatically.
(D) Its main office was relocated in State of Montana.

167. In which of the positions marked [1], [2], [3] and [4] does the following sentence best belong?

"In our product line, we have replaced the item listed above with a similar one, which appears below."

(A) [1]
(B) [2]
(C) [3]
(D) [4]

Green Clover Clothing

will be holding
its yearly "Bag of Clothes" sale
—[1]—
Thursday, 25 October
from 9 A.M. to 9 P.M.

—[2]—
Our winter merchandise
will be coming in soon!
—[3]—

Make a purchase of a shopping bag for € 50
and fill the bag
with as many last season items
as you can fit.
Sit down and enjoy complimentary coffee
or make a purchase of
our freshly baked cookies at half price.
—[4]—

The shop will be open for an extended period of time during the sale.
Registration is requested to attend. Please stop by the shop to complete a
registration form or fill it out online at www.greencloverclothing.com.

We hope to see you there!

168. What is the main purpose of the sale?
(A) To attract new clients
(B) To promote a new cloth
(C) To commemorate its 9th anniversary
(D) To make room for new merchandise

169. What can be suggested about Green
Clover Clothing?
(A) Its baked goods are offered to
customers on the house.
(B) It is usually closed on Thursdays.
(C) It has an in-house coffee shop.
(D) Its featured clothes cost € 50 each.

170. What are customers encouraged to do if
they want to take part in the event?
(A) Arrive early
(B) Fill out the form
(C) Donate a bag of clothes
(D) Bring their own shopping bag

171. In which of the positions marked [1], [2],
[3] and [4] does the following sentence
best belong?

"Help us make space on our shelves!"

(A) [1]
(B) [2]
(C) [3]
(D) [4]

GO ON TO THE NEXT PAGE

To: kdorothy@gmail.com
From: inaomi@mae.org
Date: April 20
Subject: Modern Art Festival

Dear Ms. Dorothy

We are excited that you will be participating in this year's Modern Art Festival, which is scheduled for Sunday, September 9, at Modern Art Exhibition. We received your full participation fee and you have been assigned to Booth 27.

Exhibitors should plan to arrive precisely at 8 A.M. Upon arrival, please sign in at the reception desk, which is at the west entrance. Volunteers will then escort you to the unloading spot, where you can move your items from the vehicle to your booth. Unloading and putting up booth must be completed by 10 A.M. sharp. After unloading, please park your car in the lot on Jefferson Avenue. We expect a large crowd and the parking areas at the exhibition are reserved for festival goers.

Please be reminded that participants assigned to Booth 26-30 will have to transport their merchandise a distance of approximately 300 meters. A limited number of carts are on hand, but most of them are too small. If you are assigned to this area, we require you to bring your own cart and a person to aid you with carrying your items.

We look forward to seeing you on Sunday.

Isabell Naomi
Program Coordinator
Modern Art Festival

172. What will Ms. Dorothy most likely to do
at the Modern Art Festival?
(A) Exhibit artworks
(B) Help participants carry some
merchandise
(C) Train volunteer workers
(D) Direct festival goers to the parking lot

173. What should Ms. Dorothy do first when
she arrives?
(A) Pay participation fee
(B) Check an unloading list
(C) Report directly to booth 27
(D) Go to the reception desk

174. According to the letter, what is prevented
after 10 A.M.?
(A) New enrollment
(B) Assign booth
(C) Unloading from vehicles
(D) Renting carts

175. Why is Ms. Dorothy requested to bring
someone to assist her?
(A) Most of the carts are out of order in
the present.
(B) She is not familiar with exhibition.
(C) She must carry items a long way.
(D) Modern Art Exhibition is
short-handed.

GO ON TO THE NEXT PAGE

From: k_mia@redvanilla.com
TO: alyssakayla@gmail.com
Date: January 9
Subject: Delightful News

Dear Ms. Kayla

As one of our most loyal customers, you will be glad to know that during the month of February, Red Vanilla is bringing back the popular "3 for $ 13 Lunch Special." This special includes an appetizer, entrée, and a dessert from our tasty menu – a $ 100 value for just $ 13.

You can select one item from each category:

Choice of Appetizers
Onion Ring with blue cheese Salad of the day Fried shrimp

Choice of Entrées
Tuna sandwich Chicken & mashed potatoes Seafood risotto Walnut-crushed eggplant

Choice of Desserts
Carrot cake Chocolate mousse with raspberry Ginseng ice cream

If you are interested in joining us for healthy lunch, please visit our website at www.redvanilla. com to make a reservation. This offer is available from 11:30 to 2:00 P.M. Monday through Thursday exclusively.

We hope to see you soon,

Kaitlyn Mia
Owner & Executive Chef
Red Vanilla

<table>
<tr><td>From:</td><td>alyssakayla@gmail.com</td><td>Date:</td><td>February 2, Tuesday</td></tr>
<tr><td>To:</td><td>k_mia@redvanilla.com</td><td>Subject:</td><td>Thanks</td></tr>
</table>

Dear Mia,

I would like to express my gratitude for your excellent service and delicious food.

The appetizer I had in your restaurant was so fresh that I strongly recommend it to other customers. The vinegar dressing encouraged me to take second helping of vegetables. The main entree was doubtless impeccable. Moist bread enhanced the taste of blackened tuna. Dessert proved that the chef was the perfection of genius. I've never heard of the food before the chef recommended it to me. The ginseng and jujubes in vanilla ice cream boosted my vigor.

The only disadvantage I felt yesterday was the lack of seats for dinners. The opening day was packed with lovers of your restaurant so it was hard for some to find any tables.

Alyssa Kayla

176. Why did Mia send the e-mail?
(A) To promote upcoming cooking demonstrations
(B) To announce a recent change in business hours
(C) To introduce a new award-winning chef
(D) To give information concerning a special promotion

177. What can be inferred about Ms. Kayla in the first e-mail?
(A) She is a former employer of Red Vanilla.
(B) She has recommended Red Vanilla to Mia.
(C) She is a regular customer of Red Vanilla.
(D) She made a lunch reservation at Red Vanilla.

178. What is indicated about Red Vanilla?
(A) It is closed on Thursdays.
(B) It takes reservations online.
(C) It has several branches nationwide.
(D) It is famous for its desserts.

179. Which food did not Kayla enjoy in Lunch Special?
(A) Salad of the day
(B) Tuna sandwich
(C) Seafood risotto
(D) Ginseng ice cream

180. What problem did Kayla mention in her e-mail?
(A) Vinegar dressing made the vegetable withered.
(B) Ginseng ice cream had a slightly bitter taste.
(C) There were not enough space for many visitors.
(D) Lunch Special was more expensive than the advertised price.

GO ON TO THE NEXT PAGE →

Louisiana Skyline Residence
Rentals available
Spacious one-and two-bedroom apartments
with modern kitchens and elegant dining rooms

Promotional offer for new residents
(must sign a two-year lease to qualify)

One-bedroom unit: $ 1500/month
Two-bedroom unit: $ 2000/month
Inclusive of air-conditioning and heating costs

Tenants get access to an on-site laundry room and a fully furnished lounge area and recreation room.

28 Louisiana Pl.
Louisiana, OFF HJW SHG
802-241-7819
www.skylineresidence.lo

To:	Vanessa Velvet
From:	Adolph Edith
Subject:	Recent Update
Date:	10 March
Attachment:	Apartment_612A

Dear Mr. Velvet:

I have all of the paperwork ready for Katie Kim. She is scheduled to arrive this afternoon to sign the one-year lease contract for apartment 612A, and she will bring a check of $ 1,500 for the first month's rent. I will put the completed paperwork and the check on your drawer this evening.

Could you communicate to maintenance department that this apartment needs to be ready by 10 April? A work list that should be done is attached to this e-mail. Please be reminded that Ms. Kim chose the living room for complimentary painting. (color #472, pure white)

We have just one more apartment available for rent. I have some appointments tomorrow to show the two-bedroom unit. I expect to get a lease signed before the end of this week. Once that happens, we will be at full occupancy.

Thank you.

Sincerely,

Adolph Edith

181. What is mentioned about the apartments for rent?
(A) They each have a dining area.
(B) They are equipped with fully renovated bathroom.
(C) They give complimentary paintings to renters.
(D) They each have a washing machine in the unit.

182. What is suggested about Ms. Kim?
(A) She has selected a one bed room apartment.
(B) She renewed her lease contract for one more year.
(C) She will move into her new apartment on March 10th.
(D) She insisted that an air conditioning and heating should be replaced.

183. What is Ms. Velvet requested to do?
(A) Fill in some documents
(B) Give information to maintenance staff
(C) Make an appointment with Mr. Edith
(D) Renegotiate the rental costs with a tenant

184. In the e-mail, the word "expect" in paragraph 3, line 2, is closest in meaning to
(A) solidify
(B) anticipate
(C) promote
(D) recommend

185. What does Mr. Edith suggest about apartments at Louisiana Skyline Residence?
(A) Their cooling system will be upgraded.
(B) Their yearly rental costs will be raised in April.
(C) They will all be rented shortly.
(D) They will all be painted pure white.

GO ON TO THE NEXT PAGE ▸

Adagio Computers Community Forum

Adagio PRO 1 Ultra is losing wireless internet connectivity.

Post by Alexander Lee
August 15, 8:23 A.M.

After using the Adagio MAX model for two years, I purchased the new Adagio PRO 1 Ultra laptop this Monday. For the most part, I am very satisfied with the new one. However, I am having difficulty keeping the model connected to my Internet network. The laptop is able to connect up to the network, but then following two minutes or so online, it gets disconnected. I have experimented with some remedies, including restarting my PRO 1 Ultra and reconnecting with the network. Nothing works at all.

Has anyone else experienced this? I am not sure whether the problem is with all PRO 1 laptops or just with the only one I purchased. I know my network itself is fine. My siblings, who own laptops of other brands, stay connected to the network without any problem.

Adagio Computers Community Forum
>>>>> Re: Adagio PRO 1 Ultra is losing wireless internet connectivity.

Post by Tony McGuire
August 15, 9:34 A.M.

Hi Alexander,

I just purchased PRO 1 Ultra laptop from Adagio for the first time. Unfortunately, I and several of my coworkers experienced the same problem like yours. I tried adjusting the Internet settings, inspecting and reconnecting the power cord, and restarting the computer but without any luck.

I then called the Adagio Computers Service desk. A technician named Steven was able to help straightaway. I attached the letter Steven sent me containing his direction. I hope this will address your problem.

<table>
<tr><td>From:</td><td>Steven Buck <steven@adagio.com></td><td>To:</td><td>Tony McGuire <tony@gmail.com></td></tr>
</table>

I am really sorry about the inconvenience you and your colleagues have experienced. I am the head manager of customer satisfaction department in Adagio and I can correct your problem in no time.

First of all, go to our website. All you have to do is to download and install the "update" (that is, save the file onto your laptop computers, open it, and then follow a series of messages). You can download from the software update page on the Adagio Computers website at no charge. Once you install the "update," you should have no problem remaining connected to the network.

Once again, I am sorry about the inconvenience.

Steven Buck
Head manager of customer satisfaction department

---

186. In the reply, the word "called" in paragraph 2, line 1 is closest in meaning to
(A) named
(B) appointed
(C) proved
(D) contacted

187. What problem did Alexander mention in his website post?
(A) He received the wrong computer.
(B) He was charged the wrong price.
(C) The delivery time was longer than promised.
(D) He witnessed a problem with internet access.

188. What is most likely true about Tony?
(A) The problem with internet connection was rectified by his coworkers.
(B) He sent a letter to Steven for the first time.
(C) It was his first time to use the laptop from Adagio.
(D) He claimed a refund for computer malfunction.

189. What do Alexander and Tony have in common?
(A) They are colleagues in Adagio Computer.
(B) They all have PRO 1 Ultra laptop.
(C) They once had Adagio MAX model for two years.
(D) They received letters from Steven, head manager of customer satisfaction in Adagio.

190. What does Steven ask Tony to do?
(A) Call a technician from Adagio
(B) Bring the computer to a local store near him
(C) Go to website and download the "update"
(D) Change the internet service provider

GO ON TO THE NEXT PAGE

September 1 - What is the secret of living well?

written by Elizabeth Lucy

Nicholas Hunter, founder of the Follow the One Institution, asked himself the question five years ago. He relates, "I talked with a woman on a train who got absorbed in reading a biography of Agatha Della, the famous artist. The story had somehow transported this woman back to her own childhood. I realized then how the life stories of renowned figures are often interrelated with our own experiences."

After he returned from that trip, Mr. Hunter launched Followtheone.com, an award-winning blog with more than three million readers. The website features thousands of stories about a majority of famous figures and a new story is added each day. "Success has come because of the power of these stories," Mr. Hunter says. "People understand their own lives better after reading about the personal experiences of notable members of society."

To find out more, visit www.Followtheone.com/notablepeople.

From: wdvaunt@followtheone.co.ca
To: elucy@mostmagazine.com
Subject: Error
Date: September 5

Hi, Ms. Lucy

I just wanted to thank you for your article on September 1st. However I wondered why the number of subscribers has been unchanged since the article you wrote came in the local newspaper.

I have found some errors in your story. Our website address is followtheone.co.ca but not Followtheone.com. Would you address this problem correctly?

And we will be launching a print magazine called Enlightening People. This new publication will feature inspiring stories about celebrities alongside those of remarkable everyday people.

Winnie De Vaunt
Secretary of Nicholas Hunter

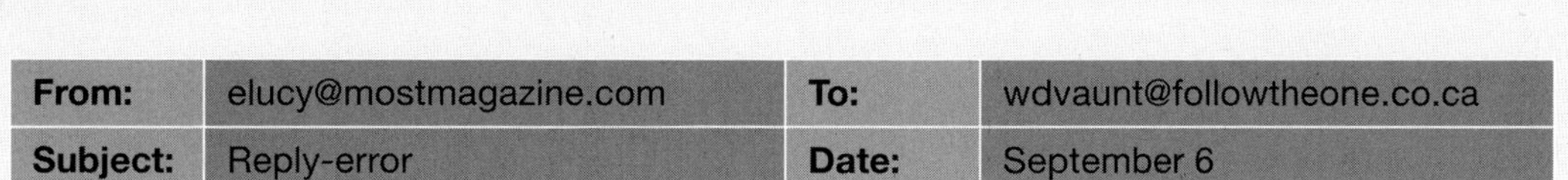

| **From:** | elucy@mostmagazine.com | **To:** | wdvaunt@followtheone.co.ca |
| **Subject:** | Reply-error | **Date:** | September 6 |

After receiving your letter and checking the article, I immediately corrected my mistakes. I am really sorry about the error I made. You can check the revised article on the website, www.mostmagazine.com/article24.business.

I am interested in your new publication, Enlightening People you mentioned in your recent letter. I want to make an arrangement for an interview with you. Can you make time for this interview this Friday at noon? You can make it in a different time if you like. Please let my assistant, Sarah know when you are available.

Thanks,

Elizabeth Lucy

191. What's the main purpose of the article?
(A) To recommend a hidden tourist attraction
(B) To describe the work of Mr. Hunter
(C) To provide advice for writers
(D) To subscribe to new publication

192. According to Mr. Hunter, why are stories so appealing?
(A) They help the readers better understand their lives.
(B) They are written by well-known celebrities.
(C) They are easy to follow and read.
(D) They familiarize readers with various blog styles.

193. What can be inferred about Enlightening People?
(A) The publication will be released soon.
(B) It features touching stories about celebrities exclusively.
(C) Readers can view it on its website.
(D) Subscription fees are free of charge to every magazine editor.

194. In the first e-mail, what does Mr. Winnie say about the article?
(A) It is recommended by remarkable people.
(B) It will be reprinted in a book.
(C) It has some crucial errors that affects the number of subscribers.
(D) It will appear in a national newspaper soon.

195. What does Elizabeth want Winnie to do?
(A) To make some time for an interview about the new publication
(B) To revise some errors in the article
(C) To interview potential job candidates
(D) To make a phone call to Nicholas Hunter

GO ON TO THE NEXT PAGE

Thank you for contracting with Excellent Partner. We are happy to be your choice for corporate environmental standards certification of your facility and look forward to working with you.

As we discussed before, the audit will determine whether or not your company is in observance of government regulations governing clean air, clean water, and waste disposal. Four main categories to be covered are attached in this letter.

Ratings for every category will be included in the report along with an overall rating of your business. We will perform separate audits and ratings for your manufacturing plant, repository and shipping center.

As you already know, the audit period lasts at least two weeks and must take place when all operations are running smoothly and normally. On your enrollment application, you requested that the audit happen during the last two weeks of July. This time frame works well for us. Unless I hear from you otherwise, I will assume that this is the best time to schedule environmental assessment of your facility.

Please call me at your earliest convenience to review the details of how to be ready for the audit.

Sincerely,

Mr. Evan
Excellent Partner

Excellent Partner
always with you

environmental standards certification
of
Green Technology

Manufacturing plant / Repository / Shipping Center			
	Rating A	Rating B	Rating C
General practices			
The quality of discharged air			
The quality of discharged water			
Waste removal and recycling			
Overall			

TO: Farrel_Lautner@greentechnology.com **FROM:** Max_Wahlberg@greentechnology.com

SUBJECT: Third quarter schedule **DATE:** July 1

ATTACHMENT: 3qschedule.pdf

Dear Mr. Lautner

I have enclosed the current draft of the company scheduled for July, August, and September. Please be reminded that staff in our repository will need to work overtime during these months depending on the plastic orders from China. We expect the orders to come in by the end of this week at the latest, at which point we should be able to finalize the schedule. All other existing orders have been finalized and entered into the schedule.

At our last meeting, you said that we might add to the schedule. I have added the July security training sessions on it already, but could you let me know what else I should add? I want to forward the schedule to the regional managers by the end of the next week.

Dwayne Douglas

196. Why did Mr. Evan write the letter?
(A) To attract a potential client
(B) To answer a customer request for information
(C) To confirm a proposed schedule
(D) To remind changes to a work procedure

197. What service does Excellent Partner provide?
(A) Searching for manufacturing and warehousing staff
(B) Preparing financial reports for technology institution
(C) Training assembly line workers
(D) Rating how well companies comply with government rules

198. According to the e-mail, what will most likely take place next month in the warehouse?
(A) Some employees will be working longer hours.
(B) Some automatic equipment will be installed.
(C) Waste materials will be properly handled and protected for recycling.
(D) Copies of the company calendar will be sent to all workers.

199. Which categories will not be covered in the audit?
(A) General Practice
(B) The quality of discharged air
(C) Waste container
(D) Clean water

200. What will Ms. Lautner probably say in her response to the e-mail?
(A) Manufacturing facilities must get ready for increased business opportunities.
(B) An audit of the company must be added to the company calendar.
(C) A security training must be arranged for August.
(D) Plastic orders from China will be completely filled.

[점수 그래프]

LC Score

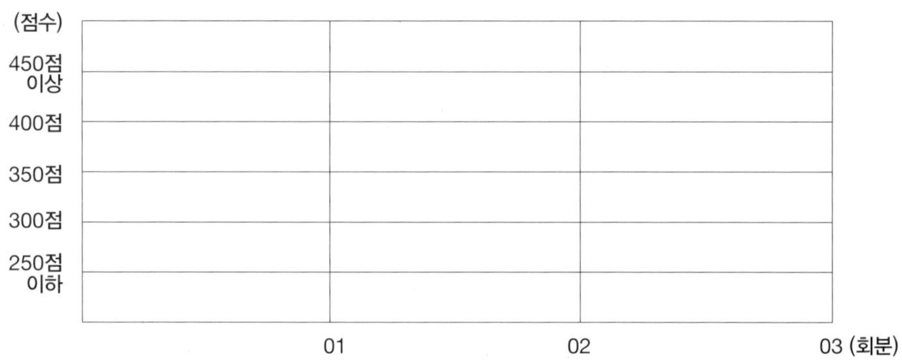

RC Score

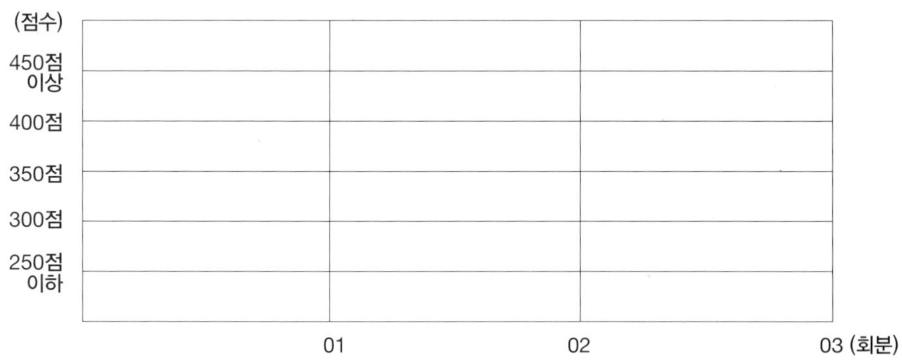

ACTUAL TEST

03

LISTENING TEST

In the listening test, you will be asked to demonstrate how well you understand spoken English. The entire listening test will last approximately 45 minutes. There are four parts, and directions are given for each part. You must mark your answers on the separate answer sheet. Do not write your answers in the test book.

PART 1

Directions: For each question in this part, you will hear four statements about a picture in your test book. When you hear the statements, you must select the one statement that best describes what you see in the picture. Then find the number of the question on your answer sheet and mark your answer. The statements will not be printed in your test book and will be spoken only one time.

Sample Answer
(A) ● (C) (D)

Example

Statement (B), "She's making a presentation," is the best description of the picture. So you should select answer (B) and mark it on your answer sheet.

1.

2.

3.

mOre
SAVINGS
every day
$2.98 kg
$1.88 ea
$7.98
$3.48
KIPFLER POTATO
$4.98 kg
POTATO SWEET

4.

5.

6.

PART 2

Directions: You will hear a question or statement and three responses spoken in English. They will not be printed in your text book and will be spoken only one time. Select the best response to the question or statement and mark the letter (A), (B), or (C) on your answer sheet.

7. Mark your answer on your answer sheet.

8. Mark your answer on your answer sheet.

9. Mark your answer on your answer sheet.

10. Mark your answer on your answer sheet.

11. Mark your answer on your answer sheet.

12. Mark your answer on your answer sheet.

13. Mark your answer on your answer sheet.

14. Mark your answer on your answer sheet.

15. Mark your answer on your answer sheet.

16. Mark your answer on your answer sheet.

17. Mark your answer on your answer sheet.

18. Mark your answer on your answer sheet.

19. Mark your answer on your answer sheet.

20. Mark your answer on your answer sheet.

21. Mark your answer on your answer sheet.

22. Mark your answer on your answer sheet.

23. Mark your answer on your answer sheet.

24. Mark your answer on your answer sheet.

25. Mark your answer on your answer sheet.

26. Mark your answer on your answer sheet.

27. Mark your answer on your answer sheet.

28. Mark your answer on your answer sheet.

29. Mark your answer on your answer sheet.

30. Mark your answer on your answer sheet.

31. Mark your answer on your answer sheet.

PART 3

Directions: You will hear some conversations between two or more people. You will be asked to answer three questions about what the speakers say in each conversation. Select the best response to each question and mark the letter (A), (B), (C), or (D) on your answer sheet. The conversations will not be printed in your test book and will be spoken only one time.

32. What is the man inquiring about?
(A) A cell phone case
(B) A wide screen TV
(C) A insurance policy
(D) A cellular phone

33. What does the man mean when he says, "Oh, that's great"?
(A) He is aware of cellular's feature.
(B) He receives a discount.
(C) He is satisfied with an item selection.
(D) He wants shop's newsletter.

34. What does the woman encourage the man to take?
(A) An employment contract
(B) A discount coupon
(C) A product manual
(D) A store newsletter

Room No.	Room Price
3rd floor(301-315)	$ 399
4th floor(401-415)	$ 499
5th floor(501-515)	$ 599
6th floor(601-615)	$ 699

35. Why is the man calling?
(A) To get directions from the hotel
(B) To ask for a refund
(C) To change a reservation
(D) To check a confirmation number

36. What will the woman e-mail the man?
(A) A confirmation information
(B) A discounted coupon
(C) An application form
(D) A complete list of menu options

37. Look at the graphic. Which floor will the man stay?
(A) 3rd floor
(B) 4th floor
(C) 5th floor
(D) 6th floor

GO ON TO THE NEXT PAGE

38. Who most likely is the woman?
(A) An award-winning florist
(B) A card designer
(C) A photographer
(D) A postal worker

39. What can't the man find?
(A) A valid credit card
(B) A delivery notice
(C) A trip itinerary
(D) A mailing list

40. What does the woman request the man to bring with him?
(A) Proof of receipt
(B) An account number
(C) Photo identification
(D) Some office supplies

Date	Class description
Monday Morning	vanilla macaroon
Tuesday Afternoon	dark chocolate cake
Friday Morning	strawberry cup cake
Saturday Afternoon	snowman cookie

41. What does the woman want to do at the store?
(A) Display her signature dishes
(B) Interview an advertising expert
(C) Apply for a cooking job
(D) Register for a class

42. What problem does the man mention?
(A) A room is not big enough.
(B) An instructor is not available right now.
(C) A kitchen utensil is missing.
(D) A cup of chocolate is out of stock.

43. Look at the graphic. Which day will the woman register for?
(A) Monday Morning
(B) Tuesday Afternoon
(C) Friday Morning
(D) Saturday Afternoon

44. Where does the man work for?
(A) An architecture firm in Mountain Park
(B) A construction company
(C) A real estate agency
(D) A multinational bank

45. What is the woman satisfied with?
(A) A house is conveniently located.
(B) A job position is opening shortly.
(C) Housing funding has been finally approved.
(D) Some renovations have been done as scheduled.

46. What is the woman planning to do next week?
(A) Fill out some documents
(B) View a property
(C) Attend a housing fair
(D) Make a reservation in advance

47. What does the man say will happen today?
(A) A thorough inspection will take place.
(B) Repair work will begin.
(C) A maintenance department will stop by.
(D) Some equipment will be installed.

48. Why does the woman say, "It's a piece of cake"?
(A) It is hard to believe, but it is actually a cake.
(B) She is eating a piece of cake.
(C) It is not a whole cake but a piece of cake.
(D) The work is easy to accomplish.

49. What will the woman do after the talk?
(A) Put out a sign
(B) Make a piece of cake
(C) Extend business hours
(D) Open the door

50. What are the speakers scheduled to do?
  (A) Arrange a filing system
  (B) Review some resume
  (C) Schedule a training seminar
  (D) Brainstorm a budget in sales

51. What does the man imply?
  (A) Dividing some work
  (B) Clarifying a complete procedure
  (C) Extending a deadline
  (D) Putting an advertisement on a web

52. What does the man expect the woman to do?
  (A) Go over a journal article
  (B) Develop an application design
  (C) Hand in a resume
  (D) Print out some documents

---

53. What is the woman's occupation?
  (A) A festival organizer
  (B) An event planner
  (C) A reporter
  (D) An accountant

54. What problem is described in the festival?
  (A) A venue is very crowded.
  (B) A trip has been called off.
  (C) Passes are much too expensive.
  (D) Musical performances do not begin on time.

55. According to the conversation, what do the men think about the festival?
  (A) They both think it is better than previous one.
  (B) The performers all live nearby.
  (C) There are many food selections.
  (D) The men have voiced different opinions.

56. What is the man interested in making a purchase?
  (A) Office stationery
  (B) Advertising space in a newspaper
  (C) Promotional products
  (D) Bathroom tiles

57. How can the man receive a discount?
  (A) By donating used products
  (B) By uploading a company image
  (C) By paying the bill well in advance
  (D) By placing a large order

58. What does the woman ask the man to do?
  (A) Speak with a advertising manager
  (B) Visit a company website
  (C) Make a payment early
  (D) Request a sample

---

59. Why does the man want to sell his car?
  (A) He has had car accidents several times.
  (B) He plans to take public transportation.
  (C) He needs a bigger vehicle.
  (D) He is transferred to an overseas branch.

60. According to the woman, why will buyers like the car?
  (A) It is a fuel efficient sedan.
  (B) It has brand new leather seats.
  (C) The model is very popular with customers now.
  (D) The outside is in good condition.

61. What will the woman most likely do next?
  (A) Repair the front seat
  (B) Find contact information
  (C) Check a catalog online
  (D) Take a measure of some fabric

GO ON TO THE NEXT PAGE ▶

62. What does the woman say she must do
by the end of today?
(A) Speak in a meeting
(B) Finalize agenda items
(C) Submit a report
(D) Check the manual for some errors

63. What problem does the man mention?
(A) Some misspellings are found.
(B) An engagement with clients is coming.
(C) The wrong equipment was used.
(D) A deadline has passed.

64. What solution does the woman offer?
(A) Looking for a different venue
(B) Meeting at a later time
(C) Dividing the work with other colleagues
(D) Asking for an extension

---

65. What is the conversation mainly about?
(A) An enlargement of manufacturing facility
(B) A dramatic increase in sales
(C) A change in company newsletter
(D) A move into the athletic apparel

66. Why does the woman say, "They didn't
seem real"?
(A) She strongly disagrees.
(B) She would like an explanation.
(C) She is happily surprised.
(D) She feels unsatisfied with the reports.

67. What will the sales team do after work?
(A) Commemorate their achievement
(B) Update their sales reports
(C) Hire new addition to their team
(D) Postpone their presentation

Green Bee Agency	
Hourly wage $ 20 per person	50 workers complete the work by 9
Central Place	
Hourly wage $ 15 per person	20 workers complete the work by 12
Mountain High	
Hourly wage $ 30 per person	30 workers complete the work by 11
Rainbow Ocean	
Hourly wage $ 9 per person	50 workers complete the work by 10

68. What does the woman ask the man to do?
(A) Order some merchandise
(B) Help her select the agency
(C) Repair the old computers
(D) Contact job candidates

69. What will happen next Tuesday?
(A) Place an order of the new computers
(B) Receive the shipment of new computers
(C) Choose the good employment agency
(D) Hire more office workers

70. Look at the graphic. Which agency will
they choose?
(A) Green Bee Agency
(B) Central Place
(C) Mountain High
(D) Rainbow Ocean

PART 4

Directions: You will hear some short talks given by a single speaker. You will be asked to answer three questions about what the speaker says in each short talk. Select the best response to each question and mark the letter (A), (B), (C), or (D) on your answer sheet. The talks will not be printed in your test book and will be spoken only one time.

71. Where is the announcement being heard?
(A) At a technology store
(B) At a workshop meeting
(C) At an international sporting event
(D) At a brunch cafe

72. What is the announcement mainly discussing?
(A) Keeping the restroom clean
(B) Correcting contact information
(C) Reclaiming a lost item
(D) Taking on a duty

73. Who most like is Mr. Dustin?
(A) An announcer
(B) A store manager
(C) A handcraft man
(D) A receptionist

74. Where does the caller work?
(A) At an organic farm
(B) At a boutique shop
(C) At a vegetarian restaurant
(D) At a flower shop

75. What problem does the caller mention?
(A) An order was filled incorrectly.
(B) An appliance is not working properly.
(C) A bulk discount has not been applied.
(D) An account has been sent to the wrong address.

76. What is Mr. Winnie requested to do?
(A) Make an arrangement
(B) Indicate his preference
(C) Contact the delivery person
(D) Make an overdue payment

77. What most likely is the speaker's job?
(A) A marketing manager
(B) A hotel janitor
(C) A renowned cook
(D) A tour guide

78. What will the listeners plan to do this evening?
(A) Visit a local night fair
(B) Move to a different hotel
(C) Change a room
(D) Attend a tea class

79. What does the speaker say is scheduled to do at eleven o'clock?
(A) A massage
(B) An outdoor concert
(C) An exciting flight
(D) A museum tour

80. Who is the speaker?
(A) A theater coordinator
(B) A tour guide
(C) A cast member
(D) A financial supporter

81. What does the speaker say is special about this performance?
(A) It has won many awards.
(B) It was written by a middle school student.
(C) Free souvenir has been given to all performers.
(D) All shows have sold out.

82. How will proceeds from the evening's sales be used?
(A) To replace computers with new ones
(B) To fund restoration of the theater
(C) To support programs in local school
(D) To repair the musical instrument

GO ON TO THE NEXT PAGE

83. What is the main purpose of the call?
(A) To announce a job opening
(B) To decline an invitation
(C) To interview job applicants
(D) To sign up for a training

84. What does the speaker plan to do next Friday?
(A) Meet with the new clients
(B) Take a rest
(C) Record a conversation
(D) Conduct some interview

85. What does the speaker request the listener to offer?
(A) Feedback about some training
(B) Details of job interview
(C) A complete list of participants
(D) Photos of regional managers

---

86. Who most likely is the speaker?
(A) A flower shop manager
(B) A city official
(C) A landscape painter
(D) A mechanical specialist

87. What does the speaker say about the color?
(A) It has increased in numbers recently.
(B) It can be viewed in an outdoor exhibit.
(C) It is recommended by a painter.
(D) It will ease one's mind.

88. What has been offered for the listeners?
(A) Some drawing tools
(B) A crab sandwich
(C) A complimentary lunch
(D) A map of the park

89. What does the business mainly focus on?
(A) Passenger buses
(B) Portable MP3 player
(C) Automobile tires
(D) Plant engines

90. According to the speaker, what will Pro Tire do in November?
(A) Hold a press conference
(B) Launch an online advertising campaign
(C) Open a new manufacturing plant
(D) Raise the public awareness in environment

91. What does the mayor hope to take place in Detroit?
(A) More traffic regulations will be passed.
(B) Employment opportunities will increase.
(C) Net profits of the plant will drop shortly.
(D) Public transportation will be added.

Welcome to the seminar

Presenter	Subject
Mr. Baek	Efficient sales skills
Ms. Oha	Marketing strategy
Break	Lunch
David S.	Business portfolio
Caren Van De	How to avoid typo

92. Look at the graphic. Who most likely is the speaker?
(A) Mr. Baek
(B) Ms. Oha
(C) David S.
(D) Caren Van De

93. According to the speaker, why is it essential to make a good first impression?
(A) To attract new clients
(B) To take advantage of sales skills
(C) To share work experience
(D) To get investor's support

94. What does the speaker advise members of the group go do?
(A) Review a business portfolio
(B) Describe past work experience
(C) Give a demonstration
(D) Make some examples

| English | German | Korean | Japanese |

Attention!

New System

1. Where - Main entrance

2. How - Touch screen

3. Benefit - Quick and Easy to use

Natural Energy Solutions

Expert area	Initial cost
Rainwater usage	$ 1,000
Steam powered electricity	$ 1,500
Waste recycling	$ 1,200

---

95. Where most likely is this announcement being heard?
(A) At an airport
(B) At a train station
(C) At a department store
(D) At a ticket booth

96. What does the speaker say is now available?
(A) A renovated cafeteria
(B) An expanded waiting area
(C) Complimentary Internet access
(D) Automated ticketing machines

97. Look at the graphic. What are Chinese passengers instructed to do for ticketing?
(A) They can get an air ticket exclusively on the website.
(B) They can use ticketing service at the air ticket booth.
(C) They can receive detailed instructions from the airport managerial office.
(D) They can use the new automated ticketing system.

98. What is the main purpose of the recorded message?
(A) To change a delivery schedule
(B) To clarify some procedures
(C) To make payment arrangements
(D) To promote a service

99. What does the speaker plan to send?
(A) A feasible solution
(B) A product sample
(C) Customer recommendations
(D) A detailed refund process

100. Look at the graphic. How much will Ms. Stella pay for the service that the speaker mentions?
(A) $ 1,000
(B) $ 1,500
(C) $ 1,200
(D) $ 3,700

GO ON TO THE NEXT PAGE

READING TEST

In the Reading test, you will read a variety of texts and answer several different types of reading comprehension questions. The entire Reading test will last 75 minutes. There are three parts, and directions are given for each part. You are encouraged to answer as many questions as possible within the time allowed.

You must mark answers on the separate answer sheet. Do not write your answer in your test book.

PART 5

Directions: A word or phrase is missing in each of the sentences below. Four answer choices are given below each sentence. Select the best answer to complete the sentence. Then mark the letter (A), (B), (C), or (D) on your answer sheet.

---

101. Super Economics magazine is the latest trade ------- for professional experts.
(A) publication
(B) publishers
(C) publish
(D) is publishing

102. The group's top executives ordered that last year's sales documents be submitted ------- the end of this week.
(A) at
(B) with
(C) throughout
(D) by

103. A global SPA brand, 7 Hours mentioned in an official press release that it is scheduled to expand ------- China.
(A) at
(B) about
(C) into
(D) of

104. The vice president, Marie De Charlotte thanked her subordinates for ------- dedication to boosting the domestic sales by 20 percent.
(A) their
(B) themselves
(C) they
(D) theirs

105. Dean Winchester will talk about a conference on personal information protection he ------- in London last week.
(A) participated
(B) attended
(C) enrolled
(D) registered

106. ------- the success of his first movie, Jeremy Lucas was offered a much bigger budget to develop his next tight plot.
(A) Because
(B) However
(C) After
(D) Already

107. The Chief Financial Officer of the Laster Rink Hospital will say a few words ------- his retirement party.
(A) except
(B) before
(C) as
(D) onto

108. The time-honored website for copyright infringements will go back online early next month with a ------- upgraded appearance.
(A) total
(B) totaling
(C) totally
(D) totaled

109. The oldest barber shop in Quebec City has ------- its business locations worldwide to serve its many customers.
(A) expansively
(B) expanded
(C) expands
(D) expand

110. A small-sized clinic -------, Big Mama Dermatology specializes in getting rid of acne scars.
(A) firm
(B) program
(C) piece
(D) chart

111. In order to make sure the freshness of each menu item, Jamba Jumbo Juice uses a variety of fruits exclusively from ------- farms.
(A) original
(B) entire
(C) casual
(D) local

112. Technicians are not able to repair the Tech Pro washing machine model as ------- parts are discontinued.
(A) our
(B) its
(C) his
(D) theirs

113. Michael Consulting Group has ------- costs and improved performance by using teleconferencing with mobile phones.
(A) examined
(B) reduced
(C) stated
(D) qualified

114. Marvel Fragrance Franchise gives approximately 30 percent discounts to first time -------.
(A) buys
(B) buyer
(C) bought
(D) buyers

115. We will ask for a refund and a written apology because ------- a month has passed since we placed an order for 100 new computers.
(A) partially
(B) immediately
(C) nearly
(D) thoroughly

116. The Space One Theater in Miami features work by Asia's top movie directors ------- make films with food themes.
(A) both
(B) who
(C) besides
(D) since

117. The faculty of the Standstill Science College will do ------- they can to make a transition to a new career as smoothly as possible.
(A) some
(B) whatever
(C) above
(D) each

118. Large bulk orders of office supplies will not be filled until the ------- business day.
(A) approximate
(B) following
(C) recent
(D) leading

119. The owner's manual for proper operating directions warns prospective users that glass with certain color may not fuse ------- with others.
(A) completion
(B) completing
(C) completely
(D) completes

120. Wentworth Brown will ------- for his immediate supervisor to meet the overseas investors this coming Saturday.
(A) conduct
(B) identify
(C) connect
(D) arrange

GO ON TO THE NEXT PAGE ▶

121. The Eaton Rosemead Library has a wide variety of ------- of over 10,000 children's paper books and e-books.
(A) collects
(B) collecting
(C) collections
(D) collected

122. A slight ------- in the processing of orders is expected this Friday as we change our overseas shipping company.
(A) package
(B) return
(C) change
(D) postage

123. Casablanca, a renowned film production firm, is organizing the audition for ------- actors this Friday at Cat Walk Theater.
(A) experience
(B) to experience
(C) experiences
(D) experienced

124. Frequent shoppers are invited to pre-use and pre-own the new line of luxury sedan before the ------- release on May 10th.
(A) constant
(B) official
(C) natural
(D) satisfactory

125. Comfort Two boasts a wide ------- of customized shoes for every age, in almost any type of leather.
(A) record
(B) solution
(C) selection
(D) preference

126. A mutually beneficial relationship was set up ------- to help both parties involved reach beyond their expectations.
(A) specifying
(B) specifically
(C) specific
(D) specify

127. Edmond Hair Salon hired ten hairdressers, most of ------- obtained beautician licenses from Patrick Anderson School.
(A) who
(B) whom
(C) them
(D) that

128. The 5th annual Kansas seminar offers participants the most ------- way to familiarize themselves with the new technology.
(A) effective
(B) reluctant
(C) concerned
(D) contained

129. Every visitor to The Cherry Popped Ice Cream Factory must ------- an identification badge at the reception desk.
(A) catch up
(B) take after
(C) pick up
(D) call on

130. ------- Anderson Darcy has been working late to meet the deadline for submission of entries.
(A) Late
(B) Later
(C) Latest
(D) Lately

PART 6

Directions: Read the texts that follow. A word, phrase, or sentence is missing in parts of each text. Four answer choices for each question are given below the text. Select the best answer to complete the text. Then mark the letter (A), (B), (C), or (D) on your answer sheet.

Questions 131-134 refer to the following press release.

The quarterly Stanford Marathon Competition ------ on September 1st.
131.

This famous national race had been held at Stanford World Stadium ever since its start in 1972 but this year, the organizing committee decided to move it to a ------ location.
132.

A shift to much bigger venue turned out to be the right decision since an unprecedented number of attendees took part.

The committee Chairman, Lim Charles attributed its success ------ international awareness of
133.
many health benefits obtained from regular exercise. ------
134.

---

131. (A) will happen
(B) happened
(C) happens
(D) were happening

132. (A) closer
(B) quieter
(C) larger
(D) sunnier

133. (A) to
(B) from
(C) with
(D) along

134. (A) He also thanked committee organizers for this great outcome.
(B) A wide variety of vendors will participate in that auction.
(C) Let them know the reason you couldn't attend the seminar.
(D) Singers, dancers, and jugglers should register in advance.

GO ON TO THE NEXT PAGE

From: sanders@hcs.com

To: madeline@ecs.com

Date: November 11

Re: A new program

Dear Ms. Adeline,

We'd like to thank you for your ------ in doing business with Hot Clip Stock to meet your office
135.
needs.

Please be reminded that we have a new ------ program. In our Frequent Shopper Club Program,
136.
any orders more than $ 25 will be offered a 10 percent discount.

137.

As you are a frequent shopper, ------ company's account has been registered for this program
138.
in automatic mode.

For more information concerning this program, visit our website at www.hotclipstock.com.

135. (A) loyalty
    (B) loyal
    (C) loyalties
    (D) loyally

136. (A) radio
    (B) travel
    (C) train
    (D) savings

137. (A) We acknowledge a receipt of your
       message.
    (B) However, excessive use of quotation
       can confuse the issue.
    (C) If you want to have further reduction
       in price, you can get much lower
       prices by ordering in bulk.
    (D) Students can get group discounts for
       classes.

138. (A) my
    (B) her
    (C) your
    (D) our

To: dcordelia@bigmail.net

From: adextor@comfortfortwo.com.ch

Date: 15 August

Subject: Please tell us how you did.

Dear Comfort for Two customer,

On behalf of all the company, I'd like to thank you for staying with Comfort for Two Hotel. I'd like to hear about your brief sojourn ------ our Chicago branch on 13 August.
139.

We would be grateful if you could fill in a short customer survey about your experience with our hotel chain. ------ should take around five minutes of your time to complete.
140.

Simply copy and paste the following URL into your browser: http://comfortfortwo.com.ch/486.cs

Your feedback will help us ------ the way we serve our guests.
141.

142.

Thank you again for your business.

---

139. (A) from
   (B) in
   (C) near
   (D) away

140. (A) Each
   (B) Both
   (C) They
   (D) This

141. (A) report
   (B) improve
   (C) value
   (D) provide

142. (A) Special courtesy buses ran from and to the Chicago airport.
   (B) Customers can request a wake-up call anytime.
   (C) As a token of our appreciation, we will give a complimentary bottle of champagne to all respondents on their next visit.
   (D) Souvenir and barber shops are near the front entrance of our hotel.

GO ON TO THE NEXT PAGE →

Questions 143-146 refer to the following notice.

The Ashton Car Rentals is planned for renovation starting March 1 and ending in late April. This project ------ storage space for our increasing collections. The store is to stay open during the
143.
process of the remodeling.

------, some electro-mobiles will be temporarily unavailable to on-site customers.
144.

A list of these ------ collections will be posted on our website at www.ashtoncarrental.com.
145.
Renters are encouraged to check the list or contact the shop manager before visiting. ------
146.

143. (A) to expand
(B) expanding
(C) expanded
(D) will expand

144. (A) Rather
(B) Nevertheless
(C) Similarly
(D) Previously

145. (A) mislabeled
(B) unassociated
(C) unvalued
(D) inaccessible

146. (A) The company plans to unveil a new compact car in May.
(B) A series of lectures on proper ventilation will be given.
(C) He is available from morning till night except on Saturdays.
(D) Over a billion bicycles are in Los Angeles.

PART 7

Directions: In this part you will read a selection of texts, such as magazine and newpaper articles, e-mails, and instant messages. Each text or st of texts is followed by several questions. Select the best answer to complete the text. Then mark the letter (A), (B), (C), or (D) on your answer sheet.

Questions 147-148 refer to the following letter.

April 24

Angela Sheen
568 Blue Bird Boulevard
Boston, MT 147050

Re: Account #790310-486

Dear Ms. Sheen,

Thank you for your letter notifying us of your new contact information. We have updated the information on your account, and all subsequent bank statements and correspondence will be mailed to your new address.

Please be reminded that we received your letter just today. And your most recent statement had already been sent to your previous address. However, you can see your account information in detail (including account balance, recent charges, and payments received) at any time simply by accessing your account on our website.

Thank you for being a valued customer.

Sincerely,

Felicia Bocelli
Customer Service Department

147. What is the letter mainly about?
(A) A late payment
(B) A newly opened savings account
(C) A change-of-address request
(D) An incorrect statement

148. What does Mr. Bocelli suggest that Ms. Sheen do?
(A) Visit a website
(B) Call the customer service department
(C) Send an overdue payment
(D) Update new contact information

GO ON TO THE NEXT PAGE

From: jstewart@marionvilledialnet.com
To: admin@marionvillemedical.com
Date: October 10
Subject: Reminder

Dear Ms. Stewart,

This is a reminder to confirm your dental appointment next week with Big Smile Medical Group. Please take a few minutes to go over the details of your appointment.

Dentist: Amanda Corby	
Date: Thursday, October 17	
Time: 10:30 A.M.	
Purpose: Tooth scaling and tooth polishing	

If any of this information seems to be incorrect, please call us at our reception desk at (802) 333-0128. In addition, if you are unable to keep this appointment, it is imperative that you contact our receptionist as soon as possible so we can reschedule yours. Appointments canceled with less than one day of advance notice will be subject to a $ 100 cancellation fee.

Sincerely,

Big Smile Medical Group

149. What is the e-mail mostly about?
(A) An upcoming appointment
(B) Medical test results
(C) Changes on a check-up process
(D) Notice about cancellation fee

150. According to the e-mail, what is one reason for Ms. Stewart to contact the office?
(A) To report inaccurate information
(B) To confirm her dental appointment
(C) To talk to Dr. Corby
(D) To request a billing statement

151. According to the e-mail, why is an extra fee charged?
(A) Receiving advance notice from receptionists
(B) Forwarding medical records to other clinics
(C) Same-day medical test results
(D) Late cancellation of an appointment

Jeffery Benet	10:13
A family emergency suddenly came up, so I missed my train in Seattle.	
Jeffery Benet	10:15
I have no choice but to take the following train scheduled for 10:40.	
Norah Jones	10:45
I just checked my message. Sorry for the late reply.	
Norah Jones	10:46
Did you board the train?	
Jeffery Benet	10:47
Definitely.	
Norah Jones	10:47
Do you think can you make it to meeting on time?	
Jeffery Benet	10:48
Sure thing. This is an express train so I can arrive way ahead of the scheduled meeting time. See you then!	

152. What is suggested about Mr. Benet?
(A) He has been to Seattle more than twice.
(B) He is currently in a Seattle airport.
(C) He boarded the train at 10:15
(D) He can be punctual for the meeting.

153. At 10:47, what does Mr. Jeffery mean when he writes, "Definitely"?
(A) He has confirmed the arrival time of a train.
(B) He is certain he can handle the family emergency.
(C) He assures Jones that he is on board that train.
(D) He knows Ms. Jones pick him up at the station.

GO ON TO THE NEXT PAGE

http://www.pinkdiamond.com

Pink Diamond
think quality first

Fill out the information below to contact our customer service department. We will promptly answer your inquiry less than a day, seven days a week.

First Name: Henry
Surname: Donavan
E-mail: bianca@officepro.com
Subject: Rocking chair-style no.325

Message:
I am interested in purchasing a wooden rocking chair, style number 325. Your website indicates that shipping charges are calculated based on the weight and dimensions of the merchandise. Could I pick up the chair myself in order not to pay for this fee? I live approximately one hour away from your warehouse, and I have a truck that can easily accommodate a large chair, thank you.

154. Why did Mr. Donavan complete the form?
(A) To ask about a delivery policy
(B) To complain about a chair he purchased
(C) To request a discounted price for a rocking chair
(D) To find out the direction to the factory

155. What does Pink Diamond promise to do?
(A) Reduce the shipping fee for large order
(B) Respond to messages less than 24 hours
(C) Refer a truck-rental agency
(D) Repair any chairs that are damaged in transit

Deadline for a Full-Page Advertisement

The deadline for placing a full-page advertisement in the World Sports Weekly is Thursday morning at 10:00 at the latest, for publication on Friday. After initial contents are received, changes will not be accepted. We reserve the right to edit any contents.

All ads should be prepaid. Ads scheduled to run for over a week may be called off after the first week for future advertising credit only. E-mail the contents of your ad to ads@worldsportsweekly. com. Discounts are available for multiple ads.

Call 346-0989 for pricing.

156. What will happen if an advertiser submits an ad on a Friday morning?
(A) The ad will appear the following Friday.
(B) The ad will be printed later that day.
(C) The ad will be declined by the newspaper.
(D) The ad will cost the advertiser much more money.

157. According to the notice, what should advertisers do to place an ad?
(A) Turn in initial contents by the deadline
(B) Contact the World Sports Weekly editor
(C) Receive a written permission from the copyright owner
(D) Meet the head editor on Thursday at 10:00

GO ON TO THE NEXT PAGE →

Welcome Bags
Available

The American Village Welcome Association (AVWA) has decided on an amazing and unique gift for new residents; a reusable shopping bag packed with helpful information regarding the American Village. These cloth bags, which will have "Welcome American Village" printed across the front, will be full of community updates, discount coupons, and home-baked cookies from association members.

Local businesses interested in helping to aid this project can pay to have their company logos printed on the back of the bags. American Village residents are expected to welcome their new neighbors by personally handing these bags to each newcomer.

To participate, please go online to visit our updated community website at americanvillage.org.

158. In which paper would this article most likely appear?
(A) In a housing design magazine
(B) In a travel journal
(C) In an entertainment newspaper
(D) In a community newsletter

159. How can local businesses support the project?
(A) By distributing complimentary samples
(B) By using reusable products
(C) By purchasing advertising space
(D) By volunteering community service

160. According to the article, what are American Village residents requested to do?
(A) Hand out greeting materials
(B) Design a new community logo
(C) Shop at local stores
(D) Share their favorite recipes

Vert et Blanc Group
announces its ambitious plan

March 2 - Vert et Blanc Group has released its plan to develop a fast-food chain called Brunch in Paris. The new chain will be managed from Vert et Blanc' Korea headquarters, and the multinational corporation hopes to eventually introduce 100 Brunch in Paris locations throughout Asia and South America.

"The convenience food sector has shown international growth for the past ten years." remarked Sandra Brienne, industry analyst at trendhunter.com.

"Vert et Blanc" is wisely taking advantage of this trend. A market survey conducted by Vert et Blanc over the last year indicated that consumers prefer to have more healthy and wholesome foods when eating out.

Edward Lee, Vert et Blanc's top executive, noted that the industry in general is placing less emphasis on fried foods and concentrating more on fresh ingredients and nutritional value. "We are offering consumers a pleasurable and satisfying experience, at an average price of US $ 5.20 for a lunch or US $ 8.20 for a dinner, with much cheaper options for breakfast and snacks" said Mr. Lee. It is much cheaper than comparable establishments.

"Moreover, we will cater chiefly to urban residents with faster-paced lifestyle. So we think that they will appreciate the convenience that our menu can offer." Vert et Blanc Group is optimistic that Brunch in Paris, its newest subsidiary, will start to turn profits by its second year of operations. The group still carries some long-term debt from funds it borrowed to start up current business.

161. Who most likely is Mr. Brienne?
(A) A legal consultant for Vert et Blanc Group
(B) A Korea bank officer
(C) A health expert
(D) A food industry researcher

162. What is reported about Vert et Blanc Group?
(A) It has hired a new executive.
(B) It has been affected by slow sales growth.
(C) It investigated people's dining preferences.
(D) It is planning to relocate its headquarters to South America.

163. What does Mr. Lee indicate about the merit at Brunch in Paris?
(A) They will be less expensive than meals at similar restaurants.
(B) They will be available around the clock.
(C) They will include locally grown ingredients.
(D) They will be served in no time.

164. What is suggested about Brunch in Paris?
(A) It replaced an unsuccessful Vert et Blanc Group.
(B) It will provide its main recipes to frequent diners.
(C) It is not expected to be profitable immediately.
(D) It puts an emphasis on fried foods.

GO ON TO THE NEXT PAGE

Scottish Village Musical Festival

Interested in donating some of your free time while enjoying the story of the greatest musical geniuses? The volunteer at the fourteenth annual Scottish Village Musical Festival! This year's festival runs from August 17 to 23 at the country fairgrounds in Scottish Village and features music performances from nearly 24 gifted artists, including local favorites; Jazz artist, Norah Brightman, ballad singer Sarah Jones, and expert string quartet Danny Cho Brothers.

Volunteers are requested to

• Help with publicity – designing and posting all brochures and handing out press releases – starting August 1.

• Greet the musicians and help escort them to their housing assignments from August 15 to 24. All out-of-town artists will be hosted by area families.

• Operate the ticket booth at the gate to the fairgrounds, direct guests to the parking areas during the festival, and provide general information.

In appreciation of your aid, all of the volunteers will receive a limited edition Scottish Village Musical Festival T-shirt and two complimentary tickets.

If you are interested in volunteering, please contact Cordelia Benny, cbenny@ scottishvillagemusical.org by July 17.

165. What can be inferred about the festival?
(A) It will take place on August 1.
(B) It features a selection of music types.
(C) It gives complimentary luncheon to performers.
(D) It may be rescheduled due to unfavorable weather.

166. What is suggested about some of the performers?
(A) They will be donating their musical instruments.
(B) They will be designing posters for the festival.
(C) They will be staying at homes in Scottish Village.
(D) They will be giving volunteers free tickets.

167. What task will probably NOT be done by volunteers?
(A) Selling tickets for festival performances
(B) Transporting equipment to the fairgrounds
(C) Directing visitors where to park
(D) Sending out publicity materials

168. What will volunteers receive at no charge?
(A) An article of clothing
(B) A pass to get access to backstage areas
(C) A video recording of all the performances
(D) Snacks and meals during festival days

http://www.mysterystory.org.uk/

The Mystery Story in the World

Archive	About MSW	Tickets	Home

The Mystery Story in the World is one of the largest novel competitions in London attracting renowned detective writers and thousands of other attendees from all over the world. Click on the "archive" tab above to see videos of readings at last competitions, along with short biographies of the featured writers.

This year, the competition will take place on 12 and 13 September at Harrods Park in London. Tickets are £ 20 for adults and £ 15 for children 13 and under. Advance sale tickets will be available for purchase online as of 18 June at http://www. mysterystory.org.uk/tickets (the "tickets" tab above).

Presentation Submissions
Anyone is entitled to submit his or her work for formal presentation at the competition. Submissions must include a work sample containing between 700 and 1000 lines; the sample may consist of one page abstract. —[1]—

Both published and unpublished work may be submitted. A video of the applicant reading the work is preferred but not required. —[2]—

Submissions must be received no later than 24 May. Please refrain from inquiring about the states of your submission. —[3]—

Due to the high volume of submissions, at the conclusion of the selection process we will be able to notify only those applicants who are invited to present. —[4]—

Send your work for consideration to the following address.
The Mystery Story in the World, c/o Harrods Park
PO Box 800109, London PEJ 3PP

169. What is NOT mentioned as something that can be done on the competition's website?
(A) View recordings of past performance
(B) Read about the lives of famous writers
(C) Buy tickets to attend the festival
(D) Register to take part in writing classes

170. What is a requirement of the novel turned in by applicants?
(A) It must be unpublished before.
(B) It must be recorded on video.
(C) It must be within a specified length.
(D) It must be written in a particular language.

171. The word "consideration" in paragraph 7, line 1, is closest in meaning to
(A) thoughtfulness
(B) evaluation
(C) compliance
(D) guidance

172. In which of the position marked [1], [2], [3] and [4] does the following sentence best belong?

"All applicants will receive a letter of acknowledgement by post, and accepted applicants will be contacted by 25 April."

(A) [1]
(B) [2]
(C) [3]
(D) [4]

GO ON TO THE NEXT PAGE

No more free parking in the city

December 11

By Rachel Bessie

In an attempt to limit congestion in the center of Chicago, the city council is announcing changes in street parking rules. —[1]—

"Our streets are often at their busiest in the evening hours." said Sophia Cara, spokesperson for the Chicago City Council. "That's because residents and nonresidents alike come to an entertainment district near our downtown area to enjoy our restaurants, theaters, and concert halls. —[2]— They drive around looking for free street parking spaces and this increases traffic congestion."

Currently, payment for parking is requested only from 8 A.M. to 6 P.M. and no parking fee is charged past 6 o'clock. —[3]— "This regulation needs to be amended," Ms. Cara said. "We'd like to follow the example of other cities, where payment is required 24 hours a day."

If the proposed change takes effect, it will be the second in recent months. In September, new parking meters were installed that accept coins and credit cards as well as special Chicago parking cards. —[4]— The cards, which became available in October, can be purchased from any markets or shopping malls in Chicago.

173. What is suggested about Chicago?
    (A) Its roads are in need of repair.
    (B) It must raise public awareness about road construction.
    (C) It has a traffic problem.
    (D) Its residents can park their cars at no cost in city parking garages.

174. What is the city council considering?
    (A) Expanding existing parking spaces
    (B) Searching for new parking areas
    (C) Raising the hourly rate for parking
    (D) Introducing evening parking fees

175. In which of the position marked [1], [2], [3], and [4] does the following sentence best belong?

"People tend to avoid the parking garages, which charge a substantial fee."

    (A) [1]
    (B) [2]
    (C) [3]
    (D) [4]

GO ON TO THE NEXT PAGE

<table>
<tr><td colspan="4" align="right">http://www.luxurylifeinvermont.com/advertising</td></tr>
<tr><td>**Home**</td><td>**Contact us**</td><td>**Place order**</td><td>**Customer reviews**</td></tr>
</table>

Advertising with Luxurylifeinvermont: Luxurylifeinvermont is an award-winning online magazine with hundreds of subscribers who look to us for dependable and beneficial information on shopping for food and eating out in the Vermont area.

Advertisement on our web page can be placed in the four designs below,

Design 1 This horizontal banner will appear on the top of a page and is the first thing that attracts the reader's eye. Audio and photographs are excluded.	**Design 2** This small-format advertisement will appear centered in the middle of a featured article. One photograph and audio can be included along with text.
Design 3 This vertical banner will be seen along the side of a featured article. Audio and photographs cannot be included.	**Design 4** Our biggest-format, this half-page advertisement can contain multiple photographs and audio along with text.

To make a purchase for advertising, please contact Sandra Jill at jill@luxurylifeinvermont.com.

From:	Nathaniel Travis [travis@bighotdog.com]	**Date:**	November 11
To:	Sandra Jill [jill@luxurylifeinvermont.com]	**Subject:**	Advertisement for Big Hot Dog

Dear Ms. Jill,

I am wondering if I put another advertisement with Luxury Life in Vermont. I am eager to place large-format advertisement once again. I want you to use the same text and audio as supplied before, but I will provide four new photographs of my recently remolded store for you. I am going to forward it to your layout managers in charge to determine where to place the photographs in an extremely thoughtful manner. Could you tell me in detail what size and shape is requested to hand in the photographs?

Sincerely,

Nathaniel Travis, head chef and a store owner
Big Hot Dog

176. Where does Ms. Jill work?
(A) At a food manufacturing company
(B) At a marketing research institute
(C) At a vegetarian restaurant
(D) At a food-related publication

177. What is mentioned about Design 1?
(A) It is reasonable.
(B) It is very easily noticed.
(C) It can include the most text and photograph.
(D) It can be prepared quickly.

178. In what advertisement format, is Mr. Travis most likely interested?
(A) Design 1
(B) Design 2
(C) Design 3
(D) Design 4

179. What is suggested about Big Hot Dog?
(A) It is being redesigned by a local artist.
(B) It has continually won awards.
(C) It has been advertised in Luxury Life in Vermont before.
(D) It will be closed while it is being renovated.

180. What does Mr. Travis inquire about the photographs?
(A) What size they should be
(B) When to send them
(C) How many can be used
(D) How much extra it will cost to publish them

GO ON TO THE NEXT PAGE

Important Notice

Did you buy canned corn last week? Aveda Energy, Inc. of San Diego has just announced that several cases of their canned vegetables (210g/7.4oz.size) were shipped to area shopping centers past week with incorrect labels. The labels for Aveda Energy's Sweet Corn and Aveda Energy's Condensed Milk Corn were switched as a result of computer malfunction. The mislabeled cans are stamped with product codes C4885 or C4886.

To ask for a full refund, return the product on or before May 10 to the shopping centers where the purchase was made. In observance of manufacturer policy, the original receipt must be submitted along with the returned merchandise.

More information in regard to this matter can be found at www.avedaenergy.com.

From: Charlie Dion <cdion@goldsuperstore.com>
To: Ally Lee <alee@lemaison.com>
Date: February 15
Subject: Refund requests

Dear Ms. Lee

We have received the shipment of canned corn from your store. In about three or four business days, you should receive a check by mail in the amount of $ 42.80. This should cover the money refunded to your savvy customers when they returned the mislabeled cans. As we promised, this includes the $ 5.20 that you refunded a customer who did not have the original receipt.

We apologize for the inconvenience this has caused you and your patrons. We hope to continue to do business with Le Maison Shopping Store.

Sincerely,

Charlie Dion
Customer Service Department
Aveda Energy, Inc.

181. Who is the notice directed to?
   (A) Consumers who bought a packaged
       product
   (B) Employees of Aveda Energy, Inc.
   (C) Manufacturers of aluminum can
   (D) Managers of supermarkets in and
       around San Diego

182. What is indicated about the cans?
   (A) They were damaged while in transit.
   (B) They are stamped with incorrect
       prices.
   (C) They can be identified by a product
       code.
   (D) They were sent to the wrong
       shopping center.

183. According to the notice, whose website
   includes more information over the
   problem?
   (A) A newspaper's
   (B) A supermarket's
   (C) A shopping center's
   (D) A canned-goods manufacturer's

184. In the e-mail, the word "cover" in
   paragraph 1, line 3, is closest in meaning
   to
   (A) detach
   (B) versatile
   (C) conceal
   (D) provide for

185. What is suggested about Ms. Lee?
   (A) She will receive additional canned
       goods.
   (B) She will send a check later than she
       initially promised.
   (C) She made an exception to the
       company policy.
   (D) She will meet with Mr. Dion.

GO ON TO THE NEXT PAGE

Singapore International Laboratory Inspection

Company name: General Laboratory
Location: 19 South Parkway
Inspection Date: December 10

S = Satisfactory
No concerns were found out.
No follow-up inspection is required.

U = Unsatisfactory
Violations were identified.
Follow-up inspection must verify remediation within a month.

R = Violations
Those noted at a previous inspection were identified again. Monetary fine will vary based on the severity of the violation. Follow-up inspection must verify remediation within a month.

If a follow-up inspection is necessary, both this form and the form for the subsequent visit must be turned in. Failure to submit both forms may result in additional penalties.

Print name: Vanessa De Van Haney
Sign name: *Vanessa De Van Haney*

Laboratory Evaluation Managing Inspector

Evaluation Form no.16 and Score

Item	Score
1. Exit signs are placed above doors.	S
2. Lab personnel should always wear identification cards.	R
3. Door locks are fully functional.	S
4. Workspaces are free of excess items.	U
5. Windows can be opened easily.	U
6. Emergency alarms are fully functional.	S
7. Floors are clean and dry.	U
Fine = $ 250 Follow-up inspection scheduled for January 10	Comments

Evaluator: Vanessa De Van Haney
Laboratory Evaluation Managing Inspector

To: All Employees
From: S. Florence, Lab Manager
Subject: New company policies
Date: December 12

Management is currently taking significant measures to address these issues indicated by the managing inspector at our recent inspection.

First, all employees will be offered photo identification badges that must be worn at all times. Tomorrow, a list will be posted for workers to sign up for a time to have their photographs taken. A photographer will be on-site from December 17 to December 19. If you are unavailable on these days, please contact me. We will also have a number of badges made for visitors. We will be available at the reception desk.

Second, over the next 5 days, additional closets and cabinetry will be added for storage of personal belongings such as coats, handbags, and briefcases. These items should be properly stowed in order that work spaces are neat and tidy.

Management will conduct periodic checks to make sure that work areas are clear and floors are clean. Please report any liquid spills to management immediately.

These new policies will take effect officially on January 3.

186. For what type of inspection is form 16 most likely expected?
(A) General safety
(B) Lab equipment check
(C) Electrical repairs
(D) Chemical storage

187. Why has General Laboratory been charged a fine?
(A) Because necessary training was not implemented
(B) Because its inspection was performed later than originally scheduled
(C) Because a previous violation has not been corrected
(D) Because a necessary form was not turned in

188. What does Ms. Florence require her employees to do?
(A) Wear protective medical gear in the laboratory
(B) Store food in designated areas
(C) Take part in a staff meeting
(D) Have their photographs taken

189. When will the sign-up list be posted?
(A) On December 13
(B) On December 17
(C) On January 3
(D) On January 10

190. What is a violation that is NOT addressed in the memo?
(A) Item 2
(B) Item 4
(C) Item 5
(D) Item 7

GO ON TO THE NEXT PAGE

Trustworthy Package Delivery Service
Customer Questions and Concerns

Check the line that best explains your problems:

✔ Mail not received	____ Contents damaged during handling
____ Mail received after	____ Parcel arrived with missing contents
✔ Unreasonable delay	

Sender information: Adrian Randolph
Addresses information: 314 Hong Kong District
Affiliation: Fresh Milk 207 Hainan Avenue
Type of mail: A small parcel
Date mailed: May 18

Description of problem:
It has been nearly 14 days since the parcel were sent from the warehouse. The contents include perishable food shelf life of approximately 30 days. I would appreciate prompt attention and feedback to this inquiry.

Name: Adrian Randolph   **Signature:** *Adrian Randolph*

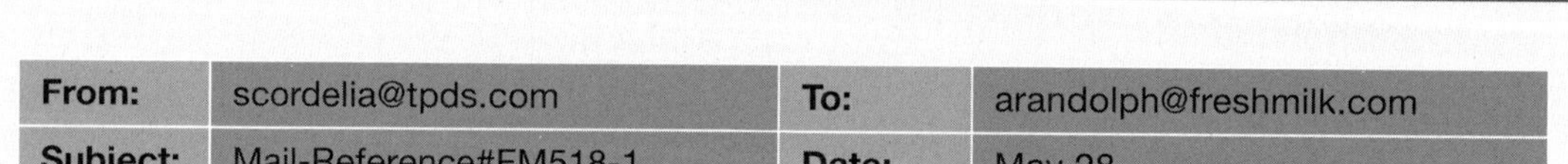

From:	scordelia@tpds.com	To:	arandolph@freshmilk.com
Subject:	Mail-Reference#FM518-1	Date:	May 28

Dear Mr. Randolph,

We have received your inquiries concerning your parcel. The two-week delay is unacceptable and our office will do its utmost to locate the package as quickly as possible. In the meantime, it may be arriving at its destination, so I ask you to continue checking with the intended recipient.

By way of apology, we would like to give you a coupon which is attached this letter. You can enroll in our VIP Delivery Service for another 6 months at no additional charge with this voucher.

In future correspondence concerning this matter, please refer to the case number listed in the subject line of this message.

With best regards,

Stella Cordelia
Trustworthy Package Delivery Service

From: arandolph@freshmilk.com
To: scordelia@tpds.com
Date: May 31
Subject: #FM518-1

Dear Ms. Cordelia,

I'd like to thank you for your prompt attention to my inquiry. We received the package on May 30 and the food in that package was fresh and in its original condition.

I have another question concerning the coupon you gave me. Should we register for your service program right now or can we enroll in that service next year?

I would appreciate prompt response to this inquiry.

Thank you,

Adrian Randolph

191. According to Mr. Randolph, what is the status of the parcel?
(A) It was forwarded with incorrect contents.
(B) It has not arrived at its destination.
(C) It was sent to the wrong address.
(D) It arrived with some contents damaged.

192. What is Mr. Randolph given?
(A) Shipping supplies at no additional cost
(B) Compensation for the value of the package
(C) A premium service plan
(D) A complimentary e-mail account

193. In the first e-mail, the word "matter" in paragraph 3, line 1, is closest in meaning to
(A) situation
(B) reason
(C) solution
(D) chore

194. What is Mr. Randolph requested to do in future communications?
(A) Include a specific identification number
(B) Contact Ms. Cordelia's assistant
(C) Make a call directly to the service department
(D) Update contact information

195. What is indicated in the second e-mail?
(A) Its main purpose is to complain about late delivery.
(B) Randolph received the package on May 31.
(C) Cordelia gave a complimentary coupon as a way of apology.
(D) The objective of this mail is to inquiry about the use of a coupon.

GO ON TO THE NEXT PAGE

From:	Catherine Dorothy <cdorothy@waterindeepwell.com>	To:	Stanley Cube <scube@marinecomputer.com>
Date:	April 20	Subject:	Water Delivery

Dear Ms. Cube,

We really appreciate your interest in our company.

We, Water in Deep Well offers the best-tasting water in Quebec. We are happy to work with you to select which dispenser system best meets your needs.

I have attached the table below so you may compare options and costs. The twelve-liter bottle sizes are typically for residential use. For businesses, we recommend a twenty-liter bottle size. If you let me know how many employees are in your company and how much percentage of them will be using the system, I can give you an estimate for the number of bottles you will need per week.

In addition to the refill costs, a one-time refundable deposit of 45,000 VND is requested when you place your initial order. Delivery drivers will pick up your empty bottles and drop off filled ones every two weeks.

Delivery fees commensurate with the number of bottles ordered as well as with how easy it is for our delivery driver to access the drop-off and pickup area. The latter can be determined with a simple site visit.

I would be glad to dispatch a sales representative to your venue to discuss our service in detail. You can reach me at (315) 425 0975 to schedule a time.

Catherine Dorothy
Water in Deep Well

Water in Deep Well

System	Dispenser Features	Bottle Size	Price per refill	Monthly dispenser fee
White	Dispenses hot water, cold water and ice	12L	45,000 VND	60,000 VND
Gold	Dispenses cold water	12L	45,000 VND	40,000 VND
Silver	Dispenses ice and cold water	20L	65,000 VND	65,000 VND
Pink	Dispenses hot and cold water	20L	65,000 VND	50,000 VND

Our software company recently relocated to 7120 Vancouver, CA, and we are interested in ordering regular drinking-water delivery. We would also plan to lease a refillable water dispenser with built-in heating and cooling. We were coming into personal contact with several different companies, but after reading positive reviews about Water in Deep Well, we decided to e-mail you first. And we think we made the right choice.

We have around 200 employees in our company and all of them are going to use your system. We want a hot and cold water dispenser. We need to use a bottle size for business use but not for residential one.

We are available from 9 to 1, Monday through Friday to discuss your service.

Sincerely,

Stanley Cube
Marine Computer

196. What is the main purpose of the first e-mail?
(A) To inquire about a billing error
(B) To notify a change of address
(C) To ask about a company
(D) To introduce a water service

197. What system most likely fits Ms. Cube's needs best?
(A) White
(B) Gold
(C) Silver
(D) Pink

198. What is mentioned about payments?
(A) The initial order includes an extra charge.
(B) Customers are billed biweekly.
(C) A discount is offered to large orders.
(D) Delivery is free for the first month.

199. What information is considered for a delivery fee estimate?
(A) The distance of delivery
(B) The number of users
(C) The customer's venue
(D) The preferred dispenser

200. According to the second e-mail, why should Ms. Cube reach Ms. Dorothy?
(A) To confirm a delivery date
(B) To respond to a request
(C) To make a cash deposit
(D) To cancel an order

정답표

<table>
<tr><th colspan="20" style="text-align:center">Actual Test 01</th></tr>
<tr><td>1</td><td>(B)</td><td>21</td><td>(B)</td><td>41</td><td>(A)</td><td>61</td><td>(B)</td><td>81</td><td>(A)</td><td>101</td><td>(C)</td><td>121</td><td>(C)</td><td>141</td><td>(C)</td><td>161</td><td>(B)</td><td>181</td><td>(B)</td></tr>
<tr><td>2</td><td>(B)</td><td>22</td><td>(C)</td><td>42</td><td>(D)</td><td>62</td><td>(D)</td><td>82</td><td>(D)</td><td>102</td><td>(A)</td><td>122</td><td>(C)</td><td>142</td><td>(A)</td><td>162</td><td>(C)</td><td>182</td><td>(C)</td></tr>
<tr><td>3</td><td>(D)</td><td>23</td><td>(B)</td><td>43</td><td>(C)</td><td>63</td><td>(B)</td><td>83</td><td>(B)</td><td>103</td><td>(D)</td><td>123</td><td>(D)</td><td>143</td><td>(B)</td><td>163</td><td>(C)</td><td>183</td><td>(D)</td></tr>
<tr><td>4</td><td>(C)</td><td>24</td><td>(A)</td><td>44</td><td>(C)</td><td>64</td><td>(A)</td><td>84</td><td>(B)</td><td>104</td><td>(C)</td><td>124</td><td>(C)</td><td>144</td><td>(D)</td><td>164</td><td>(A)</td><td>184</td><td>(C)</td></tr>
<tr><td>5</td><td>(A)</td><td>25</td><td>(C)</td><td>45</td><td>(B)</td><td>65</td><td>(C)</td><td>85</td><td>(B)</td><td>105</td><td>(D)</td><td>125</td><td>(A)</td><td>145</td><td>(D)</td><td>165</td><td>(C)</td><td>185</td><td>(A)</td></tr>
<tr><td>6</td><td>(A)</td><td>26</td><td>(B)</td><td>46</td><td>(A)</td><td>66</td><td>(B)</td><td>86</td><td>(C)</td><td>106</td><td>(C)</td><td>126</td><td>(D)</td><td>146</td><td>(D)</td><td>166</td><td>(D)</td><td>186</td><td>(B)</td></tr>
<tr><td>7</td><td>(A)</td><td>27</td><td>(C)</td><td>47</td><td>(B)</td><td>67</td><td>(C)</td><td>87</td><td>(A)</td><td>107</td><td>(C)</td><td>127</td><td>(D)</td><td>147</td><td>(A)</td><td>167</td><td>(B)</td><td>187</td><td>(C)</td></tr>
<tr><td>8</td><td>(C)</td><td>28</td><td>(B)</td><td>48</td><td>(D)</td><td>68</td><td>(A)</td><td>88</td><td>(B)</td><td>108</td><td>(A)</td><td>128</td><td>(A)</td><td>148</td><td>(C)</td><td>168</td><td>(C)</td><td>188</td><td>(C)</td></tr>
<tr><td>9</td><td>(C)</td><td>29</td><td>(B)</td><td>49</td><td>(A)</td><td>69</td><td>(C)</td><td>89</td><td>(D)</td><td>109</td><td>(C)</td><td>129</td><td>(A)</td><td>149</td><td>(D)</td><td>169</td><td>(D)</td><td>189</td><td>(B)</td></tr>
<tr><td>10</td><td>(C)</td><td>30</td><td>(A)</td><td>50</td><td>(C)</td><td>70</td><td>(C)</td><td>90</td><td>(B)</td><td>110</td><td>(D)</td><td>130</td><td>(B)</td><td>150</td><td>(B)</td><td>170</td><td>(C)</td><td>190</td><td>(B)</td></tr>
<tr><td>11</td><td>(B)</td><td>31</td><td>(B)</td><td>51</td><td>(D)</td><td>71</td><td>(B)</td><td>91</td><td>(D)</td><td>111</td><td>(A)</td><td>131</td><td>(D)</td><td>151</td><td>(B)</td><td>171</td><td>(C)</td><td>191</td><td>(A)</td></tr>
<tr><td>12</td><td>(A)</td><td>32</td><td>(A)</td><td>52</td><td>(C)</td><td>72</td><td>(C)</td><td>92</td><td>(D)</td><td>112</td><td>(C)</td><td>132</td><td>(C)</td><td>152</td><td>(A)</td><td>172</td><td>(A)</td><td>192</td><td>(B)</td></tr>
<tr><td>13</td><td>(C)</td><td>33</td><td>(A)</td><td>53</td><td>(A)</td><td>73</td><td>(D)</td><td>93</td><td>(C)</td><td>113</td><td>(C)</td><td>133</td><td>(B)</td><td>153</td><td>(D)</td><td>173</td><td>(B)</td><td>193</td><td>(A)</td></tr>
<tr><td>14</td><td>(C)</td><td>34</td><td>(C)</td><td>54</td><td>(A)</td><td>74</td><td>(A)</td><td>94</td><td>(C)</td><td>114</td><td>(B)</td><td>134</td><td>(D)</td><td>154</td><td>(B)</td><td>174</td><td>(D)</td><td>194</td><td>(D)</td></tr>
<tr><td>15</td><td>(A)</td><td>35</td><td>(B)</td><td>55</td><td>(C)</td><td>75</td><td>(B)</td><td>95</td><td>(A)</td><td>115</td><td>(B)</td><td>135</td><td>(B)</td><td>155</td><td>(B)</td><td>175</td><td>(A)</td><td>195</td><td>(D)</td></tr>
<tr><td>16</td><td>(B)</td><td>36</td><td>(D)</td><td>56</td><td>(C)</td><td>76</td><td>(D)</td><td>96</td><td>(C)</td><td>116</td><td>(D)</td><td>136</td><td>(C)</td><td>156</td><td>(C)</td><td>176</td><td>(B)</td><td>196</td><td>(C)</td></tr>
<tr><td>17</td><td>(A)</td><td>37</td><td>(A)</td><td>57</td><td>(A)</td><td>77</td><td>(A)</td><td>97</td><td>(C)</td><td>117</td><td>(C)</td><td>137</td><td>(D)</td><td>157</td><td>(A)</td><td>177</td><td>(D)</td><td>197</td><td>(A)</td></tr>
<tr><td>18</td><td>(A)</td><td>38</td><td>(C)</td><td>58</td><td>(B)</td><td>78</td><td>(D)</td><td>98</td><td>(C)</td><td>118</td><td>(B)</td><td>138</td><td>(B)</td><td>158</td><td>(B)</td><td>178</td><td>(C)</td><td>198</td><td>(B)</td></tr>
<tr><td>19</td><td>(C)</td><td>39</td><td>(B)</td><td>59</td><td>(C)</td><td>79</td><td>(B)</td><td>99</td><td>(D)</td><td>119</td><td>(A)</td><td>139</td><td>(D)</td><td>159</td><td>(A)</td><td>179</td><td>(C)</td><td>199</td><td>(C)</td></tr>
<tr><td>20</td><td>(C)</td><td>40</td><td>(A)</td><td>60</td><td>(D)</td><td>80</td><td>(C)</td><td>100</td><td>(D)</td><td>120</td><td>(A)</td><td>140</td><td>(C)</td><td>160</td><td>(D)</td><td>180</td><td>(A)</td><td>200</td><td>(C)</td></tr>
</table>

<table>
<tr><th colspan="20" style="text-align:center">Actual Test 02</th></tr>
<tr><td>1</td><td>(C)</td><td>21</td><td>(B)</td><td>41</td><td>(B)</td><td>61</td><td>(A)</td><td>81</td><td>(D)</td><td>101</td><td>(D)</td><td>121</td><td>(B)</td><td>141</td><td>(A)</td><td>161</td><td>(C)</td><td>181</td><td>(A)</td></tr>
<tr><td>2</td><td>(B)</td><td>22</td><td>(B)</td><td>42</td><td>(C)</td><td>62</td><td>(A)</td><td>82</td><td>(C)</td><td>102</td><td>(A)</td><td>122</td><td>(A)</td><td>142</td><td>(C)</td><td>162</td><td>(D)</td><td>182</td><td>(A)</td></tr>
<tr><td>3</td><td>(D)</td><td>23</td><td>(A)</td><td>43</td><td>(D)</td><td>63</td><td>(D)</td><td>83</td><td>(D)</td><td>103</td><td>(A)</td><td>123</td><td>(D)</td><td>143</td><td>(D)</td><td>163</td><td>(D)</td><td>183</td><td>(B)</td></tr>
<tr><td>4</td><td>(C)</td><td>24</td><td>(A)</td><td>44</td><td>(A)</td><td>64</td><td>(C)</td><td>84</td><td>(C)</td><td>104</td><td>(B)</td><td>124</td><td>(B)</td><td>144</td><td>(D)</td><td>164</td><td>(D)</td><td>184</td><td>(B)</td></tr>
<tr><td>5</td><td>(D)</td><td>25</td><td>(C)</td><td>45</td><td>(D)</td><td>65</td><td>(A)</td><td>85</td><td>(C)</td><td>105</td><td>(B)</td><td>125</td><td>(D)</td><td>145</td><td>(A)</td><td>165</td><td>(B)</td><td>185</td><td>(C)</td></tr>
<tr><td>6</td><td>(C)</td><td>26</td><td>(A)</td><td>46</td><td>(B)</td><td>66</td><td>(B)</td><td>86</td><td>(A)</td><td>106</td><td>(A)</td><td>126</td><td>(C)</td><td>146</td><td>(D)</td><td>166</td><td>(A)</td><td>186</td><td>(D)</td></tr>
<tr><td>7</td><td>(C)</td><td>27</td><td>(C)</td><td>47</td><td>(B)</td><td>67</td><td>(D)</td><td>87</td><td>(D)</td><td>107</td><td>(B)</td><td>127</td><td>(D)</td><td>147</td><td>(D)</td><td>167</td><td>(B)</td><td>187</td><td>(D)</td></tr>
<tr><td>8</td><td>(C)</td><td>28</td><td>(C)</td><td>48</td><td>(C)</td><td>68</td><td>(B)</td><td>88</td><td>(A)</td><td>108</td><td>(B)</td><td>128</td><td>(B)</td><td>148</td><td>(C)</td><td>168</td><td>(D)</td><td>188</td><td>(C)</td></tr>
<tr><td>9</td><td>(A)</td><td>29</td><td>(A)</td><td>49</td><td>(A)</td><td>69</td><td>(C)</td><td>89</td><td>(D)</td><td>109</td><td>(B)</td><td>129</td><td>(C)</td><td>149</td><td>(A)</td><td>169</td><td>(C)</td><td>189</td><td>(B)</td></tr>
<tr><td>10</td><td>(A)</td><td>30</td><td>(B)</td><td>50</td><td>(C)</td><td>70</td><td>(B)</td><td>90</td><td>(D)</td><td>110</td><td>(A)</td><td>130</td><td>(C)</td><td>150</td><td>(B)</td><td>170</td><td>(B)</td><td>190</td><td>(C)</td></tr>
<tr><td>11</td><td>(C)</td><td>31</td><td>(C)</td><td>51</td><td>(D)</td><td>71</td><td>(C)</td><td>91</td><td>(B)</td><td>111</td><td>(D)</td><td>131</td><td>(A)</td><td>151</td><td>(C)</td><td>171</td><td>(C)</td><td>191</td><td>(B)</td></tr>
<tr><td>12</td><td>(B)</td><td>32</td><td>(C)</td><td>52</td><td>(B)</td><td>72</td><td>(B)</td><td>92</td><td>(D)</td><td>112</td><td>(C)</td><td>132</td><td>(C)</td><td>152</td><td>(B)</td><td>172</td><td>(A)</td><td>192</td><td>(A)</td></tr>
<tr><td>13</td><td>(B)</td><td>33</td><td>(B)</td><td>53</td><td>(C)</td><td>73</td><td>(D)</td><td>93</td><td>(B)</td><td>113</td><td>(D)</td><td>133</td><td>(A)</td><td>153</td><td>(D)</td><td>173</td><td>(D)</td><td>193</td><td>(A)</td></tr>
<tr><td>14</td><td>(B)</td><td>34</td><td>(D)</td><td>54</td><td>(B)</td><td>74</td><td>(D)</td><td>94</td><td>(A)</td><td>114</td><td>(A)</td><td>134</td><td>(A)</td><td>154</td><td>(A)</td><td>174</td><td>(C)</td><td>194</td><td>(C)</td></tr>
<tr><td>15</td><td>(C)</td><td>35</td><td>(C)</td><td>55</td><td>(D)</td><td>75</td><td>(A)</td><td>95</td><td>(B)</td><td>115</td><td>(D)</td><td>135</td><td>(A)</td><td>155</td><td>(D)</td><td>175</td><td>(C)</td><td>195</td><td>(A)</td></tr>
<tr><td>16</td><td>(C)</td><td>36</td><td>(C)</td><td>56</td><td>(B)</td><td>76</td><td>(A)</td><td>96</td><td>(D)</td><td>116</td><td>(C)</td><td>136</td><td>(B)</td><td>156</td><td>(D)</td><td>176</td><td>(D)</td><td>196</td><td>(C)</td></tr>
<tr><td>17</td><td>(A)</td><td>37</td><td>(A)</td><td>57</td><td>(D)</td><td>77</td><td>(A)</td><td>97</td><td>(B)</td><td>117</td><td>(D)</td><td>137</td><td>(C)</td><td>157</td><td>(B)</td><td>177</td><td>(C)</td><td>197</td><td>(D)</td></tr>
<tr><td>18</td><td>(B)</td><td>38</td><td>(C)</td><td>58</td><td>(C)</td><td>78</td><td>(D)</td><td>98</td><td>(A)</td><td>118</td><td>(D)</td><td>138</td><td>(C)</td><td>158</td><td>(B)</td><td>178</td><td>(B)</td><td>198</td><td>(A)</td></tr>
<tr><td>19</td><td>(A)</td><td>39</td><td>(C)</td><td>59</td><td>(D)</td><td>79</td><td>(B)</td><td>99</td><td>(D)</td><td>119</td><td>(D)</td><td>139</td><td>(B)</td><td>159</td><td>(A)</td><td>179</td><td>(C)</td><td>199</td><td>(C)</td></tr>
<tr><td>20</td><td>(B)</td><td>40</td><td>(B)</td><td>60</td><td>(C)</td><td>80</td><td>(B)</td><td>100</td><td>(B)</td><td>120</td><td>(C)</td><td>140</td><td>(C)</td><td>160</td><td>(D)</td><td>180</td><td>(C)</td><td>200</td><td>(B)</td></tr>
</table>

1	(B)	21	(C)	41	(D)	61	(B)	81	(D)	101	(A)	121	(C)	141	(B)	161	(D)	181	(A)
2	(B)	22	(B)	42	(A)	62	(C)	82	(C)	102	(D)	122	(C)	142	(C)	162	(C)	182	(C)
3	(D)	23	(C)	43	(B)	63	(A)	83	(B)	103	(C)	123	(D)	143	(D)	163	(A)	183	(D)
4	(C)	24	(C)	44	(C)	64	(B)	84	(D)	104	(A)	124	(B)	144	(B)	164	(C)	184	(D)
5	(D)	25	(B)	45	(A)	65	(B)	85	(A)	105	(B)	125	(C)	145	(D)	165	(B)	185	(C)
6	(A)	26	(A)	46	(B)	66	(C)	86	(B)	106	(C)	126	(B)	146	(C)	166	(C)	186	(A)
7	(A)	27	(A)	47	(B)	67	(A)	87	(D)	107	(B)	127	(B)	147	(C)	167	(B)	187	(C)
8	(B)	28	(A)	48	(D)	68	(B)	88	(A)	108	(C)	128	(A)	148	(A)	168	(A)	188	(D)
9	(B)	29	(C)	49	(A)	69	(B)	89	(C)	109	(B)	129	(C)	149	(A)	169	(D)	189	(A)
10	(A)	30	(B)	50	(B)	70	(D)	90	(C)	110	(A)	130	(D)	150	(A)	170	(C)	190	(C)
11	(C)	31	(A)	51	(A)	71	(B)	91	(B)	111	(D)	131	(B)	151	(D)	171	(B)	191	(B)
12	(B)	32	(D)	52	(D)	72	(C)	92	(C)	112	(B)	132	(C)	152	(D)	172	(C)	192	(C)
13	(C)	33	(C)	53	(C)	73	(D)	93	(D)	113	(B)	133	(A)	153	(C)	173	(C)	193	(A)
14	(B)	34	(D)	54	(A)	74	(D)	94	(B)	114	(D)	134	(A)	154	(A)	174	(D)	194	(A)
15	(A)	35	(C)	55	(D)	75	(A)	95	(A)	115	(C)	135	(A)	155	(B)	175	(B)	195	(D)
16	(C)	36	(A)	56	(C)	76	(B)	96	(D)	116	(B)	136	(D)	156	(A)	176	(D)	196	(D)
17	(B)	37	(B)	57	(D)	77	(D)	97	(B)	117	(B)	137	(C)	157	(A)	177	(B)	197	(D)
18	(A)	38	(D)	58	(B)	78	(A)	98	(D)	118	(B)	138	(C)	158	(D)	178	(D)	198	(A)
19	(A)	39	(B)	59	(C)	79	(A)	99	(C)	119	(C)	139	(B)	159	(C)	179	(C)	199	(A)
20	(B)	40	(C)	60	(D)	80	(A)	100	(A)	120	(D)	140	(D)	160	(A)	180	(A)	200	(B)

 # 점수 그래프

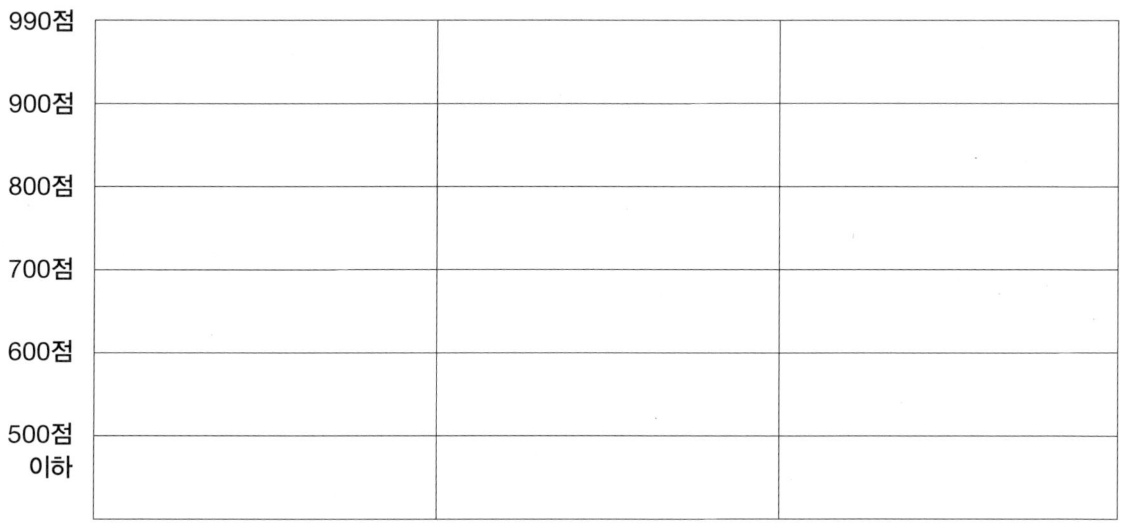

ANSWER SHEET

TOEIC 실전 테스트

수험번호   고사장   고사실

성명 한글 / 한자

Listening Comprehension Part I ~ Part IV

No.	ANSWER A B C D	No.	ANSWER A B C D	No.	ANSWER A B C D	No.	ANSWER A B C D	No.	ANSWER A B C D
1	Ⓐ Ⓑ Ⓒ Ⓓ	21	Ⓐ Ⓑ Ⓒ	41	Ⓐ Ⓑ Ⓒ Ⓓ	61	Ⓐ Ⓑ Ⓒ Ⓓ	81	Ⓐ Ⓑ Ⓒ Ⓓ
2	Ⓐ Ⓑ Ⓒ Ⓓ	22	Ⓐ Ⓑ Ⓒ	42	Ⓐ Ⓑ Ⓒ Ⓓ	62	Ⓐ Ⓑ Ⓒ Ⓓ	82	Ⓐ Ⓑ Ⓒ Ⓓ
3	Ⓐ Ⓑ Ⓒ Ⓓ	23	Ⓐ Ⓑ Ⓒ	43	Ⓐ Ⓑ Ⓒ Ⓓ	63	Ⓐ Ⓑ Ⓒ Ⓓ	83	Ⓐ Ⓑ Ⓒ Ⓓ
4	Ⓐ Ⓑ Ⓒ Ⓓ	24	Ⓐ Ⓑ Ⓒ	44	Ⓐ Ⓑ Ⓒ Ⓓ	64	Ⓐ Ⓑ Ⓒ Ⓓ	84	Ⓐ Ⓑ Ⓒ Ⓓ
5	Ⓐ Ⓑ Ⓒ Ⓓ	25	Ⓐ Ⓑ Ⓒ	45	Ⓐ Ⓑ Ⓒ Ⓓ	65	Ⓐ Ⓑ Ⓒ Ⓓ	85	Ⓐ Ⓑ Ⓒ Ⓓ
6	Ⓐ Ⓑ Ⓒ Ⓓ	26	Ⓐ Ⓑ Ⓒ	46	Ⓐ Ⓑ Ⓒ Ⓓ	66	Ⓐ Ⓑ Ⓒ Ⓓ	86	Ⓐ Ⓑ Ⓒ Ⓓ
7	Ⓐ Ⓑ Ⓒ Ⓓ	27	Ⓐ Ⓑ Ⓒ	47	Ⓐ Ⓑ Ⓒ Ⓓ	67	Ⓐ Ⓑ Ⓒ Ⓓ	87	Ⓐ Ⓑ Ⓒ Ⓓ
8	Ⓐ Ⓑ Ⓒ Ⓓ	28	Ⓐ Ⓑ Ⓒ	48	Ⓐ Ⓑ Ⓒ Ⓓ	68	Ⓐ Ⓑ Ⓒ Ⓓ	88	Ⓐ Ⓑ Ⓒ Ⓓ
9	Ⓐ Ⓑ Ⓒ Ⓓ	29	Ⓐ Ⓑ Ⓒ	49	Ⓐ Ⓑ Ⓒ Ⓓ	69	Ⓐ Ⓑ Ⓒ Ⓓ	89	Ⓐ Ⓑ Ⓒ Ⓓ
10	Ⓐ Ⓑ Ⓒ Ⓓ	30	Ⓐ Ⓑ Ⓒ	50	Ⓐ Ⓑ Ⓒ Ⓓ	70	Ⓐ Ⓑ Ⓒ Ⓓ	90	Ⓐ Ⓑ Ⓒ Ⓓ
11	Ⓐ Ⓑ Ⓒ	31	Ⓐ Ⓑ Ⓒ	51	Ⓐ Ⓑ Ⓒ Ⓓ	71	Ⓐ Ⓑ Ⓒ Ⓓ	91	Ⓐ Ⓑ Ⓒ Ⓓ
12	Ⓐ Ⓑ Ⓒ	32	Ⓐ Ⓑ Ⓒ	52	Ⓐ Ⓑ Ⓒ Ⓓ	72	Ⓐ Ⓑ Ⓒ Ⓓ	92	Ⓐ Ⓑ Ⓒ Ⓓ
13	Ⓐ Ⓑ Ⓒ	33	Ⓐ Ⓑ Ⓒ	53	Ⓐ Ⓑ Ⓒ Ⓓ	73	Ⓐ Ⓑ Ⓒ Ⓓ	93	Ⓐ Ⓑ Ⓒ Ⓓ
14	Ⓐ Ⓑ Ⓒ	34	Ⓐ Ⓑ Ⓒ	54	Ⓐ Ⓑ Ⓒ Ⓓ	74	Ⓐ Ⓑ Ⓒ Ⓓ	94	Ⓐ Ⓑ Ⓒ Ⓓ
15	Ⓐ Ⓑ Ⓒ	35	Ⓐ Ⓑ Ⓒ	55	Ⓐ Ⓑ Ⓒ Ⓓ	75	Ⓐ Ⓑ Ⓒ Ⓓ	95	Ⓐ Ⓑ Ⓒ Ⓓ
16	Ⓐ Ⓑ Ⓒ	35	Ⓐ Ⓑ Ⓒ	56	Ⓐ Ⓑ Ⓒ Ⓓ	76	Ⓐ Ⓑ Ⓒ Ⓓ	96	Ⓐ Ⓑ Ⓒ Ⓓ
17	Ⓐ Ⓑ Ⓒ	37	Ⓐ Ⓑ Ⓒ	57	Ⓐ Ⓑ Ⓒ Ⓓ	77	Ⓐ Ⓑ Ⓒ Ⓓ	97	Ⓐ Ⓑ Ⓒ Ⓓ
18	Ⓐ Ⓑ Ⓒ	38	Ⓐ Ⓑ Ⓒ	58	Ⓐ Ⓑ Ⓒ Ⓓ	78	Ⓐ Ⓑ Ⓒ Ⓓ	98	Ⓐ Ⓑ Ⓒ Ⓓ
19	Ⓐ Ⓑ Ⓒ	39	Ⓐ Ⓑ Ⓒ	59	Ⓐ Ⓑ Ⓒ Ⓓ	79	Ⓐ Ⓑ Ⓒ Ⓓ	99	Ⓐ Ⓑ Ⓒ Ⓓ
20	Ⓐ Ⓑ Ⓒ	40	Ⓐ Ⓑ Ⓒ	60	Ⓐ Ⓑ Ⓒ Ⓓ	80	Ⓐ Ⓑ Ⓒ Ⓓ	100	Ⓐ Ⓑ Ⓒ Ⓓ

Reading Comprehension Part V ~ Part VII

No.	ANSWER A B C D	No.	ANSWER A B C D	No.	ANSWER A B C D	No.	ANSWER A B C D	No.	ANSWER A B C D
101	Ⓐ Ⓑ Ⓒ Ⓓ	121	Ⓐ Ⓑ Ⓒ Ⓓ	141	Ⓐ Ⓑ Ⓒ Ⓓ	161	Ⓐ Ⓑ Ⓒ Ⓓ	181	Ⓐ Ⓑ Ⓒ Ⓓ
102	Ⓐ Ⓑ Ⓒ Ⓓ	122	Ⓐ Ⓑ Ⓒ Ⓓ	142	Ⓐ Ⓑ Ⓒ Ⓓ	162	Ⓐ Ⓑ Ⓒ Ⓓ	182	Ⓐ Ⓑ Ⓒ Ⓓ
103	Ⓐ Ⓑ Ⓒ Ⓓ	123	Ⓐ Ⓑ Ⓒ Ⓓ	143	Ⓐ Ⓑ Ⓒ Ⓓ	163	Ⓐ Ⓑ Ⓒ Ⓓ	183	Ⓐ Ⓑ Ⓒ Ⓓ
104	Ⓐ Ⓑ Ⓒ Ⓓ	124	Ⓐ Ⓑ Ⓒ Ⓓ	144	Ⓐ Ⓑ Ⓒ Ⓓ	164	Ⓐ Ⓑ Ⓒ Ⓓ	184	Ⓐ Ⓑ Ⓒ Ⓓ
105	Ⓐ Ⓑ Ⓒ Ⓓ	125	Ⓐ Ⓑ Ⓒ Ⓓ	145	Ⓐ Ⓑ Ⓒ Ⓓ	165	Ⓐ Ⓑ Ⓒ Ⓓ	185	Ⓐ Ⓑ Ⓒ Ⓓ
106	Ⓐ Ⓑ Ⓒ Ⓓ	126	Ⓐ Ⓑ Ⓒ Ⓓ	146	Ⓐ Ⓑ Ⓒ Ⓓ	166	Ⓐ Ⓑ Ⓒ Ⓓ	186	Ⓐ Ⓑ Ⓒ Ⓓ
107	Ⓐ Ⓑ Ⓒ Ⓓ	127	Ⓐ Ⓑ Ⓒ Ⓓ	147	Ⓐ Ⓑ Ⓒ Ⓓ	167	Ⓐ Ⓑ Ⓒ Ⓓ	187	Ⓐ Ⓑ Ⓒ Ⓓ
108	Ⓐ Ⓑ Ⓒ Ⓓ	128	Ⓐ Ⓑ Ⓒ Ⓓ	148	Ⓐ Ⓑ Ⓒ Ⓓ	168	Ⓐ Ⓑ Ⓒ Ⓓ	188	Ⓐ Ⓑ Ⓒ Ⓓ
109	Ⓐ Ⓑ Ⓒ Ⓓ	129	Ⓐ Ⓑ Ⓒ Ⓓ	149	Ⓐ Ⓑ Ⓒ Ⓓ	169	Ⓐ Ⓑ Ⓒ Ⓓ	189	Ⓐ Ⓑ Ⓒ Ⓓ
110	Ⓐ Ⓑ Ⓒ Ⓓ	130	Ⓐ Ⓑ Ⓒ Ⓓ	150	Ⓐ Ⓑ Ⓒ Ⓓ	170	Ⓐ Ⓑ Ⓒ Ⓓ	190	Ⓐ Ⓑ Ⓒ Ⓓ
111	Ⓐ Ⓑ Ⓒ Ⓓ	131	Ⓐ Ⓑ Ⓒ Ⓓ	151	Ⓐ Ⓑ Ⓒ Ⓓ	171	Ⓐ Ⓑ Ⓒ Ⓓ	191	Ⓐ Ⓑ Ⓒ Ⓓ
112	Ⓐ Ⓑ Ⓒ Ⓓ	132	Ⓐ Ⓑ Ⓒ Ⓓ	152	Ⓐ Ⓑ Ⓒ Ⓓ	172	Ⓐ Ⓑ Ⓒ Ⓓ	192	Ⓐ Ⓑ Ⓒ Ⓓ
113	Ⓐ Ⓑ Ⓒ Ⓓ	133	Ⓐ Ⓑ Ⓒ Ⓓ	153	Ⓐ Ⓑ Ⓒ Ⓓ	173	Ⓐ Ⓑ Ⓒ Ⓓ	193	Ⓐ Ⓑ Ⓒ Ⓓ
114	Ⓐ Ⓑ Ⓒ Ⓓ	134	Ⓐ Ⓑ Ⓒ Ⓓ	154	Ⓐ Ⓑ Ⓒ Ⓓ	174	Ⓐ Ⓑ Ⓒ Ⓓ	194	Ⓐ Ⓑ Ⓒ Ⓓ
115	Ⓐ Ⓑ Ⓒ Ⓓ	135	Ⓐ Ⓑ Ⓒ Ⓓ	155	Ⓐ Ⓑ Ⓒ Ⓓ	175	Ⓐ Ⓑ Ⓒ Ⓓ	195	Ⓐ Ⓑ Ⓒ Ⓓ
116	Ⓐ Ⓑ Ⓒ Ⓓ	135	Ⓐ Ⓑ Ⓒ Ⓓ	156	Ⓐ Ⓑ Ⓒ Ⓓ	176	Ⓐ Ⓑ Ⓒ Ⓓ	196	Ⓐ Ⓑ Ⓒ Ⓓ
117	Ⓐ Ⓑ Ⓒ Ⓓ	137	Ⓐ Ⓑ Ⓒ Ⓓ	157	Ⓐ Ⓑ Ⓒ Ⓓ	177	Ⓐ Ⓑ Ⓒ Ⓓ	197	Ⓐ Ⓑ Ⓒ Ⓓ
118	Ⓐ Ⓑ Ⓒ Ⓓ	138	Ⓐ Ⓑ Ⓒ Ⓓ	158	Ⓐ Ⓑ Ⓒ Ⓓ	178	Ⓐ Ⓑ Ⓒ Ⓓ	198	Ⓐ Ⓑ Ⓒ Ⓓ
119	Ⓐ Ⓑ Ⓒ Ⓓ	139	Ⓐ Ⓑ Ⓒ Ⓓ	159	Ⓐ Ⓑ Ⓒ Ⓓ	179	Ⓐ Ⓑ Ⓒ Ⓓ	199	Ⓐ Ⓑ Ⓒ Ⓓ
120	Ⓐ Ⓑ Ⓒ Ⓓ	140	Ⓐ Ⓑ Ⓒ Ⓓ	160	Ⓐ Ⓑ Ⓒ Ⓓ	180	Ⓐ Ⓑ Ⓒ Ⓓ	200	Ⓐ Ⓑ Ⓒ Ⓓ

ANSWER SHEET

TOEIC 실전 테스트

수험번호						고사장	고사실
성명 한글							
성명 한자							

Listening Comprehension Part I ~ Part IV

No.	ANSWER A B C D	No.	ANSWER A B C D	No.	ANSWER A B C D	No.	ANSWER A B C D	No.	ANSWER A B C D
1	Ⓐ Ⓑ Ⓒ Ⓓ	21	Ⓐ Ⓑ Ⓒ	41	Ⓐ Ⓑ Ⓒ Ⓓ	61	Ⓐ Ⓑ Ⓒ Ⓓ	81	Ⓐ Ⓑ Ⓒ Ⓓ
2	Ⓐ Ⓑ Ⓒ Ⓓ	22	Ⓐ Ⓑ Ⓒ	42	Ⓐ Ⓑ Ⓒ Ⓓ	62	Ⓐ Ⓑ Ⓒ Ⓓ	82	Ⓐ Ⓑ Ⓒ Ⓓ
3	Ⓐ Ⓑ Ⓒ Ⓓ	23	Ⓐ Ⓑ Ⓒ	43	Ⓐ Ⓑ Ⓒ Ⓓ	63	Ⓐ Ⓑ Ⓒ Ⓓ	83	Ⓐ Ⓑ Ⓒ Ⓓ
4	Ⓐ Ⓑ Ⓒ Ⓓ	24	Ⓐ Ⓑ Ⓒ	44	Ⓐ Ⓑ Ⓒ Ⓓ	64	Ⓐ Ⓑ Ⓒ Ⓓ	84	Ⓐ Ⓑ Ⓒ Ⓓ
5	Ⓐ Ⓑ Ⓒ Ⓓ	25	Ⓐ Ⓑ Ⓒ	45	Ⓐ Ⓑ Ⓒ Ⓓ	65	Ⓐ Ⓑ Ⓒ Ⓓ	85	Ⓐ Ⓑ Ⓒ Ⓓ
6	Ⓐ Ⓑ Ⓒ Ⓓ	26	Ⓐ Ⓑ Ⓒ	46	Ⓐ Ⓑ Ⓒ Ⓓ	66	Ⓐ Ⓑ Ⓒ Ⓓ	86	Ⓐ Ⓑ Ⓒ Ⓓ
7	Ⓐ Ⓑ Ⓒ Ⓓ	27	Ⓐ Ⓑ Ⓒ	47	Ⓐ Ⓑ Ⓒ Ⓓ	67	Ⓐ Ⓑ Ⓒ Ⓓ	87	Ⓐ Ⓑ Ⓒ Ⓓ
8	Ⓐ Ⓑ Ⓒ Ⓓ	28	Ⓐ Ⓑ Ⓒ	48	Ⓐ Ⓑ Ⓒ Ⓓ	68	Ⓐ Ⓑ Ⓒ Ⓓ	88	Ⓐ Ⓑ Ⓒ Ⓓ
9	Ⓐ Ⓑ Ⓒ Ⓓ	29	Ⓐ Ⓑ Ⓒ	49	Ⓐ Ⓑ Ⓒ Ⓓ	69	Ⓐ Ⓑ Ⓒ Ⓓ	89	Ⓐ Ⓑ Ⓒ Ⓓ
10	Ⓐ Ⓑ Ⓒ Ⓓ	30	Ⓐ Ⓑ Ⓒ	50	Ⓐ Ⓑ Ⓒ Ⓓ	70	Ⓐ Ⓑ Ⓒ Ⓓ	90	Ⓐ Ⓑ Ⓒ Ⓓ
11	Ⓐ Ⓑ Ⓒ	31	Ⓐ Ⓑ Ⓒ	51	Ⓐ Ⓑ Ⓒ Ⓓ	71	Ⓐ Ⓑ Ⓒ Ⓓ	91	Ⓐ Ⓑ Ⓒ Ⓓ
12	Ⓐ Ⓑ Ⓒ	32	Ⓐ Ⓑ Ⓒ	52	Ⓐ Ⓑ Ⓒ Ⓓ	72	Ⓐ Ⓑ Ⓒ Ⓓ	92	Ⓐ Ⓑ Ⓒ Ⓓ
13	Ⓐ Ⓑ Ⓒ	33	Ⓐ Ⓑ Ⓒ	53	Ⓐ Ⓑ Ⓒ Ⓓ	73	Ⓐ Ⓑ Ⓒ Ⓓ	93	Ⓐ Ⓑ Ⓒ Ⓓ
14	Ⓐ Ⓑ Ⓒ	34	Ⓐ Ⓑ Ⓒ	54	Ⓐ Ⓑ Ⓒ Ⓓ	74	Ⓐ Ⓑ Ⓒ Ⓓ	94	Ⓐ Ⓑ Ⓒ Ⓓ
15	Ⓐ Ⓑ Ⓒ	35	Ⓐ Ⓑ Ⓒ	55	Ⓐ Ⓑ Ⓒ Ⓓ	75	Ⓐ Ⓑ Ⓒ Ⓓ	95	Ⓐ Ⓑ Ⓒ Ⓓ
16	Ⓐ Ⓑ Ⓒ	35	Ⓐ Ⓑ Ⓒ	56	Ⓐ Ⓑ Ⓒ Ⓓ	76	Ⓐ Ⓑ Ⓒ Ⓓ	96	Ⓐ Ⓑ Ⓒ Ⓓ
17	Ⓐ Ⓑ Ⓒ	37	Ⓐ Ⓑ Ⓒ	57	Ⓐ Ⓑ Ⓒ Ⓓ	77	Ⓐ Ⓑ Ⓒ Ⓓ	97	Ⓐ Ⓑ Ⓒ Ⓓ
18	Ⓐ Ⓑ Ⓒ	38	Ⓐ Ⓑ Ⓒ	58	Ⓐ Ⓑ Ⓒ Ⓓ	78	Ⓐ Ⓑ Ⓒ Ⓓ	98	Ⓐ Ⓑ Ⓒ Ⓓ
19	Ⓐ Ⓑ Ⓒ	39	Ⓐ Ⓑ Ⓒ	59	Ⓐ Ⓑ Ⓒ Ⓓ	79	Ⓐ Ⓑ Ⓒ Ⓓ	99	Ⓐ Ⓑ Ⓒ Ⓓ
20	Ⓐ Ⓑ Ⓒ	40	Ⓐ Ⓑ Ⓒ	60	Ⓐ Ⓑ Ⓒ Ⓓ	80	Ⓐ Ⓑ Ⓒ Ⓓ	100	Ⓐ Ⓑ Ⓒ Ⓓ

Reading Comprehension Part V ~ Part VII

No.	ANSWER A B C D	No.	ANSWER A B C D	No.	ANSWER A B C D	No.	ANSWER A B C D	No.	ANSWER A B C D
101	Ⓐ Ⓑ Ⓒ Ⓓ	121	Ⓐ Ⓑ Ⓒ Ⓓ	141	Ⓐ Ⓑ Ⓒ Ⓓ	161	Ⓐ Ⓑ Ⓒ Ⓓ	181	Ⓐ Ⓑ Ⓒ Ⓓ
102	Ⓐ Ⓑ Ⓒ Ⓓ	122	Ⓐ Ⓑ Ⓒ Ⓓ	142	Ⓐ Ⓑ Ⓒ Ⓓ	162	Ⓐ Ⓑ Ⓒ Ⓓ	182	Ⓐ Ⓑ Ⓒ Ⓓ
103	Ⓐ Ⓑ Ⓒ Ⓓ	123	Ⓐ Ⓑ Ⓒ Ⓓ	143	Ⓐ Ⓑ Ⓒ Ⓓ	163	Ⓐ Ⓑ Ⓒ Ⓓ	183	Ⓐ Ⓑ Ⓒ Ⓓ
104	Ⓐ Ⓑ Ⓒ Ⓓ	124	Ⓐ Ⓑ Ⓒ Ⓓ	144	Ⓐ Ⓑ Ⓒ Ⓓ	164	Ⓐ Ⓑ Ⓒ Ⓓ	184	Ⓐ Ⓑ Ⓒ Ⓓ
105	Ⓐ Ⓑ Ⓒ Ⓓ	125	Ⓐ Ⓑ Ⓒ Ⓓ	145	Ⓐ Ⓑ Ⓒ Ⓓ	165	Ⓐ Ⓑ Ⓒ Ⓓ	185	Ⓐ Ⓑ Ⓒ Ⓓ
106	Ⓐ Ⓑ Ⓒ Ⓓ	126	Ⓐ Ⓑ Ⓒ Ⓓ	146	Ⓐ Ⓑ Ⓒ Ⓓ	166	Ⓐ Ⓑ Ⓒ Ⓓ	186	Ⓐ Ⓑ Ⓒ Ⓓ
107	Ⓐ Ⓑ Ⓒ Ⓓ	127	Ⓐ Ⓑ Ⓒ Ⓓ	147	Ⓐ Ⓑ Ⓒ Ⓓ	167	Ⓐ Ⓑ Ⓒ Ⓓ	187	Ⓐ Ⓑ Ⓒ Ⓓ
108	Ⓐ Ⓑ Ⓒ Ⓓ	128	Ⓐ Ⓑ Ⓒ Ⓓ	148	Ⓐ Ⓑ Ⓒ Ⓓ	168	Ⓐ Ⓑ Ⓒ Ⓓ	188	Ⓐ Ⓑ Ⓒ Ⓓ
109	Ⓐ Ⓑ Ⓒ Ⓓ	129	Ⓐ Ⓑ Ⓒ Ⓓ	149	Ⓐ Ⓑ Ⓒ Ⓓ	169	Ⓐ Ⓑ Ⓒ Ⓓ	189	Ⓐ Ⓑ Ⓒ Ⓓ
110	Ⓐ Ⓑ Ⓒ Ⓓ	130	Ⓐ Ⓑ Ⓒ Ⓓ	150	Ⓐ Ⓑ Ⓒ Ⓓ	170	Ⓐ Ⓑ Ⓒ Ⓓ	190	Ⓐ Ⓑ Ⓒ Ⓓ
111	Ⓐ Ⓑ Ⓒ Ⓓ	131	Ⓐ Ⓑ Ⓒ Ⓓ	151	Ⓐ Ⓑ Ⓒ Ⓓ	171	Ⓐ Ⓑ Ⓒ Ⓓ	191	Ⓐ Ⓑ Ⓒ Ⓓ
112	Ⓐ Ⓑ Ⓒ Ⓓ	132	Ⓐ Ⓑ Ⓒ Ⓓ	152	Ⓐ Ⓑ Ⓒ Ⓓ	172	Ⓐ Ⓑ Ⓒ Ⓓ	192	Ⓐ Ⓑ Ⓒ Ⓓ
113	Ⓐ Ⓑ Ⓒ Ⓓ	133	Ⓐ Ⓑ Ⓒ Ⓓ	153	Ⓐ Ⓑ Ⓒ Ⓓ	173	Ⓐ Ⓑ Ⓒ Ⓓ	193	Ⓐ Ⓑ Ⓒ Ⓓ
114	Ⓐ Ⓑ Ⓒ Ⓓ	134	Ⓐ Ⓑ Ⓒ Ⓓ	154	Ⓐ Ⓑ Ⓒ Ⓓ	174	Ⓐ Ⓑ Ⓒ Ⓓ	194	Ⓐ Ⓑ Ⓒ Ⓓ
115	Ⓐ Ⓑ Ⓒ Ⓓ	135	Ⓐ Ⓑ Ⓒ Ⓓ	155	Ⓐ Ⓑ Ⓒ Ⓓ	175	Ⓐ Ⓑ Ⓒ Ⓓ	195	Ⓐ Ⓑ Ⓒ Ⓓ
116	Ⓐ Ⓑ Ⓒ Ⓓ	135	Ⓐ Ⓑ Ⓒ Ⓓ	156	Ⓐ Ⓑ Ⓒ Ⓓ	176	Ⓐ Ⓑ Ⓒ Ⓓ	196	Ⓐ Ⓑ Ⓒ Ⓓ
117	Ⓐ Ⓑ Ⓒ Ⓓ	137	Ⓐ Ⓑ Ⓒ Ⓓ	157	Ⓐ Ⓑ Ⓒ Ⓓ	177	Ⓐ Ⓑ Ⓒ Ⓓ	197	Ⓐ Ⓑ Ⓒ Ⓓ
118	Ⓐ Ⓑ Ⓒ Ⓓ	138	Ⓐ Ⓑ Ⓒ Ⓓ	158	Ⓐ Ⓑ Ⓒ Ⓓ	178	Ⓐ Ⓑ Ⓒ Ⓓ	198	Ⓐ Ⓑ Ⓒ Ⓓ
119	Ⓐ Ⓑ Ⓒ Ⓓ	139	Ⓐ Ⓑ Ⓒ Ⓓ	159	Ⓐ Ⓑ Ⓒ Ⓓ	179	Ⓐ Ⓑ Ⓒ Ⓓ	199	Ⓐ Ⓑ Ⓒ Ⓓ
120	Ⓐ Ⓑ Ⓒ Ⓓ	140	Ⓐ Ⓑ Ⓒ Ⓓ	160	Ⓐ Ⓑ Ⓒ Ⓓ	180	Ⓐ Ⓑ Ⓒ Ⓓ	200	Ⓐ Ⓑ Ⓒ Ⓓ

ANSWER SHEET

TOEIC 실전 테스트

수험번호 | 고사장 | 고사실

성명 — 한글 / 한자

Listening Comprehension Part I ~ Part IV

No.	ANSWER	No.	ANSWER	No.	ANSWER	No.	ANSWER	No.	ANSWER
1	A B C D	21	A B C	41	A B C D	61	A B C D	81	A B C D
2	A B C D	22	A B C	42	A B C D	62	A B C D	82	A B C D
3	A B C D	23	A B C	43	A B C D	63	A B C D	83	A B C D
4	A B C D	24	A B C	44	A B C D	64	A B C D	84	A B C D
5	A B C D	25	A B C	45	A B C D	65	A B C D	85	A B C D
6	A B C D	26	A B C	46	A B C D	66	A B C D	86	A B C D
7	A B C D	27	A B C	47	A B C D	67	A B C D	87	A B C D
8	A B C D	28	A B C	48	A B C D	68	A B C D	88	A B C D
9	A B C D	29	A B C	49	A B C D	69	A B C D	89	A B C D
10	A B C D	30	A B C	50	A B C D	70	A B C D	90	A B C D
11	A B C	31	A B C	51	A B C D	71	A B C D	91	A B C D
12	A B C	32	A B C	52	A B C D	72	A B C D	92	A B C D
13	A B C	33	A B C	53	A B C D	73	A B C D	93	A B C D
14	A B C	34	A B C	54	A B C D	74	A B C D	94	A B C D
15	A B C	35	A B C	55	A B C D	75	A B C D	95	A B C D
16	A B C	35	A B C	56	A B C D	76	A B C D	96	A B C D
17	A B C	37	A B C	57	A B C D	77	A B C D	97	A B C D
18	A B C	38	A B C	58	A B C D	78	A B C D	98	A B C D
19	A B C	39	A B C	59	A B C D	79	A B C D	99	A B C D
20	A B C	40	A B C	60	A B C D	80	A B C D	100	A B C D

Reading Comprehension Part V ~ Part VII

No.	ANSWER	No.	ANSWER	No.	ANSWER	No.	ANSWER	No.	ANSWER
101	A B C D	121	A B C D	141	A B C D	161	A B C D	181	A B C D
102	A B C D	122	A B C D	142	A B C D	162	A B C D	182	A B C D
103	A B C D	123	A B C D	143	A B C D	163	A B C D	183	A B C D
104	A B C D	124	A B C D	144	A B C D	164	A B C D	184	A B C D
105	A B C D	125	A B C D	145	A B C D	165	A B C D	185	A B C D
106	A B C D	126	A B C D	146	A B C D	166	A B C D	186	A B C D
107	A B C D	127	A B C D	147	A B C D	167	A B C D	187	A B C D
108	A B C D	128	A B C D	148	A B C D	168	A B C D	188	A B C D
109	A B C D	129	A B C D	149	A B C D	169	A B C D	189	A B C D
110	A B C D	130	A B C D	150	A B C D	170	A B C D	190	A B C D
111	A B C D	131	A B C D	151	A B C D	171	A B C D	191	A B C D
112	A B C D	132	A B C D	152	A B C D	172	A B C D	192	A B C D
113	A B C D	133	A B C D	153	A B C D	173	A B C D	193	A B C D
114	A B C D	134	A B C D	154	A B C D	174	A B C D	194	A B C D
115	A B C D	135	A B C D	155	A B C D	175	A B C D	195	A B C D
116	A B C D	135	A B C D	156	A B C D	176	A B C D	196	A B C D
117	A B C D	137	A B C D	157	A B C D	177	A B C D	197	A B C D
118	A B C D	138	A B C D	158	A B C D	178	A B C D	198	A B C D
119	A B C D	139	A B C D	159	A B C D	179	A B C D	199	A B C D
120	A B C D	140	A B C D	160	A B C D	180	A B C D	200	A B C D

문제집+해설집
정가 12,800원(mp3 CD 포함)
ISBN 978-89-7172-804-8

新

최신의 토익 출제경향을 그대로 반영한
최종 마무리 테스트

이지투

오해원, 박은주, 최서원 외 3인 저

토익 급상승

퍼펙트 600제

[LC + RC 실전문제집 3세트]

mp3 CD 포함

• 신토익 예상 출제경향과 난이도를 반영한 실전문제 3세트 수록
• 실제 토익과 같은 성우 구성의 LC 음원 + RC 주요 문제 음성강의 CD 제공
• 복습용 문제별 음원 홈페이지(www.bansok.co.kr) 제공

제1라운드 [해설집]

Bansok

퍼펙트 600제

제 ❶ 라운드 · 해설집

新 이지투 토익 급상승 퍼펙트 600제 제❶라운드

저 자 오해원, 박은주, 최석원 외 3인
발행인 고본화
발 행 반석출판사
2016년 6월 15일 초판 1쇄 인쇄
2016년 6월 20일 초판 1쇄 발행
홈페이지 www.bansok.co.kr
이메일 bansok@bansok.co.kr
블로그 blog.naver.com/bansokbooks

157-779 서울시 강서구 양천로 583번지 B동 904호
　　　　　(서울시 강서구 염창동 240-21번지 우림블루나인 비즈니스센터 B동 904호)
대표전화 02) 2093-3399 **팩 스** 02) 2093-3393
출 판 부 02) 2093-3395 **영업부** 02) 2093-3396
등록번호 제315-2008-000033호

Copyright ⓒ 오해원, 박은주, 최석원 외 3인

ISBN 978-89-7172-804-8 (13740)

목차

정답표

Actual Test 01

#		#		#		#		#		#		#		#		#		#	
1	(B)	21	(B)	41	(A)	61	(B)	81	(A)	101	(C)	121	(C)	141	(C)	161	(B)	181	(B)
2	(B)	22	(C)	42	(D)	62	(D)	82	(D)	102	(A)	122	(C)	142	(A)	162	(C)	182	(C)
3	(D)	23	(B)	43	(C)	63	(B)	83	(B)	103	(D)	123	(D)	143	(B)	163	(C)	183	(D)
4	(C)	24	(A)	44	(C)	64	(A)	84	(B)	104	(C)	124	(C)	144	(D)	164	(A)	184	(C)
5	(A)	25	(C)	45	(B)	65	(C)	85	(B)	105	(D)	125	(A)	145	(D)	165	(C)	185	(A)
6	(A)	26	(B)	46	(A)	66	(B)	86	(C)	106	(C)	126	(D)	146	(D)	166	(D)	186	(B)
7	(A)	27	(C)	47	(B)	67	(C)	87	(A)	107	(C)	127	(D)	147	(A)	167	(B)	187	(C)
8	(C)	28	(B)	48	(D)	68	(A)	88	(B)	108	(A)	128	(A)	148	(C)	168	(C)	188	(C)
9	(C)	29	(B)	49	(A)	69	(C)	89	(D)	109	(C)	129	(A)	149	(D)	169	(D)	189	(B)
10	(C)	30	(A)	50	(C)	70	(C)	90	(B)	110	(D)	130	(B)	150	(B)	170	(C)	190	(B)
11	(B)	31	(B)	51	(D)	71	(B)	91	(D)	111	(A)	131	(D)	151	(B)	171	(C)	191	(A)
12	(A)	32	(A)	52	(C)	72	(C)	92	(D)	112	(C)	132	(C)	152	(A)	172	(A)	192	(B)
13	(C)	33	(A)	53	(A)	73	(D)	93	(C)	113	(C)	133	(B)	153	(D)	173	(B)	193	(A)
14	(C)	34	(C)	54	(A)	74	(A)	94	(C)	114	(B)	134	(D)	154	(B)	174	(D)	194	(D)
15	(A)	35	(B)	55	(C)	75	(B)	95	(A)	115	(B)	135	(B)	155	(B)	175	(A)	195	(D)
16	(B)	36	(D)	56	(C)	76	(D)	96	(C)	116	(D)	136	(C)	156	(C)	176	(B)	196	(C)
17	(A)	37	(A)	57	(A)	77	(A)	97	(C)	117	(C)	137	(D)	157	(A)	177	(D)	197	(A)
18	(A)	38	(C)	58	(B)	78	(D)	98	(C)	118	(B)	138	(B)	158	(B)	178	(C)	198	(B)
19	(C)	39	(B)	59	(C)	79	(B)	99	(D)	119	(A)	139	(D)	159	(A)	179	(C)	199	(C)
20	(C)	40	(A)	60	(D)	80	(C)	100	(D)	120	(A)	140	(C)	160	(D)	180	(A)	200	(C)

Actual Test 02

#		#		#		#		#		#		#		#		#		#	
1	(C)	21	(B)	41	(B)	61	(A)	81	(D)	101	(D)	121	(B)	141	(A)	161	(C)	181	(A)
2	(B)	22	(B)	42	(C)	62	(A)	82	(C)	102	(A)	122	(A)	142	(C)	162	(D)	182	(A)
3	(D)	23	(A)	43	(D)	63	(D)	83	(D)	103	(A)	123	(D)	143	(D)	163	(D)	183	(B)
4	(C)	24	(A)	44	(A)	64	(C)	84	(C)	104	(B)	124	(B)	144	(D)	164	(D)	184	(B)
5	(D)	25	(C)	45	(D)	65	(A)	85	(C)	105	(B)	125	(D)	145	(A)	165	(B)	185	(C)
6	(C)	26	(A)	46	(B)	66	(B)	86	(B)	106	(A)	126	(C)	146	(D)	166	(A)	186	(D)
7	(C)	27	(C)	47	(B)	67	(D)	87	(D)	107	(B)	127	(D)	147	(D)	167	(B)	187	(D)
8	(C)	28	(C)	48	(C)	68	(B)	88	(A)	108	(B)	128	(B)	148	(C)	168	(D)	188	(C)
9	(A)	29	(A)	49	(A)	69	(C)	89	(D)	109	(B)	129	(C)	149	(A)	169	(C)	189	(B)
10	(A)	30	(B)	50	(C)	70	(B)	90	(D)	110	(A)	130	(C)	150	(B)	170	(B)	190	(C)
11	(C)	31	(C)	51	(D)	71	(C)	91	(B)	111	(D)	131	(A)	151	(C)	171	(C)	191	(B)
12	(B)	32	(C)	52	(B)	72	(B)	92	(D)	112	(C)	132	(C)	152	(B)	172	(A)	192	(A)
13	(B)	33	(B)	53	(C)	73	(D)	93	(B)	113	(D)	133	(A)	153	(D)	173	(D)	193	(A)
14	(B)	34	(D)	54	(B)	74	(D)	94	(A)	114	(A)	134	(A)	154	(A)	174	(C)	194	(C)
15	(C)	35	(C)	55	(D)	75	(A)	95	(B)	115	(D)	135	(A)	155	(D)	175	(C)	195	(A)
16	(C)	36	(C)	56	(B)	76	(A)	96	(D)	116	(C)	136	(B)	156	(C)	176	(D)	196	(C)
17	(A)	37	(A)	57	(D)	77	(A)	97	(B)	117	(D)	137	(C)	157	(B)	177	(C)	197	(D)
18	(B)	38	(C)	58	(C)	78	(D)	98	(A)	118	(D)	138	(C)	158	(B)	178	(B)	198	(A)
19	(A)	39	(C)	59	(D)	79	(B)	99	(D)	119	(D)	139	(B)	159	(A)	179	(C)	199	(C)
20	(B)	40	(B)	60	(C)	80	(B)	100	(B)	120	(C)	140	(C)	160	(D)	180	(C)	200	(B)

Actual Test 03

1	(B)	21	(C)	41	(D)	61	(B)	81	(D)	101	(A)	121	(C)	141	(B)	161	(D)	181	(A)
2	(B)	22	(B)	42	(A)	62	(C)	82	(C)	102	(D)	122	(C)	142	(C)	162	(C)	182	(C)
3	(D)	23	(C)	43	(B)	63	(A)	83	(B)	103	(C)	123	(D)	143	(D)	163	(A)	183	(D)
4	(C)	24	(C)	44	(C)	64	(B)	84	(D)	104	(A)	124	(B)	144	(B)	164	(C)	184	(D)
5	(D)	25	(B)	45	(A)	65	(B)	85	(A)	105	(B)	125	(C)	145	(D)	165	(B)	185	(C)
6	(A)	26	(A)	46	(B)	66	(C)	86	(B)	106	(C)	126	(B)	146	(C)	166	(C)	186	(A)
7	(A)	27	(A)	47	(B)	67	(A)	87	(D)	107	(B)	127	(B)	147	(C)	167	(B)	187	(C)
8	(B)	28	(A)	48	(D)	68	(B)	88	(A)	108	(C)	128	(A)	148	(A)	168	(A)	188	(D)
9	(B)	29	(C)	49	(A)	69	(B)	89	(C)	109	(B)	129	(C)	149	(A)	169	(D)	189	(A)
10	(A)	30	(B)	50	(B)	70	(D)	90	(C)	110	(A)	130	(D)	150	(A)	170	(C)	190	(C)
11	(C)	31	(A)	51	(A)	71	(B)	91	(B)	111	(D)	131	(B)	151	(D)	171	(B)	191	(B)
12	(B)	32	(D)	52	(D)	72	(C)	92	(C)	112	(B)	132	(C)	152	(D)	172	(C)	192	(C)
13	(C)	33	(C)	53	(C)	73	(D)	93	(D)	113	(B)	133	(A)	153	(C)	173	(C)	193	(A)
14	(B)	34	(D)	54	(A)	74	(D)	94	(B)	114	(D)	134	(A)	154	(A)	174	(D)	194	(A)
15	(A)	35	(C)	55	(D)	75	(A)	95	(A)	115	(C)	135	(A)	155	(B)	175	(B)	195	(D)
16	(C)	36	(A)	56	(C)	76	(B)	96	(D)	116	(B)	136	(D)	156	(A)	176	(D)	196	(D)
17	(B)	37	(B)	57	(D)	77	(D)	97	(B)	117	(B)	137	(C)	157	(A)	177	(B)	197	(D)
18	(A)	38	(D)	58	(B)	78	(A)	98	(D)	118	(B)	138	(C)	158	(D)	178	(D)	198	(A)
19	(A)	39	(B)	59	(C)	79	(A)	99	(C)	119	(C)	139	(B)	159	(C)	179	(C)	199	(A)
20	(B)	40	(C)	60	(D)	80	(A)	100	(A)	120	(D)	140	(D)	160	(A)	180	(A)	200	(B)

 ## 점수 그래프

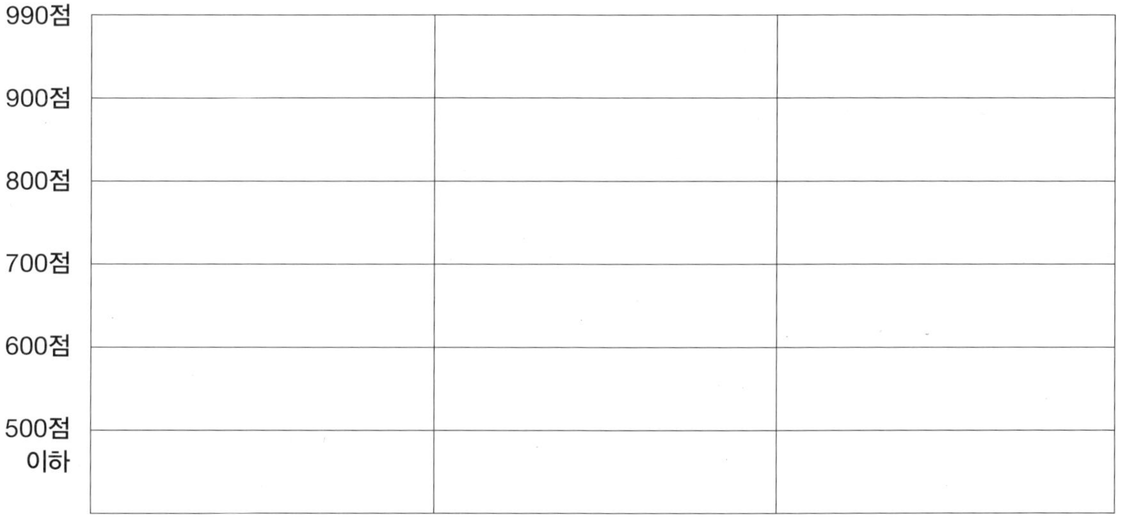

Actual Test 01

1. (B)

(A) The man is repairing the car door.
(B) The man is looking under the hood of the car.
(C) The man is parking the vehicle on the road.
(D) The man is taking the engine out of the car.

(A) 남자가 자동차 문을 수리 중이다.
(B) 남자가 보닛 아래를 보는 중이다.
(C) 남자가 도로에 주차하는 중이다.
(D) 남자가 자동차에서 엔진을 꺼내는 중이다.

어휘_ repair 수리하다 hood of the car 자동차 보닛 take A out of ~를 꺼내다

분석_ 사람 1인 사진으로 등장인물의 동작, 외모, 배경을 보고 정답을 고르는 유형의 문제이다. 이 문제는 자동차의 보닛을 열고 정비하는 동작에 맞는 표현을 고른다. (B) 사진에 등장한 사람의 동작과 일치하므로 정답이다. **오답분석** (A) 자동차의 문이 보이지 않으므로 오답이다. 또한 남자는 보닛 아래를 보고 있다. (C) 주차하고 있는 중이 아니므로 오답이다. 이미 자동차는 주차되어 있는 걸로 볼 수 있다. (D) 사진과 맞지 않는 동작 불일치 오답이다.

2. (B)

(A) She's turning on the light.
(B) She's holding up a book.
(C) She's speaking to the audience.
(D) She's rearranging the bookshelf.

(A) 여자가 불을 켜는 중이다.
(B) 여자가 책을 쥐고 있다.
(C) 여자가 청중에게 연설하는 중이다.
(D) 여자가 책꽂이를 정리하는 중이다.

어휘_ turn on ~를 켜다 hold ~를 쥐다 audience 청중 rearrange ~를 재배열하다

분석_ 사람 1인 사진으로 도서관에서 책을 보고 있으며 책꽂이에 책들이 정리되어 있다는 표현을 고른다. (B) 여자가 책을 들고 있다는 설명으로 사진과 일치하므로 정답이다. **오답분석** (A) 불을 켜는 동작이 아니므로 동작 불일치 오답이다. (C) 사진에 청중이 없으므로 오답이다. (D) 단순히 책을 보고만 있으므로 동작 불일치 오답이다.

3. (D)

(A) The couple is standing next to each other.
(B) The road is closed to traffic.
(C) A tree has fallen onto the road.
(D) Some cars are parked along the road.

(A) 커플이 길을 건너는 중이다.
(B) 도로가 막혀 있다.
(C) 나무가 도로에 쓰러져 있다.
(D) 몇몇 자동차가 도로를 따라 주차되어 있다.

어휘_ stand 서 있다 fall 쓰러지다 along ~를 따라서

분석_ 사람 없는 사진으로 배경과 사물의 위치를 파악해두어야 한다. 이 사진에서는 자동차가 다니고 있고 길가로 주차가 되어 있다는 표현을 고른다. (D) 길을 따라서 자동차가 주차되어 있다는 표현이므로 정답이다. **오답분석** (A) 길을 건너는 사람이 없으므로 오답이다. (B) 도로가 막혀 있지 않으므로 오답이다. (C) 도로에 쓰러져 있는 나무가 없으므로 오답이다.

4. (C)

(A) The waves are hitting the shore.
(B) A boat has been pulled onto the beach.
(C) The boats are floating on the water.
(D) The ducks are flying over the sea.

(A) 해변으로 파도가 치는 중이다.
(B) 한 대의 보트가 해변에 올라와 있다.
(C) 물위에 보트들이 떠 있다.
(D) 오리가 바다 위를 나는 중이다.

어휘_ wave 파도 hit ~를 치다 shore 해변 be pulled onto ~에 정박되어 있다 float 떠 있다

분석_ 사람 없는 사진이므로 배경과 사물에 대한 표현을 미리 알아두어야 한다. 이 문제에서는 부두에 여러 대의 배가 정박되어 있다는 표현을 골라준다. (C) 배가 물위에 떠 있다는 표현으로 정답이다. **오답분석** (A) 파도가 등장하지 않았으므로 오답이다. (B) 사진에 해변이 없으므로 오답이다. (D) 오리가 나오지 않는 사진이므로 오답이다.

5. (A)

(A) Dishes have been set on the table.
(B) The people have finished their meals.
(C) They are waiting for their food to arrive.
(D) All of the seats are unoccupied.

(A) 음식들이 식탁에 마련되어 있다.
(B) 사람들이 식사를 끝냈다.
(C) 그들이 음식이 나오길 기다리는 중이다.
(D) 모든 좌석이 비어 있다.

어휘_ dish 요리 finish ~를 끝내다 unoccupied 비어 있는

분석_ 사람이 다수 등장하는 사진으로 공통된 동작이나 두드러지는 한 명에 대한 설명이 주로 출제된다. 이 사진에서는 단체로 식사하고 있다거나 식탁에 음식이 준비되어 있다는 표현을 고른다. (A) 식탁에 음식이 준비되어 있다는 표현으로 정답이다. **오답분석** (B) 식사가 아직 끝나지 않았으므로 오답이다. (C) 음식이 이미 나와 있으므로 오답이다. (D) 비어 있는 좌석이 없으므로 오답이다.

6. (A)

(A) The people are strolling on the sidewalk.
(B) The people are crossing the street.
(C) Commuters are waiting for the bus.
(D) They are waiting for the traffic light to change.

(A) 사람들이 인도를 걷는 중이다.
(B) 사람들이 도로를 건너는 중이다.
(C) 통근자들이 버스를 기다리는 중이다.
(D) 그들이 신호등이 바뀌길 기다리는 중이다.

어휘_ stroll 걷다 cross ~를 건너다 commuters 통근자 traffic light 신호등

분석_ 다수의 사람들이 나오는 사진이다. 공통된 동작을 정답으로 골라준다. 이 사진에서는 사람들이 같은 방향으로 인도를 걷고 있다는 내용을 골라준다. (A) 인도를 걷고 있다는 표현이므로 정답이다. **오답분석** (B) 도로를 건너는 사람이 없으므로 동작 불일치 오답이다. (C) 사진에 버스가 없으므로 오답이다. (D) 사진에 신호등이 없으므로 오답이다.

Part 2　　본문 p.20

7. (A)
Where's the supply room?
(A) On the lower level.
(B) No, it wasn't supplied yet.
(C) Some mushrooms, please.

사무용품실이 어디인가요?
(A) 아래층에 있어요.
(B) 아니요. 아직 공급되지 않았어요.
(C) 버섯 조금 주세요.

어휘_ supply room 사무용품실 supply ~를 공급하다

분석_ where로 시작하는 의문사 문제이며 주로 장소 전치사(at, on, in, around, near 등)가 정답의 단서가 된다. 또한 장소를 나타내는 부사(there, here, upstairs 등)도 함께 기억해보자. (A) 장소 전치사(on)와 아래층을 나타내는 표현(lower level)이 만나서 정답이 되고 있다. **오답분석** (B) 의문사 의문문의 경우 Yes/No의 대답이 불가능하다. (C) 질문의 room이라는 단어와 유사한 발음인 mushrooms가 함정으로 등장하여 오답을 유도하고 있다.

8. (C)
When will today's computer training end?
(A) At the Washington Station.
(B) Mr. Bonds trained us.
(C) Around 12 P.M.

오늘 컴퓨터 교육 언제 끝나요?
(A) 워싱턴 역에서요.
(B) Bonds 씨가 우리를 훈련시켰어요.
(C) 12시쯤이요.

어휘_ computer training 컴퓨터 교육 train ~를 훈련시키다

분석_ when으로 시작하는 의문사 문제이며 주로 시간 접속사(when, once, as soon as, before 등), 시간 전치사(at, on, in, during 등) 그리고 시간 부사(tomorrow, yesterday 등)가 정답이 된다. (C) 시간 전치사(around)와 시간 표현(12 P.M.)이 만나서 정답이 되고 있다. **오답분석** (A) 장소 표현이 등장하였으므로 where 질문에 적절한 대답이다. (B) 질

문의 training과 유사 발음인 train이 함정으로 등장했다.

9. (C)
What kind of hotel did Mike choose for the annual banquet?
(A) Yes, it was near the bank.
(B) I made a choice.
(C) The same one we used last year.

연례 연회를 위해 Mike가 어떤 종류의 호텔을 골랐나요?
(A) 네, 은행이랑 가까웠어요.
(B) 제가 선택했어요.
(C) 작년에 우리가 이용했던 호텔이요.

어휘_ choose 선택하다 annual 연례적인 banquet 연회

분석_ what으로 시작하는 의문사 문제이며 뒤에 따라오는 명사(hotel)가 중요한 정답의 단서가 된다. (C) what 혹은 which 질문에서 정답률이 높은 유형으로 대명사 one이 등장했다. 앞에 나온 명사를 가리키는 단어로 거의 매달 출제될 만큼 빈도가 높은 표현이다. **오답분석** (A) what 질문에 Yes/No 대답은 불가능하다. (B) 질문에 나온 choose라는 단어와 유사한 표현인 choice가 함정으로 등장했다.

10. (C)
Who's in charge of the next year's advertising budget?
(A) In the newspaper advertisement.
(B) The final changes.
(C) I heard Julia is.

내년 광고 예산 업무는 누가 맡고 있나요?
(A) 신문 광고에서요.
(B) 최종 변경사항이요.
(C) Julia라고 들었어요.

어휘_ in charge of ~를 책임지는 budget 예산

분석_ who로 시작하는 의문사 문제로 주로 사람 이름, 직책, 회사명, 그리고 부서명을 정답으로 출제한다. (C) 사람 이름인 Julia가 등장하므로 정답이 될 수 있다. **오답분석** (A) 장소 전치사(in)가 등장하여 where 질문에 대한 답으로 볼 수 있다. (B) 질문의 charge와 유사 발음인 changes가 함정으로 등장했다.

11. (B)
Is the workshop for new employees in this room or in the room C?
(A) Beginning on Tuesday.
(B) Ask Marcel.
(C) For the new employees.

신입사원 워크숍이 이 방인가요 아니면 C번 방인가요?
(A) 화요일에 시작합니다.
(B) Marcel에게 물어보세요.
(C) 신입사원들을 위해서요.

어휘_ beginning on ~부터 시작하는

분석_ 문중에 or이 들어가는 선택의문문으로 두 가지 선택사항 중 한 가지를 고른 대답이 정답이 될 가능성이 높은 유형이다. (B) 만능 정답으로 불리는 회피형 대답이다. 타인에게

물어보라는 대답은 거의 모든 질문에서 정답이 될 수 있다. **오답분석** (A) 시간에 대한 답으로 when 질문에 대한 정답이 될 수 있다. (C) 질문의 new employees와 동일 발음인 new employees가 함정으로 등장했다.

12. (A)

Have you talked with the project organizer yet?
(A) We're meeting tomorrow.
(B) 40 organizations.
(C) That's a nice project.
프로젝트 관리자와 이야기해봤어요?
(A) 우리는 내일 만날 겁니다.
(B) 40개의 단체입니다.
(C) 훌륭한 프로젝트군요.
어휘_ organizer 기획자, 관리자 organization 단체
분석_ have동사 의문문으로 완료나 경험을 묻는 질문으로 출제된다. 주로 '아직 덜했다(not yet, still)'와 '이미 다했다(already finish, done, complete)'는 표현이 정답률이 높다. (A) 이야기해봤냐는 질문에 내일 만나기로 했다는 자연스러운 대답으로 정답이 된다. **오답분석** (B) 질문의 organizer와 유사 발음인 organizations가 함정으로 등장했다. (C) 질문의 project가 다시 등장해 오답을 유도하고 있다.

13. (C)

Aren't you going to see that horror movie with Jennifer this weekend?
(A) I've moved a few of them.
(B) A recently renovated theater.
(C) Actually, we just saw it.
이번 주말에 Jennifer랑 그 공포영화 볼 거 아니에요?
(A) 제가 그것 중 몇 개를 옮겼어요.
(B) 최근에 수리된 영화관이요.
(C) 사실, 방금 봤어요.
어휘_ horror 공포 renovate 개조하다
분석_ be동사 의문문으로 일반적인 경우 보어를 듣고 풀이한다. 하지만 이 문제의 경우 going to 구문을 이용하여 앞으로 할 일에 대해서 묻고 있다. (C) 영화를 볼 것인지를 묻는 질문에서 방금 보았다는 반전의 대답을 하고 있으므로 정답이 가능하다. **오답분석** (A) 질문의 movie와 유사 발음인 move를 함정으로 등장시켰다. (B) 질문에 등장한 영화의 연관 어휘(theater)를 함정으로 출제하여 오답을 유도하고 있다.

14. (C)

This new refrigerator is going to be on sale until the end of the month, won't it?
(A) It holds more than seven liters.
(B) It's a specialty store.
(C) Yes, until 30th.
이 새로운 냉장고가 월말까지 할인되죠, 그렇죠?
(A) 이것은 7리터 이상 저장합니다.
(B) 그것은 전문점입니다.
(C) 네, 30일까지요.

어휘_ refrigerator 냉장고 on sale 할인 중인 hold 쥐다, 보관하다 specialty store 전문점
분석_ 문장의 마지막에 다시 물어보는 부가의문으로 평서문과 더불어 가장 어려운 난이도의 유형에 속한다. 반드시 주어, 동사, 목적어를 모두 들어야만 질문의 의도가 전달되므로 높은 청취력을 요구한다. (C) 제품의 할인이 월말까지인지를 확인하는 질문에서 정확하게 일자를 알려주는 대답으로 정답이 된다. **오답분석** (A) 냉장고와 연관성이 있는 저장 용량이 함정으로 등장했다. (B) 전문점이라는 장소 표현으로 보아 where 질문에 적절한 대답으로 볼 수 있다.

15. (A)

Where can I leave these additional charts?
(A) Right there on the desk is fine.
(B) You must do it by Monday.
(C) Ms. Green lives there.
이 추가 차트를 어디에 둘까요?
(A) 바로 저기 책상 위가 좋겠네요.
(B) 당신은 월요일까지 그것을 해야만 합니다.
(C) Green 씨는 거기에 살아요.
어휘_ leave 남겨두다 additional 추가적인
분석_ where로 시작하는 의문사 문제이며 주로 장소 전치사(at, on, in, around, near 등)가 중요 정답의 단서가 된다. 또한 장소를 나타내는 부사(there, here, upstairs 등)도 함께 기억해보자. (A) 장소 표현인 right there과 on the desk가 등장하여 정답이다. **오답분석** (B) 월요일까지 꼭 해야 한다는 대답은 where 질문보다는 when 질문에 더 어울린다. (C) 질문에 나온 leave와 동일 발음이지만 다른 의미를 가진 live가 함정으로 등장했다.

16. (B)

Can you please turn off the copier when you're done with the job?
(A) Yes, I can get you some coffee.
(B) It's already off.
(C) Please turn down the volume.
당신 작업 끝내면 복사기를 꺼주실래요?
(A) 네, 커피 가져다드릴게요.
(B) 이미 꺼져 있어요.
(C) 소리 줄여주세요.
어휘_ turn off ~를 끄다 turn down ~를 줄이다, 거절하다
분석_ 부탁하는 의미로 조동사 can을 이용한 질문이다. 흔히 조동사를 이용하는 의문문의 경우 흔쾌히 수락(OK, of course, be happy to)하거나 정중히 거절(sorry, afraid)하는 표현이 정답률이 높다. (B) 작업이 끝나면 기기를 꺼달라는 부탁에 이미 껐다는 대답을 하고 있으므로 정답이다. **오답분석** (A) 질문의 copier와 유사 발음인 coffee가 함정으로 등장했다. (C) 질문의 turn과 동일 발음이 함정으로 등장하여 오답을 유도하고 있다.

17. (A)

Would you rather work here or in the accounting department?
(A) I prefer to stay here.
(B) I will count them down.
(C) Yes, for ten years.
당신은 여기와 회계부서 중 어디서 일하기를 더 선호하세요?
(A) 저는 여기 머무르고 싶어요.
(B) 제가 그것을 셀 겁니다.
(C) 네, 10년 동안이요.

어휘_ accounting department 회계부서 prefer 선호하다 count down ~를 세다

분석_ 문중에 or이 들어가는 선택의문문으로 두 가지 선택사항 중 한 가지를 고른 대답이 정답이 될 가능성이 높은 유형이다. (A) 선택의문문에서 prefer, would like, wish 등 무언가를 선호하거나 원한다는 표현이 등장하면 정답률이 높다. 오답분석 (B) 질문의 accounting과 유사 발음인 count가 함정으로 등장했다. (C) 선택의문문의 경우 Yes/No의 대답이 불가능하다.

18. (A)

Which of the candidates did the committee select?
(A) I think we'll find out today.
(B) The selection committee.
(C) I'm going out with him.
위원회가 어떤 후보자를 골랐나요?
(A) 제 생각에 오늘 알 수 있을 거예요.
(B) 선발 위원회입니다.
(C) 그와 데이트할 거예요.

어휘_ candidate 후보자 committee 위원회 selection committee 선발 위원회

분석_ which로 시작하는 의문사 의문문으로 what 의문문과 대답의 유형이 비슷하다. (A) 위원회가 어떤 후보자를 뽑았냐는 질문에 오늘 알게 될 것이라는 말로 대답을 회피하고 있다. 질문에 대해 곧장 대답하지 않고 회피하는 유형의 대답은 정답률이 높다. 오답분석 (B) 질문의 committee와 동일 발음을 함정으로 이용하여 오답을 유도하고 있다. (C) 선택지에 등장한 him이 누구인지 알 수 없는 경우로 대명사 불일치 함정에 해당한다. 이처럼 누구인지 알 수 없는 인칭대명사가 등장하면 오답이 된다.

19. (C)

The ferry to Fukuoka departs every thirty minutes, doesn't it?
(A) 30 dollars round trip.
(B) Please turn left at the dock.
(C) No, it's every 40 minutes.
후쿠오카행 여객선이 30분마다 출발하죠, 그렇죠?
(A) 30달러짜리 왕복여행입니다.
(B) 부두에서 왼쪽으로 도세요.
(C) 아니요, 40분마다 출발합니다.

어휘_ depart 출발하다 round trip 왕복여행 dock 부두

분석_ 문장의 마지막에 다시 물어보는 부가의문문으로 평서문과 더불어 가장 어려운 난이도에 속한다. 반드시 주어, 동사, 목적어를 모두 들어야만 질문의 의도가 전달되므로 높은 청취력을 요구한다. (C) 30분마다 출발하느냐는 질문에 40분마다라고 올바른 시간을 알려주고 있으므로 정답이다. 오답분석 (A) 금액 표현이 등장하는 경우 보통 how much 질문에 대한 답이 될 수 있다. (B) 질문의 여객선(ferry)이라는 표현과 연관성이 있는 부두(dock)를 함정으로 등장시켜 오답을 유도하고 있다.

20. (C)

Who should I talk to about changing my e-mail address?
(A) At the mall on Bell Street.
(B) That's my password.
(C) Contact the Human Resources.
이메일 주소를 변경하려면 누구에게 이야기해야 하나요?
(A) Bell Street에 있는 상점에서요.
(B) 그것은 제 비밀번호입니다.
(C) 인사부에 연락해보세요.

어휘_ change 변경하다 address 주소 password 비밀번호 contact 연락하다

분석_ who로 시작하는 의문사 문제로 주로 사람 이름, 직책, 회사명, 그리고 부서명을 정답으로 출제한다. (C) 부서명(Human Resources)이 등장하였으므로 who 질문에 대한 명확한 답이 될 수 있다. 오답분석 (A) 장소 표현이므로 who보다는 where 질문에 대한 답이 된다. (B) 사람을 물어보는 질문에 대해 비밀번호를 이야기하고 있으므로 질문과 연관성이 없어 오답이다.

21. (B)

Shouldn't we order some more sandwiches for the presentation?
(A) No, they're not.
(B) Yes, we need more.
(C) Present them to me.
발표회를 위해 샌드위치를 좀 더 주문해야 하지 않을까요?
(A) 아니요, 그렇지 않습니다.
(B) 네, 더 필요하겠네요.
(C) 그것들을 저에게 보여주세요.

어휘_ order 주문하다 presentation 발표(회) present ~를 보여주다, 발표하다

분석_ 제안의 의미로 조동사 should를 이용한 질문이다. 흔히 조동사를 이용하는 의문문의 경우 흔쾌히 수락(OK, of course, be happy to)하거나 정중히 거절(sorry, afraid)하는 표현이 정답률이 높다. (B) 샌드위치를 더 주문하자는 제안에 더 필요하다는 말을 하고 있으므로 수락의 의미로 볼 수 있다. 동사 의문문은 수락의 표현들이 정답이 잘 된다. 오답분석 (A) 샌드위치 주문과 연관성이 없는 대답이므로 오답이다. (C) 질문의 presentation과 유사 발음인 present를 함정으로 이용한 오답유형이다.

22. (C)

The facility will be closed for the month of May.
(A) Close it carefully.
(B) The latest shipment.
(C) Can you tell me why?

그 시설은 5월 한 달 동안 문을 닫을 겁니다.
(A) 조심스럽게 닫아주세요.
(B) 최근 배송품이요.
(C) 왜 그런지 말씀해주실래요?

어휘_ facility 시설 carefully 조심스럽게 shipment 배송(품)

분석_ 파트2에서 가장 어려운 난이도로 불리는 평서문이다. 부가의문문과 마찬가지로 주어, 동사, 목적어를 반드시 듣고 의미를 파악해야 하므로 높은 청취력이 요구된다. (C) 평서문의 경우 오히려 되묻는 대답이 정답률이 높다. 오답분석 (A) 질문의 closed와 유사 발음인 close가 함정으로 등장했다. (B) 시설 문 닫는 이야기와 연관이 없는 배송품을 말하고 있다.

23. (B)

Why was the routine inspection for the quality control delayed?
(A) I'll take the route.
(B) The inspector was out of town.
(C) The controller's office is upstairs.

정기 품질 관리 조사가 왜 지연되었나요?
(A) 저는 그 길로 갈 겁니다.
(B) 검사관이 자리를 비웠어요.
(C) 통제 사무실은 위층입니다.

어휘_ routine 정기적인 inspection 검사 delay 지연시키다 route 경로

분석_ 의문사 why를 이용하여 이유를 묻는 유형으로 의문사 의문문 중에서 가장 까다롭다. 다른 의문사들과 달리 정답의 패턴이 일정하지 않으므로 주어와 동사를 집중 청취하여 의미를 파악해야 한다. (B) 검사가 지연된 이유에 대해 검사관이 자리를 비웠다는 대답을 하고 있으므로 정답이다. 오답분석 (A) 질문의 routine과 유사 발음인 route가 함정으로 등장했다. (C) 질문의 control과 유사 발음인 controllers가 함정으로 등장, 오답을 유도하고 있다.

24. (A)

How will Lois get to Seoul?
(A) She's flying there from New Mexico.
(B) Sure, I'll return the key.
(C) It'll only last for a few weeks.

Lois는 어떻게 서울에 갈 건가요?
(A) 그녀는 멕시코에서 거기로 비행기 타고 갈 거예요.
(B) 물론이죠, 열쇠 돌려드릴게요.
(C) 몇 주 동안 지속될 겁니다.

어휘_ get to ~에 도착하다 return ~를 되돌려주다 last 지속되다

분석_ how로 시작하여 방법을 묻는 문제이다. 주로 교통, 통신, 지불 수단(by bus, by phone, by cash)이 등장하면 정답률이 높다. (A) 교통수단을 묻는 질문에 대해 비행기를 이용한다는 답을 하고 있으므로 정답이다. 오답분석 (B) 교통수단 질문과 전혀 연관성이 없으므로 오답이다. (C) 특정 기간 지속된다는 표현은 how long 질문에 대한 답이 될 수 있다.

25. (C)

We have to finish painting the second floor by the end of the week.
(A) The door on the right.
(B) On Armenian Street.
(C) Why don't we find more workers?

우리는 이번 주까지 2층 도색 작업을 끝내야 합니다.
(A) 오른쪽에 있는 문입니다.
(B) Armenian Street에 있습니다.
(C) 인력을 더 찾아보는 게 어때요?

어휘_ finish ~를 끝내다 paint ~를 칠하다

분석_ 파트2에서 가장 어려운 난이도로 불리는 평서문이다. 부가의문문과 마찬가지로 주어, 동사, 목적어를 반드시 듣고 의미를 파악해야 하므로 높은 청취력이 요구된다. (C) 평서문의 경우 오히려 되묻는 대답이 정답률이 높다. 오답분석 (A) 문에 대한 이야기로 작업을 끝내야 한다는 질문과 연관성이 없으므로 오답이다. (B) 거리명을 이야기하고 있으므로 장소를 묻는 where 질문에 대한 답으로 더 적절하다.

26. (B)

Was Jenny at the orientation on Friday?
(A) It was extremely informative.
(B) I'll check the attendance list.
(C) Open Tuesday to Sunday.

Jenny가 금요일에 오리엔테이션에 왔었나요?
(A) 매우 유익했어요.
(B) 참가자 명단을 확인해볼게요.
(C) 화요일부터 일요일까지 열려 있어요.

어휘_ extremely 꽤 informative 유익한 attendance 참석(율)

분석_ be동사 의문문으로 일반적인 경우 보어를 듣고 풀이한다. 질문에서 at the orientation이 보어에 해당하므로 오리엔테이션 참석 여부를 묻는다고 볼 수 있다. (B) check가 들어가서 확인해보겠다는 뉘앙스의 대답이 등장하면 정답률이 높다. 오답분석 (A) 오리엔테이션에 대한 느낌을 답하고 있으므로 상태를 물어보는 how 질문에 대한 답으로 적절하다. (C) 시간에 대한 이야기를 하고 있으므로 when 질문에 대한 답으로 더 적절하다.

27. (C)

Is it cheaper to buy a sedan, or to lease one?
(A) Around 5000 euros.
(B) A one-year warranty.
(C) I think lease is more competitive.

세단을 구매하는 것과 임대하는 것 중 어느 것이 더 저렴할까요?
(A) 약 5000유로예요.
(B) 1년짜리 보증이에요.
(C) 임대가 더 저렴하다고 생각해요.

어휘_ lease 임대하다 warranty 보증 competitive 경쟁력 있는, 저렴한

분석_ 문중에 or이 들어가는 선택의문문으로 두 가지 선택사항 중 한 가지를 고른 대답이 정답이 될 가능성이 높은 유형이다. 이 문제의 경우 선택지에 구매 혹은 임대라는 표현이 등장하면 정답률이 높다. (C) 구매와 임대 중 임대에 대한 의견을 나타내고 있으므로 정답으로 적절하다. 오답분석 (A) 금

액을 나타내는 표현은 how much 질문에 더 어울린다. (B) 구매, 임대와 연관성이 있는 듯한 보증(서)에 대한 이야기가 함정으로 등장하여 오답을 유도하고 있다.

28. (B)
Why wasn't Ms. Geller's package delivered on Thursday?
(A) From that electronics store in Eastern district.
(B) She wasn't home to sign for it.
(C) Sometime this afternoon.
왜 목요일에 Geller의 소포가 배송되지 않았나요?
(A) 동부 지역의 전자제품 매장으로부터 옵니다.
(B) 그녀가 확인을 위해 집에 있지 않았어요.
(C) 오늘 오후 언젠가요.
어휘_ package 소포 deliver ~를 배송하다 sign for ~에 등록하다
분석_ 의문사 why를 이용하여 이유를 묻는 유형으로 의문사 의문문 중에서 가장 까다롭다. 다른 의문사들과 달리 정답의 패턴이 일정하지 않으므로 주어와 동사를 집중 청취하여 의미를 파악해야 한다. (B) 소포가 배달되지 않은 이유를 묻고 있으므로 받아야 할 사람이 집에 없었다는 대답이 적절하다. 오답분석 (A) 장소에 대한 이야기를 하고 있으므로 where 질문에 대한 답으로 더 어울린다. (C) 시간에 대한 표현으로 when 질문에 대한 답으로 더 어울린다.

29. (B)
Can't I just pick that up at the event supply store?
(A) I don't think he's been there before.
(B) Yes, it must be in stock now.
(C) We all had a great time.
행사용품 가게에서 그거 가지고 올까요?
(A) 그는 예전에 거기 가본 적이 없는 것 같아요.
(B) 네, 지금 재고가 있을 거예요.
(C) 우리 모두 즐거운 시간이었어요.
어휘_ pick up ~를 가져오다 in stock 재고가 있는
분석_ 제안의 의미로 조동사 can을 이용한 질문이다. 흔히 조동사를 이용하는 의문문의 경우 흔쾌히 수락(OK, of course, be happy to)하거나 정중히 거절(sorry, afraid)하는 표현이 정답률이 높다. (B) 물건을 가져올까라는 질문에 지금 재고가 있을 것이라는 대답을 하고 있다. 즉, 가져오라고 시키는 말을 대신하고 있으므로 정답이 된다. 오답분석 (A) 누군지 알 수 없는 대명사(he)가 등장하였으므로 오답이 된다. 정체를 알 수 없는 인칭대명사가 등장하면 함정이 되므로 주의한다. (C) 물건 가져오는 것과 연관성이 없는 대답으로 정답이 될 수 없다.

30. (A)
How many volunteers are working on the Asian Travel Project?
(A) Let me call the manager right away.
(B) There's a heavy workload.
(C) A variety of products.
Asian Travel Project에 몇 명의 자원봉사자가 일하고 있나요?

(A) 지금 바로 관리자에게 전화해볼게요.
(B) 엄청난 업무가 있어요.
(C) 다양한 제품이에요.
어휘_ volunteer 지원자, 자원봉사자 workload 업무 a variety of 다양한
분석_ how로 시작하지만 뒤에 many가 붙어서 개수를 물어보는 의문문이다. 이때 주로 숫자가 등장하면 정답률이 높다. (A) 스스로 대답하지 않고 타인에게 물어보겠다는 회피형 대답으로 정답률이 매우 높은 표현이다. 오답분석 (B) 몇 명인지를 물어보는 질문과 관계없이 업무가 많다는 이야기를 하고 있으므로 오답이다. (C) 질문의 project와 유사 발음인 products가 함정으로 등장했다.

31. (B)
I'd like your comments on our new production line.
(A) Go through the front door.
(B) I can review it later today.
(C) Let's order some products.
우리의 새 생산라인에 대한 당신의 의견을 듣고 싶어요.
(A) 앞문을 지나가세요.
(B) 오후에 그것을 검토해볼게요.
(C) 몇몇 제품들을 주문합시다.
어휘_ comment 언급, 의견 production 생산 review 검토하다
분석_ 파트2에서 가장 어려운 난이도로 불리는 평서문이다. 부가의문문과 마찬가지로 주어, 동사, 목적어를 반드시 듣고 의미를 파악해야 하므로 높은 청취력이 요구된다. (B) 나중에 검토해보겠다는 대답에 의견을 나중에 주겠다는 뉘앙스가 담겨 있으므로 정답이 될 수 있다. 오답분석 (A) 방향을 지시하는 대답으로 where 질문에 대한 답으로 적절하다. (C) 질문의 production과 유사 발음인 products가 함정으로 등장했다.

Questions 32-34 refer to the following conversation.

W: 32 *I am wondering if you have any apple sandwiches available.* I can't see any in the display case.

M: 33 *I'm sorry, but all the apple sandwiches we had today were sold out.* We still have a nice selection of other sandwiches, though.

W: Hmm... It's for a mother's birthday party tomorrow and she really likes apple.

M: 34 *If you don't need the sandwiches until tomorrow, I can place an order for it right now. Why don't you specify exactly what you want? And we can have it ready for you first thing tomorrow in the morning.*

W: 사과 샌드위치가 있는지 궁금한데요. 진열상자에서는 찾을 수가 없어요.

Actual Test 1 | Actual Test 2 | Actual Test 3 | LC Script

M: 죄송하지만 오늘 우리가 가지고 있던 사과 샌드위치는 다 팔렸어
   요. 그래도 괜찮은 다른 샌드위치가 남아 있어요.
W: 흠… 내일 있을 어머니 생신파티을 위한 건데요, 사과를 아주 좋
   아하세요.
M: 만약 샌드위치가 내일 필요하다면 지금 당장 주문을 넣을게요. 정
   확히 원하는 게 무엇인지 말씀해주실래요? 그러면 내일 아침 가
   장 먼저 준비해둘게요.
어휘_ wonder if ~인지 아닌지 궁금해하다 display case 진열상자 a
   selection of 다양한 place an order 주문을 넣다

32. (A)

Where most likely are the speakers?
(A) At a bakery
(B) At a flower shop
(C) At a concert hall
(D) At a party supply store
화자는 어디에 있는 것 같은가?
(A) 제과점
(B) 꽃가게
(C) 콘서트장
(D) 파티용품점
분석_ 샌드위치가 있는지 없는지를 물어보고 있으므로 제과점임
   을 알 수 있다.

33. (A)

Why does the man apologize?
(A) A product has sold out.
(B) A reservation wasn't correct.
(C) An order was sent to the wrong address.
(D) A bill was not accurate.
남자는 왜 사과하는가?
(A) 제품이 매진되었다.
(B) 예약이 제대로 되지 않았다.
(C) 주문품이 다른 주소로 보내졌다.
(D) 청구서가 잘못되었다.
분석_ 남자의 첫 대화에서 여자가 찾는 제품이 다 팔렸음을 알
   수 있다.

34. (C)

What does the man suggest?
(A) Contacting another shop
(B) Requesting a replacement
(C) Placing an order
(D) Cancelling an event
남자는 무엇을 제안하는가?
(A) 다른 매장에 연락해보기
(B) 대체품 요청하기
(C) 주문하기
(D) 행사 취소하기
분석_ 마지막 남자의 언급에서 원하는 것을 정확히 알려주면 준
   비해두겠다는 것으로 보아 주문을 하라고 제안함을 알 수
   있다.

Questions 35-37 refer to the following conversation.

M: Excuse me, 35 *I'm here to repair the computer in
   your lab.* It should only take me about 30 minutes.
W: Right now? But 36 *I didn't get any notice informing
   me that you would be coming.* I don't think this is a
   good time. I'm very busy now. Why don't you come
   back later today?
M: Actually, I have several other work orders today, so
   I am not sure I'll have the time. 37 *I'll send another
   technician to help you today at 4 o'clock.*

M: 실례합니다, 여기 연구실에 있는 컴퓨터를 수리하려고 왔는데요.
   대략 30분 정도 걸릴 것 같습니다.
W: 지금이요? 하지만 당신이 온다는 내용의 어떤 공지도 받지 못했
   는데요. 지금은 안 될 것 같아요. 지금 매우 바쁘거든요. 오늘 오후
   에 다시 오실 수 있나요?
M: 사실 오늘 다른 작업 주문이 있어서, 시간이 될지 모르겠네요. 4시
   에 도와줄 수 있는 다른 기술자를 보내드릴게요.
어휘_ repair 수리하다 lab 연구실 notice 공지문 inform 알려주다
   busy 바쁜 several 몇몇의 work order 작업주문 technician
   기술자

35. (B)

Why is the man at the woman's office?
(A) To do some cleaning
(B) To make a repair
(C) To bring a package
(D) To ask about holidays
남자는 왜 여자의 사무실에 있는가?
(A) 청소하기 위해서
(B) 수리하기 위해서
(C) 소포를 가져다주기 위해서
(D) 휴일에 대해 문의하기 위해서
분석_ 남자의 대화 시작부분에서 수리를 하기 위해 왔음을 알 수
   있다.

36. (D)

Why is the woman surprised by the man's visit?
(A) She canceled a delivery of shipments.
(B) She just saw the man last week.
(C) She was expecting someone else.
(D) She didn't receive notification.
여자는 왜 남자의 방문에 놀랐는가?
(A) 그녀는 배송품 배달을 취소했다.
(B) 그녀는 지난주에 남자를 만났다.
(C) 그녀는 다른 누군가를 예상했다.
(D) 그녀는 통보를 받지 못했다.
분석_ 남자의 방문에 대해서 아무런 통보도 받은 적이 없다는 말
   에서 정답을 알 수 있다.

37. (A)

What does the man offer to do?

(A) Send another employee
(B) Refund an item
(C) Provide a complimentary delivery
(D) Revise an estimate
남자는 무엇을 제안하는가?
(A) 또 다른 직원 보내기
(B) 제품 환불해주기
(C) 무료 배송해주기
(D) 견적서 수정하기

분석_ suggest의 제안은 타인에게 시키는 경우이지만 offer의 제안은 직접 해주겠다는 것이므로 주의한다. 마지막 대화 내용에서 남자가 바빠서 다른 사람을 보내겠다고 언급하고 있다.

Questions 38-40 refer to the following conversation.

M: Hi, I'm staying here at the hotel on business, but I've decided to extend my trip to do some shopping. **38** *Is it possible for me to keep my room another day?*

W: Of course. We're not fully booked this week. I can extend the reservation for you. And **39** *if you'd like, I can book a city shopping tour for you.*

M: Oh, thanks, but that won't be necessary. Actually, a brother of mine lives in the area, **40** *so I'm going for shopping together with him tomorrow.*

- -

M: 안녕하세요, 저는 사업차 여기 호텔에서 머무르고 있는데요, 하지만 쇼핑을 위해 여행기간을 연장하기로 결정했어요. 제 방을 하루 더 연장할 수 있을까요?

W: 물론입니다. 이번 주에 예약이 다 차지 않았어요. 당신의 예약을 연장해드릴게요. 그리고 원하신다면, 도시 쇼핑 투어를 예약해드릴게요.

M: 오, 고마워요, 하지만 필요 없을 것 같아요. 사실 남동생 한 명이 이 지역에 살고 있어요, 그래서 내일 그와 함께 쇼핑할 거예요.

38. (C)
What does the man ask the woman about?
(A) Rescheduling a calendar
(B) Visiting a local museum
(C) Extending a reservation
(D) Placing a phone call
남자는 여자에게 무엇을 문의하는가?
(A) 일정 수정하기
(B) 지역 박물관 방문하기
(C) 예약 연장하기
(D) 전화하기

분석_ 대화 초반 남자가 방을 하루 더 연장할 수 있는지 묻고 있다.

39. (B)
What does the woman offer to do?
(A) Remove a charge from a credit card
(B) Book a sightseeing tour

(C) Contact with a director
(D) Apply a discounted rate
여자는 무엇을 제안하는가?
(A) 신용카드의 청구금 공제하기
(B) 관광 예약하기
(C) 디렉터에게 연락하기
(D) 할인가 적용하기

분석_ 대화 중반에서 투어 예약을 제안하는 부분에서 정답을 알 수 있다.

40. (A)
What does the man say he plans to do?
(A) Meet a brother
(B) Register a complaint
(C) Participating in a meeting
(D) Rent a vehicle
남자는 무엇을 계획하는가?
(A) 남동생 만나기
(B) 불만 제기하기
(C) 회의 참석하기
(D) 차량 빌리기

분석_ 대화 마지막에 남동생과 쇼핑을 할 것이라 말하고 있다.

Questions 41-43 refer to the following conversation.

M: I'm here to locate an article that was published in the local newspaper about four or five years ago. **41** *Is there a copy in the library?* I don't know how far back you keep newspapers.

W: We only keep issues of the local paper for the last 3 months. But articles from the last 5 years are kept on our website. So, I can help you find an electronic copy of the article.

M: Great! How much will it cost to print?

W: It's 5 cents a page. But unfortunately, **42** *our printer is out of order right now.* A technician will come in any minute, and it should be fixed by noon, **43** *so you can come back anytime this afternoon.*

- -

M: 약 4, 5년 전 지역신문에 발행된 기사를 찾으려는데요. 도서관에 사본이 있나요? 이 도서관이 얼마나 오래된 것까지 보관하는지를 모르겠네요.

W: 우리는 지난 3개월간 발행된 지역신문들만 보관합니다. 하지만 지난 5년간의 기사들은 웹사이트에 보관되어 있어요. 그러니까 제가 기사 사본 찾는 것을 도와드릴 수 있어요.

M: 좋아요. 인쇄비용은 얼마인가요?

W: 페이지당 5센트예요. 하지만 불행히도 지금 인쇄기가 고장 났어요. 수리공이 몇 분 안에 올 거예요. 그러니 정오까지는 수리될 거예요. 그러니까 오후 언제든 다시 오시면 됩니다.

어휘_ locate ~를 찾다 publish 발행하다 library 도서관 keep 보관하다 cost 비용이 ~만큼 들다 unfortunately 불행하게도 out of order 고장 난 fix 수리하다

41. (A)

Where are the speakers?
(A) At a library
(B) At a newspaper company
(C) At a publishing company
(D) At a print shop
화자들은 어디에 있는가?
(A) 도서관
(B) 신문사
(C) 출판사
(D) 인쇄소
분석_ 대화 장소를 묻고 있다. 도서관에 사본이 있냐는 물음에서
　　　정답을 알 수 있다.

42. (D)

What problem does the woman mention?
(A) A book is out of stock.
(B) A newspaper delivery is late.
(C) A facility is under renovation.
(D) A printer is not working.
여자가 언급하고 있는 문제점은 무엇인가?
(A) 책이 재고가 없다.
(B) 신문 배달이 늦다.
(C) 시설이 개조 중이다.
(D) 복사기가 고장 났다.
분석_ 여자의 마지막 대화에서 복사기의 고장을 언급하고 있다.

43. (C)

What does the woman suggest the man do?
(A) Cancel a subscription
(B) Call technical support
(C) Come back later
(D) Visit another branch
여자는 남자에게 무엇을 제안하는가?
(A) 구독 취소하기
(B) 기술지원팀에 전화하기
(C) 나중에 다시 오기
(D) 다른 지점 방문하기
분석_ 마지막 대화에서 복사기 고장을 말한 다음 오후에 다시 오
　　　라고 언급하고 있다.

Questions 44-46 refer to the following conversation.

M: Hello, *44 I'm calling because I'd like to register for the economics workshop.* I have a group of 20 people who would like to participate in the event.

W: Unfortunately, we don't process group registrations over the phone. *45 You should complete a form online.*

M: You know, I just tried filling out that form several times, but whenever I pressed the submit button, I got an error message. Is there any other way to register?

W: Oh, I'm so sorry to hear that. *46 Could you please give me your name, e-mail address and phone number?* I'll have our technical support team contact you right away.

M: 안녕하세요. 경제 워크숍에 등록하려고 전화 드립니다. 행사에 참여하길 원하는 20명으로 이루어진 그룹이 저희 쪽에 있습니다.

W: 안타깝게도, 저희는 전화상으로는 단체 등록을 처리하지 않습니다. 온라인으로 양식을 작성하셔야 합니다.

M: 그런데요, 몇 번이나 온라인 양식을 작성하려고 시도했습니다. 하지만 제출 버튼을 누를 때마다 오류메세지가 뜨던데요. 등록할 수 있는 다른 방법이 있나요?

W: 오, 죄송합니다. 이름, 이메일 주소 그리고 전화번호 주실래요? 기술팀에게 곧장 연락하라고 할게요.

어휘_ register for ~에 등록하다 participate in ~에 참여하다
　　　precess 처리하다 form 양식 fill out 작성하다 several 몇몇의
　　　press 누르다 technical support team 기술지원팀 contact
　　　연락하다

44. (C)

Why is the man calling?
(A) To obtain a report
(B) To pay an invoice
(C) To sigh up for an event
(D) To order some software
남자는 왜 전화했는가?
(A) 보고서를 받기 위해
(B) 송장 금액을 지불하기 위해
(C) 행사에 등록하기 위해
(D) 소프트웨어를 주문하기 위해
분석_ 남자가 첫 번째 대화에서 등록하기 위해 걸었다는 이야기
　　　를 하고 있다.

45. (B)

According to the woman, what does the man have to do?
(A) Make an appointment
(B) Complete a task online
(C) Submit a proposal
(D) Approve an expense
여자에 따르면, 남자는 무엇을 해야 하는가?
(A) 약속을 잡기 위해
(B) 온라인으로 양식 작성하기
(C) 제안서 제출하기
(D) 비용 승인하기
분석_ 여자가 언급한 내용 중 남자가 해야 할 일이 무엇인지 묻고
　　　있다. 전화상 등록할 수가 없고 온라인으로 해야 한다고 언
　　　급하고 있다.

46. (A)

What does the woman request?
(A) Some contact information
(B) Presentation slides

(C) Details from a bill
(D) Proof of employment
여자는 무엇을 요청하는가?
(A) 연락처
(B) 발표 슬라이드
(C) 청구서의 세부사항
(D) 고용의 증거
분석_ 마지막 대화에서 조동사(could)를 이용하여 개인정보를 요구한다는 것을 알 수 있다.

Questions 47-49 refer to the following conversation.

W: Hi, Jacob. It's Melissa. I just arrived at the sales department office in corporation headquarters to meet with their sales team. **47 But I can't find my files in client folder. I think I left it on my desk. Can you check and see if it is there?** It's red.

M: OK, Melissa. Let me have a look. Yes, it's here on your desk. **48 Do you want me to scan any of the files for you?**

W: No, that won't be necessary. I just need some data. If you look on the last page, **49 you'll see the figures for item sales for this year. Can you read those numbers to me?**

W: 안녕 Jacob. Melissa야. 나 영업팀 만나려고 방금 본사 영업부서에 도착했어. 하지만 고객 폴더에서 내 파일을 못 찾겠어. 내 생각에 책상 위에 둔 거 같아. 거기 있는지 없는지 확인해줄래? 빨간색이야.

M: 그래 Melissa. 한번 볼게. 그래 여기 책상 위에 있어. 스캔해줄까?

W: 아니야, 그럴 필요는 없어. 몇 가지 정보가 필요할 뿐이야. 맨 뒷장 보면, 올해 제품 판매량 수치가 보일 거야. 그 숫자들을 불러줄래?

어휘_ arrive 도착하다 sales department 영업부서 headquarters 본사 leave 남겨두다 have a look 보다 necessary 필요한 figure 수치 increase rate 증가율

47. (B)
Why is the woman calling?
(A) To get driving directions
(B) To ask about a missing item
(C) To arrange a meeting
(D) To discuss a contract
여자는 왜 전화했는가?
(A) 길 안내를 받기 위해
(B) 잃어버린 물건에 대해 문의하기 위해
(C) 회의를 잡기 위해
(D) 계약서에 대해 이야기하기 위해
분석_ 여자의 처음 대화에서 파일을 못 찾아서 확인을 부탁하는 내용에서 정답을 알 수 있다.

48. (D)
What does the man offer to do?
(A) Order a chair

(B) Call a client
(C) Obtain a report
(D) Scan some documents
남자는 무엇을 제안하는가?
(A) 의자 주문하기
(B) 고객에게 연락하기
(C) 보고서 받기
(D) 문서 스캔하기
분석_ 남자가 해주겠다고 제안하는 것이 무엇인지 묻고 있다. Do you want me to ~ 구문으로 스캔을 해주겠다는 의사를 밝히고 있다.

49. (A)
What information does the woman ask for?
(A) Some sales figures
(B) A phone number
(C) A street name
(D) Some project dates
여자가 요구하는 정보는 무엇인가?
(A) 판매량 수치
(B) 전화번호
(C) 도로명
(D) 프로젝트 일정
분석_ 여자가 마지막 대화에서 판매량 수치를 읽어달라고 부탁하고 있다.

Questions 50-52 refer to the following conversation.

W: Hello, and welcome to the monthly resume-building workshop. Today, **50 you'll have the opportunity to learn what makes your resume more competitive than others.** Are there any questions before we begin?

M: Yes, **51 are we also going to discuss job interviews? That part of the application process has always been the most challenging to me.**

W: I'm sorry, but today's workshop doesn't have that part. **52 But we'll be offering a separate workshop for those who want to know about interviews next week.** You might want to attend that session as well.

W: 안녕하세요, 월간 이력서 작성 워크숍에 오신 것을 환영합니다. 오늘, 당신은 다른 사람들보다 더 경쟁력 있는 이력서를 만드는 것이 무엇인지에 대해서 배울 것입니다. 시작하기 전에 질문 있나요?

M: 네, 면접에 대한 것도 이야기하나요? 지원절차 중에서 그 부분이 저에겐 항상 가장 까다로웠거든요.

W: 죄송하지만, 오늘 워크숍에선 그 부분을 다루지 않습니다. 하지만 면접에 대해 알고 싶어 하는 분들을 위해 다음 주에 별도의 워크숍을 제공할 겁니다. 당신은 그 워크숍에 참석하시면 될 것 같아요.

어휘_ welcome 환영하다 resume-building 이력서 작성하기 opportunity 기회 learn 배우다 competitive 경쟁력이 있는 application 지원 process 절차 challenging 까다로운, 도전적인 separate 분리된, 별도의

50. (C)

What is the topic of the workshop?
(A) Recruiting training expert
(B) Developing presentation skills
(C) Writing resumes
(D) Taking an annual inventory
워크숍의 주제는 무엇인가?
(A) 훈련 전문가 고용하기
(B) 발표 기술 개발하기
(C) 이력서 쓰기
(D) 연간 재고 조사하기
분석_ 대화 초반 워크숍에서 배울 내용에 대해서 언급하고 있다.

51. (D)

What does the man find challenging?
(A) Leading small-group activities
(B) Obtaining letters of reference
(C) Learning new computer programs
(D) Interviewing for a position
남자가 까다로워하는 것은 무엇인가?
(A) 소그룹 활동을 이끌기
(B) 추천서 받기
(C) 새로운 컴퓨터 프로그램 배우기
(D) 직책에 대한 면접 보기
분석_ 남자의 대화에서 면접에 대해 물음과 동시에 그 부분이 가장 까다롭다고 언급하고 있다.

52. (C)

What does the woman say will happen next week?
(A) Some jobs will be posted online.
(B) A follow-up survey will be distributed.
(C) Another workshop will be held.
(D) An instruction manual will be published.
여자는 다음 주에 무슨 일이 일어날 것이라고 이야기하는가?
(A) 일자리가 온라인에 게시될 것이다.
(B) 후속 설문조사지가 배분될 것이다.
(C) 다른 워크숍이 열릴 것이다.
(D) 지침서가 발행될 것이다.
분석_ 여자의 마지막 대화에서 면접에 대한 워크숍이 이루어진다고 언급하고 있다.

Questions 53-55 refer to the following conversation with three speakers.

M1: That laser show was just the best way to end this party.
W: Yes, I think so!
M2: **53** *It is amazing that the company's been in business for 30 years.* I've worked here since it opened its first store. **54** *And I've grown with this firm since then.*

W: I'm happy to hear that, Tony. Haven't you been here for a long time too, Kross?
M1: Certainly. **54** *It's a fulfilling job,* and the company is generous to employees.
W: According to my supervisor, **53 55** *the company is offering heavy discounts on furniture in celebration of its anniversary.*
M2: I heard that, too. The catalog released last week included the list of furniture.

M1: 그 레이저 쇼는 파티를 끝내기에 최고의 방법이었어.
W: 그래, 나도 그렇게 생각해!
M2: 회사가 30년이나 운영됐다니 놀라워. 나는 첫 번째 매장이 오픈한 이후로 지금까지 여기서 일을 했거든. 그리고 그 이후로 이 회사와 함께 성장했어.
W: 그 얘길 들으니 기뻐, Tony. 너도 여기 오래 있었지 않아 Kross?
M1: 물론이지. 만족스러운 일이야, 그리고 회사도 직원들에게 지원을 아끼지 않아.
W: 상사가 말하길, 창립을 기념해서 회사가 가구를 할인한대.
M2: 나도 들었어. 지난달에 발행된 카탈로그에 가구 목록이 나와 있었어.
어휘_ way 방법 amazing 놀라운 in business 사업을 운영중인 grow 성장하다 fulfilling 만족감을 주는 generous 관대한 according to ~에 따르면 discount 할인 in celebration of ~를 기념하여 release 발행하다

53. (A)

What kind of event is being discussed?
(A) A company's founding anniversary
(B) A store opening
(C) An executive's promotion
(D) A laser display
어떤 종류의 행사가 논의되고 있는가?
(A) 회사의 창립 기념일
(B) 매장 오픈
(C) 임원의 승진
(D) 레이저 전시회
분석_ 대화 중반과 마지막에서 나온 회사가 30년 되었다는 부분과 창립 기념 할인에 대한 언급에서 정답을 알 수 있다.

54. (A)

What do the men imply about the company?
(A) The work is rewarding.
(B) It leads the laser show industry.
(C) It offers affordable benefits.
(D) All of its items are not cheap.
남자들은 회사에 대해 무엇을 암시하는가?
(A) 일이 보람차다.
(B) 회사가 레이저 쇼 산업을 주도한다.
(C) 회사가 합리적인 복지혜택을 제공한다.
(D) 모든 제품들이 비싸다.

분석_ 두 남자가 각각 회사와 함께 성장했다는 이야기와 만족스러운 업무라는 이야기를 하는 부분에서 정답을 알 수 있다.

55. (C)

According to the woman, what is the company giving staff members?
(A) Complimentary furniture
(B) Cash refund
(C) Merchandise discounts
(D) Extra holidays

여자에 따르면, 회사는 직원들에게 무엇을 제공하는가?
(A) 무료 가구
(B) 현금 환불
(C) 제품 할인
(D) 추가 휴가

분석_ 여자의 마지막 언급에서 창립 기념일을 맞이하여 할인을 제공한다는 사실을 알 수 있다.

Questions 56-58 refer to the following conversation.

W: Hi, Paul. You're an organizer for the museum's charity event this year, right? **56 I have a suggestion for the event. A friend of mine is a member of the community musical band, and I think they'd be great for this event.**

M: Oh, Monica, that's a great idea! **57 Unfortunately, our budget is not enough to pay them for an event.**

W: No problem. My friend told me they'd be happy to volunteer their services. The exposure would be good for them. And it might bring future jobs to them.

M: **58 OK, I'll ask my supervisor about it first, and let you know.**

- -

W: 안녕, Paul. 네가 올해 박물관 자선행사 기획자잖아, 그렇지? 행사에 대해서 제안할 게 있어. 내 친구 중 한 명이 지역 음악밴드부 멤버인데, 내 생각에 그들이 행사에 어울릴 것 같아.

M: 오, Monica, 좋은 생각이야! 안타깝게도, 그들에게 행사비를 지급할 만큼 예산이 충분하지가 않아.

W: 문제없어. 내 친구가 말하길 그들이 기꺼이 공연을 지원하겠대. 노출되는 것이 그들에게 좋은 거잖아. 그게 아마도 그들에겐 미래의 일자리를 가져다줄지도 몰라.

M: 그래, 상사에게 먼저 물어보고 나서 알려줄게.

어휘_ organizer 기획자 charity 자선 suggestion 제안 professional 전문적인 budget 예산 volunteer 자원하다 exposure 노출 bring 가져다주다

56. (C)

What aspect of a charity event are the speakers discussing?
(A) Booking a room
(B) Contacting a caterer
(C) Providing entertainment
(D) Recruiting volunteers

화자들은 자선행사의 어떤 면에 대해 논의하고 있는가?
(A) 방 예약하기
(B) 출장 요리업체에 연락하기
(C) 연주회 제공하기
(D) 봉사자 구하기

분석_ 여자의 첫 대화에서 밴드 멤버인 친구를 언급하고 그들을 행사에 초대하자는 의견을 나타내고 있다.

57. (A)

What concern does the man have?
(A) Funding is limited.
(B) Invitations have not been sent.
(C) The weather condition is bad.
(D) A meeting room is too crowded.

남자는 어떤 것을 우려하는가?
(A) 자금이 제한적이다.
(B) 초대장이 발송되지 않았다.
(C) 날씨가 안 좋다.
(D) 회의장이 너무 붐빈다.

분석_ 여자의 제안에 대해 남자가 예산이 충분하지 않다는 언급을 하고 있다.

58. (B)

What does the man say he will do?
(A) Advertise on the website
(B) Consult with a supervisor
(C) Cancel an event
(D) Meet a decorator

남자는 무엇을 할 것이라고 이야기하는가?
(A) 웹사이트에 광고하기
(B) 상사에게 물어보기
(C) 행사 취소하기
(D) 장식업자 만나기

분석_ 남자의 마지막 대화에서 상사에게 물어보고 연락해준다고 언급하고 있다.

Questions 59-61 refer to the following conversation.

M: Hello, it's James Turker. **59 I'd like to ask about the delivery of some materials for construction. I've been waiting for it since Thursday.**

W: Hello, Mr. Turker. I'll check it. Oh... This is embarrassing. Our records indicate your order hasn't been processed yet. It seems like our warehouse didn't receive it.

M: Seriously? I didn't get any notice about it.

W: I apologize, Mr. Turker. There must have been some mistakes among our staff members.

M: **60 I need the supplies the day after tomorrow. My client is waiting for them. 61 Can you deliver them tomorrow?**

W: Definitely, Mr. Turker. **61** *I promise. I will have your order delivered right now and contact you again.*

M: Okay. I'll look forward to your call.

M: 안녕하세요. James Turker입니다. 공사장 자재 배송에 대해 문의를 드리고자 하는데요. 목요일 이후로 배송을 기다리고 있습니다.

W: 안녕하세요. Turker 씨. 확인해볼게요. 오... 당황스럽네요. 우리 기록에 당신의 주문이 아직 처리되지 않은 걸로 나와 있네요. 저희 창고가 아직 주문을 받지 못한 것 같습니다.

M: 정말요? 저는 어떤 통보도 받지 못했는데요.

W: 사과드립니다, Turker 씨. 직원들 사이에 실수가 있었음이 틀림없습니다.

M: 저는 모레 그 공급품이 필요합니다. 제 고객이 기다리고 있거든요. 내일 배송해주실 수 있나요?

W: 물론입니다, Turker 씨. 제가 약속할게요. 당장 당신의 주문품이 배송되도록 하고 다시 연락드릴게요.

M: 좋습니다. 전화 기다리고 있을게요.

어휘_ ask about ~에 대해 문의하다 delivery 배송 material 재료 construction 공사 embarrassing 당황스러운 record 기록 indicate 나타내다 process 처리하다 warehouse 창고 mistake 실수 promise 약속하다 client 고객 look forward to ~를 기대하다

59. (C)

What are the speakers talking about?
(A) A procedure for delivery
(B) Missing items
(C) A delayed order
(D) Wrong client information

화자들은 무엇에 대해 이야기하고 있는가?
(A) 배송 절차
(B) 분실된 물건
(C) 지연된 주문
(D) 잘못된 고객정보

분석_ 대화 주제를 묻고 있다. 주제는 대화 초반에 나오는 명사로 유추 가능하다. 대화 초반 남자가 물건을 배송받지 못했다고 언급하고 있다.

60. (D)

What does the man imply about the supplies?
(A) They should be heavily discounted.
(B) They will be picked up at the warehouse.
(C) They must be repaired as soon as possible.
(D) They are necessary for his business.

남자는 공급품에 대해 무엇을 암시하는가?
(A) 그것들은 크게 할인되어야 한다.
(B) 그것들은 창고에서 픽업될 것이다.
(C) 그것들은 가능한 한 빨리 수리되어야 한다.
(D) 그것들은 그의 사업에 필요하다.

분석_ 대화 중간에서 남자가 모레까지 물건이 필요하며 자신의 고객이 기다리고 있다고 언급하고 있다.

61. (B)

Why does the woman say, "I promise"?
(A) She wants a quick response.
(B) She will get the goods shipped.
(C) She should explain her problem.
(D) She supports the man's stance.

여자는 왜 "제가 약속할게요"라고 말하는가?
(A) 그녀는 빠른 대답을 원한다.
(B) 그녀는 물건을 배송되게 할 것이다.
(C) 그녀는 그녀의 문제점을 설명해야 한다.
(D) 그녀는 남자의 입장을 지지한다.

분석_ 여자의 마지막 대화에서 지연된 물건을 곧장 배송하겠다는 내용이 언급되고 있다.

Questions 62-64 refer to the following conversation with three speakers.

W: **62** *I'm pleased to tell you that both of you accepted my offer to lead our new sales teams.*

M1: It's our pleasure, Ms. Geller.

M2: Thank you for the opportunity to work here. It means a lot.

M1: So, when do we start hiring new employees?

W: Personnel Department told me that some applicants are scheduled for interviews next week.

M1: Great! **63** *We need additional salespeople for the launch of our latest cars in March.*

M2: That's two months from now. I hope we'll finish hiring by the end of the month, so we can train new people.

W: Of course. **64** *Also, the two of you will interview applicants with me.* Personnel Department will send you the resume they received.

W: 두 분께서 새로운 영업팀을 이끌어달라는 저의 제안을 받아주셔서 정말 기쁩니다.

M1: 저희가 기쁘죠, Geller 씨.

M2: 여기서 일할 수 있는 기회를 주셔서 감사합니다. 이건 의미하는 바가 많아요.

M1: 그래서, 언제부터 우리가 신입사원을 고용하기 시작하나요?

W: 인사부가 말하길 다음 주에 몇몇 지원자들이 면접 보기로 했대요.

M1: 좋아요. 3월에 있을 신차 출시를 위해 추가적인 영업사원들이 필요해요.

M2: 지금으로부터 2개월 후예요. 우리가 이달 말까지 고용을 끝내길 바랍니다, 그래야 신입사원들을 교육시킬 수가 있어요.

W: 물론이에요. 또한 두 분은 저와 함께 지원자들을 면접 볼 거예요. 인사부가 받았던 이력서를 두 분에게 보내줄 거예요.

어휘_ be pleased to + V ~하게 되어서 기쁘다 accept 받아들이다 lead 이끌다 mean 의미하다 hire 고용하다 Personnel Department 인사부서 additional 추가적인 launch 출시 latest 최신의 finish 끝내다 train 훈련시키다 resume 이력서 receive ~를 받다

62. (D)

What are the speakers talking about?
(A) Training for job applicants
(B) A marketing event
(C) The prices of cars
(D) The organization of new teams
화자들은 무엇에 대해 이야기하고 있는가?
(A) 지원자들 교육
(B) 마케팅 행사
(C) 자동차 가격
(D) 새로운 팀의 구성
분석_ 주제는 주로 대화 초반에 등장한다. 처음 대화에서 여자 가 팀을 이끌어달라는 제안을 받아줘서 기쁘다는 말을 하 고 있다.

63. (B)

What will the company do in March?
(A) Increase staff
(B) Release new products
(C) Give training to staff
(D) Reward employees
회사는 3월에 무엇을 할 것인가?
(A) 직원 충원하기
(B) 신제품 출시하기
(C) 직원 훈련시키기
(D) 직원들에게 보상해주기
분석_ 대화 중반에 남자가 새로운 자동차의 출시에 대해서 언급 하고 있다.

64. (A)

What does the woman imply about the interviews?
(A) They will be attended by team managers.
(B) They are conducted once a week.
(C) They will be rescheduled for next week.
(D) They will be held at a car showroom.
여자는 면접에 대해 무엇을 암시하는가?
(A) 면접에 팀 관리자들이 참석할 것이다.
(B) 일주일에 한 번씩 이루어진다.
(C) 면접 일정이 다음 주로 변경될 것이다.
(D) 면접이 자동차 전시장에서 열릴 것이다.
분석_ 여자의 마지막 대화에서 두 명의 남자와 함께 면접에 임할 것이라 언급하고 있다.

Questions 65-67 refer to the following conversation and schedule.

W: 65 *Excuse me, Mr. Evans. I have to tell you something about your schedule tomorrow.*
M: Do we need to change it?
W: I think so. 65 *Mr. Hill of Simmons Furniture called this morning. He would like to discuss our office desks.* His company needs them for its next furniture convention.

M: 66 *Simmons Furniture is our main account, so we can't say no.* 65 *Do I have an appointment I can reschedule?*
W: There are two meetings you can cancel now.
M: Hmm. I must meet the budget committee. 67 *I'll just skip the second one. Please call Mr. Hill and say that I'll meet him then.*

Mr. Evans' Schedule (March 25, Friday)	
Speech at Convention	9:00 A.M.
Budget committees' meeting	10:00 A.M.
Look over reports	2:00 P.M.
Weekly meeting	4:00 P.M.
Employee party	7:00 P.M.

W: 실례합니다, Evans 씨. 내일 일정에 대해서 이야기할 게 있는 데요.
M: 변경해야 할 것이 있나요?
W: 그렇습니다. Simmons 가구에서 Hill 씨가 오늘 아침에 전화를 했어요. 그는 우리의 사무실 책상에 대해서 이야기하고 싶어 합 니다. 그의 회사가 다음 가구 컨벤션에서 그것들을 필요로 하고 있어요.
M: Simmons 가구는 우리의 중요한 고객이에요, 그래서 우리는 거 절할 수가 없어요. 제가 취소할 수 있는 약속이 있나요?
W: 지금 취소하실 수 있는 회의가 2개 있습니다.
M: 흠. 예산위원회는 만나야만 해요. 두 번째 회의를 생략해야겠어요. Hill 씨에게 연락해서 그 시간에 만나겠다고 이야기해줘요.

Evans 씨의 일정 (3월 25일 금요일)	
컨벤션에서 연설	오전 9:00
예산위원회 회의	오전 10:00
보고서 검토	오후 2:00
주간 회의	오후 4:00
직원 파티	오후 7:00

어휘_ schedule 일정 change 변경하다 call 전화하다 discuss ~ 에 대해 이야기하다 account 고객 appointment 일정, 약속 reschedule 일정을 조정하다 budget committee 예산위원회 skip 건너뛰다

65. (C)

Who most likely is the woman?
(A) A computer expert
(B) A sales representative
(C) A personal assistant
(D) A furniture artisan
여자는 아마도 누구일 것인가?
(A) 컴퓨터 전문가
(B) 판매사원
(C) 개인 비서
(D) 가구 장인

분석_ 전반적인 대화 내용으로 보아 여자가 남자의 일정에 대해 조정해주고 있으므로 비서임을 알 수 있다.

66. (B)

What does the man imply about Mr. Hill?
(A) He works with Mr. Evans.
(B) He is an important client.
(C) He is an office supply developer.
(D) He sells user-friendly software.

남자는 Hill 씨에 대해 무엇을 암시하는가?
(A) 그는 Evans 씨와 함께 일을 한다.
(B) 그는 중요한 고객이다.
(C) 그는 사무용품 개발자이다.
(D) 그는 이용자에게 편리한 소프트웨어를 판매한다.

분석_ 대화 중반 남자가 중요한 고객이라서 No라는 말을 할 수 없다고 언급하고 있다.

67. (C)

Look at the graphic. What time will the man meet Mr. Hill?
(A) 9:00 A.M.
(B) 10:00 A.M.
(C) 4:00 P.M.
(D) 7:00 P.M.

그래픽을 보자. 남자는 Hill 씨를 몇 시에 만날 것인가?
(A) 오전 9시
(B) 오전 10시
(C) 오후 4시
(D) 오후 7시

분석_ 대화 마지막에 두 개의 회의 중 두 번째 것을 취소하고 대신 그 시간에 Hill을 만나는 걸로 일정을 수정해달라는 언급이 있다.

Questions 68-70 refer to the following conversation and schedule.

M: It's been a long day! **68** *Are there any other client meetings we should attend this week?*
W: **69 70** *The last one is on Thursday at 1:00 P.M. It's a brief meeting, so it'll probably be over by 2 P.M.* Afterwards, we will visit one of our branches in London.
M: Oh, you're right. What railway are we using?
W: Newtown Railways. **70** *It takes about two hours to get there by train.*
M: **70** *The branch manager told me that someone will pick us up at London Train Station at 7:00 P.M. We should arrive before then.*
W: I see. I'll reserve two ticket right away.

Daily Train Schedule (Oxford-London)	
Train	Departure
B301	10:07 A.M.
B302	11:40 A.M.
B303	3:30 P.M.
B304	5:22 P.M.

M: 힘든 하루였어요! 이번 주에 우리가 참석해야 하는 다른 회의가 있나요?
W: 목요일 오후 1시에 마지막 하나가 있습니다. 그것은 짧습니다. 그래서 오후 2시 전에는 끝날 것 같습니다. 그 후에 우리는 런던에 있는 우리 지사 중 하나를 방문할 것입니다.
M: 오, 그렇군요. 어느 철로를 이용할 건가요?
W: 뉴타운 철로예요. 열차로 거기에 도착하는 데 대략 2시간이 걸립니다.
M: 지사 관리자가 말하기를 저녁 7시에 런던역에 누가 우릴 데리러 온다더군요. 우리는 그 전에 도착해야 해요.
W: 알겠어요. 지금 바로 열차표 두 장 예약할게요.

일일 열차 일정표 (옥스퍼드-런던)	
열차 번호	출발시간 오전
B301	오전 10:07
B302	오전 11:40
B303	오후 3:30
B304	오후 5:22

어휘_ attend 참석하다 brief 짧은, 간단한 afterwards 그 이후로 branch 지점 railway 철도 pick up 데려가다 reserve 예약하다

68. (A)

What are the speakers mainly discussing?
(A) A work schedule
(B) A new train service
(C) A tourist attraction
(D) An annual event

화자들이 주로 논의하고 있는 것은 무엇인가?
(A) 근무 일정
(B) 새로운 열차 서비스
(C) 관광명소
(D) 연례행사

분석_ 대화 주제를 묻고 있다. 주제는 대화 초반에 주로 등장한다. 맨 처음 대화에서 남자가 앞으로 참석해야 하는 회의가 있냐는 물음으로 일정에 대해 언급하고 있다.

69. (C)

What will the speakers do on Thursday afternoon?
(A) Pick up a branch manager
(B) Review a travel expense report
(C) Attend a business meeting
(D) Look around headquarters

화자들은 목요일 낮에 무엇을 할 것인가?
(A) 지점 관리자 데려오기
(B) 출장비용 보고서 검토하기
(C) 사업회의에 참석하기
(D) 본사 둘러보기
분석_ 여자의 첫 번째 대화에서 목요일의 일정을 언급하고 있다.

70. (C)
Look at the graphic. What train will the speakers most likely take on Thursday?
(A) B301
(B) B302
(C) B303
(D) B304
그래픽을 보자. 화자들은 목요일에 어떤 열차를 탈 것인가?
(A) B301
(B) B302
(C) B303
(D) B304
분석_ 회의는 1시에 시작하여 2시 전에 끝이 나고, 목적지 도착에 2시간이 걸리고, 7시 전까지 도착해야 한다. B301과 B302는 회의보다 이른 시간이라서 탈 수 없고, B304는 탔을 경우 7시 전에 도착하지 못하므로 탈 수 없다. 정답은 B303이 된다.

<table><tr><td>**Part 4**</td><td>본문 p.25</td></tr></table>

Questions 71-73 refer to the following introduction.

You're watching our local history on Fellows television. **72 Today we're fortunate to have a special guest, John Smith who recently wrote a book 'A Great Starting.' 71 John's book talks about a detailed and interesting description of when our community was established.** In honor of John's appearance on today's show, we will arrange for a special game where callers will be encouraged to answer questions about the community's past. **73 Give the right answers, and you'll win a free coupon for two at Roll's Restaurant.** And now, please welcome John Smith.

여러분은 지금 Fellows 텔레비전의 지역 역사를 보고 있습니다. 운이 좋게도 오늘 우리는 최근에 '위대한 시작'이라는 책을 쓴 John Smith를 특별손님으로 모셨습니다. John의 책은 우리 공동체가 언제 설립되었는지에 대해서 자세하고 재미있는 이야기를 다루고 있습니다. 오늘 쇼에 John이 출연한 것을 기념하여, 우리는 특별한 게임을 준비할 것입니다. 게임에서 전화를 건 사람들은 공동체의 과거에 대해 대답을 하게 됩니다. 정확한 답을 주세요, 그러면 당신은 2명이 이용할 수 있는 Roll's Restaurant 무료 쿠폰을 받을 것입니다. 그러면 지금 John Smith 씨를 환영해주십시오.

어휘_ history 역사 fortunate 운이 좋은 special 특별한 recently 최근에 write 글을 쓰다 detailed 자세한 interesting 흥미로운 description 설명, 묘사 establish 설립하다 in honor of ~를 기념하여 appearance 등장, 출현 arrange for ~를 준비하다

71. (B)
What topic is the TV show discussing?
(A) Weekend Entertainment
(B) The history of a community
(C) The opening of a local restaurant
(D) Traffic updates
TV 쇼가 논의하고 있는 주제는 무엇인가?
(A) 주말 오락프로
(B) 지역 공동체의 역사
(C) 지역 식당 개점
(D) 교통 정보
분석_ 대화 초반 손님으로 작가를 소개하면서 작가의 책에 대한 내용을 언급하고 있다.

72. (C)
Who is John Smith?
(A) A tour guide
(B) A city official
(C) An author
(D) A food critic
John Smith는 누구인가?
(A) 여행 가이드
(B) 시 공무원
(C) 작가
(D) 음식 비평가
분석_ 처음에 특별손님으로 소개하면서 최근에 책을 썼다고 언급하고 있다.

73. (D)
How can viewers win a prize?
(A) By registering on the station's website
(B) By becoming a sponsor
(C) By participating in a special meeting
(D) By answering questions correctly
시청자들은 어떻게 하면 상품을 탈 수 있는가?
(A) 방송국 웹사이트에 등록함으로써
(B) 후원자가 됨으로써
(C) 특별 회의에 참석함으로써
(D) 질문에 올바르게 대답함으로써
분석_ 대화 마지막 부분에서 정답을 말하면 쿠폰을 받을 수 있다고 언급하고 있다.

Questions 74-76 refer to the following broadcast.

Now, Radio KTDT is pleased to announce that a special event is going to be held in town this weekend. **74 *As most of you already know, the local youth gym has recently been renovated.* 75 *And it is expected to open this Thursday.*** At the event, staff will be ready to show the new yoga facility, basketball courts and fitness rooms to every community member. Parents will also have the opportunity to sign their children up for fitness classes at the center. **76 *And those who pay for class registration at the event will get a free gym suit.***

지금, 라디오 KTDT는 이번 주말 시에서 열리는 특별 행사를 발표하게 되어 기쁩니다. 여러분 대부분이 이미 알고 있듯이, 지역 청소년 체육관은 최근에 개조되었습니다. 그리고 이번 목요일에 개장할 예정입니다. 행사에서, 새로운 요가 시설, 농구장 그리고 헬스장을 모든 지역민들에게 보여주기 위해 직원들이 준비하고 있을 것입니다. 부모님들은 자녀들을 센터에서 열리는 운동 수업에 등록시킬 수도 있습니다. 그리고 행사에서 수업료를 내는 분들은 무료 운동복을 받을 것입니다.

어휘_ announce 발표하다 hold 개최하다 gym 체육관 renovate 개조하다 sign A for B A를 B에 등록시키다 pay for 돈을 지급하다 registration 등록 gym suit 운동복

74. (A)

What has recently been renovated?
(A) A local gym
(B) A hospital
(C) An community park
(D) A department store

최근에 개조된 것은 무엇인가?
(A) 지역 체육관
(B) 병원
(C) 지역 공동체 공원
(D) 백화점

분석_ 최근에 개조된 것이 무엇인지 묻고 있다. 방송 초반 지역 청소년 체육관이 개조되었다고 언급하고 있다.

75. (B)

What event will take place on Thursday?
(A) A sports competition
(B) A grand opening
(C) A training workshop
(D) An annual festival

목요일에 어떤 행사가 있을 것인가?
(A) 스포츠 시합
(B) 개업식
(C) 훈련 워크샵
(D) 연례 축제

분석_ 체육관의 개조에 대한 내용을 이야기한 후 목요일에 개장할 것이라고 언급하고 있다.

76. (D)

What can the event attendees receive?
(A) Tickets to a sports match
(B) An autographed program
(C) Free refreshments
(D) Complimentary sportswear

행사 참석자들은 무엇을 받을 수 있는가?
(A) 스포츠 경기에 대한 티켓
(B) 자필 서명된 프로그램
(C) 무료 다과
(D) 무료 운동복

분석_ 방송 마지막에 등록을 하면 무료로 운동복을 받을 수 있다고 언급하고 있다.

Questions 77-79 refer to the following announcement.

77 *Attention all Merriam Tang Shoes factory workers.* This is your senior manager, Johnny Peterson. **78 *Because mechanical problem with a leather-cutting machine occurs again,*** production will be shut down tomorrow so that maintenance work can be done. Tomorrow is pay day, but your paychecks are available today. **79 *Please pick them up at the payroll department before leaving this evening.***

모든 Merriam Tang 신발 공장 직원들은 들어주세요. 저는 상급관리자 Johnny Peterson입니다. 가죽 절단 기계에 기계적인 결함이 또 발생했기 때문에, 내일 생산이 중단되고 수리가 이루어질 것입니다. 내일은 급여일입니다, 하지만 여러분의 급여는 오늘 받으실 수 있습니다. 오늘 저녁 퇴근 전에 급여부에 가서 급여를 챙겨가세요.

어휘_ factory 공장 senior manager 상급 관리자 mechanical 기계상의 occur 발생하다 production 생산 shut down 중단시키다 maintenance work 수리, 보수 작업 paycheck 급여 payroll department 급여부서

77. (A)

Where is the announcement most likely taking place?
(A) At a manufacturing plant
(B) At a repair shop
(C) At a footwear store
(D) At a department store

방송이 나오는 곳은 어디인 것 같은가?
(A) 제조 공장
(B) 수리 가게
(C) 신발 가게
(D) 백화점

분석_ 장소를 묻는 문제는 지문의 초반에 나오는 명사로 유추 가능하다. 방송 처음 인사말에서 공장 직원들이라는 표현을 사용하고 있다.

78. (D)

What problem does the speaker mention?

(A) Accounting error
(B) A missing item
(C) A scheduling conflict
(D) An equipment malfunction
화자가 언급하는 문제점은 무엇인가?
(A) 회계 오류
(B) 분실된 물건
(C) 일정상 문제
(D) 장비 오작동
분석_ 화자가 자기소개를 한 이후 기계에 문제가 생겼음을 언급
하고 있다.

79. (B)

What does the speaker ask the listeners to do before leaving?
(A) Clean their work area
(B) Pick up their paychecks
(C) Consult a supervisor
(D) Check a work schedule
화자가 청자들에게 퇴근 전 할 것을 요구하는 것은 무엇인가?
(A) 작업장 청소하기
(B) 급여 가져가기
(C) 상관에게 이야기하기
(D) 근무 일정 확인하기
분석_ 방송 마지막에 급여부서에서 급여를 챙겨가라고 언급하고
있다.

Questions 80-82 refer to the following excerpt from a meeting.

80 *I'd like to start today's meeting by welcoming our hospital's new chief financial officer Tony Chang.* Mr. Chang has more than 20-year experience as a chief financial officer. With abilities to speak both English and German, **81** *his first official duty here at Coastal Hospital will be to help negotiate a business contract with one of our Germany-based medical suppliers.* **82** *Tomorrow, there will be a welcoming reception for Mr. Chang beginning at 1 P.M. in conference room on the fourth floor.* I hope you will all join us for that.

우리 병원의 새로운 재무 책임자인 Tony Chang을 환영하면서 오늘의 회의를 시작하겠습니다. Chang 씨는 재무 책임자로서 20년 이상의 경험을 갖고 있습니다. 영어와 독일어 말하기 능력을 이용하여, 이곳 Coastal 병원에서 그가 맡을 첫 번째 공식 업무는 독일 기반 의료 공급업체와의 사업 계약 협상을 돕는 것입니다. 내일, 오후 1시 4층 회의장에서 Chang 씨를 위한 환영 파티가 있을 것입니다. 여러분 모두 참석해주시기 바랍니다.

어휘_ hospital 병원 official 공식적인 negotiate 협상하다 business contract 사업 계약 supplier 공급업자 reception 연회 join 합류하다

80. (C)

Where does the speaker most likely work?
(A) At a supply store
(B) At a real estate firm
(C) At a hospital
(D) At a catering company
화자는 어디에서 일하는 것 같은가?
(A) 물품 창고
(B) 부동산
(C) 병원
(D) 출장요리 회사
분석_ 처음 인사말에서 병원의 재무 책임자라고 언급을 하고 있다.

81. (A)

According to the speaker, what will Mr. Chang's first assignment be?
(A) Negotiating a contract
(B) Hiring more staff
(C) Reviewing a regulation
(D) Planning a relocation
화자에 따르면, Chang 씨의 첫 번째 업무는 무엇이 될 것인가?
(A) 계약 협상하기
(B) 추가 직원 고용하기
(C) 규정 검토하기
(D) 이전 계획하기
분석_ 유창한 언어능력을 이용하여 계약 협상을 돕는 것이 첫 번째
업무라고 언급하고 있다.

82. (D)

What event will take place tomorrow?
(A) An awards dinner
(B) A grand opening ceremony
(C) A retirement celebration
(D) A welcoming reception
내일은 어떤 행사가 있을 것인가?
(A) 시상 연회
(B) 개업식
(C) 은퇴 기념식
(D) 환영 파티
분석_ 마지막 부분에 환영 파티가 몇 시에 어디서 열리는지 언급
하고 있다.

Questions 83-85 refer to the following telephone message.

I'm calling to ask about your advertisement for an apartment with a short-term lease in Seoul city center. **83** *I'm moving to Seoul because I was offered a teaching job at a local school.* And I'd be interested in renting your apartment starting March 25. **84** *The ad mentioned that the lease is only for nine months. I'm really glad about that. Because I'd like to get familiar* *with the area for a few months before committing to a longer lease, I think the apartment is perfectly suitable for me.* **85** *But I'm wondering if your building is pet-friendly or if pets are not allowed.*

서울 도심지에서 단기간 아파트 임대에 대한 당신의 광고에 대해 문의 드립니다. 저는 지역 학교에서 교직을 제안받아서 서울로 이사를 갑니다. 그리고 저는 3월 25일부터 당신의 아파트를 임대하고 싶습니다. 광고에는 임대가 오직 9개월 동안만이라고 되어 있던데요. 저는 그 부분이 정말 좋습니다. 장기 임대에 들어가기 전에 몇 개월간 이 지역에 대해서 익숙해지고 싶어서, 제 생각에 그 아파트는 저한테 가장 적합한 것 같아요. 하지만 당신의 건물에서 애완동물을 키울 수 있는지 아닌지 알고 싶습니다.

어휘_ ask about ~에 대해 문의하다 advertisement 광고 lease 임대 offer 제공하다 rent 빌리다 mention 언급하다 get familiar with ~에 익숙하다 suitable 적합한 pet-friendly 애완동물에 친화적인(애완동물을 키울 수 있는)

83. (B)

Why is the speaker moving to Seoul?
(A) To live near her family
(B) To teach at a school
(C) To study Korean
(D) To start a real estate business
화자는 왜 서울로 이사하는가?
(A) 그녀의 가족과 가까이 살기 위해
(B) 학교에서 강의하기 위해
(C) 한국어를 배우기 위해
(D) 부동산 사업을 시작하기 위해
분석_ 화자는 대화 초반 교직을 제안받아서 서울로 간다고 언급하고 있다.

84. (B)

What does the man mean when he says, "I'm really glad about that"?
(A) He can live with his family.
(B) He found the place he was looking for.
(C) He doesn't have to move.
(D) He can advertise a property.
남자가 "저는 그 부분이 정말 좋습니다"라고 말한 것의 의미는 무엇인가?
(A) 그는 가족과 함께 살 수 있게 되었다.
(B) 그가 찾던 장소를 발견했다.
(C) 그는 이사 갈 필요가 없다.
(D) 그가 땅을 광고할 수 있다.
분석_ 화자는 장기 임대를 하기 전 단기적으로 계약을 맺길 원하고 있으며 광고에서 단기 임대를 보고 연락했다는 언급을 하고 있다. 또한 그런 이유로 가장 적합하다는 이야기도 하고 있으므로 원하던 장소를 찾은 것임을 알 수 있다.

85. (B)

What additional information does the speaker want to know?

(A) What parking options are available
(B) Whether residents are allowed to have pets
(C) The amount of the security deposit
(D) Where the nearest supermarket is
화자가 추가적으로 알고 싶어 하는 정보는 무엇인가?
(A) 이용 가능한 주차 옵션
(B) 거주자들이 애완동물을 기를 수 있는지 여부
(C) 보증금의 액수
(D) 가장 가까운 슈퍼마켓 위치
분석_ 마지막 부분에서 화자가 애완동물들이 허용되는지 여부를 물어보고 있다.

Questions 86-88 refer to the following announcement.

86 *Good afternoon, Myungseong Gym members. I'm sorry to announce that we need to temporarily close the health club* **87** *because a water pipe in the locker room is now broken.* So, please gather your belongings and exit the building. Plumbers are coming in to fix the pipe soon, but it may take three or four days for the repairs to be completed. **88** *Please visit our website at msgym.com for updated information on the status of the repair job and when we will open again.* We are sorry for this inconvenience. Thank you for your cooperation.

안녕하세요, Myungseong 체육관 회원님들. 지금 라커룸의 송수관이 파열돼서 잠정적으로 헬스장 문을 닫아야 함을 알리게 되어 유감입니다. 그러므로 여러분의 소지품을 챙기셔서 건물을 나가주시기 바랍니다. 배관공이 곧 수리하러 올 것입니다, 하지만 수리가 완료되려면 3, 4일 정도 걸릴 것입니다. 수리작업 상태와 언제 다시 문을 여는지에 대한 최신 정보는 웹사이트 msgym.com에 가면 알 수 있습니다. 불편함을 드려 죄송합니다. 협조해주셔서 감사합니다.

어휘_ temporarily 임시적으로 close 폐쇄하다 pipe 파이프 locker room 사물함 gather 모으다 belongings 소지품 plumber 배관공 fix 수리하다 repair 수리 status 상태

86. (C)

Where is the announcement being made?
(A) At a butcher shop
(B) At a sporting goods store
(C) At a fitness center
(D) At a post office
방송이 나오는 장소는 어디인가?
(A) 정육점
(B) 운동 장비 매장
(C) 헬스장
(D) 우체국
분석_ 처음 인사말에서 체육관임을 언급하고 있다.

87. (A)

What problem does the speaker mention?

(A) A pipe needs to be fixed.
(B) A shipment was sent to a wrong address.
(C) An office is not for sale.
(D) A schedule is incorrect.

화자가 언급하는 문제점은 무엇인가?
(A) 파이프가 수리되어야 한다.
(B) 배송품이 잘못된 주소로 보내졌다.
(C) 사무실은 판매되지 않는다.
(D) 일정이 잘못되었다.

분석_ 처음 인사말 이후 임시로 문을 닫는 이유로 파이프가 파열되어서임을 언급하고 있다.

88. (B)

Why are the listeners asked to visit the website?
(A) To find other branch locations
(B) To learn when a facility will reopen
(C) To sign up for a mailing list
(D) To provide a review on a service

청자들은 왜 웹사이트에 방문할 것을 요구받는가?
(A) 다른 지점을 찾기 위해
(B) 언제 시설을 다시 여는지 알기 위해
(C) 정기 메일 서비스에 가입하기 위해
(D) 서비스에 대한 후기를 남기기 위해

분석_ 웹사이트에 가면 수리 상태에 대한 정보와 언제 문을 다시 여는지에 대한 정보가 있다고 언급하고 있다.

Questions 89-91 refer to the following news.

In business news, World Smith, Inc., has grown over the last three years. **89** *And now it has been trying to expand its capacity abroad.* To do so, it attempted to merge with newspaper provider Neo International. This would have helped sales, especially in Europe. **90** *However, Jimmy Carter, a spokesperson for World Smith, Inc., announced the status of the firm's business arrangement with Neo International, and it won't happen.* **91** *Instead of pursuing the merger, Neo International accepted an investment from another company.* World Smith, Inc., is starting over, looking for solutions to be competitive.

재계 뉴스입니다. World Smith, Inc.는 지난 3년간 성장해왔습니다. 그리고 현재는 영업력을 해외로 확장하려고 시도하고 있습니다. 이를 위해, 회사는 신문 공급업체인 Neo International과 합병하려고 시도했었습니다. 이것은 특히 유럽시장에서 판매량을 도와줄 수 있었을 겁니다. 하지만, World Smith, Inc.의 대변인인 Jimmy Carter가 Neo International과의 사업 협상 상태에 대해 발표를 했고, 그것은 일어나지 않을 것이라고 이야기했습니다. 합병을 추진하는 대신, Neo International은 다른 회사로부터 투자를 받았습니다. World Smith, Inc.는 처음부터 시작하여 경쟁력을 가질 수 있는 해결책을 찾고 있습니다.

89. (D)

What does the speaker mention about World Smith, Inc.?
(A) It has experienced problems with leadership.
(B) Its new product will be launched soon.
(C) It sells products made by Neo International.
(D) It has tried to expand overseas.

화자는 World Smith, Inc.에 대해 무엇이라 언급하는가?
(A) 회사는 지도력에 문제를 겪고 있다.
(B) 회사의 신제품이 곧 출시될 것이다.
(C) 회사는 Neo International에 의해 만들어진 제품을 판매한다.
(D) 회사는 해외 확장을 시도해왔다.

분석_ 처음 부분에서 회사가 해외로 확장을 시도해왔음을 언급하고 있다.

90. (B)

What does the man mean when he says, "it won't happen"?
(A) He doesn't agree with a proposal.
(B) He is reporting on a plan's failure.
(C) He doesn't support a policy.
(D) He thinks a product will be unpopular.

남자가 "그것은 일어나지 않을 거예요"라고 말한 것의 의미는 무엇인가?
(A) 그는 제안에 동의하지 않는다.
(B) 그는 계획의 실패를 보고한다.
(C) 그는 정책을 지지하지 않는다.
(D) 그는 제품이 인기 없을 것이라 생각한다.

분석_ 지문 마지막 부분에 합병하는 것 대신에 다른 회사로부터 투자를 받았음을 언급하고 있으므로 먼저 언급되었던 계획이 실행되지 않았음을 알 수 있다.

91. (D)

What is indicated about Neo International?
(A) It changed its product price.
(B) It opened other branches.
(C) Its CFO left the company.
(D) It received investment funds.

Neo International에 대해 나타난 것은 무엇인가?
(A) 회사가 제품 가격을 바꿀 것이다.
(B) 회사가 다른 지점을 열 것이다.
(C) CFO가 회사를 떠날 것이다.
(D) 회사가 투자를 받았다.

분석_ 90번 문제에서 나온 계획의 실패에 대한 이유를 묻는 문제와 동일하다. 다른 회사로부터 투자를 받았다는 내용이 지문 마지막에 언급되고 있다.

Questions 92-94 refer to the following event advertisement and list.

Spring is around the corner. Are you looking for something exciting? **92** *You can join the community celebration on Sunday, March 25, at Dalseong Park.* This special event will begin at 1 P.M. and **93** *will feature dance performances, craft workshops, and live music.* Besides, celebration attendees can register for the prize drawing to be held at 6 P.M. This will include prizes sponsored by some local companies: Hunde Motors, Toyoda Electronics, and Hummel Fashions. **94** *There will be one grand prize, three gold prizes, ten silver prizes, and twenty bronze prizes.* So, there are lots of chances to be a winner!

Category	Prize
Grand Prize	3D TV
Gold Prize	Vacuum Cleaner
94 Sliver Prize	**Blender**
Bronze Prize	Two Movie tickets

봄이 다가왔습니다. 신나는 뭔가를 찾고 계십니까? 3월 25일 일요일 Dalseong 공원에서 열리는 공동체 축하행사에 참석하세요. 이 특별 행사는 1시에 시작하며 댄스공연, 공예 워크샵과 라이브 음악이 준비되어 있습니다. 게다가, 축하행사 참석자들은 6시에 열리는 상품 추첨에도 등록할 수 있습니다. 이것은 Hunde 자동차, Toyoda 전자, 그리고 Hummel 패션과 같은 몇몇 지역 회사들로부터 후원을 받은 상품들을 포함합니다. 상품은 하나의 대상, 3개의 금상, 10개의 은상, 그리고 20개의 동상이 준비되어 있습니다. 그러므로 수상자가 될 수 있는 많은 기회가 있습니다.

분류	상품
대상	3D TV
금상	청소기
은상	믹서기
동상	영화표 2장

어휘_ around the corner ~가 가까이 있는 exciting 흥미로운 celebration 축하행사 feature ~를 특별하게 다루다 attendee 참가자 register for ~에 등록하다 prize drawing 상품 추첨 include ~를 포함하다 sponsor ~를 후원하다

92. (D)
What is being advertised?
(A) A local workshop
(B) A sports competition
(C) An art gallery
(D) A community event
광고되고 있는 것은 무엇인가?
(A) 지역 워크샵
(B) 운동 경기
(C) 미술 갤러리
(D) 지역 공동체 행사
분석_ 광고 초반 장소와 시간을 이야기하며 지역 공동체 축하 행사임을 언급하고 있다.

93. (C)
According to the advertisement, what can visitors do at the event?
(A) Attend a debate
(B) Sample international cuisine
(C) Watch live performers
(D) Meet a famous writer
광고에 따르면, 방문자들은 행사에서 무엇을 할 수 있는가?
(A) 토론에 참석하기
(B) 세계적인 요리 시식하기
(C) 라이브 연주자 보기
(D) 유명 작가 만나기
분석_ 행사가 특별히 다루는 것들 중에 댄스 공연, 공예 워크샵, 라이브 음악 등이 있다고 언급하고 있다.

94. (C)
Look at the graphic. How many people will receive a blender?
(A) One
(B) Three
(C) Ten
(D) Twenty
그래픽을 보자. 몇 명의 사람이 믹서기를 받을 것인가?
(A) 1명
(B) 3명
(C) 10명
(D) 20명
분석_ 표를 보고 얼마나 많은 사람들이 믹서기를 받을 수 있는지를 알아내는 문제이다. 표에서 믹서기는 은상에 해당한다는 것을 알 수 있고, 광고 마지막에 10개의 은상이 있다고 언급하고 있으므로 정답은 10명이 된다.

Questions 95-97 refer to the following telephone message and list.

Hello, Ms. Yang. **95** *Thanks for your interest in Pears Electronics.* **95 96** *Our records indicate that one of our representatives visited your store on March 25. I heard she demonstrated our desktop products.* I just wanted to see if you decided to stock our products. You may also want to know that since that visit, we have expanded our product line to include mobile phones, tablet computers, and laptops. These are perfectly compatible with our popular desktop products. **97** *I'm going to ask one of our representatives to tell you more about the new tablet line.* If you have any questions, please contact me at 231-4723.

Representative	Product Line
Chris	Desktop
Green	Mobile Phone
97 *Max*	Tablet Computer
Brian	Laptop

안녕하세요, Yang 씨. Pears 전자에 관심을 보여주셔서 감사합니다. 우리 기록에 사원들 중 한 명이 3월 25일 당신의 매장을 방문했다고 나와 있습니다. 제가 듣기로는 그녀가 우리 데스크탑 제품을 시연해 보였다는데요. 당신이 저희 제품을 들여놓기로 결정하셨는지 알고 싶습니다. 그 방문 이후로 당신은 우리가 제품 라인을 확장하여 핸드폰, 태블릿 컴퓨터, 그리고 노트북 컴퓨터까지 추가했다는 사실을 알고자 하실 수 있습니다. 이 제품들은 우리의 인기 있는 데스크탑 컴퓨터와 완벽하게 호환됩니다. 저는 직원들 중 한 명을 시켜서 당신에게 새로운 태블릿 컴퓨터 라인에 대해서 알려드리라고 할 겁니다. 만약 궁금한 게 있으시면, 231-4723으로 연락 주세요.

사원	제품 라인
Chris	데스크탑
Green	휴대폰
Max	태블릿 컴퓨터
Brian	노트북 컴퓨터

어휘_ interest 관심 record 기록 indicate ~를 나타내다 representative 사원 demonstrate ~를 시연하다 decide 결정하다 stock ~를 저장하다 expand 확장하다 be compatible with ~와 호환되는

95. (A)

Why is the speaker calling?
(A) To follow up on a business proposal
(B) To announce an ongoing renovation
(C) To request some product samples
(D) To thank a customer for reporting a problem

화자는 왜 전화하고 있는가?
(A) 사업 제안에 대해 후속조치를 하기 위해
(B) 진행 중인 수리에 대해 알리기 위해
(C) 제품 샘플을 요청하기 위해서
(D) 문제를 보고해준 고객에게 감사를 표하기 위해

분석_ 지문 초반 인사말과 함께 관심을 보여주어서 감사하다는 이야기를 하고 있다. 또한 그 뒤로 사원 중 하나가 제품을 시연해 보이기 위해 매장을 방문했음을 언급하고, 매장에 자기 회사의 제품을 들일 것인지를 묻고 있으므로 청자가 먼저 사업 제안을 해왔고, 화자는 거기에 응했다는 것을 알 수 있다.

96. (C)

What happened on March 25?
(A) A new electronic line was launched.
(B) A computer products store was opened.
(C) A product demonstration took place.
(D) A tablet computer workshop was held.

3월 25일에 무슨 일이 있었는가?
(A) 새로운 전자제품 라인이 출시되었다.
(B) 컴퓨터 제품 매장이 열렸다.
(C) 제품 시연이 있었다.
(D) 태블릿 컴퓨터 워크샵이 개최되었다.

분석_ 95번 문제와 정답에 대한 단서가 중복되고 있다. 화자의 회사 직원 중 한 명이 3월 25일에 청자의 매장을 방문하여 제품을 시연해 보였음을 언급하고 있다.

97. (C)

Look at the graphic. Who will be talking to Ms. Yang?
(A) Chris
(B) Green
(C) Max
(D) Brian

그래픽을 보자. 누가 Yang 씨에게 이야기할 것인가?
(A) Chris
(B) Green
(C) Max
(D) Brian

분석_ 표 안에서 Yang에게 누가 이야기할 것인지를 찾는 문제이다. 지문 마지막에 사원들 중 한 명을 시켜서 태블릿에 대해 이야기하도록 시키겠다는 말을 하고 있다. 또한 표 안에서 태블릿을 담당하는 사람이 Max이므로 정답이 누구인지 알 수 있다.

Questions 98-100 refer to the following broadcast and schedule.

I hope you all enjoyed that cooking demonstration by Grace Kent, the head chef for Willa Hotel. **98 *The next guest at the show will be Selina Blond. I'm sure many of you are familiar with Ms. Blond's dishes, as she is the leading chef and the host on a popular TV cooking show.* 99 *Today she'll be sharing her method for easily making healthy food in today's busy life. Using these tips, you can keep your body healthy.* 100 *And after Ms. Blond finishes her demonstration, we will have our scheduled break. Let's give her big applause.***

Schedule	
Demonstration 1	9:00-9:40
100 *Demonstration 2*	9:40-10:40
Morning Break	10:40-11:00
Demonstration 3	11:00-11:50
Demonstration 4	11:50-12:10

여러분 모두 Willa 호텔 주방장인 Grace Kent가 보여준 요리 시연회를 즐겼기를 바랍니다. 쇼의 다음 손님은 Selina Blond입니다. 저는

여러분들이 Blond 씨의 요리를 잘 알 거라 확신합니다, 왜냐하면 그녀는 대표적인 요리사이자 유명한 TV 요리쇼의 호스트이기 때문입니다. 오늘 그녀는 오늘날의 바쁜 삶 속에서 건강한 음식을 쉽게 만들 수 있는 방법을 공유할 것입니다. 그 팁을 이용해서, 여러분은 건강을 유지할 수 있습니다. 그리고 Blond 씨가 시연회를 끝낸 이후에, 우리는 예정된 휴식시간을 가질 것입니다. 박수 부탁드립니다.

일정	
시연 1	9:00-9:40
시연 2	9:40-10:40
오전 휴식	10:40-11:00
시연 3	11:00-11:50
시연 4	11:50-12:10

어휘_ enjoy ~를 즐기다 demonstration 시연회 guest 손님 be familiar with ~에 익숙한 leading 선도하는 popular 인기 있는 share ~를 공유하다 method 방법 healthy 건강한 finish ~를 끝내다 break 휴식시간 applause 박수

98. (C)

Who is Selina Blond?
(A) A business owner
(B) An government official
(C) A show host
(D) A famous author
Selina Blond는 누구인가?
(A) 기업 경영자
(B) 정부 공무원
(C) 쇼 호스트
(D) 유명한 작가
분석_ Selina Blond가 누구인지 묻고 있다. 지문 초반 Selina Blond가 요리사이면서 동시에 쇼 호스트라고 언급하고 있다.

99. (D)

What will Ms. Blond give a demonstration about?
(A) Managing hotels for a long time
(B) Keeping in shape
(C) Writing a cook book
(D) Making use of healthful ingredients
Blond 씨는 어떤 것에 대한 시연회를 하는가?
(A) 장기간 호텔 경영하기
(B) 몸매 유지하기
(C) 요리책 쓰기
(D) 몸에 좋은 재료 이용하기
분석_ 지문 중반 Blond 씨가 건강한 음식을 만드는 방법을 공유한다고 이야기하고 있으며 그 팁을 이용하여 건강을 유지할 수 있다고 언급하는 부분에서 정답을 알 수 있다.

100. (D)

Look at the graphic. How long will Ms. Blond's demonstration last?

(A) 20 minutes
(B) 40 minutes
(C) 50 minutes
(D) 60 minutes
그래픽을 보자. Blond 씨의 시연회는 얼마나 지속될 것인가?
(A) 20분
(B) 40분
(C) 50분
(D) 60분
분석_ 표를 보고 발표 진행 시간을 고르는 문제이다. 지문 마지막에 Blond 씨의 시연 이후 휴식시간을 갖는다는 것으로 보아 휴식 직전 일정이 Blond 씨의 시연임을 알 수 있다. 즉 Blond 씨의 시연은 일정상 2번째 것이 되므로 정답은 60분이 된다.

101. (C) relocation 음성강의

해석_ 개인 투자자들에게 승인을 받는다면, Proton Appliance Facility의 Birmingham 지역으로의 이전은 5월에 일어날 것이다.
분석_ 품사 문제이다. 관사 the 뒤에 명사가 와야 하므로 (C)가 가장 적절하다.

102. (A) for 음성강의

해석_ Green 씨는 5년 이상 동안 Lemona Cecome Company에서 일을 해왔다.
분석_ 기간명사와 어울리는 전치사를 고르는 문제이다. (B), (C)는 시점명사와 어울린다.

103. (D) it 음성강의

해석_ 제안서가 고객에게 전달되기 최소 이틀 전에 Choi 씨는 그것을 검토해야 한다.
분석_ 동사 앞 주격 대명사를 넣는 문제이다. 앞에서 언급된 명사(proposal)를 받아오는 대명사는 it이다.

104. (C) supply 음성강의

해석_ Kovoelo Construction은 Washington Community의 확장 프로젝트에 필요한 모든 재료를 공급하기로 동의할 것이다.
분석_ 동사 어휘 문제이다. 건설사가 확장공사에 필요한 재료를 공급한다는 내용이 적절하다. (A) 넓히다 (B) 시작하다 (D) 무시하다 모두 해석이 부자연스럽다.

105. (D) finished 음성강의

해석_ 원래 예정된 대로, 지난 화요일 North Lincoln Avenue에서 몇몇 측량기사들이 대지 경계선 측량을 끝냈다.
분석_ 문장의 동사가 들어갈 자리이다. (B)는 동사가 아니므로 오답이다. 시제의 단서(last)가 있으므로 과거가 정답이다.

106. (C) because of

해석_ 예기치 못한 우천으로 경기장을 이용하지 못하게 되어 대학의 풋볼 게임이 취소되었다.

분석_ 전치사 어휘 문제이다. 경기가 취소된 이유를 말해야 하므로 '때문에'라는 의미를 가진 because of가 적절하다.

107. (C) generously
해석_ Samdong Bread는 시의 봉사활동을 위해 매주 스낵 한 상자를 기부하는 데에 흔쾌히 동의했다.
분석_ 현재완료 시제인 have p.p 사이는 부사 자리이다.

108. (A) while
해석_ 새로운 보안 시스템이 설치되는 동안 Skytech Telecom은 1주일간 문을 닫기로 했다.
분석_ 접속사 어휘 문제이다. (B), (C)는 전치사, (D)는 명사절 접속사이므로 오답이다.

109. (C) detailed
해석_ 만약 지금 등록한다면, 당신은 Hamnar Motors의 자동차에 대한 자세한 정보가 담긴 무료 카탈로그를 받을 수 있습니다.
분석_ 명사 앞 형용사가 들어갈 자리이다. 동사의 V-ing 형태와 V-ed 형태는 형용사로 사용할 수 있다.

110. (D) summary
해석_ 기획자가 지난 목요일에 있었던 American Bank와의 회의에 대한 요약안을 검토하길 원한다.
분석_ 명사 어휘 문제이다. 회의의 요약안을 검토한다는 내용이 적절하다. (A) 거래 (B) 능력 (C) 요구사항 모두 의미가 적절하지 못하다.

111. (A) their
해석_ 배송 규정에 따라서, Kao Corporation의 음료는 맛과 영양을 보존하기 위해 유리병에 포장된다.
분석_ 명사(flavor) 앞에 들어가는 대명사는 소유격이 적절하다.

112. (C) eagerly
해석_ Kyunghee Aluminum Co.의 CEO인 Mark Hunter는 모든 부서로부터 수익 보고서를 열렬히 기다리고 있다.
분석_ 부사 어휘 문제이다. eagerly await(열렬히 기다리다) 짝꿍 표현을 기억해보자.

113. (C) updating
해석_ 선택사항들에 대해 주의 깊게 고려한 이후에, Ehdores Plastics는 생산라인 과정을 개선함으로써 전반적인 생산 수준을 증가시킬 계획이다.
분석_ 전치사와 명사 사이 동명사 자리이다.

114. (B) seasonal
해석_ 고객으로부터 피드백 받기를 좋아하는 요리사 Rangsh는 계절별 과일과 채소를 제공하기 위해 한해 내내 식당의 메뉴를 교체한다.
분석_ 형용사 어휘 문제이다. 계절별 과일이라는 표현이 적절하다. (A) 내부적인 (D) 낭비하는

115. (B) his
해석_ 홍보 담당자에 따르면, Steve 씨가 도시의 새로운 다리를 건설할

것으로 선정되었다.
분석_ 명사(publicist) 앞 소유격 대명사가 적절하다.

116. (D) significantly
해석_ 몇몇 연구는 의사들이 Stingheal의 새로운 수술용 레이저를 이용함으로써 환자들의 회복기간을 상당히 줄일 수 있음을 보여준다.
분석_ 조동사(can)와 동사원형(reduce) 사이 부사가 들어갈 자리이다.

117. (C) historically
해석_ 지역 정부와 협력을 맺어서, Cerena 국립 박물관은 역사적으로 상당한 세계의 고대 예술품들을 소장하고 있다.
분석_ 부사 어휘 문제이다. 박물관이 소장하는 것으로 역사적 예술품이 적절하다.

118. (B) What
해석_ 주주들을 가장 감동시킨 것은 Ronson King Corporation이 올해에 브랜드에 대한 국가적 인식을 개선시켰다는 것이다.
분석_ 명사절 문법 문제이다. 빈칸부터 is 앞까지를 하나의 명사덩어리로 만들어줄 명사절 접속사가 필요하다. (C), (D)는 접속사가 아니므로 제외한다. 빈칸 뒤로 주어가 없이 곧바로 impresses라는 동사가 있으므로 불완전한 문장을 이끄는 what이 정답이 된다. what과 which는 주로 선택의 폭 존재 여부로 구분한다. 둘 중, 혹은 셋 중에서라는 범위가 주어지면 which를 사용하고 그 외엔 what을 사용하도록 한다.

119. (A) About
해석_ 최고 경영진으로 승진하기 전에, 약 50퍼센트의 임원들은 관련분야에서 상급 수준의 직책을 맡았다.
분석_ 부사 어휘 문제이다. 숫자 앞에서 '대략'이라는 의미로 사용되는 부사인 about이 정답이다. 동의어로 approximately, almost, around 등이 있다.

120. (A) successful
해석_ High Developments Today의 최신판의 한 기사는 성공적인 *grant writing에 대한 좋은 아이디어들을 담고 있다.
분석_ 형용사 어휘 문제이다. 기사에 담겨진 내용으로 성공적으로 글을 쓰는 것에 대한 것이 적절하다. (B) 추정된 (C) 이전의 등은 적절하지 않다. (D)는 복수명사와 어울리므로 오답이다.
*정부부처, 기업, 재단 또는 신탁과 같은 기관들에 의해서 기금의 이용 과정을 작성해내는 실무

121. (C) impact
해석_ Metropolitan Transportation Authority는 예정된 도로 보수작업이 지역 공동체에 미치는 영향을 조사할 것이다.
분석_ 명사 어휘 문제이다. impact on(~에 대한 영향) 짝꿍표현을 기억하자. 또한 have an impact on(~에 영향을 미치다)이라는 관용어구도 함께 기억해보자.

122. (C) necessitates
해석_ Heven Gow Building의 리모델링은 Dal-sung Avenue의 일시적인 폐쇄를 필요로 한다.

분석_ 동사 문법 문제이다. 동사가 없는 문장은 존재할 수 없고 빈칸 앞뒤에 동사가 없기 때문에 동사가 필요한 자리이다. (A), (B)는 각각 부사, 형용사이므로 제외된다. (C), (D)를 주어(Heven Gow Building)에 맞추어보면 단수형 동사가 정답이다.

123. (D) Even though

해석_ 회의에서 인수 조건이 구두상의 동의를 받기는 했지만 여전히 공식적으로 승인을 받아야만 한다.

분석_ 접속사 어휘 문제이다. (A)는 뒤에 절대 주어, 동사를 사용하지 않는 특징이 있다. (B), (C)는 전치사이므로 오답이다.

124. (C) several

해석_ 유명한 패션 디자이너인 Tomas Geller는 몇몇 가족구성원들을 위한 옷을 만듦으로써 새로운 재단 기술을 개발했다.

분석_ 수량형용사 문제이다. 복수명사(members)와 어울리는 several이 정답이다. (A), (B)는 그 자체로 명사이므로 명사 앞에 사용할 수 없다. (D)는 가산 단수명사와 어울린다.

125. (A) through

해석_ Manhattan National Bank의 온라인 채팅 서비스를 통해서, 하루 24시간 내내 보안직원에게 연락할 수 있다.

분석_ 전치사 어휘 문제이다. 수단이나 방법과 어울리는 전치사는 through이다. between은 '둘 사이'라는 의미로 복수명사와 어울린다.

126. (D) impressive

해석_ Fierce Vrosnan은 새로운 연구팀의 관리직으로 선택되었다. 왜냐하면 그의 배경이 매우 인상적이기 때문이다.

분석_ 형용사 어휘 문제이다. (A), (B), (C) 모두 사람명사와 어울리는 형용사들이다. 반면 (D)는 토익에서 절대 사람과 어울려 사용되지 않는다. (A) 자격 있는 (B) 기쁜 (C) 지식이 풍부한 (D) 인상적인

127. (D) portion

해석_ 다음 주, Yogoyo 서점의 모든 판매 수익의 일부가 지역 고아원에 전달될 것이다.

분석_ 명사 어휘 문제이다. 지역 고아원에 기부된다는 의미이므로 '판매 수익의 일부'라는 표현이 적절하다.

128. (A) complete

해석_ 오늘 밤 건설 직원들이 도로 재포장 프로젝트를 마무리하는 동안 Ereetian 다리의 교통 정체를 피하세요.

분석_ 동사 문법 문제이다. 접속사(while)가 있고 동사(avoid)가 하나뿐이므로 동사가 들어갈 자리이고, 목적어가 존재하므로 능동태 동사가 정답이다.

129. (A) reconsider

해석_ Worldwide Network Times 구독을 취소하기 전에 시간을 내서 당신의 결정을 다시 고려해보세요.

분석_ 동사 어휘 문제이다. 구독 취소 전 결정을 한 번 더 고민해보라는 내용이 적절하다.

130. (B) in order to

해석_ 새로운 규정을 준수하기 위해서 Feders 공장의 환기시스템은 작년에 수정되었다.

분석_ 전치사로 사용되는 to인지 부정사를 만들어주는 to인지를 고르는 문제이다. 빈칸 뒤 동사원형(comply)이 있으므로 부정사를 만들어줄 수 있는 in order to가 정답이다. (A), (C), (D)는 모두 전치사로 뒤에 명사 혹은 동명사가 따라온다.

Part 6　　　　본문 p.31

Questions 131-134 refer to the following article.　음성강의

Reading Pleasure Bookstore으로 Eric Jackson이 온다
New York(3월25일) – New York Voice의 서평가인 Clark Kent는 Reading Pleasure Bookstore에서 3월 27일 오전 10시에 Eric Jackson을 인터뷰할 것이다. 대담 이후에, Jackson 씨는 「Snow in Alaska」라는 신간 여행기를 낭독할 것이다. 또한 참석한 사람들을 위해 도서 사인회를 가질 것이다. *점심식사시간과 담화를 포함한 모든 일정은 오후 5시까지 진행될 것이다.*
Jackson 씨는 여행기 수상작인 「Leave Suddenly」와 몇몇 여행 수필집의 작가이다. 그의 작품은 New Revolution of Journey Literature의 비평가들에 의해서 뛰어난 업적으로 지명되었다.
만약 당신이 행사에 대한 세부사항을 필요로 한다면 www.readingpleasure.com를 방문할 수도 있고 더 많이 알아보기 위해 (473) 293-5839번으로 서점에 전화를 할 수도 있다.

131. (D) interview

분석_ 동사 어휘 문제이다. 아래에 유명 작가가 최신 책과 사인회를 연다는 내용이 있으므로 (D)가 어울린다. (A) 추천하다 (B) 초대하다 (C) 대체하다 (D) 인터뷰하다

132. (C) also

분석_ 부사 어휘 문제이다. 작가가 서점에 방문해서 하는 일들을 나열하고 있으므로 (C)가 적합하다. (A) 오늘 (B) 앞선 (C) 또한 (D) 다소

133. (B)

(A) 그의 서적은 대부분의 비평가들이 기대했던 것과 달리 두 배 이상 팔렸다.
(B) 점심식사시간과 담화를 포함한 모든 일정은 오후 5시까지 진행될 것이다.
(C) 그는 New York City에서 태어나고 자랐다.
(D) 출판사는 그의 서적 판매를 통해 상당한 수익을 벌어들였다.

분석_ 앞에서 언급된 내용들이 행사의 시간 순서로 배열되고 있으므로 행사의 마무리로 단락을 마무리 짓는 것이 문맥상 자연스럽다.

134. (D) achievement

분석_ 명사 문법 문제이다. 관사 a 오른쪽에 명사가 필요한 자리

이며 (A)와 (D) 중에 골라준다. 여행 작품은 성취한 사람 (achiever)이라기보다 성취한 업적(achievement)에 해당 된다.

Questions 135-138 refer to the following e-mail.

발신: Remington Steel
수신: 장기 근무 직원들
참조: Taylor Momson
제목: 근무 기념일
날짜: 10월 10일
첨부: 선물 목록
직원들에게:
축하드립니다. Jeepson Advertising Company에 대한 당신의 근 무를 치하하게 되어 기쁩니다. 오랫동안 근무해온 회사의 전문직원들 은 우리의 성공에 크게 기여하고 있습니다.
사실은, 우리가 나라 안에서 영향을 미치는 최고의 회사들 중 하나로 널리 인정받는 것은 Jeepson에 대한 여러분의 엄청난 헌신적인 자 세 때문입니다. *그러므로 여러분의 소중한 헌신에 대한 감사의 표시 로서, 중역 위원들은 여러분에게 선물로 보상해드리게 되어 기쁩니다.* 11월 11일까지 첨부된 목록에서 당신이 선택한 것을 Taylor Momson에게 알려주세요.
Remington Steel
최고 경영자

135. (B) contribute

분석_ 동사 문법 문제이다. 문장의 동사가 필요한 자리이므로 (A) 는 오답이다. 주어(professionals)에 수일치시키면 (C)도 오 답이다. 〈contribute to + 명사〉는 '~에 기여하다'라는 의미 로 사용된다는 것을 기억해두자. 전문가들이 성공에 헌신되 는 수동의 의미라기보다 성공에 기여하는 능동의 의미이므 로 수동태인 are contributed는 오답이다. contribute는 자 동사와 타동사 모두 활용된다.

136. (C) In fact

분석_ 부사 어휘 문제이다. 문장과 문장을 연결하는 접속부사 문 제는 앞뒤 문장의 문맥을 따져야 한다. 앞 문장에서 회사의 성공을 언급하고 있고 다음 문장에서 앞 문장의 내용을 부 가적으로 설명하고 있기 때문에 대조나 반전의 의미를 지닌 (A), (D)는 오답이다. (A) 대조적으로 (B) 견주어 보면 (C) 사실은 (D) 그러나

137. (D)

(A) 직원들 대부분은 그들의 관심사를 판매량 증대에 초점을 맞춰야 합 니다.
(B) 경영진은 모든 직원에게 회사 인지도를 높일 수 있는 많은 기회들을 제공해왔습니다.
(C) 우리는 예기치 못한 판매량 감소로 인해 경기침체로부터 재정적으로 어려움을 겪을 것입니다.
(D) 여러분의 소중한 헌신에 대한 감사의 표시로서, 중역 위원들은 여러분 에게 선물로 보상해드리게 되어 기쁩니다.
분석_ 회사가 인정받는 것이 직원들의 헌신 때문이었다는 내용

이 앞 문장에서 언급되어 있다. 연결사 therefore는 인과 관계를 의미하므로 헌신으로 인한 보상을 주는 내용이 문 맥상 자연스럽다.

138. (B) notify

분석_ 동사 어휘 문제이다. (A)는 뒤에 사람을 취할 때 반드시 전 치사 to를 필요로 한다. 〈announce + to + 사람〉〈notify + 사람 + of 명사〉 '사람에게 ~를 통보하다' (A) 발표하다 (B) 알리다 (C) 배우다 (D) 추천하다

Questions 139-142 refer to the following letter.

Geneva Networking
3030-2nd Ave. S.W.
Calgary AB T2N 5N7
Geneva Elrond 씨
부동산 투자 회사
Toronto, ON M7Y 2C5
Elrond 씨에게,
이 편지는 우리 회사에 낸 당신의 지원서가 마침내 승인되었음을 알 리기 위한 것입니다. 직무 안내서에 나와 있고 면접 때 언급된 것처 럼, 당신은 퇴임을 하게 될 매니저가 책임졌던 모든 업무를 떠맡게 될 것입니다.
고용되고 처음 5개월 동안, 면접 때 만났던 Britny Spears가 진행하 는 오리엔테이션 과정을 거치게 될 것입니다.
우리의 제안을 수락한다면, 당신은 9월 3일에 업무를 시작하게 될 것 입니다.
늦어도 8월 31일까지 우리에게 제안의 수락 여부를 알려주세요.
Richard Aragon
인사부장

139. (D) job

분석_ 앞으로 고용될 직원의 업무와 관련된 것이므로 (D) job이 적절하다.

140. (C) met

분석_ 이미 채용이 결정된 시점이기 때문에, Britny Spears를 만 난 면접은 과거에 일어난 것이므로 과거시제 (C) met이 적 절하다

141. (C) accept

분석_ 9월 3일에 업무를 시작하기 위해서는 제안을 받아들여야 하 므로 (C) accept가 적절하다.

142. (A)

(A) 늦어도 8월 31일까지 우리에게 제안의 수락 여부를 알려주세요.
(B) 당신은 다가올 은퇴식에 정중히 초대받으셨습니다.
(C) 8월 31일까지 지원서를 제출하여주십시오.
(D) 당신이 언제 면접을 볼지 곧 통보받으실 겁니다.
분석_ 면접 후 합격을 알리는 통지서이므로 지원자의 고용 제안 수 락 여부로 글을 마무리하는 것이 문맥상 자연스럽다.

Questions 143-146 refer to the following e-mail.

수신: Ian Holmes
발신: Peter Jackson
보낸 날짜: 2016년 5월 15일
제목: 다음 회의
Ian Holmes 씨에게
안녕하세요. Holmes 씨. 저는 지난주에 있었던 프레젠테이션이 성공적이었다는 좋은 소식을 전합니다. Kintex Inc.는 우리의 성과에 완전히 만족했고, 차기 공사작업을 우리와 함께하기를 원했습니다. 그들은 거래를 마무리 짓기 위해 이달 말에 우리와 만나고자 합니다. *다음 주쯤에 우리가 만나서 계약과 다른 세부사항들을 검토해보는 게 어떨까요?* 제가 생각하기에 우리가 그들에게 계약서를 보여주기 전에 변경해야 할 몇 가지 사항들이 있습니다.
조속한 답신 바랍니다.
Peter Jackson

143. (B) success
분석_ 좋은 소식과 관련해서 적절한 의미인 (B) success가 자연스럽다.

144. (D) would like
분석_ 함께 작업하기를 원한다는 의미이므로 (D) would like가 적절하다.
어휘_ would like to + V ~하기를 원하다

145. (D)
(A) 협력사가 우리에게 재발표를 요구할 것임을 알 수 있습니다.
(B) 마감시한 전까지 계약을 마무리 짓는 데 다소 어려움이 있었습니다.
(C) 조만간 우리 회사의 재정 상태에 상당한 영향을 끼칠 것으로 기대됩니다.
(D) 다음 주쯤에 우리가 만나서 계약과 다른 세부사항들을 검토해보는 게 어떨까요?
분석_ 이달 말에 계약을 마무리 짓자는 내용이 앞 문장에 언급되었다. 뒤의 문장에서 수정해야 할 몇몇 내용이 있다는 걸로 봐서 그 전에 만나서 내용 검토를 제안하는 내용이 문맥상 적절하다.

146. (D) them
분석_ '계약서를 Kindex Inc.(they로 본문에 언급되고 있음)에 보여주기 전에'라는 의미이므로 (D) them이 적절하다. 회사 자체를 본다면 단수형의 대명사인 it으로 대신할 수 있지만, 회사에서 근무하는 직원들을 의미하는 경우에는 복수형의 대명사인 them을 사용한다.

Questions 147-148 refer to the following text message.

발신: Eplus Telecom
일시: 9월 3일
제목: 지불만기일
귀하의 월간 청구금액 55.50달러가 오늘 날짜 9월 3일부로 0304번호로 끝나는 신용카드에서 자동이체됩니다. 이체 만기일 혹은 지불 방법의 변경을 원할 시, 온라인 홈페이지 www.eplustelecom.com으로 방문해주세요. 귀하는 문자 알람을 수령하는 데 동의하셨기 때문에 이 자동 문자 메시지를 받으셨습니다. 문자 거부 시, '정지'라는 글자와 함께 문자를 보내주세요.
귀하의 지속적인 거래에 감사드립니다.

147. (A)
이 문자는 왜 작성되었는가?
(A) 알림사항을 발송하기 위해
(B) 신규 고객을 유치하기 위해
(C) 연체를 확인하기 위해
(D) 회의 날짜를 잡기 위해
분석_ 첫 단락에서 자동이체 내역을 확인시켜주고 있다.

148. (C)
고객은 웹페이지에서 무엇을 할 수 있는가?
(A) 수수료 프로그램 등록 해지
(B) 새로운 신용카드 수령에 동의
(C) 이체일정 변경
(D) 문자 수령을 해지
분석_ 웹페이지는 온라인(online)을 의미하므로 첫 단락에 언급된 이체날짜 변경(change your due date)에서 정답을 찾을 수 있다.

Questions 149-150 refer to the following advertisement.
음성강의

Carson Entertainment
사무실에서 파티를 개최하실 건가요?
저희가 바로 그 답입니다.
Carson Entertainment는 간편한 저녁식사부터 공식만찬에 이르기까지 어떠한 종류의 행사건 특별한 음식을 제공해드리고 있습니다. 중국요리, 멕시코요리 그리고 인도요리 등 매운 음식을 전문으로 취급하며, 저희의 후식은 이 도시에서 최고로 알려져 있습니다.
웹사이트에서 모든 메뉴를 확인해보시거나 혹은 Wellington 31번가에 직접 방문하셔서 저희 서비스 사원과 상담하시고 선택하신 요리를 무료로 시식해보십시오.
당신은 분명 왜 우리가 특별한 비즈니스 행사에 대해서 지역업체들로부터 최고라는 등급을 받았는지 아시게 될 겁니다.
www.carsonentertainment.com

149. (D)
Carson Entertainment는 무슨 종류의 사업을 하고 있는가?

(A) 영화 제작
(B) 주방용품 가게
(C) 웹디자인
(D) 음식 제공 업체

분석_ 첫 단락에서 제공하는 요리(dishes)를 제공하는 내용이 언급되어 있다. dish는 접시뿐만 아니라 음식을 의미하기도 한다.

150. (B)

회사는 무료로 무엇을 제공하는가?
(A) 영화 샘플본
(B) 상품 샘플
(C) 특급배송
(D) 마케팅 상담

분석_ at no charge는 본문의 for free와 동의표현으로서 '무료'라는 의미를 지닌다. product는 흔히 알고 있는 공산품뿐만 아니라 사람 손으로 만들어진 모든 산물을 일컫는다.

Questions 151-153 refer to the following advertisement.

Bom Bom Cafe
일요일을 제외한 모든 요일에 오전 8시부터 오후 2시까지 영업
삶은 혹은 구운 계란 2개·················4.5달러
블루베리 와플
구운 와플, 신선한 블루베리와 휘핑크림 ··········4.5달러
팬케이크 세트
감자칩 또는 딸기 추가 1달러·············4.5달러
Bom Bom 오믈렛 특선
계란 3개, 그릴로 구운 마늘과 얇게 썬 토마토가 토스트와 함께 제공
베이컨 추가 1달러 ················5.25달러
소시지 특선
구운 계란 3개, 네모로 썬 소시지, 토스트 그리고 튀긴 당근
···················5.75달러
조조 특선
구운 팬케이크 한 조각, 계란 2개, 후라이드 치킨 그리고 신선한 토마토
베이컨 추가 1달러 ················5.75달러
그 유명한 돼지고기 소시지를 판매한 지 5주년임을 축하하면서!

151. (B)

Bom Bom Cafe에 관해 진술한 것은?
(A) 새로운 식사공간이다.
(B) 저녁에는 문을 닫는다.
(C) 다양한 야채와 과일을 판매한다.
(D) 저렴한 가격에 제품을 판매한다.

분석_ 영업시간이 오전 8시부터 오후 2시까지(open 8 A.M. to 2 P.M.)이므로 저녁에는 영업하지 않음을 알 수 있다.

152. (A)

고객이 추가요금을 내고 과일을 추가할 수 있는 것은 무엇인가?
(A) 팬케이크 세트
(B) 소시지 특선
(C) 블루베리 와플
(D) 조조 특선

분석_ 단순히 과일이 담긴 제품을 찾는 것이 아니라 추가요금을 내고 과일을 더한 세트를 묻고 있으므로 팬케이크(Pancake set Potato chips or strawberries for $ 1 more)가 정답이다.

153. (D)

모든 특선 요리에 공통으로 들어가는 재료는 무엇인가?
(A) 토마토
(B) 감자
(C) 토스트
(D) 계란

분석_ 조리방식이나 수량은 다르지만 계란이 모든 세트에 들어간다.

Questions 154-155 refer to the following text message chain.

Jessica Simpson	(13:05)
첫 번째 비행기가 지연되어서 LA에서의 연결편을 놓쳤어요.	
Jessica Simpson	(13:06)
그래서 Honolulu에 저녁 7시에 도착하는 다른 비행편을 타려고 해요.	
Jason Cruise	(13:11)
네 동일한 비행편인가요?	
Jessica Simpson	(13:12)
여전히 Pacific Airway입니다. 늦을 겁니다.	
Jessica Simpson	(13:13)
그래도 회의 시간에 딱 맞출 듯합니다.	
Jason Cruise	(13:18)
좋아요. 도착시간을 확인할게요.	
Jason Cruise	(13:19)
혹시 화물로 부친 수화물 있나요?	
Jessica Simpson	(13:25)
네. 세관통과대 옆문에서 저를 픽업해주세요.	
Jason Cruise	(13:27)
물론이죠. 그곳에서 뵐게요.	
Jessica Simpson	(13:29)
도와준다니 고마워요. 그때 봐요.	

154. (B)

Simpson 씨에 관해 나타난 것은?
(A) 그녀는 LA에 한 번 와본 적이 있다.
(B) 그녀는 출장 중이다.
(C) 그녀는 Pacific Airway에서 근무하고 있다.
(D) 그녀는 현재 Honolulu에서 근무 중이다.

분석_ 비행편(flight)과 회의(conference)에서 출장 중임을 유추할 수 있다.

155. (B)

13시 27분에 Cruise 씨가 "물론이죠"라고 쓴 의도는 무엇인가?
(A) 그는 그녀의 도착시간을 확인하였다.
(B) 세관장소 가까이에서 기다리는 것에 동의한다.
(C) 그의 손님이 세관을 통과할 수 없을지도 모른다고 생각한다.
(D) 그는 세관공무원을 만날 것이다.

분석_ be my guest는 상대방의 부탁을 들어주는 경우에 하는 말이기 때문에 앞선 상대방의 부탁(up at the door next to customs clearance office.)의 내용을 담고 있는 (B)가 정답이다.

Questions 156-157 refer to the following information.

대문	예약	수화물 수송	후기

Easy Transport

The One Airline을 이용하는 승객들에게 편리한 수화물 수송을 제공하게 되어 기쁩니다. Australia 내에 어디든지 귀하의 수화물을 수령하거나 맡길 수 있습니다. 출발하기 최대 24시간 전에 매표소에서 표를 구매하실 때, Easy Transport에 쉽게 등록하실 수 있습니다.
서비스 요금은 수화물 개수와 크기에 따라 다릅니다.
9월 3일부터 Easy Transport는 해외로 서비스를 확장합니다. 고객들은 조만간 이 서비스를 제공하는 해외 도시의 총 목록을 확인하실 수 있을 겁니다.

156. (C)
이 정보란에 무엇이 광고 중인가?
(A) 변경된 비행일정
(B) 확장된 매표소
(C) 수화물 취급 서비스
(D) 개선된 승객불만처리체계

분석_ 수송(transport), 수화물(baggage)에서 쉽게 정답을 찾을 수 있다. baggage와 luggage는 동의어다.

157. (A)
Easy Transport에 관해 옳은 것은?
(A) 사전 등록이 필요하다.
(B) 9월 3일에 시작할 것이다.
(C) 해외에서 이용 가능하다.
(D) 고객들은 Australia 안에서는 무료로 이용 가능하다.

분석_ 첫 단락에 등록(sign up for Easy Transport)이라는 표현이 등장하므로 등록 후 사용 가능함을 유추할 수 있다. 해외에서 이용 가능한 시점은 미래(will expand abroad)이므로 (C)는 오답이다.

Questions 158-160 refer to the following letter.

EZ PROPERTY
10 Pitt Street, Hong Kong 43025

12월 17일
Zenith Tower 거주민들에게
공동체 월모임이 3층 커뮤니티 센터에서 12월 18일 금요일 오전 10시에 열립니다. 지난달 동안에 이사 온 새로운 거주민들을 환영해드릴 겁니다. 간략한 자기소개 후에, 우리는 다음 달로 다가오는 주차장과 체력단련실에 보수공사에 대해 토론할 겁니다. 또한 Zenith Tower를 확장하고자 제안된 계획을 검토할 겁니다. 커뮤니티 센터의 폐쇄와 임대료의 소폭 인상이 Zenith Tower 거주민들에게 어떤 영향을 끼칠지에 대해 논의할 겁니다.

참가하실 수 없는데 혹시 질문이나 우려사항이 있으시다면, mao0903@rocketmail.com로 이메일 연락을 하시거나 혹은 오전 9시부터 오후 8시 사이 관리사무소에 들러주시기 바랍니다.
Mao Chuddung
관리소장

158. (B)
EZ Property에 대해서 나타난 것은?
(A) 고비용 거주공간을 제공하고 있다.
(B) 정기적으로 거주민들을 위한 회의를 제공하고 있다.
(C) 최근에 복합단지를 리모델링하였다.
(D) 임대를 위한 상업용 공간을 가지고 있다.

분석_ 첫 단락에서 매월 개최하는 모임(monthly community gathering)이라는 표현에서 정기적인 회의임을 알 수 있다. commercial area는 식당, 가게와 같은 상업용도의 공간을 의미한다.

159. (A)
다음 달에 무슨 일이 발생할 것인가?
(A) 유지보수공사가 시작할 것이다.
(B) 임대료가 소폭 상승할 것이다.
(C) 관리소장이 개인적인 담화를 할 것이다.
(D) 복합단지가 확장될 것이다.

분석_ 다음 달로 예정된 것은 주차장 및 체력단련실 보수공사(the upcoming renovation work to the parking area and the fitness center, both scheduled next month)이다. renovation work는 remodeling 또는 maintenance work와 동일한 표현이다.

160. (D)
편지에 따르면, 왜 거주민들은 걱정이 있을 수도 있는가?
(A) 체력단련실이 두 달 동안 문을 닫을 것이다.
(B) 모임 날짜가 변경될 것이다.
(C) 도시를 바라보는 장관을 가릴 수도 있다.
(D) 몇몇 시설에 대한 접근권한을 잃을 수도 있다.

분석_ 논의 내용이 주차장 및 체력단련실 보수공사가 언급되고 커뮤니티 센터의 폐쇄(closure of the community center)가 언급되므로 시설이용에 제한이 생김을 유추할 수 있다.

Questions 161-163 refer to the information on a web page.

소개	초기화면	연락	교수진

교수진 프로필
London 캠퍼스

Antonio Najar 박사
경영학
najar@hilton.edu

Antonio Najar 박사는 Chelsea에 위치한 Mohito 대학을 경영학과 영국 역사학 복수전공으로 졸업하였다. 그는 교육자로서의 커리어에 첫발을 내딛었다. 그때가 바로 Manchester에 위치한 Cambridge 대학의 대학원생으로서 학생들에게 개인과외를 하면서 비즈니스 개론을 이끌 때였다. Cambridge 대학으로부터 경영학 학위를 받은 후, 그는 Hilton 대학의 London 캠퍼스에 비즈니스 교수진으로 왔다. 그는 Hilton 대학출판에서 출간된 「왜 당신의 사업은 항상 망하는가」의 대표저자이다. 또한 Big Ben 비즈니스 위원회의 고문을 역임하고 있다. Najar 박사는 Hilton 대학을 떠나서 지금은 독일 Frankfurt시에 있는 유럽 비즈니스 협회에서 다양한 국제 비즈니스 학술회의를 이끌고 있다.

161. (B)
이 정보의 목적은 무엇인가?
(A) 비즈니스 학술회의를 홍보하기 위해
(B) 직원에 관한 사실을 묘사하기 위해
(C) 기업체 임원들에게 도서 구매를 장려하기 위해
(D) 지원서에 대한 세부사항을 제공하기 위해
분석_ 인터넷 웹페이지 글이며 직원 소개글이 담긴 글이다.

162. (C)
Najar 교수는 어디에서 교육 커리어를 시작하였는가?
(A) Chelsea에서
(B) London에서
(C) Manchester에서
(D) Frankfurt에서
분석_ 다른 곳에서도 교육일을 하지만 맨 처음 시작한 곳은 Manchester이다.(He embarked on his academic career as an educator when, as the graduate student in Cambridge University located in Manchester, he led Business introductory courses, tutoring the students.) embark는 원래 배가 항해를 처음 시작할 때 배를 띄운다는 의미이지만 지금은 처음 시작하는 의미도 지닌다.

163. (C)
Najar 교수에 대해 제시된 것은?
(A) 그는 지금 영국역사학의 교수이다.
(B) 그는 Big Ben 비즈니스 위원회에서 근무를 하곤 했었다.
(C) 그는 잠시 독일에서 근무 중이다.
(D) 그는 출판사를 소유하고 있다.
분석_ Hilton의 현 소속이기에 홈페이지에 교수진으로 소개되고 있지만 현재 독일에서 학술행사를 이끌고 있다고 언급되었다.(currently conducts a range of international business seminars at Europe Business Association at Frankfurt, German.)

Questions 164-167 refer to the following e-mail.

제목: Great Island 음악회
첨부자료: 자원봉사 확인서
안녕하세요, Honolulu 음악팬 여러분!
음악회에 대한 지원 관심을 다시 한번 표현하고자 많은 자원봉사자들이 저에게 연락을 취해왔습니다. 3일 내내 다양한 환상의 공연을 즐기는 것은 하와이에서 주말을 보내는 완벽한 방법임이 확실합니다.
항상 그래왔던 것처럼, 음악회 자원봉사들은 자원봉사활동에 대한 대가로 무료 식사쿠폰과 출입증을 수령하게 됩니다.
올해는 더 많은 관객이 몰릴 것으로 예상되어 만반의 준비가 이미 갖춰졌습니다. 사실, 지난해보다 훨씬 더 많은 사전예약티켓을 이미 판매하였습니다.
다시 참여하는 모든 자원봉사자들은 9월 10일로 예정된 오리엔테이션 교육에 참가해야 합니다. 늦어도 9월 9일까지는 첨부된 자원봉사 확인서를 제게 다시 보내야 합니다. 아울러 당신이 참여하고자 하는 자원봉사업무와 당신이 선호하는 상위 세 개의 근무팀을 표시해주세요. 지난해의 체계와 마찬가지로, 정보안내 데스크에 직원을 배치하고, 식품가판대를 운영하며, 무대 설치 및 철거를 관리하며, 주차관리를 지원하는 업무를 주요 팀들이 맡게 될 겁니다. 안타깝게도, 저희는 모든 지원자를 각자의 최우선 선호 팀으로 보장해드릴 순 없습니다만 최선을 다해 수용해보도록 하겠습니다.
감사합니다. 더 많은 내용으로 곧 연락을 드리겠습니다. 올해 다시 여러분을 뵙는 것을 고대하고 있습니다.
Andy Oh

164. (A)
이메일 수령인에 대해 옳지 않은 것은?
(A) 그들은 음악회에서 연주할 음악가들이다.
(B) 그들은 작년에 음악회에 무료로 참여했었다.
(C) 그들은 Andy Oh를 이전에 본 적이 있다.
(D) 그들은 관중이 많은 행사에서의 업무에 익숙하다.
분석_ 첫 단락에 이메일을 받는 사람들이 자원봉사자임이 진술되었다.(As always, concert volunteers will receive free meal coupons and passes in exchange for your volunteer work.)

165. (C)
올해의 Great Island 음악회는 작년과 어떻게 다른가?
(A) 실내에서 열릴 것이다.
(B) 3일 동안 개최될 것이다.
(C) 보다 많은 사람들이 참가할 것이다.
(D) 참가하는 데 비용이 덜 비쌀 것이다.
분석_ 두 번째 단락에서 보다 많은 관객(larger crowd)을 예상하고 있으며, 작년보다 많은 사전예약티켓을 팔았으므로(far more advance tickets than last year.) 작년보다 관객이 늘어남을 알 수 있다.

166. (D)
자원봉사 확인서에는 무슨 정보가 요구되는가?
(A) 요청된 출입증 장수
(B) 선호하는 음식
(C) 개인 은행정보
(D) 희망하는 팀 업무

분석_ 자원봉사 확인서가 언급된 문장에서 가장 좋아하는 업무 세 가지를 표시하라는 내용이 첨가되어 있다.(indicating your volunteer job in which you want to participate and your three top choices in regard to a work team.)

167. (B)
무슨 자원봉사활동이 언급되어 있는가?
(A) 음식 요리
(B) 공연 설비 설치
(C) 음악회 홍보
(D) 연주가들을 위한 숙박업체 예약
분석_ 무대 설치 및 철거(managing the stage set up and breakdown)가 주요 업무임이 서술되어 있다.

Questions 168-171 refer to the following article.

경제위원회의 전망

5월 10일 – Mexico City 경제위원회는 최신 지역고용전망을 내놓았다. 보고서는 가장 빠르게 성장 중인 산업과 직업 그리고 하락 중인 것들에 대한 세부사항을 담고 있다. [1] 보고서는 정보가 Mexico City 및 인근 지역에서의 고용시장을 정확히 반영할 수 있도록 일 년에 두 번, 5월과 10월에 발표된다.
[2] 명백하게도 외과의사, 치과의사, 간호인력 그리고 건강용품업체들이 다가올 2분기 동안에 걸쳐서 가장 큰 성장을 이룰 것으로 기대된다. 관광 및 숙박산업이 지속적으로 성장세를 보이고 휴가시즌이 시작됨에 따라 숙박 관련 모든 분야에서의 점진적인 성장이 예상된다. *반면, IT 제품들에 대한 국내 판매량이 지속적으로 감소함에 때라 제조 분야 업체들은 9퍼센트가량 감소할 것으로 예상된다.*
[3] 전체 내용을 보려면 www.mexicicity.go.or/economic_board를 방문하면 그곳에서 10개 이상의 산업에 대한 예상전망치를 확인할 수 있다. [4]

168. (C)
보고서에서 무엇이 논의되었는가?
(A) 지역에서의 급여 증가
(B) 직장 안전 문제점
(C) Mexico City와 인근 지역의 일자리 미래 전망
(D) 제조업체들의 전략 변화
분석_ 서두에서 최신 지역 고용 전망을 발표하고 그 세부내용이 아래에 기술되어 있음을 알 수 있다.(Mexico City Economic Board has announced its latest Regional Work Forecast.)

169. (D)
보고서는 얼마나 자주 출간되는가?
(A) 매 분기마다
(B) 매년마다
(C) 한 달에 한 번
(D) 일 년에 두 번

170. (C)
2번째 문단 2행에 있는 "over"와 의미가 가장 가까운 것은?
(A) 넘어서서
(B) 가까운
(C) 동안에
(D) 위에
분석_ over는 선택지에 나온 의미를 모두 가지는데, 시간단위 명사와 어울려 사용되는 경우(over the following two quarters)에는 '~ 동안'이라는 기간의 의미로 쓰인다.

171. (C)
[1], [2], [3] 그리고 [4]라고 표시된 곳 중, 다음 문장이 들어가기에 가장 적합한 곳은?
"반면, IT 제품들에 대한 국내 판매량이 지속적으로 감소함에 때라 제조 분야 업체들은 9퍼센트가량 감소할 것으로 예상된다."
(A) [1]
(B) [2]
(C) [3]
(D) [4]
분석_ '반면에'라는 의미를 지닌 on the other hand가 중요한 단서이다. 감소(decreasing)의 내용과 반전을 이룰 만한 내용이 앞에서 언급되어야 하므로 점진적 성장(Moderate growth is anticipated for almost all positions in the accommodation sector)이 기술된 문장 뒤에 나오는 것이 문맥상 자연스럽다.

Questions 172-175 refer to the following e-mail.

수신: Mark Jordan 〈markjordan@rocketmail.com〉
발신: Chris Brown 〈chris1980@navel.com〉
일시: 3월 5일
제목: 배송 문제
Jordan 씨에게
Adidas Sports Gear 쪽으로 귀하께서 최근에 하셨던 주문의 오류에 대해 저희가 관심을 가질 수 있도록 해주신 점 감사드립니다. 귀하가 주문하신 대략 400벌의 여성 의류가 도착하지 않았음을 말씀하셨습니다.
불행하게도, 시스템상 오류가 3월 1일 오전 이른 시간에 발생하였습니다. 고장은 한동안 웹사이트의 오작동을 일으켰을 뿐만 아니라, 그날에 이루어진 주문을 몇몇 삭제시켰습니다. 결국, 청구부서가 귀하의 주문을 접수하는 동안 저희 배송부서는 그렇게 하지 못했습니다.
받지도 못했던 주문품에 대해서 요금이 부과되었을 때 귀하가 분명 실망스러워했을 거라 생각합니다. 귀하는 신규 고객이라는 것을 저희는 또한 알고 있으며 귀하가 또 다른 거래를 위해 저희 업체를 떠나는 것을 원치 않습니다. 이런 결과로, 이 문제점을 보상하기 위해, 빠뜨린 모든 물품을 초특급배송으로 무료로 보내드리겠습니다. 이런 불쾌한 경험에 대한 보상으로, 귀하께서는 다음 주문에 이용 가능한 무제한 이용 상품권을 수령하실 겁니다. 또한, 2개월 이내에 어떤 주문이든 30퍼센트의 추가 할인을 받으실 겁니다.
이번 일이 야기한 불편에 대해 사과드리며 저희의 마음을 담은 후속조치에 만족하신다면 좋겠습니다. 질문이 있으시다면 주저하지 마시고 연락 주십시오. 감사합니다.
Chris Brown
고객관리 책임자

172. (A)

Brown 씨는 왜 이메일을 보냈는가?

(A) 사과의 말을 전하기 위해

(B) 불만서식을 제출하기 위해

(C) 이메일 수령인에게 주문서를 다시 발송하도록 재촉하기 위해

(D) 지원자의 지원서를 수락하기 위해

분석_ 서두에서 주문서상에 오류가 있음을 지적하는 문의를 받았다는 내용(Thank you for bringing to our attention the inaccuracy in the order)이 언급되어 있다. 대략 아래에 후속조치와 아울러 사과의 말이 언급됨을 유추할 수 있다.

173. (B)

Jordan 씨에 대해 나타난 것은?

(A) 그는 스포츠용품 회사에서 근무하고 있다.

(B) 그는 3월 1일에 주문하였다.

(C) 그는 스포츠용품을 온라인으로 구매하는 것을 선호한다.

(D) 그는 새로운 배송품을 받자마자 청구금액을 지불할 것이다.

분석_ 이메일을 작성한 것은 3월 5일이지만 주문시스템 오류가 발생한 것은 3월 1일(a system error did happen early in the evening of March 1)이기 때문에, 고객이 이 시점에 주문을 해서 주문품을 받지 못했음을 유추할 수 있다.

174. (D)

3번째 문단 1행에 있는 "recognize"와 의미가 가장 가까운 것은?

(A) 기억하다

(B) 동의하다

(C) 승인하다

(D) 인정하다

분석_ recognize는 '인식하다'라는 의미 외에도 that절을 취하면서 어떠한 사실을 인정하고 받아들이는 경우에 사용되는데 acknowledge로 대신할 수 있다.

175. (A)

Chris 씨가 Jordan 씨에게 제공하지 않는 것은 무엇인가?

(A) 기존 주문품에 대한 부분적 환불

(B) 다음 번 주문에 대한 제한적 가격 할인

(C) 또 다른 구매에 대한 가격 할인

(D) 이미 구매된 물품들에 대한 특급배송

분석_ 할인은 현재의 주문품이 아니라 앞으로의 주문에서만 가능하다. 현재 주문품은 배송만 무료인 것으로 언급되어 있다.(we will send all missing items by overnight delivery free of charge.)

Questions 176-180 refer to the following brochure and e-mail.

Kansas 대학 종합병원(KUGH)이 후원하는 무료강연 시리즈 KUGH는 지역 의료 전문가들을 위한 가을 강연시리즈를 알리게 되어 기쁩니다. 그 강연들은 의료 시스템을 관리하는 헬스케어 분야의 선도적인 인물들 몇 분을 만나실 수 있는 기회를 제공해드립니다. 모든 강좌는 Kansas 대학 강의 캠퍼스에서 이용 편리한 곳에서 개최되며, 선착순으로 이용 가능합니다. 강좌들은 강의 시작 한 시간 전에 개방됩니다.

수요일, 9월 1일, 오후 6시, 21호 강의실 강사: Jake Mercedes, Jake's 의료 진료실 의료시간 관리 – 당신의 의료시간을 효율적으로 관리하는 방법에 대해 알아보자.
수요일, 9월 8일, 오후 6시, 19호 강의실 강사: Nancy Orlando, Orlando 건강관리센터 효과적인 의사소통 – 사무직원들과의 소통을 보다 효율적으로 만드는 간단한 기술을 알아보자.
토요일, 9월 11일, 오후 9시, 19호 강의실 강사: Mora Kano, Digital Medical Records 정보관리 – 환자기록 관리지침과 정보보안에 관한 정보를 배워보자.
월요일, 9월 13일, 오후 5시 30분, 34호 강의실 강사: Sul Hyun, Kansas 보험협회 재무관리 – 환자 및 보험사들이 제때 돈을 지불하는 것을 새로운 청구기법이 어떤 식으로 가능하게 만드는지를 배워보자.
추가로 알고 싶은 세부사항은 Gary Lesmore에게 이메일 gary09@netian.com로 연락해주세요.

수신: Gary Lesmore 〈gary09@netian.com〉

발신: Onigiri Jo 〈icecreamjoa@freechal.com〉

제목: 강의 일정

일시: 9월 12일

Lesmore 씨에게

가을 강연 시리즈에 대한 안내책자를 수령하였습니다. Digital Medical Records의 대표자가 나오는 발표가 무척 기대되었습니다. 최근에 제가 라이센스받은 소프트웨어를 설치했지만 사용에 익숙하지 않기 때문이죠. 그러나 제가 어제 School of Public Health에 갔었을 때, 19호 강의실에는 아무도 없었습니다. 안내데스크에 문의했으나 보안 요원은 그 강좌에 대한 어떠한 정보도 알고 있지 않았습니다. 강좌의 일정이 조정되었다면 언제 어디서 열리는지 알려주세요.

Onigiri Jo

176. (B)

안내책자의 1번째 문단 3행에 있는 "figures"와 의미상 가장 가까운 것은?

(A) 숫자

(B) 사람들

(C) 정보

(D) 연구자료 및 수치

분석_ figure는 수치, 자료, 정보 등의 의미를 가지기도 하나, 본문에서는 선도적인 인물로 표현되고 있으므로 사람을 의미하는 people로 바꾸어 사용하는 것이 적절하다.

177. (D)

강좌들에 관해서 무엇이 언급되었는가?

(A) 참가자는 50명으로 제한되어 있다.

(B) Kansas 대학병원에서 개최될 것이다.

(C) 강의 후 질의 응답시간이 뒤따를 것이다.

(D) 의료 진료실을 운영하는 사람들을 위한 강좌다.

178. (C)

9월 13일자 강의에서 무엇이 논의될 것인가?

(A) 함께 효율적으로 일하는 방법

(B) 환자들의 건강기록을 관리하는 방법

(C) 청구액이 즉시 지불되도록 확실히 만드는 방법

(D) 환자들과 효율적으로 의사소통하는 방법

179. (C)

Onigiri Jo 씨는 누구의 강의에 참가하길 원하는가?

(A) Mercedes 씨의 강의

(B) Orlando 씨의 강의

(C) Kano 씨의 강의

(D) Oh 씨의 강의

분석_ 이메일을 쓴 날짜는 9월 12일이며 그 전날에 강의를 들으러 갔다(When I went to the School of Public Health yesterday morning, no one was in room 19.)는 내용으로 봐서 9월 11일 강의를 들으려 했음을 알 수 있다. 강의 스케줄상 9월 11일 강사를 찾으면 된다.

180. (A)

Onigiri Jo 씨는 왜 이메일을 작성하였는가?

(A) 새로운 소식을 요청하기 위해

(B) 강의를 등록하기 위해

(C) 우편목록에 가입하기 위해

(D) 그의 근무일정을 변경하기 위해

분석_ 이메일은 강의에 갔었으나 아무도 없었기 때문에 혹시 변경이 있었는지 문의하는(If this lecture has been rescheduled, please let me know when and where it will be) 내용이다. 변경된 일정은 새로운 소식(update)에 해당되므로 (A)가 정답이다.

Questions 181-185 refer to the following web pages.

<table>
<tr><td colspan="5" align="center">**Oz Castle로 환영합니다**</td></tr>
<tr><td>소개</td><td>여행상품</td><td>예약</td><td>연락</td><td>후기</td></tr>
<tr><td colspan="5">Oz Castle은 베트남 Hanoi에 있는 가장 유명한 호수인 Hoam Quiem이라는 호수 근처에 지어진 화려한 고품격 호텔입니다. 조용한 거리인 Hoam Quiem가의 끝자락에 위치하고 있습니다. 저희는 실외 커피라운지와 무선 인터넷 설비를 갖춘 30개의 큰 객실을 제공하고 있습니다.
편안한 휴일을 즐기시건 모험을 떠나시건 저희 호텔을 방문해주세요. 도심과 태평양 해안의 중간지점 편리한 곳에 위치하고 있으며, Ha Long Bay의 수려한 해변가와 Hanoi의 유명한 쇼핑지구로 가는 무료 셔틀버스를 제공해드립니다. 또한 호텔의 우거진 수풀을 가로지르는 가벼운 산책이나 미지의 땅으로 가는 투어상품에 가이드가 동반 가능합니다.
장마기간 동안에 요금은 훨씬 더 저렴하므로 정확한 객실요금 문의를 위해 저희에게 연락해주세요.</td></tr>
</table>

<table>
<tr><td colspan="5" align="center">**Oz Castle로 환영합니다**</td></tr>
<tr><td>소개</td><td>여행상품</td><td>예약</td><td>연락</td><td>후기</td></tr>
<tr><td colspan="5">저는 항상 호텔 객실을 예약하기 전에 다양한 숙박업소들을 온라인으로 비교하지만 이번만은 달랐어요. Ghana Car Rental Service로부터 Oz Castle 무료 쿠폰을 받았어요. 그래서 이용해보기로 했죠. 온라인 동호회에서 몇몇 후기를 이미 읽어봤기 때문에, Oz Castle에 감동한 사람이 저뿐만이 아니라는 것을 알고 있답니다. 주요 여행 사이트들로부터 높은 등급을 받았더라고요.
Oz Castle에서 머무른 것은 환상적이었어요. 그리고 평화로운 휴가 장소를 찾는 이라면 누구든지 Oz Castle을 심각히 고려해봐야 한다고 생각해요. 객실은 너무나도 아늑했고 편안했어요. 신선하게 마련된 음식은 저로 하여금 집에서 요리한 베트남 음식을 처음으로 맛보게끔 만들었죠. 또한, Ha Long Bay로의 편안한 한나절 여행을 마음껏 즐겼어요.
호텔이 위치한 거리가 몇몇 구덩이가 깊게 패인 먼지 낀 도로였다는 점이 제가 말할 수 있는 유일한 단점이에요. 그렇다고 심각한 문제는 아니었어요. 왜냐하면 도로상에 차들이 별로 없었거든요.
고마워요.
Lisa White</td></tr>
</table>

181. (B)

Oz Castle에 대해서 나타난 것은?

(A) 다양한 크기의 객실을 제공한다.

(B) 가격이 계절별로 상이하다.

(C) 베트남 정부에 의해 운영된다.

(D) 365일 24시간 이용 가능하다.

분석_ 첫 번째 지문 세 번째 단락에서 장마시즌에는 더 저렴하다(prices are considerably lower during the monsoon season.)는 내용으로 비추어 가격 변동이 있음을 알 수 있다.

182. (C)

Oz Castle에서 제공되는 것이 아닌 것은?

(A) 실외 좌석공간

(B) 인터넷 접속

(C) 무료 객실 업그레이드

(D) 집에서 만든 요리

분석_ 무료 객실 업그레이드는 본문에서 전혀 언급이 없다.

183. (D)

Lisa White 씨는 후기에서 무엇을 언급하고 있는가?

(A) 온라인 후기들에 대해 동감하지 못하고 있다.

(B) 베트남에서는 보통 친지들과 머물고 있다.

(C) 웹사이트를 통해서 Oz Castle을 알게 되었다.

(D) Oz Castle을 다른 이들에게 추천하고 있다.

분석_ 지저분한 도로가 유일한 단점(a dusty dirt road with some deep holes is my only negative comment.)이라면 나머지는 긍정의 표현임을 의미하므로 (D)가 정답임을 유추할 수 있다.

184. (C)

Lisa White 씨는 무슨 야외활동에 참가했다고 명시하고 있는가?

(A) 정글에서의 산책

(B) Hanoi에서의 쇼핑

(C) 해변 방문

(D) 미지의 대지 탐험

분석_ 두 번째 지문에서 Ha Long Bay에서 한나절 보냈다는 내용이 언급되었다.(I thoroughly enjoyed my relaxing day trip to Ha Long Bay.) 첫 번째 지문 두 번째 단락에서 Ha Long Bay에 아름다운 해변(gorgeous beaches)이 있음을 알 수 있는 연계형 문제이다.

185. (A)

Hoam Quiem가에 대해 암시된 것은?

(A) 비포장도로이다.

(B) 찾기가 어렵다.

(C) 해변가에 있다.

(D) 밤 동안에 사람들로 북적인다.

분석_ 호텔이 Hoam Quiem가에 위치하고 있음을 첫 번째 지문에서 알 수 있다.(It is located at the end of Hoam Quiem Avenue.) 또한 두 번째 지문에서 호텔이 있는 거리에 먼지 구덩이 도로가 있다는 내용으로 보아 비포장도로임을(the street where the hotel is located is covered with a dusty dirt road) 유추할 수 있다.

Questions 186-190 refer to the following text message chain, e-mail and schedule.　음성강의

Oz Katok
Takoyaki (16:35)
Jonathan 씨, Haywood 씨와의 회의시간 확인해주실래요?
Jonathan (16:40)
네, 잠시만요.
Jonathan (16:41)
Haywood 씨는 예정대로 8시 30분에 법무팀을 만날 거예요. 됐나요?
Takoyaki (16:43)
미안하지만 안 되겠어요. 제가 위원회로부터 호출받았거든요. 목요일 아침 일찍 하청업체와의 긴급회의에 참가해야 해요.
Jonathan (16:44)
듣고 보니 안타깝네요. 회의일정을 좀 더 편한 시간대로 변경할 필요가 있겠어요.
Takoyaki (16:45)
제 말이요, 그 회의는 다음 주 월요일 아침으로 연기해달라고 요청해야겠어요.
Jonathan (16:46)
그럼 Oh 씨의 일정부터 확인해볼게요.
Jonathan (16:48)
대박! 그 시간대에 일정이 없네요. 변경된 회의시간을 그에게 통보할게요.

Takoyaki (16:49)
진심 감사해요. Oh 씨한테 급변경된 일정에 대해 미안하다고 전해주세요.

발신: andrewjonathan@ez2group.com
수신: haywood@ez2group.com
일시: 9월 4일
제목: 일일 업데이트
첨부자료: 이메일 복사본

Oh 씨에게

이번 주 당신의 일정에 관한 급한 소식 몇 개를 첨부해드립니다. 우선 회의 일정이 변경 가능한지에 대해 법무팀장이 물어왔습니다. [1] 당신이 인터뷰를 위해 만나고 싶어 하는 사진작가 Charles Duff를 그 시간대에 넣어드릴 수 있습니다. 당신이 Calgary 프로젝트에 대해 그를 만나서 작업이 가능한지 확인해보고 싶다고 언급했습니다. [2] 인터뷰일정으로 제가 그에게 전화를 해야 할지 말지를 알려주십시오. 추가적으로, 재무위원회에서 온 Oltega Gonzales가 영상전화회의에 참여하기 위해 금요일 회의에 합류하는 것을 확인해주었습니다. [3] 저는 이미 멀티미디어 회의실을 예약해두었습니다.

마지막으로, 당신은 오늘 오후에 출장을 나설 것이므로 Omega City Hotel로부터 예약을 확인하는 이메일사본을 전송해드리겠습니다. [4] 이미 비행기 티켓과 세부일정표는 가지고 계신 것으로 알고 있습니다. 혹시 그러지 않으시면 제가 이메일로 전송해드리겠습니다.

Andrew Jonathan

The EZ2 Group-Haywood Oh의 일정– 9월 3일~7일				
목요일	화요일	수요일	목요일	금요일
오전 9:00 마케팅회의 오후 1:15 Jaydong Kim과 점심식사 오후 4:00 중역위원회 회의	오전 8:45 부서장들과 예산 심의 오후 2:40 브리스번행 기차로 출발 4시 45분에 도착	오전 9:15 다가올 광고캠페인 기획을 위해 브리스번 지사팀과 회의 오후 1:00 골드코스트로 복귀 2시 5분에 도착 오후 5:30 분기 중역회의 준비	오전 8:30 Mimi Takoyaki와 미팅 (법무팀) 오후 1:45 Martha Stone과 그녀의 수정안을 가지고 미팅 오후 4:30 월간 중역회의 오후 5:30 서울 지사 전화회의	오전 8:00 뉴욕 지사 전화회의 오전 10:00 웹사이트 검토를 위해 IT직원 미팅 오후 2:00 영상홍보자료 검토 위해 미팅

186. (B)

EZ2 Group에 대해 나타난 것은?

(A) 오픈한 지 1년이 넘지 않았다.

(B) 몇몇 도시에 지사를 가지고 있다.

(C) 50명 이상의 직원을 보유하고 있다.

(D) 나라에서 가장 큰 마케팅 회사이다.

분석_ 근무 일정에서 브리스번, 골드코스트, 서울과 뉴욕지사에서의 전화회의 일정이 있는 것으로 봐서 최소 4개 이상의 도시에 지사가 있음을 알 수 있다.

187. (C)

무슨 전자 파일이 이메일과 함께 보내지는가?

(A) 기차표

(B) 디지털 사진

(C) 호텔 예약확인서

(D) 위원회 일정표

분석_ 두 번째 지문 세 번째 단락에서 호텔 예약확인서를 같이 보낸다는 내용이 언급된다.(I am sending a copy of the e-mail from Omega City Hotel that confirms the reservation.)

188. (C)

Oh 씨는 아마도 법무팀 직원을 언제 만날 것인가?

(A) 9월 3일

(B) 9월 6일

(C) 9월 10일

(D) 10월 6일

분석_ 메신저와 일정표를 동시에 보고 풀어야 하는 연계형 문제이다. 메신저에서 Takoyaki가 긴급회의가 잡혀서 목요일 아침 일찍 예정된 일정에 참여할 수 없음을 알린다. 일정표에서 그 시각의 일정은 법무팀과의 일정으로 되어 있기 때문에 Takoyaki가 법무팀 직원임을 알 수 있다. 그리고는 그 일정을 다음 주 월요일로 연기하길 원하고 있으므로(Takoyaki: of course, I want to ask to postpone that meeting to Monday morning next week.) 추후 만남이 9월 10일인 것으로 유추 가능하다.

189. (B)

Oh 씨와 Gonzales 씨는 금요일 몇 시에 회의에 참가할 것인가?

(A) 수요일 오전 9시 15분

(B) 금요일 오전 8시

(C) 금요일 오후 2시

(D) 목요일 5시 30분

분석_ 두 번째 지문 두 번째 단락에서 Gonzales가 언급되면서 금요일의 영상전화회의에 참가하는 의도를 알리고 있다.(he meeting on Friday to attend the video conference.) 일정표상에 금요일의 전화회의는 오전 8시에 있음을 알 수 있다.

190. (B)

[1], [2], [3] 그리고 [4]로 표시된 곳 중에서 다음 문장이 들어가기에 가장 적합한 곳은?

"인터뷰 일정으로 제가 그에게 전화를 해야 할지 말지를 알려주십시오."

(A) [1]

(B) [2]

(C) [3]

(D) [4]

분석_ 인터뷰 통보를 위해 전화받는 대상인 그(him)가 누구(Charles Duff)인지 알기 위해서는 그 앞 문장들을 확인해야 한다. 인터뷰 대상자를 찾으면 그 뒤에 위치하기 적절한 문장이다.(I can fill that time slot with Charles Duff, photographer whom you want to meet for an interview.)

Questions 191-195 refer to the following letter, information and e-mail.

Armani Publishing
335 George Street
Dallas, Houston 10034

4월 27일
Laura Johns
31 Elizabeth Avenue
Arizona, Nevada 30453
Johns 씨에게

저희는 귀하가 Armani Travel Guides Services의 신입 기고가이자 계약작가로 활동하시는 것을 환영합니다. 모든 비용에 대한 정산을 위해서, 프로젝트의 편집작가로부터 이미 승인받은 업무에 대한 증거 서식을 제출해야 합니다. 제출되는 송장은 당신의 연락처, 프로젝트 번호 및 상사 이름을 필수적으로 포함해야 합니다. 저에게 보내주시면 경리과로 전달될 겁니다. 사진 관련 송장에 대한 세부적인 지침에 대해서는 Trump 씨에게 연락을 취해보세요. 곧 당신이 수령하실 거라 생각되는 송장에 대한 견본은 사진촬영부서가 보여드릴 겁니다.
Mike Tyson

Armani PUBLISHING
현재의 주요 프로젝트와 팀원 할당

프로젝트명 / 핵심 인력 할당	휴가 시리즈	Armani 여행가이드북 시리즈	** 도심 시리즈
편집 작가	Julia Ridell	Isabel Tompson	Eric Kim
기사 및 사진 편집자	Benjamin Franklin	Eaton Jackson	Benjamin Franklin
행정 지원	Kate Homes	Ray Williams	Mike Tyson

**표시의 세부 지침은 이메일로 곧 발송됩니다.

발신: sakurai5@armanipublishing.com
수신: erickim@armanipublishing.com
일시: 5월 2일
제목: 추가 세부 지침
첨부자료: 업무 사본
Kim 씨에게
새로운 팀원인 Laura Johns이 즉시 당신의 프로젝트팀으로 합류될

것임을 기억하세요. 그렇게 함으로써 Franklin 씨가 그녀의 다른 할당
된 팀인 휴가촬영팀에 총력을 둘 수 있게끔 시간적 여유를 줄 겁니다.
그것은 또한 다가온 다음 호 출간업무도 포함합니다. 팀 리더로서, 당
신이 새로운 팀원을 위한 상세한 업무표가 필요한 경우에 대비하여 이
메일과 함께 첨부해드리겠습니다. 확실히 팀원들을 보다 효율적으로
감독하는 데 도움을 줄 겁니다.
Sakurai Oh
Armani Publishing 인사 담당자

191. (A)

편지는 무엇을 설명하고 있는가?
(A) 지불금액을 수령하는 방법
(B) 여행기사를 제출하는 방법
(C) 기사 작성 업무를 얻는 방법
(D) 프로젝트 공석에 지원하는 방법
분석_ 신입 기고가가 경비에 대한 정산을 받는(For reimbursement
of all expenses) 절차가 언급된 편지이다.

192. (B)

Tyson 씨와 Johns 씨에 대해 옳지 않은 것은?
(A) Tyson 씨는 작성된 기사 업무에 대한 송장을 수령한다.
(B) Tyson 씨는 여행 사진 프로젝트를 감독한다.
(D) Johns 씨는 처음으로 Armani Publishing을 위한 기사를 작성하
였다.
(D) Johns 씨는 그녀가 직접 쓴 기사에 대한 사진을 촬영하였다.
분석_ Tyson 씨는 도심촬영 프로젝트의 행정 지원을 하고 있음을
두 번째 지문의 업무할당표에서 알 수 있다.

193. (A)

편지의 8행에 있는 "suspect"와 의미가 가장 가까운 것은?
(A) 믿다
(B) 희망하다
(C) 불신임하다
(D) 고소하다
분석_ suspect은 '의심하다'라는 의미 외에도 어떠한 사실을 어렴
풋이 알아차리거나 믿고 있을 때 사용 가능하므로 believe
가 대신해서 사용될 수 있다.

194. (D)

Ridell 씨에 대해 아마도 올바른 것은?
(A) 그녀는 Armani Publishing에서 신임 편집장으로 근무하고 있다.
(B) 그녀는 Jackson 씨와 함께 작업해왔다.
(C) 그녀는 John 씨의 계약서를 사전 승인하였다.
(D) 그녀는 Kate Homes의 업무를 감독한다.
분석_ 두 번째 지문에서 Ridell 씨는 편집 작가(writing editor)이
며 Kate Homes는 행정 지원인력(administrative assistant)
이다. 편집 작가가 팀 리더인 것은 마지막 지문에서 같은 직
급의 편집인인 Eric Kim이 팀원들을 관리 감독하는 내용
이 언급되어 있다.(They will surely help you oversee your
team members effectively.)

195. (D)

프로젝트 과제에 무슨 변화가 발생할 것인가?
(A) 휴가 시리즈에 할당된 팀은 더 이상 존재하지 않을 것이다.
(B) 네 번째 프로젝트가 탄생 중이다.
(C) Kim 씨는 다른 회사에서 근무하러 떠날 것이다.
(D) 신입 기사 및 사진 편집자가 팀에 추가될 것이다.
분석_ 마지막 지문에서 새로운 팀원이 합류될 것임을 알리고 있
다.(your new team member, Ms. Laura Johns will be
joined shortly to your project team.)

Questions 196-200 refer to the following notice, form and list.

아시아 의료인 협의회 워크숍

아시아 의료인 협의회는 11월 4일부터 10일까지 방콕에서 열리는 제
9차 연례 건강워크숍에 1,000자가 넘지 않는 발표요약문을 귀하께서
제출하도록 요청합니다. 회의는 다양한 건강관리 및 의료 분야의 아시
아 의사들과 전문직 종사자들을 소집합니다.
올해의 주제는 '의료사업 확장: 의료서비스를 확대하고, 대중 인지도를
높여라'입니다. 의료사업 확장은 모든 종류의 의료활동들과 의료 서비
스 및 설비의 분배를 포함합니다. 주제의 모든 면이 논의될 것입니
다. 그러는 동안, 워크숍은 새로운 의학 기술을 의학적 치료, 의료기기
및 의료 서비스 전파로 적용시키는 것에 대해 면밀히 들여다보는 모든
노력들을 논의합니다. 각각의 발표는 40분을 초과하지 말아야 합니다.
개인이나 단체 모두 한 장만 발표요약문 제출이 가능합니다.
발표자들 각자 워크숍을 위한 자신의 교통편과 숙박편을 준비해야 합
니다. 참가자들을 위해 할인가를 제공하는 호텔들의 종합명단은 웹
사이트 www.asiandoctorcouncil.com/workshop에서 이용 가
능합니다. 사이트에서 등록서식도 이용하실 수 있습니다. 비영리기
관을 위한 제한적인 자금 지원도 가능합니다. 자격을 갖춘 지원자들
은 지원서를 작성하셔서 10월 24일부터 11월 7일까지 보내주시기
바랍니다. 발표자의 이름과 이메일 주소를 지원서에 잊지 마시고 포
함시켜주세요.

이름: Alfred Kline
이메일 주소: alfredkline@ez.net
발표 주제: 환자들을 위한 편리한 모바일 문자서비스의 개략적인 설
명요약문
우리의 발표는 의료서비스에 대해 문외한인 대중에게 그 인지도를 높
여주기 위한 수단으로서 휴대폰문자의 활용을 주장할 것이다. 나를 고
용한 업체인 태국 방콕의 비영리기관인 방콕 의료클리닉은 새로운 의
료서비스를 홍보할 필요가 있었다. 그때, 휴대폰에 초점을 두었다. 수
상 경험이 있는 홍보대행사와 협력하여 우리 기술팀에 의해 3년 전에
취해졌던 그 노력은 그 새로운 서비스에 대한 상당한 수요를 창출하였
다. 더 나아가, 우리의 웹사이트뿐만 아니라 병원으로 더 많은 환자 유
입을 이끌어냈다. 독특한 전략을 실행하면서 극복해야 했던 장애물,
개선된 의사-환자 간의 관계에 대한 결과물, 그리고 환자들과 편리하
게 의사소통할 수 있는 문자 발송의 모든 면을 발표에서 설명하겠다.

아시아 의료인 협의회 워크숍 시리즈

아시아 의료인 협의회는 건강관리 전문가들을 위한 제9차 연례 건강 워크숍을 알리게 되어 기쁩니다. 이 분야에서 의료활동과 건강관리 시스템을 감독해온 다양한 선두주자들로부터 배움을 얻을 수 있는 기회를 워크숍이 제공합니다. 모든 발표의 좌석예약은 온라인 예약을 통해서 가능합니다. 모든 참가자들은 각각의 강연 최소 20분 전부터 발표회에 입장 가능합니다.

월요일, 11월 4일, 오후 3시, 다이아몬드 홀
발표자: Gary Nelson, Singapore 종합병원
의학계 새로운 소식 – 아시아 의료 기술이 얼마나 진보했는지 그리고 얼마나 많은 환자들이 의료기술 발전국으로 의료관광을 떠나려 하는지 알아보자.

수요일, 11월 6일, 오후 6시, 골드 홀
발표자: Jessica Johnson, Johnson's 건강 관리 컨설팅
효과적인 의사소통 – 여러분이 의료진과 효율적으로 소통하는 데 도움이 되는 간단한 기술들을 배워보자.

일요일, 11월 10일, 오전 11시, 다이아몬드 홀
발표자: Alfred Kline, 방콕 의료클리닉
모바일 의료서비스 – 환자들을 위한 편리한 휴대폰문자서비스의 대략적인 설명을 들어보자.

추가정보는 Andy Oh에게 andyoh@asiandoctorcouncil.net 로 연락해주세요.

196. (C)

아시아 의료인 협의회에 관해 나타나지 않은 것은?
(A) 11월 10일에 제출된 발표요약문을 접수하지 않을 것이다.
(B) 과거 수년간 워크숍을 기획했었다.
(C) 한 단체로부터 하나 이상의 제출자료를 허용할 것이다.
(D) 아시아 의사들에게 참여를 장려할 것이다.

분석_ 첫 번째 지문에서 한 단체로부터 한 장의 발표요약문의 제출이 가능하다고 언급된다.(One entry of presenter or group of presenters is allowed.)

197. (A)

공지에 따르면, 참가자는 왜 웹사이트에 방문해야 하는가?
(A) 숙박업체의 할인가격을 알아보기 위해
(B) 일대일 토론의 예시안을 보기 위해
(C) 완전한 회의 일정표를 확인하기 위해
(D) 발표요약문을 작성하는 방법을 배우기 위해

분석_ 첫 번째 지문 두 번째 단락에서 할인가격을 제공하는 호텔 명단이 웹사이트에 있음을 명시하고 있다.(A complete list of hotels offering discounted prices for the participants is available on our website.)

198. (B)

방콕 의료클리닉에 대해 제시된 것은?
(A) 수많은 상을 타왔다.
(B) 의료확장에 대한 선도적인 움직임이 성공적이었다.
(C) 최근에 웹사이트를 업데이트하였다.
(D) 태국에서 가장 유명한 의료센터들 중 하나이다.

분석_ 두 번째 지문에서 방콕 의료클리닉이 소개되고 있다. 3년 전에 기술팀에 의해 문자서비스가 만들어졌으므로 다른 업체보다 일찍 의료 확장에 대한 노력을 기울였으므로 initiative 로 볼 수 있다. 또한 상당한 수요와 많은 환자들을 이끌어 냈으므로 성공적이었다고 볼 수 있다.(led to significant demand for the new service, and furthermore attracted more traffic to our clinic as well as website.)

199. (C)

오전 발표에 대해 제시된 것은?
(A) 의료진과의 효과적인 의사소통을 설명할 것이다.
(B) 워크숍 시리즈 첫날에 다이아몬드 홀에서 개최될 것이다.
(C) 참가자들에게 환자들의 수를 늘리는 방법을 알려줄 것이다.
(D) 40분 이상 지속할 것이다.

분석_ 오전 강의는 Alfred Kline의 강의다. 모바일의료서비스의 자세한 내용은 두 번째 지문에서 설명하고 있다. 발표 요약문의 작성자가 오전 강의하는 사람과 동일함을 확인하자. 환자수를 늘린다는 내용도 언급된다.(attracted more traffic to our clinic as well as website.)

200. (C)

Kline 씨에 대해서 아마도 사실인 것은?
(A) 그는 3년 전에 방콕 의료클리닉에 입사하였다.
(B) 그는 혁신적인 광고물로 상을 탔다.
(C) 그는 회의 기획기관으로부터 제공되는 재정적 지원에 자격을 갖추고 있다.
(D) 그는 휴대폰 문자 전송을 이용하는 아이디어를 최초로 제안하였다.

분석_ 발표요약문에서 작성자가 일하고 있는 병원이 비영리기관임을 알리고 있다.(Bangkok Medical Clinic, a nonprofit organization) 첫 번째 지문에서 비영리기관을 위한 기금 지원이 언급되었으므로(Limited fund support for the nonprofit organization is available.) 재정적 지원(financial aid)의 자격을 갖추고 있음을 알 수 있다.

Actual Test 02

1. (C)

(A) She is wearing a hat.
(B) She is trying on clothes.
(C) She is examining an article of clothing.
(D) She is standing in front of a store.

(A) 여자는 모자를 쓰고 있다.
(B) 여자는 옷을 입어보고 있다.
(C) 여자는 의류 한 점을 살펴보고 있다.
(D) 여자는 가게 앞에 서 있다.

어휘_ wear ~를 착용하다 try ~을 시도하다 examine ~를 살펴보다 an article of ~ 한 점 stand 서 있다

분석_ 사람 1인 사진으로 등장인물의 동작, 외모, 배경을 보고 정답을 고르는 유형의 문제이다. 이 문제는 매장에서 물건을 살펴보는 동작에 맞는 표현을 고른다. (C) 사진에 등장한 사람의 동작과 일치하므로 정답이다. 오답분석 (A) 모자를 쓰고 있지 않으므로 동작 불일치 오답이다. (B) 옷을 입어보지 않고 들고만 있으므로 동작 불일치 오답이다. (D) 여자가 가게 안에 들어와 있으므로 상태 불일치 오답이다.

2. (B)

(A) She is plugging in the cord.
(B) She is facing some equipment.
(C) She is looking at a clock.
(D) The test tubes are being labeled.

(A) 여자가 코드를 콘센트에 꽂고 있다.
(B) 여자가 장비를 보고 있다.
(C) 여자가 시계를 보고 있다.
(D) 시험관에 라벨이 붙여지고 있다.

어휘_ plug 콘센트를 꽂다 face 마주하다 equipment 장비 look at ~를 보다 test tube 시험관 label 라벨을 부착하다

분석_ 사람 1인이 등장하여 실험실에서 장비를 이용하는 동작에 맞는 표현을 고르는 문제이다. (B) 여자가 장비를 보고 있으므로 동작이 일치하여 정답이다. 오답분석 (A) 여자의 손에 콘센트가 쥐어져 있지 않으므로 정답이 될 수 없다. (C) 사진에 시계가 없으므로 오답이다. (D) 시험관과 라벨이 사진상에 없으므로 오답이다.

3. (D)

(A) The audience is standing up to applaud.
(B) Some musicians are leaving the stage.
(C) All of the seats at the concert hall are being cleaned.
(D) Some people are attending a concert.

(A) 관중들이 기립 박수를 치고 있다.
(B) 연주가들이 무대를 떠나고 있다.
(C) 콘서트 홀의 모든 좌석이 청소되고 있다.
(D) 사람들이 콘서트에 참석하고 있다.

어휘_ audience 관중 applaud 박수치다 leave 떠나다 stage 무대 clean 청소하다 attend 참석하다

분석_ 사람이 다수 나오는 사진으로 단체의 공통된 동작이나 상황을 표현하는 것을 정답으로 고르는 문제이다. (D) 사람들이 콘서트 장에 참석하여 구경하고 있으므로 정답이다. 오답분석 (A) 관중들이 박수를 치고 있지 않으므로 동작 불일치 오답이다. (B) 연주가들이 무대를 떠나지 않으므로 동작 불일치 오답이다. (C) 콘서트 홀의 좌석이 청소되고 있지 않으므로 동작 불일치 오답이다.

4. (C)

(A) The women are standing by a wall.
(B) One woman is stacking shelves with items.
(C) One woman is paying for her purchase.
(D) The women are filling up a bag.

(A) 여자들이 벽에 기대어 서 있다.
(B) 한 여자가 선반에 물품을 채우고 있다.
(C) 한 여자가 구매에 대한 비용을 지불하고 있다.
(D) 여자들이 가방을 물건으로 채우고 있다.

어휘_ wall 벽 stack ~를 채우다 shelf 선반 pay for 지불하다 purchase 구매품 fill ~를 채우다

분석_ 손님이 마트에서 구매 비용을 지불하는 모습이다. 결제한다는 표현이 정답률이 높은 사진이다. (C) 구매 비용을 지불하는 장면이므로 정답이 된다. 오답분석 (A) 여자들이 벽에 기대고 있지 않으므로 동작 불일치 오답이다. (B) 선반에 물품을 채우고 있지 않으므로 동작 불일치 오답이다. (D) 가방을 채우는 모습이 아니므로 동작 불일치 오답이다.

5. (D)

(A) There are blankets lying on the table.
(B) The mirror is next to a television.
(C) The beds are on opposite sides of the room.
(D) A picture has been placed over the beds.

(A) 담요가 탁자에 놓여 있다.
(B) 거울이 텔레비전 옆에 있다.
(C) 방 안의 침대가 마주보게 놓여 있다.
(D) 사진이 침대 위에 걸려 있다.

어휘_ blanket 담요 lie ~에 놓여 있다 mirror 거울 on opposite side 맞은편에 place ~를 두다

분석_ 사람이 없는 사진으로 두드러지는 사물이나 배경이 주로 출제된다. (D) 침대 위쪽에 사진이 걸려 있으므로 정답이다. 오답분석 (A) 사진에 탁자가 없으므로 오답이다. (B) 거울은 있으나 텔레비전이 없으므로 오답이다. (C) 침대가 하나밖에 없어서 마주볼 수 없으므로 오답이다.

6. (C)

(A) A ladder is lying on the floor.
(B) The windows are being opened.
(C) Stools have been placed beside the table.
(D) Tables have been arranged under the lights.

(A) 사다리가 바닥에 놓여 있다.

(B) 창문들이 열리고 있다.
(C) 등이 없는 의자가 탁자 옆에 놓여 있다.
(D) 식탁들이 전등 아래에 가지런히 놓여 있다.

어휘_ ladder 사다리 stool 등받이 없는 의자 beside ~옆에 arrange ~를 정리하다

분석_ 사람이 없는 사진으로 사물과 배경을 정확히 묘사하는 선택지가 정답이 된다. (C) 등받이가 없는 의자가 테이블 옆에 있으므로 정답이다. `오답분석` (A) 사진에 사다리가 없으므로 오답이다. (B) 창문을 열고 있는 사람이 없으므로 오답이다. (D) 식탁이 하나밖에 없으므로 복수형의 표현은 오답이다.

Part 2   본문 p.62

7. (C)

How much is the whole package including an air fare?
(A) Three miles from here.
(B) Yes, it includes all of them.
(C) It comes to 95 dollars.

항공료를 포함하는 전체 패키지는 얼마죠?
(A) 여기서 3마일이요.
(B) 네, 그것은 모두를 포함하고 있습니다.
(C) 95달러입니다.

어휘_ whole 전체의 package 패키지 including 포함하는 airfare 항공요금

분석_ 주로 dollar, cent, euro 등의 화폐단위명사가 나오면 how much 의문문의 정답유형이 된다. `오답분석` (A) three miles는 길이를 표현하므로 how far/long의 정답유형이 된다. (B) 의문사 문제는 yes나 no로 대답할 수 없는 전형적인 오답유형이다.

8. (C)

Where could I find some really interesting souvenirs?
(A) Oh, did you buy any interesting ones?
(B) Are you sure you checked out your room?
(C) Have you tried the craft stalls in the market?

정말 재미있는 기념품은 어디서 살 수 있나요?
(A) 아, 재미있는 것을 샀어요?
(B) 방은 찾아본 것이 틀림없어요?
(C) 시장의 판매점을 들러보셨나요?

어휘_ souvenir 기념품 search 탐색하다 craft stall 진열대, 매점

분석_ 문제에서 기념품을 어디서 구할 수 있는지 물어보고 있으며 in the market(시장에서)이 중요한 단서가 되어 (C)를 정답으로 골라야 한다. `오답분석` (A) 질문에 이미 나온 interesting이 한 번 더 반복되는데 동일한 어휘가 나오는 경우 거의 오답에 속한다. (B) 기념품과 당신의 방이 어울리지 않는 관계이므로 해석상 오답이다.

9. (A)

When is the board meeting in Chicago?

(A) At the end of the month, but not for sure.
(B) I lost my boarding pass.
(C) To select the new director.

시카고의 이사회는 언제이지요?
(A) 월말일 텐데, 확실하지는 않아요.
(B) 탑승권을 잃어버렸어요.
(C) 새로운 이사를 뽑기 위해서요.

어휘_ board 위원회 select 선출하다 director 부장 pass 통행권

분석_ 회의가 언제인지 물어보고 있으며 회의가 열리는 시점을 나타내는 at the end / at the beginning / at the first 등의 표현이 주로 정답유형이다. `오답분석` (B) 질문에 나오는 boarding이 한 번 더 반복되는 오답유형이다. (C) to부정사 형태의 대답은 '~하기 위해서'라는 목적의 의미를 지니게 되므로 이유를 물어보는 why 문제의 정답유형이며 다른 문제에서는 오답유형이다.

10. (A)

Which building is the library?
(A) It's the one next door.
(B) I came from the library.
(C) Thanks, but I'll do it by myself.

어느 건물이 도서관이죠?
(A) 옆문 나가면 있는 거요.
(B) 도서관에서 왔어요.
(C) 감사합니다만, 제가 혼자서 할게요.

어휘_ library 도서관 by self 홀로 스스로

분석_ which 문제이며 어느 건물인지 물어보고 있으므로 the one next door(옆문 쪽의 건물)이 적절한 대답이다. `오답분석` (B) 질문에 나온 library가 대답에서 한 번 더 반복되는 오답유형이다. (C) thanks는 주로 제안문의 정답유형에 속하며 여기서는 어울리지 않는다.

11. (C)

Who's responsible for purchasing office supplies?
(A) They're very reliable suppliers.
(B) We've just bought an office.
(C) That would be the manager.

사무 비품을 구매하는 것을 누가 맡고 있지요?
(A) 그들은 매우 신뢰할 만한 공급업체입니다.
(B) 우리가 사무실을 막 구입하였습니다.
(C) 과장님일 겁니다.

어휘_ responsible for ~를 책임지는 purchase 구매하다 supply 공급품, 비품 reliable 신뢰할 만한 supplier 공급업자(체)

분석_ who 문제이며 누구의 책임인지 물어보고 있으며 직위 명사인 manager(과장)가 정답이다. `오답분석` (A) 질문에 나온 supplies가 대답에서 파생형태인 suppliers(공급업체)로 나왔으며, 파생형태는 대표적인 오답유형에 속한다. (B) 질문에 나온 office가 대답에서 한 번 더 반복되는 오답유형이다.

12. (B)

When should I call back tomorrow?

(A) No, it's on the front.
(B) Between the hours of 10 A.M and 5 P.M.
(C) You must return it in three days.

제가 내일 언제쯤 전화할까요?
(A) 아니요, 그건 앞쪽에 있어요.
(B) 오전 10시와 오후 5시 사이에요.
(C) 3일 후에 돌려주셔야 해요.

어휘_ call back 전화에 답신하다 front 앞 between 사이에 return 돌려주다

분석_ when 문제이며 내일 언제 전화할지를 묻고 있다. 오전 10시부터 오후 5시 사이가 좋다는 표현이 가장 적절한 대답이다. A.M. 및 P.M. 등이 중요한 단서가 된다. 오답분석 (A) 의문사 문제에서는 Yes/No 등은 오답유형에 속한다. 긍정과 부정으로 대답하지 않는다. (C) in three days(3일 후에)는 속기 쉬운 함정유형이다. 3일 후에 반납하겠다는 의미로 물건을 빌렸을 경우에 발생할 답변이다.

13. (B)

Has your vehicle been repaired or is still being worked on?
(A) Please go ahead.
(B) It was fixed today.
(C) I'd like to walk, thanks.

당신의 차를 수리했나요? 아니면 아직도 수리 중인가요?
(A) 계속하세요.
(B) 어제 수리했어요.
(C) 전 걷고 싶네요. 고마워요.

어휘_ vehicle 자동차 repair 수리하다 work on ~에 대해 작업하다 fix 수리하다

분석_ 선택의문문 문제이며 수리가 완료되었는지 혹은 여전히 수리 중인지 물어보고 있다. 오늘 수리가 이루어졌다는 의미의 (B)가 정답이다. 오답분석 (A) go ahead는 "그렇게 하세요." 혹은 "먼저 하세요."라는 의미이며, 보통 질문자 자신이 어떠한 행위를 하겠다는 표현에 대한 응답으로 사용된다. (C) Would you want me to give you a ride?(제가 태워드릴까요?)의 정답으로 적당한 표현이다. 주로 제안문의 완곡한 거절의 표현으로, 제안문에 대한 응답은 I'd like 및 thanks를 사용할 수 있다.

14. (B)

Who was the guest of honor at the banquet?
(A) It was held in honor of the retiring president.
(B) It was Jeff Edwards.
(C) Yes, guest lectures were cancelled.

연회의 귀빈은 누구였습니까?
(A) 사직하는 사장을 기념하여 열렸습니다.
(B) Jeff Edwards였습니다.
(C) 네, 초청 강연은 취소되었습니다.

어휘_ guest 손님 honor 명예 banquet 연회 hold 개최하다 retire 은퇴하다 guest lecture 초청강연 cancel 취소하다

분석_ 게스트가 누구인지 물어보는 문제이며 Jeff Edwards라는 사람 이름이 정답이다. 영문 성 및 이름을 따로 정리해서 기억해두는 요령이 필요하다. 오답분석 (A) retiring president

(은퇴하는 회장)에 속기 쉬운 문제이다. 문제는 연회에 참가할 게스트를 묻는 문제이며, 대답은 "누구를 위한 연회인가"의 정답유형이다. 동일한 어휘인 honor가 다시 반복되는 오답유형이다. (C) 의문사 문제에 나올 수 없는 Yes/No의 오답유형이다. 또한 guest가 다시 반복되는 오답유형이기도 하다.

15. (C)

Excuse me, does anyone have an extra pen?
(A) She needs an extra charge.
(B) No, it closes early on Sunday.
(C) You can borrow mine.

죄송합니다만, 누가 여분의 펜이 있나요?
(A) 그녀는 추가 요금을 달래요.
(B) 아니요, 일요일에는 일찍 문을 닫습니다.
(C) 제 것을 빌려 쓰세요.

어휘_ extra 추가적인, 여분의 charge 수수료 close (문을) 닫다 borrow 빌려오다

분석_ 여분의 펜을 갖고 있는 사람을 묻는 문제이며 내 것을 사용하라는 의미의 (C)가 정답이다. 의문사가 없는 문제는 의문사가 있는 문제보다 정답유형이 훨씬 다양하기 때문에 보다 정확한 청취력이 필요하며 요령보다는 받아쓰기 및 따라 읽기와 같은 순수한 듣기공부가 병행되어야 한다. 오답분석 (A) 질문에 나왔었던 extra가 반복되는 오답유형이다. (B) 부정의 의미인 No가 나왔지만 뒤에 따라오는 내용이 질문과 어울리는 표현이 아니다. 일요일에 일찍 문을 닫는다는 내용은 Does the store always stay open late?(가게가 항상 늦게까지 문을 여나요?)라는 질문에 어울릴 만한 대답이다.

16. (C)

Have you already turned in your application form?
(A) No, make a left turn.
(B) It's on the form.
(C) Yes, I have.

지원서를 이미 제출했나요?
(A) 아니요. 좌회전하세요.
(B) 양식에 기재되어 있어요.
(C) 네, 그렇습니다.

어휘_ already 벌써 turn in 제출하다 application from 신청서 left turn 좌회전

분석_ (C) Have you로 묻는 문제이며 대명사에 유의해야 한다. 대답에서는 I로 대답해야 하며 you로 답하는 경우는 대부분 오답유형이 된다. Have I로 묻는 경우에도 유의하자. 오답분석 (A) 질문에 나온 동사 turned가 대답에서 명사 turn으로 파생된 유형이며 오답유형에 속한다. turn in은 '제출하다'이며 make a turn은 '회전하다'이다. (B) 질문에 나온 form이 대답에서 한 번 더 반복된 오답유형이다.

17. (A)

How would you feel about going to the lake this weekend?
(A) That sounds like a good plan.

(B) I felt the price was better than last weekend.
(C) Mostly, I work in the garden.
이번 주말에 호수에 가는 것 어때요?
(A) 그것 좋겠네요.
(B) 가격이 지난 주말보다 더 좋은 것 같아요.
(C) 주로, 저는 정원에서 일해요.

어휘_ lake 호수 sound like ~처럼 들리다 mostly 주로

분석_ 호수로 가는 게 어떤지 물어보고 있으며 That sounds good/ great. 혹은 It's a good/great idea.(좋은 생각이네요.)가 제 안문의 빈번한 정답유형이다. **오답분석** (B) feel의 과거동사 인 felt가 대답에 나온 파생어휘 오답유형이다. weekend가 중복된 동일어휘 오답유형이기도 하다. (C) 질문과 어울리 지 않는 대답이다. Where do you spend your time?(어디 에 시간을 할애하시나요?)의 대답으로 적절하다.

18. (B)

Why don't we review this case next?
(A) My suitcase is located right next to yours.
(B) If you insist, that's O.K.
(C) The view isn't so important.
이 경우를 다음에 검토하는 것이 어때요?
(A) 내 가방은 당신 것 옆에 있습니다.
(B) 원하시면 그렇게 하겠습니다.
(C) 전망은 그렇게 중요한 것이 아닙니다.

어휘_ review 검토하다 case 사건, 경우 suitcase 서류 가방 locate 놓다 next to ~ 옆에 insist 주장하다 view 관점, 장관

분석_ 검토해달라는 요청에 대해 긍정의 의미로 OK가 적당한 대답이다. 또한 조건의 의미인 If you want(원하시면), If possible(가능하다면), If time is allowed(시간이 허락된다 면) 등도 제안문의 정답유형이다. **오답분석** (A) 질문에 나온 case가 대답에서 suitcase로 파생된 오답이다. 또한, next to(~ 옆에)는 주로 where의 정답유형이다. (C) 질문에 나온 review가 대답에서 view로 파생된 오답이다. 유사 발음은 항상 오답유형임을 잊지 말자.

19. (A)

What's the charge for dry-cleaning a tie?
(A) It depends on the condition of a tie.
(B) No, it supposed to rain.
(C) There's one at the post office.
넥타이를 드라이클리닝하는 비용은 얼마인가요?
(A) 타이의 상태에 따라 다릅니다.
(B) 아니오, 비가 올 것 같습니다.
(C) 우체국에 하나 있습니다.

어휘_ charge 요금, 수수료 tie 타이 depend on 의존하다, 따르다 condition 상태 supposed 예정인 post office 우체국

분석_ 가격을 묻는 문제이지만 구체적인 답변이 아닌 회피성 정답 It depends on(~한 경우에 따라 달라요)이 정답이 된다. 이 러한 회피성 정답은 다양한 문제에서 정답이 된다. **오답분석** (B) 의문사로 묻는 의문문에서는 Yes/No로 대답하지 않는 다. (C) 드라이클리닝 가격을 묻는 질문과 어울리지 않는 대 답이며 순수한 청취력이 필요한 문제이다.

20. (B)

Mr. Petal will be in charge of the Sales and Marketing.
(A) No, he didn't sell much.
(B) I don't think he is the best qualified.
(C) I believe it costs 5 dollars.
Petal 씨는 영업과 마케팅을 책임지게 될 겁니다.
(A) 아니오, 그는 많이 팔지 못합니다.
(B) 그가 가장 적격이라고 생각하지 않습니다.
(C) 그게 5달러일 겁니다.

어휘_ in charge of ~를 책임지는 sales 영업 sell 팔다 qualified 유능한, 자격을 갖춘 cost 비용이 들다

분석_ Patel 씨가 부서를 맡을 거라는 얘기에 대한 의견을 담은 (B)가 정답으로 적절하다. 평서문은 상대방의 의견을 물어 보는 경향이 강하므로 I think so. / I agree ~(나도 그렇게 생각해.)와 같은 동의의 표현이 정답이 되는 경우가 많다. **오답분석** (A) sales가 영업이라는 의미로 질문에서 활용되 었지만, 대답에서는 판매량이라는 의미로 사용된 잘못된 대 답이다. 정확한 청취력 및 해석이 필요한 까다로운 문제이 다. (C) 5달러가 소요된다는 의미로 How much 및 What charge(얼마입니까)의 정답으로 적당한 대답이다. charge 는 '요금'이라는 의미 외에도 '책임, 몫'이라는 의미로도 활 용되는데 이중적인 의미를 지닌 어휘의 활용에 유의해야 할 문제이다.

21. (B)

When will the performance start?
(A) All players will come soon.
(B) As soon as all audience is seated.
(C) It started five years ago.
공연은 언제 시작합니까?
(A) 모든 참가자가 곧 올 겁니다.
(B) 모든 청중이 착석하자마자요.
(C) 5년 전에 시작되었습니다.

어휘_ performance 공연 start 시작하다 seat (좌석에) 앉히다

분석_ 언제 공연이 시작하는지에 대한 질문에 모든 사람이 좌석 에 앉고 나서라고 대답하는 (B)가 정답이다. 시간의 부사 절은 현재동사가 사용되어도 미래의 의미를 지니게 된다. **오답분석** (A) 질문과 대답과의 관계가 부적절하다. 시제는 적절하지만 공연시작과 공연자가 곧 올 것이라는 내용이 어울리지 않는다. (C) when 문제의 전형적인 오답유형이다. ago가 나오는 대답은 과거시제로 물어본 경우에 가능하다. will start와 started의 시제가 어울리지 않는 오답유형이다.

22. (B)

Would you prefer to meet over lunch, or another time?
(A) I prefer fish.
(B) Today's not good for me.
(C) It was delicious, thank you.
점심 식사를 하며 만나겠습니까 아니면 다른 시간이 좋겠습니까?
(A) 전 생선이 좋습니다.
(B) 오늘은 사양하겠습니다.
(C) 맛있었습니다. 감사합니다.

어휘_ prefer 선호하다 delicious 맛있는

분석_ 오늘 점심과 다른 시간대 중 하나를 고르는 문제에서 오늘은 좋지 않다는 의미로 another time을 선택한 (B)가 가장 적당하다. **오답분석** (A) 질문에 나온 동사 prefer가 대답에서 반복된 오답유형이다. Which do you prefer, fish or meat?에서 어울릴 대답이다. (C) delicious와 같은 상태 관련 형용사는 how로 시작하는 의문문의 정답유형이다. How about meal we served?(저희가 제공한 식사가 어땠습니까?)의 대답으로 어울리는 표현이다.

23. (A)

Where do you plan to stay while you're in Seoul?
(A) Our company has an arrangement with the Holiday Inn.
(B) I have a conference there next week.
(C) I'll be in Korea for four days.

서울에 있는 동안 어디에서 머물 계획합니까?
(A) 우리 회사는 Holiday Inn에 예약되어 있습니다.
(B) 다음 주에 회의가 있습니다.
(C) 난 4일 동안 한국에 있을 겁니다.

어휘_ stay 머물다 arrangement 약속, 예약 conference 회의

분석_ 머물 장소를 묻는 문제이며 호텔의 한 종류인 Holiday Inn에서 머물 것이라고 말하는 (A)가 정답이다. inn은 숙박업소를 말하는데 lodge, hotel과 함께 accommodation의 한 종류이다. **오답분석** (B) 어디 머물 예정이냐는 질문에 어울리지 않는 표현이다. 다음 주에 회의가 있다는 말로 When do you plan to visit Seoul?(언제 서울에 방문할 예정입니까?)의 대답에 어울릴 표현이다. (C) 4주간 한국에 머물겠다는 말로 장소를 묻는 where 의문문과 어울리지 않는다. How long do you plan to stay?(얼마나 오래 머물 예정입니까?)의 대답으로 어울릴 표현이다.

24. (A)

How long have you been supervising this project?
(A) For almost 5 years.
(B) Overhead projectors seem too expensive.
(C) Yes, my supervisor has.

얼마나 오래 이 프로젝트를 관리해왔습니까?
(A) 거의 5년 동안이요.
(B) 프로젝터는 너무 비싸 보입니다.
(C) 네, 저의 상관이 했습니다.

어휘_ supervise 관리하다, 감독하다 almost 거의 overhead projector 프로젝터기 seem ~처럼 보이다 supervisor 감독관, 상관

분석_ 기간을 묻는 문제이며 거의 5년 동안이라고 대답하는 (A)가 정답이다. how long으로 시작하는 문제의 정답유형은 a day, two minutes, many hours, weeks, a few years 등의 시간의 단위명사이다. **오답분석** (B) project와 유사한 발음인 projector가 나와서 혼란스럽게 하는 오답유형이다. (C) 의문사 문제는 Yes/No로 대답하지 않는다.

25. (C)

What time are we going to the theater?
(A) In the entrance of the theater.
(B) Yes, you always have to go to the theater.
(C) We will leave right after dinner.

우리 극장에 몇 시에 갑니까?
(A) 극장의 입구에서요.
(B) 네, 당신은 극장에 가야 합니다.
(C) 우리는 저녁 먹은 후에 떠날 겁니다.

어휘_ theater 극장 leave 떠나다 right after 직후에 entrance 출입구

분석_ 극장 갈 시간을 묻는 문제이며 저녁식사 직후에 간다는 표현이 적절하다. right after는 '직후에'라는 의미로 as soon as와 유사한 표현이며, what time 및 when으로 시작하는 의문문의 정답으로 자주 출제된다. **오답분석** (A) 질문에 나온 theater가 대답에서 반복된 오답유형이다. 〈in + 장소명사〉는 where 의문문의 정답유형이다. (B) 의문사 의문문이므로 Yes/No로 대답할 수 없다.

26. (A)

John was supposed to have finished that market review by last Wednesday, wasn't he?
(A) No, it's not due yet.
(B) I review the contract.
(C) Yes, he will.

John은 지난 수요일까지 시장 조사를 끝내기로 되어 있었지요, 그렇죠?
(A) 아니오. 아직 마감이 아닙니다.
(B) 저는 계약을 검토합니다.
(C) 네, 그가 할 거예요.

어휘_ supposed to V ~해야 하는 market review 시장 조사 due 만기의 yet 아직 review 검토하다 contract 계약

분석_ 수요일이 시장조사 마감날이지 않냐고 물어보는 문제이며, 아직 마감이 아니라고 말한 (A)가 정답이다. due는 기한의 마감을 의미하는 표현이다. **오답분석** (B) 질문에 나온 review가 대답에서 반복된 오답유형이며, 특히 동사와 명사의 형태가 같은 어휘가 질문과 대답에서 품사가 다르게 쓰인 보기는 절대 고르지 말자. (C) wasn't he로 묻는 부가의문문 문제에서 시제가 맞지 않은 오답유형이다. 질문과 대답에서 과거와 미래는 어울리지 않는 대표적 오답유형이다.

27. (C)

Is this year's trade conference going to be in Canada?
(A) I don't know anyone in our office.
(B) They have a good trade relationship.
(C) Why don't you ask Matilda, staff member in human resource?

올해의 무역 회의가 캐나다에서 열리나요?
(A) 사무실에 아는 사람이 없어요.
(B) 그들은 좋은 무역 관계를 갖고 있습니다.
(C) 인사부 직원인 Matilda에게 물어보시겠어요?

어휘_ trade 교역 conference 회의 relationship 관계 ask 묻다 human resources 인사부서

분석_ 회의가 Canada에서 열릴 예정이냐고 묻는 문제이며 본인은 잘 모르니 Matilda에게 물어보라는 회피성 답안인 (C)가 정답이다. 어떠한 의문문이든지 ask가 나온 대답은 거의 정답이 된다. 무엇을 묻든지 누구에게 물어보면 알게 될 거

라는 회피성 정답이다. **오답분석** (A) 질문과 어울리지 않는
표현이며, 정확한 청취력 및 의미 파악이 필요하다. I don't
know.(잘 모르겠어요.)는 정답이 될 수 있지만, 사무실에
아는 사람이 없다는 (A)는 정답이 될 수 없다. 빈번한 정답
유형인 I don't know가 오답유형으로 나온 함정이다. (B)
문제에서 나온 trade가 대답에서 반복되는 오답유형이다.

28. (C)

Is the agenda prepared?
(A) No, it's still out of order.
(B) Yes, they compared very well.
(C) Not yet, the vice president needs to review it.
일정이 준비되었나요?
(A) 아니오. 아직 고장 중입니다.
(B) 네, 그들은 매우 잘 비교되었습니다.
(C) 아직이요. 부사장이 검토해야 합니다.
어휘_ agenda 회의 일정 prepare 준비하다 out of order 고장 난
compare 비교하다 vice president 부회장 review 검토하다
분석_ 회의 일정이 준비되었는지 물어보고 있으며, 아직 준비
가 덜 되었다는 의미의 (C)가 정답이다. No, it's not yet
prepared(아직 준비가 안 되었습니다.)의 줄임말로 not
yet이 정답으로 출제되었는데 특히 have로 시작하는 의문
문에서 already(벌써)와 함께 매우 빈번한 정답유형이다.
오답분석 (A) still은 빈번한 정답유형이지만 위 문제에서는
함정으로 쓰였다. 회의 일정과 고장 난(out of order)의 의
미가 어울리지 않는다. 청취력 및 의미 파악이 필요한 문제
이다. (B) 질문의 prepared와 대답의 compared의 발음이
유사한 오답유형이다.

29. (A)

I heard the parking garage is near the conference center.
(A) Yes, it's across the street.
(B) The park is gorgeous.
(C) No, move it to the left.
주차장이 컨퍼런스 센터 가까이 있다고 들었는데요.
(A) 네, 길 건너편에 있습니다.
(B) 공원은 멋집니다.
(C) 아니오. 그것을 왼쪽으로 옮기세요.
어휘_ parking garage 주차장 near 가까이에 gorgeous 우아한 move
옮기다
분석_ 질문에서 주차장이 어디에 있다고 개인의 의견을 말하고 있
으며, 거기에 대한 동의를 하면서 보다 세부적인 설명을 담
고 있는 (A)가 정답이다. **오답분석** (B) 질문에 나온 parking
이 대답에서 파생어휘인 park로 나온 오답유형이다. (C) 왼
쪽으로 옮기라는 내용이 질문과 전혀 어울리지 않는 순수한
의미 파악 문제이다.

30. (B)

Did you hear that the product trial was just cancelled?
(A) I planned to visit the castle in Rome.
(B) Everyone has been talking about it.
(C) Try on the shoes.

제품 시연이 막 취소된 사실을 들었나요?
(A) 로마에 있는 성에 방문할 계획입니다.
(B) 모든 직원이 그에 관해 이야기하고 있어요.
(C) 신발 한번 신어보세요.
어휘_ hear 듣다 trial 시연 cancel 취소하다 castle 성 try 시험 삼아 해
보다
분석_ 어떠한 사실을 들었는지에 대한 여부를 묻는 문제이며 모든
사람이 그 일에 대해 이야기하고 있다는 말로 이미 알고 있
다는 의미를 담은 (B)가 정답이다. **오답분석** (A) 질문에 나
온 cancel과 대답에 나온 castle이 유사발음으로 오답유형
이다. (C) 질문에 나온 trial가 대답에서 파생어휘인 try로
나온 오답유형이다.

31. (C)

You're not going to be in the office this Thursday, are
you?
(A) Yes, the new offices are very nice.
(B) Yes, that would be fine.
(C) No, I'm leaving on vacation that day.
이번 주 목요일에 사무실에 안 계시죠, 그렇죠?
(A) 네, 새로운 사무실은 좋습니다.
(B) 네, 그거 좋겠네요.
(C) 네, 전 그날 휴가를 떠납니다.
어휘_ leave 떠나다 vacation 휴가 that day 그날에
분석_ 목요일에 사무실에 없을 거냐고 물어보는 질문에 대해,
그날에 휴가를 떠난다는 대답이 적절한 (C)가 정답이다.
오답분석 (A) 질문에 나온 office가 대답에 반복되는 오답유
형이다. (B) 제안문에서 긍정의 대답으로 어울리는 대답이다.

Questions 32-34 refer to the following conversation.

W: **32** *I'm going to be away on holiday starting Friday,
March 25 and I'd like you to put a hold on my mail.*
M: Certainly. **32** *We can keep your mail here at the
post office until you get back.* **33** *Ms. Taylor, did
you hear that you could have your mail delivered
to another address instead?*
W: **33** *Yes, I know about that. But I'm actually going to
be traveling overseas. So, I don't think I could use
that service.* I'd like you to keep everything at the
post office while I am out of town.
M: **34** *OK. So when do you want the delivery to restart?*

W: 3월 25일 금요일부터 저는 휴가를 떠나요. 그래서 당신이 제 우편
물을 보관해주셨으면 해요.
M: 물론이죠. 당신이 돌아올 때까지 우리가 우편물을 여기 우체국에
보관해드릴게요. Taylor 씨, 메일을 원래 주소 대신 다른 주소지로
배송할 수 있는데 들으셨어요?

W: 네, 알고 있습니다. 하지만 저는 사실 해외로 여행을 가는 거예요.
그래서 제가 그 서비스를 이용할 수는 없을 것 같아요. 제가 도시
에 없는 동안 당신이 우체국에 모든 것을 보관해주셨으면 해요.
M: 알겠어요. 그럼 배송서비스가 언제부터 재개되길 원하세요?
어휘_ away on holiday 휴가 중인 put a hold on ~를 보관하다
post office 우체국 deliver 배송하다 instead 대신에 travel
여행 가다, 출장 가다 overseas 해외에서, 해외로 restart 다
시 시작하다

32. (C)

What is the conversation mainly about?
(A) Reserving a meeting
(B) Renovating an office
(C) Stopping mail delivery
(D) Finding a lost product
대화는 주로 어떤 것에 대한 것인가?
(A) 모임 예약하기
(B) 사무실 개조하기
(C) 우편 배송 중단하기
(D) 분실물 찾기
분석_ 대화 주제를 묻고 있다. 주제는 대화의 초반에 제시된다. 처
음 부분에서 여자가 휴가를 떠나기 때문에 돌아올 때까지
우편물을 우체국에서 보관해달라고 요청하고 있다.

33. (B)

Why does the woman decline the man's suggestion?
(A) She has already received an item.
(B) She will be out of the country.
(C) The room is quite small.
(D) The price for service is too high.
여자가 남자의 제안을 거절한 이유는 무엇인가?
(A) 여자가 이미 물건을 받았다.
(B) 여자가 다른 나라에 있을 것이다.
(C) 방이 너무 작다.
(D) 서비스 비용이 너무 높다.
분석_ 남자가 다른 주소로 우편물이 배송되게끔 해주려고 했으나
여자가 해외로 나가는 탓에 서비스를 이용할 수 없다고 언
급하고 있다.

34. (D)

What will the woman most likely tell the man next?
(A) Her office expansion project
(B) Her temporary address
(C) The purpose of her speech
(D) The date of her return
여자는 다음에 남자에게 아마도 무엇을 말할 것인가?
(A) 여자의 사무실 확장 프로젝트
(B) 여자의 임시 주소
(C) 여자의 발표 목적
(D) 여자가 돌아오는 날짜
분석_ 대화의 마지막에 언제부터 우편물을 보내기 시작할지 남자

가 질문하고 끝이 났으므로 여자는 돌아오는 날짜를 이야
기해야 한다.

Questions 35-37 refer to the following conversation.

W: Hi, I've never been here before, **35 but your watch
repair shop was strongly recommended.** Can you
fix these watches? The hour hand is broken and I'd
like to have it replaced with new one.
M: We have a large selection of parts for watches.
Unfortunately, I don't think I have the exact same
item. But if you want, I can replace both the hour
and minute hand so they match. **36 Here, take a
look in the display case.**
W: Oh, I really like red ones up there. I will go with those
ones. Are they very expensive?
M: Well, it's one of our most expensive styles. **37 But
since I'm not able to fulfill your original request, I'll
give 20% off the price.**

W: 안녕하세요, 저는 여기가 처음인데요, 하지만 당신의 시계 수리점
은 엄청 추천받더군요. 이 시계도 수리 가능할까요? 시침이 망가
져서 새로운 것으로 교체하고 싶어요.
M: 우리는 많은 종류의 시계 부품을 가지고 있습니다. 안타깝게도, 제
생각에 정확히 똑같은 제품은 없는 것 같군요. 하지만 원하신다면,
시침과 분침 둘 다 교체해서 일치시켜드릴 수 있습니다. 여기 진
열상자를 한번 보세요.
W: 오, 저기 빨간색이 정말 맘에 들어요. 저것들로 결정할게요. 많
이 비싼가요?
M: 글쎄요, 가장 비싼 스타일 중에 하나입니다. 하지만 손님의 원래 요
구사항을 충족시키지 못했으니 20% 할인해드릴게요.
어휘_ repair shop 수리점 strongly 강력하게 recommend 추천하다
fix 수리하다 hour hand 시침 replace 교체하다 a selection
of 다양한 part 부품 unfortunately 불행하게도, 안타깝게도
exact 정확한 same 동일한 minute hand 분침 match ~에
적합하다 take a look ~를 보다 expensive 비싼 fulfill 충족
시키다

35. (C)

Where does the man most likely work?
(A) At a technical school
(B) At a clothing factory
(C) At a watch repair store
(D) At a flower shop
남자는 아마도 어디에서 일하는가?
(A) 기술 학교
(B) 의류 공장
(C) 시계 수리점
(D) 꽃가게
분석_ 첫 대화부터 여자가 시계 수리점을 언급하고 있다.

36. (C)

What does the man show the woman?
(A) A piece of machinery
(B) A list of courses
(C) Items in a display case
(D) A product catalog

남자는 여자에게 무엇을 보여주는가?
(A) 한 대의 기계
(B) 과정 목록
(C) 진열함 안의 물건들
(D) 제품 카탈로그

분석_ 여자가 요구하는 것과 동일한 것은 없지만 차선책으로 진열
함을 보여주고 고르게 하고 있다.

37. (A)

What does the man offer the woman?
(A) A discounted price
(B) A later appointment
(C) A business recommendation
(D) A training session

남자는 여자에게 무엇을 제안하는가?
(A) 할인된 가격
(B) 나중의 약속
(C) 사업 추천
(D) 교육 시간

분석_ 대화 마지막에서 여자의 원래 요구를 들어주지 못했다는 이
유로 남자는 여자에게 할인을 제공하고 있다.

Questions 38-40 refer to the following conversation.

M: **38** *Hi, Laurence. My senior manager on the technical support team just told me again about Mr. Steve's orientation next week.* I'm still leading the job training, right?
W: That's correct.
M: And all of my sessions meet in the morning...
W: Right. **39** *Here's the full schedule for the orientation. You need to check it out.*
M: Sure thing.
W: Great. There is one more thing. **40** *You can coordinate your job training with Ms. Lee's afternoon training session. It may be helpful to meet her briefly to get information about the training material.*
M: Thanks a lot. I'll do that today.

- -

M: 안녕, Laurence. 방금 기술 지원팀 상사가 나한테 다음 주에 있
을 Steve 씨의 오리엔테이션에 대해서 또 이야기했어. 여전히 내
가 실무 교육을 맡고 있는 거 맞지?
W: 맞아.
M: 그리고 모든 일정은 아침에 있고...
W: 그래, 여기 오리엔테이션에 대한 전체 일정이 있어, 너 그거 확인
할 필요가 있어.

M: 물론이야.
W: 좋아. 근데 한 가지 더 고려할 것이 있어. 너의 실무 교육이랑 Lee
씨의 오후 교육과정을 같이 준비해도 돼. 아마도 잠시 그녀를 만나
서 교육 자료에 대한 정보를 얻는 것이 도움이 될 거야.
M: 정말 고마워. 오늘 그렇게 해야겠다.

어휘_ senior manager 상급 관리자 technical support team 기술
지원팀 lead 이끌다 job training 직업훈련 helpful 도움이 되는
briefly 잠시 동안 material 재료, 자료

38. (C)

In what department does the man most likely work?
(A) Personnel
(B) Accounting
(C) Technical Support
(D) Product Development

남자는 아마도 무슨 부서에서 일하는가?
(A) 인사 부서
(B) 회계 부서
(C) 기술지원 부서
(D) 제품개발 부서

분석_ 남자가 어느 부서에서 일하는지 묻고 있다. 기술지원팀에 자
신의 상사가 있다고 언급하고 있다.

39. (C)

What does the woman give the man?
(A) A new employee directory
(B) A job application form
(C) A training schedule
(D) Survey findings

여자는 남자에게 무엇을 주는가?
(A) 새로운 직원 인명부
(B) 근무 지원 양식
(C) 훈련 일정
(D) 설문조사 결과

분석_ 일정에 대해 확신을 하지 못하는 남자에게 여자가 전체 일정
표를 건네주면서 확인을 권장하고 있다.

40. (B)

What does the woman suggest the man do?
(A) Book a conference room
(B) Go over plans with a colleague
(C) Delay a workshop
(D) Develop a software program

여자는 남자에게 무엇을 제안하는가?
(A) 회의장 예약하기
(B) 동료와 계획 검토하기
(C) 워크샵 연기하기
(D) 소프트웨어 프로그램 개발하기

분석_ 대화 마지막에 여자는 남자에게 동료와 함께 준비해서 도움
을 얻으라고 조언해주고 있다.

Questions 41-43 refer to the following conversation.

M: **41** *I'm calling to know about a new furniture for the waiting room of my law firm. I've found the four piece set from a copy of your spring catalog and I'm interested in purchasing it.*

W: **42** *Great! Have you had a chance to visit our website yet? We have an online tool that will enable you to upload your photo of your waiting room and to see what the furniture will look like in your office.*

M: Oh, I'll do that right away. **43** *But before I do, I'd like to make sure it'll fit in the room. I don't see any measurements listed for the furniture in your catalog.*

W: Oh, please check the page 28 in the back of the catalog. You can see all the dimensions of items.

M: 제 법률 사무소의 대기실에 사용할 새로운 가구에 대해 문의하려고 전화드렸습니다. 당신의 봄 책자에서 가구 4점 세트를 봤는데요. 그것에 관심이 있어요.

W: 좋습니다! 웹사이트에는 가보셨나요? 우리는 온라인상에서 당신이 대기실 사진을 업로드할 수 있고, 그 가구가 당신의 사무실에서 어떤 모습일지를 확인해볼 수 있는 기능을 가지고 있습니다.

M: 오, 지금 바로 해볼게요. 하지만 그 전에, 가구가 공간에 맞는지를 확인하고 싶어요. 카탈로그상에는 가구에 대한 어떤 치수도 명시되어 있지 않더라고요.

W: 오, 카탈로그 뒷면 28쪽을 확인해보세요. 제품들의 모든 치수를 볼 수 있을 거예요.

어휘_ furniture 가구 waiting room 대기실 law firm 법률회사 purchase 구매하다 tool 도구 enable A to do A가 ~하도록 만들다 measurement 치수 in the back of ~의 뒷면 dimension 치수

41. (B)

What is the man interested in purchasing?
(A) Computer program
(B) Office furniture
(C) Spring clothing collection
(D) Advertising space

남자가 구매하고 싶어 하는 것은 무엇인가?
(A) 컴퓨터 프로그램
(B) 사무가구
(C) 봄옷 컬렉션
(D) 광고 공간

분석_ 대화 초반에서 가구 때문에 전화를 걸었고 사무실의 대기실에서 사용할 것이라 언급하고 있다.

42. (C)

Why does the woman direct the man to a website?
(A) To read a review from customers
(B) To purchase a store credit card
(C) To try a new viewing feature
(D) To enter a serial number

여자는 남자에게 왜 웹사이트에 가보라고 말하는가?
(A) 고객들의 평가를 읽어보라고
(B) 매장 신용카드를 구매하라고
(C) 새로운 시각 자료를 둘러보라고
(D) 시리얼 번호를 입력하라고

분석_ 웹사이트에 가봤는지 물어본 후에 그곳에서 이용 가능한 기능을 언급하고 있다.

43. (D)

What additional information does the man ask for?
(A) Warranty terms
(B) A free delivery service
(C) Available sizes
(D) Product measurements

남자가 추가적으로 요구하는 정보는 무엇인가?
(A) 보증 기한
(B) 무료 배송 서비스
(C) 이용 가능한 크기
(D) 제품 치수

분석_ 대화 마지막에 남자는 가구가 사무실에 들어갈 수 있을지에 대한 것을 확인하고자 치수 정보에 대해서 언급하고 있다.

Questions 44-46 refer to the following conversation.

W: **44** *Brian, I'm having a problem using our restaurant's new coffee maker.* **45** *I noticed that the red light on the side of the machine came on after I poured ingredients into it.* Do you know what that means?

M: Oh, that light warns you that you need to put more ingredients into it. This new machine has a larger capacity and makes a bigger batch than the previous one.

W: I was just following the recipe for the old device that we used. **46** *Do you have a new recipe with an amount just for this machine? If you can get that for me, I'll finish making coffee right now.*

W: Brian, 우리 식당의 새 커피 기계를 사용하는 데 문제가 있어. 재료를 안에다 붓고 난 이후에 기계 옆면에 빨간색 불이 들어오는 걸 알게 됐어. 그게 무슨 의미인지 알고 있어?

M: 오, 그 불은 너가 더 많은 재료를 넣어야 한다는 의미야. 이 새로운 기계는 더 큰 공간을 가지고 있고 이전 기계보다 한 번에 더 많은 양을 만들어내.

W: 나는 그저 이전에 사용했던 장치에 대한 조리법을 따라 했거든. 이 기계에 대한 양이 표시된 새로운 조리법을 가지고 있어? 만약 네가 날 위해 그걸 얻을 수 있다면, 지금 바로 커피 제조를 끝낼게.

44. (A)

What are the speakers discussing?
(A) A piece of equipment
(B) A work list
(C) A power failure
(D) A customer review
화자들은 무엇에 대해 논의하고 있는가?
(A) 하나의 기계
(B) 작업 목록
(C) 정전
(D) 고객 평가
분석_ 대화 초반 여자가 기계를 사용하는 데 어려움이 있다고 언급하고 있다.

45. (D)

What has the woman noticed?
(A) An item was missing.
(B) An order was placed.
(C) A colleague is away.
(D) A warning light is on.
여자는 무엇을 알아차렸는가?
(A) 제품이 분실되었다.
(B) 주문이 이루어졌다.
(C) 동료가 멀리 있다.
(D) 경고등이 켜졌다.
분석_ 기계에 대한 어려움을 호소하면서 빨간색 불이 들어온 것을 알아차렸다고 언급했다.

46. (B)

What does the woman ask the man to do?
(A) Contact a factory manager
(B) Provide an up-to-date recipe
(C) Turn on a machine
(D) Prepare for a customer order
여자는 남자에게 무엇을 할 것을 요구하는가?
(A) 공장 관리자에게 연락하기
(B) 최신 조리법 제공하기
(C) 기계 작동시키기
(D) 고객 주문 준비하기
분석_ 새로운 기계에 맞는 조리법이 있는지를 물어보고 그것이 있다면 일을 끝내겠다고 언급하고 있다.

Questions 47-49 refer to the following conversation.

M: Hi, my name is Raymond Wang. *47 I'm calling about the advertisement I saw online for the job opening in your graphic design division.* Are you still accepting applications?
W: Yes, we are. There's been a lot of positions you may be interested in. *48 If applicants want to be considered for the positions, they have experience using several different kinds of design software.*
M: Well, I know how to use all the major design software programs. So, that's not a problem. I also worked as a freelance artist. So, I have a lot of experience of drawing and painting.
W: Then, you sound like a qualified candidate. Can you submit your resume right now? *49 The interviews are scheduled for next week.*

M: 안녕하세요, 저는 Raymond Wang입니다. 온라인에서 당신이 그래픽 디자인 부서에 공석이 있다는 광고를 보고 전화 드렸습니다. 여전히 지원을 받으시나요?
W: 네, 그렇습니다. 당신이 관심을 가질 만한 많은 직책이 있습니다. 만약 지원자가 그 자리에 뽑히고 싶다면, 몇몇 다른 종류의 소프트웨어를 사용한 경험이 있어야 합니다.
M: 아, 저는 모든 주요 디자인 소프트웨어 프로그램을 사용하는 방법을 알고 있습니다. 그래서 그것은 문제없습니다. 또한 저는 프리랜스 미술가로 일을 했습니다. 그래서 도면과 그림에 많은 경험을 갖고 있습니다.
W: 그렇다면 당신은 자격이 있는 후보자 같군요. 지금 바로 이력서를 제출해주실래요? 면접은 다음 주에 예정되어 있습니다.

47. (B)

What position is the man inquiring about?
(A) A magazine writer
(B) A graphic designer
(C) A sales clerk
(D) A computer programmer
남자가 문의하는 자리는 무엇인가?
(A) 잡지 기자
(B) 그래픽 디자이너
(C) 판매 사원
(D) 컴퓨터 프로그래머
분석_ 대화 초반 남자가 그래픽 디자인 부서의 일자리에 대한 광고를 보고 연락했다고 언급하고 있다.

48. (C)

What job qualification does the woman mention?

(A) Recommendation from past employers
(B) A portfolio of art samples
(C) Knowledge of special software
(D) A certificate from a design academy
여자는 어떤 근무 자격에 대해 언급하는가?
(A) 이전 고용주의 추천서
(B) 미술 샘플 포트폴리오
(C) 특정 소프트웨어에 대한 지식
(D) 디자인 학교의 자격증
분석_ 일자리에 뽑히고 싶다면 다양한 소프트웨어를 사용한 경험
이 있어야 한다고 언급하고 있다.

49. (A)

What does the woman say will happen next week?
(A) Excellent candidates will be interviewed.
(B) Computer programs will be upgraded.
(C) A new office branch will be open.
(D) A recruiting manager will lead an orientation session.
여자는 다음 주에 무슨 일이 있을 것이라고 말하는가?
(A) 훌륭한 후보자들이 면접을 볼 것이다.
(B) 컴퓨터 프로그램이 업그레이드될 것이다.
(C) 새로운 지점이 오픈될 것이다.
(D) 고용 관리자가 오리엔테이션을 이끌 것이다.
분석_ 대화 마지막에 다음 주 면접이 있으니 당장 이력서를 제출
해달라고 언급하고 있다.

Questions 50-52 refer to the following conversation.

W: David, I'm looking for a new fitness center for jogging. **50** *I really like the one I currently go to, but I heard yesterday that it's closing down in March.*
M: Why don't you join mine? The monthly fee is affordable and the gym is equipped with some new exercise machines. **51** *Actually, I go there to run, too. I usually go there first in the morning because the track is almost empty then.*
W: Oh, that sounds good. I prefer going to the gym when it's less crowded too. Can I try out the equipment before applying for membership?
M: Yes, it offers one-day trials. **52** *And now it has promotion for new members. When you sign up, mention my name, and you'll get a discount on the first month.*

W: David, 나 조깅하려고 새로운 헬스장을 찾고 있어. 지금 다니는 곳도 정말 좋아, 하지만 어제 듣기로는 3월에 문을 닫는대.
M: 내가 다니는 곳에 다니지 그래? 월회비도 저렴하고 몇몇 최신 운동기구들도 갖추어져 있어. 사실 나도 달리기하러 가거든. 나는 보통 아침에 먼저 가. 왜냐하면 그때 트랙이 거의 비어 있거든.
W: 오, 좋아. 나 역시 덜 붐빌 때 운동하러 가는 걸 선호해. 회원으로 등록하기 전에 장비들을 한번 이용해볼 수 있을까?

M: 그래, 그곳은 하루는 시험 삼아 이용하게 해줘. 그리고 지금 신입 회원들에게 프로모션을 진행 중이야. 등록할 때 내 이름을 말해, 그러면 첫 달에 할인을 받을 거야.

어휘_ look for ~를 찾다 jogging 조깅 close down 폐쇄하다 affordable 합리적인, 저렴한 be equipped with ~를 갖춘 exercise machine 운동기구 empty 비어있는 prefer ~를 선호하다 crowded 붐비는 apply for ~에 지원하다, 등록하다 trial 시도, 시험(판) promotion 판촉상품 mention 언급하다

50. (C)

What problem does the woman mention?
(A) She has many assignments.
(B) A fee is too high.
(C) A fitness center is closing.
(D) A building is under renovation.
여자가 언급하는 문제점은 무엇인가?
(A) 여자는 할 일이 많다.
(B) 요금이 너무 높다
(C) 피트니스 센터가 문을 닫는다.
(D) 건물이 개조공사 중이다.
분석_ 대화 초반 지금 다니는 곳을 좋아하지만 3월에 문을 닫는다
는 이야기를 하고 있다.

51. (D)

What does the man say about the running track?
(A) It will not be open this month.
(B) It has running instructors available.
(C) It was recently renovated.
(D) It is not used a lot in the morning.
남자는 러닝트랙에 대해 무엇이라고 말하는가?
(A) 이번 달에 개장되지 않을 것이다.
(B) 달리기 강사가 있다.
(C) 최근에 개조되었다.
(D) 아침에 많이 사용되지 않는다.
분석_ 대화 중간 남자 역시 달리기를 위해서 헬스장에 다닌다고 언
급하면서 아침시간대에 주로 비어 있다고 이야기하고 있다.

52. (B)

How can a woman obtain a discount?
(A) By showing a proof of employment
(B) By providing a friend's name
(C) By using a facility on weekends only
(D) By paying in cash
여자는 어떻게 할인을 얻어낼 수 있는가?
(A) 고용의 증거를 보여줌으로써
(B) 친구의 이름을 제공함으로써
(C) 주말에만 시설을 이용함으로써
(D) 현금으로 결제함으로써
분석_ 대화 마지막에 남자가 지금 헬스장이 신입회원에 대해 프로
모션 중이며 자기의 이름을 말하면 할인받을 수 있을 것이
라 언급하고 있다.

Questions 53-55 refer to the following conversation.

W: Hi, I saw on a television commercial that your shop gives guitar lessons, and I'd like to sign up.

M: Great. Do you have any previous experience playing the guitar?

W: 53 *Well, I played a little in my university band.*

M: I think you'll probably fit into our intermediate class, then. Those classes start next week.

W: Excellent.

M: 54 *And there are instructional videos on our website.* 55 *You can watch them if you sign up for our monthly e-mails. Would you like to join?*

W: 55 *Oh, that would be helpful.* My e-mail address is tony25@hatmail.net.

M: All right, you're signed up, and the first lesson will be next Thursday at 6 P.M. See you then!

W: 안녕하세요, 텔레비전 광고에서 당신의 가게가 기타 수업을 진행한다는 걸 봤는데요, 등록하고 싶어요.

M: 좋습니다. 예전에 기타를 쳐보신 경험이 있으세요?

W: 음. 대학교 밴드에서 조금 쳤었어요.

M: 그렇다면 제 생각에 당신은 중급반에 맞을 것 같아요. 그 수업은 다음 주에 시작합니다.

W: 좋아요.

M: 그리고 웹사이트에 교육용 비디오가 있습니다. 우리의 월간 이메일 서비스에 등록하시면 그것을 보실 수 있습니다. 등록하시겠어요?

W: 오, 그게 도움이 될 것 같아요. 제 이메일 주소는 tony25@hatmail.net입니다.

M: 좋습니다, 당신은 등록되었어요, 그리고 첫 수업은 다음 주 목요일 오후 6시입니다. 그때 봐요!

어휘_ television commercial 텔레비전 광고 guitar lesson 기타 수업 sign up 등록하다 intermediate 중급의 instructional video 교육용 비디오

53. (C)

What does the woman say she did in university?
(A) She led a band.
(B) She created a web page.
(C) She played in a musical group.
(D) She taught guitar.

여자는 대학시절 무엇을 했다고 말하는가?
(A) 여자는 밴드를 이끌었다.
(B) 여자는 웹 페이지를 만들었다.
(C) 여자는 음악 그룹에서 연주했다.
(D) 여자는 기타를 가르쳤다.

분석_ 기타를 쳐본 경험이 있느냐는 물음에 대학시절 해본 적이 있다고 언급하고 있다.

54. (B)

What is available on the store website?
(A) Complimentary instruments
(B) Instruction videos
(C) Comments from musicians
(D) A list of local festivals

가게 웹사이트에서 무엇이 이용 가능한가?
(A) 무료 악기
(B) 교육 비디오
(C) 음악가들로부터 조언
(D) 지역 축제 목록

분석_ 대화 중반 웹사이트에 교육 비디오가 있으며 이메일 서비스에 등록하면 이용할 수 있다고 언급하고 있다.

55. (D)

What does the woman imply when she says, "Oh, that would be helpful"?
(A) An e-mail address is not needed.
(B) A lesson seems competitively prices.
(C) An instrument was already tuned.
(D) She can join a mailing list.

여자가 "오, 그게 도움이 될 것 같아요"라고 말한 것이 암사하는 것은 무엇인가?
(A) 이메일 주소가 필요하지 않다.
(B) 수업료가 적절하다.
(C) 악기가 이미 조율되어 있다.
(D) 여자가 정기 메일 서비스에 가입할 수 있다.

분석_ 이메일 서비스에 등록하면 교육용 비디오를 이용할 수 있다는 이야기에 이메일 주소를 알려준 것으로 보아 흔쾌히 서비스에 가입할 의사를 보인 것으로 유추 가능하다.

Questions 56-58 refer to the following conversation.

M: 56 *Hi Lisa, can we talk about the budget presentation you're giving at next week's executive meeting? How's the preparation going?* Has the accounting department sent their expense report to you?

W: 57 *Yes, they did. But there are some calculation errors in the report. It's taking longer than I expected to check the figures and make corrections.*

M: Oh, I'm sorry to hear that. Well, the meeting is on Tuesday. 58 *I think we need someone to help finish the presentation on time. I'll assign colleagues to assist you.*

W: Thank you. I'm sure this will go quickly if there is someone to help me.

M: 안녕하세요 Lisa, 다음 주 임원 회의에서 당신이 진행할 예산 발표에 대해서 이야기할 수 있을까요? 준비 어떻게 진행 중이에요? 회계부서가 당신에게 비용 보고서를 보냈나요?

W: 네, 그랬어요. 하지만 보고서에 몇 가지 계산 오류가 있어요. 그 수치들을 확인하고 수정하는 데에 제 예상보다 더 오래 걸릴 것 같아요.

M: 오, 그렇다니 유감이에요. 음, 회의는 목요일이죠. 내 생각에 발표 준비를 제때에 끝내는 걸 도와줄 누군가가 필요할 것 같아요. 제가 동료들한테 당신을 도와주라고 할게요.

W: 고마워요. 만약 누가 저를 도와준다면 준비가 더 빨리 진행될 거라 확신해요.

어휘_ talk about ~에 대해 이야기하다 budget presentation 예산 발표 executive meeting 임원회의 preparation 준비 accounting department 회계부서 expense report 비용 보고서 calculation 계산 figure 수치 make a correction 수정하다 finish ~를 끝내다 assign 할당하다

56. (B)

What is the woman preparing to do?
(A) Visit a customer
(B) Give a presentation
(C) Hire a new department manager
(D) Correct a pricing policy

여자가 준비하고 있는 것은 무엇인가?
(A) 고객 방문하기
(B) 발표하기
(C) 새로운 부서장 고용하기
(D) 가격 정책 수정하기

분석_ 대화 초반 남자가 여자에게 발표 준비 상태에 대해 묻고 있다는 점에서 정답을 유추할 수 있다.

57. (D)

Why is the woman's work taking extra time to finish?
(A) Some resumes have not been sent.
(B) A computer is outdated.
(C) A colleague is away on holiday.
(D) Some data are incorrect.

여자의 업무가 마치는 데 추가 시간이 필요한 이유는 무엇인가?
(A) 몇몇 이력서가 보내지지 않았다.
(B) 컴퓨터가 구식이다.
(C) 동료가 휴가를 떠났다.
(D) 몇몇 정보가 잘못되었다.

분석_ 여자가 일을 끝내는 데에 시간을 더 가져야 하는 이유를 묻고 있다. 여자의 예상보다 시간이 더 걸릴 것 같다는 이야기를 하기 전 계산상의 오류가 있다는 언급을 먼저 하고 있다.

58. (C)

What does the man say he will do?
(A) Schedule a meeting
(B) Prepare a job description
(C) Add another person to a project
(D) Contact department head

남자는 무엇을 하겠다고 말하는가?
(A) 회의 일정 잡기
(B) 직무 설명서 준비하기
(C) 프로젝트에 다른 사람 추가하기
(D) 부서장에게 연락하기

분석_ 발표 준비를 제때에 끝내기 위해 누군가가 필요하다는 이야기를 하면서 동료에게 도와주라고 시키겠다는 언급을 하고 있다.

Questions 59-61 refer to the following conversation with three speakers.

W: Good evening. 59 *Welcome to the Fairfield Inn and Suites.*

M1: Hi, good evening. 59 *I'd like to make a reservation.* Do you have any vacancies?

W: Let me see what I can do for you. Oh, you are in luck. We do have two rooms available. How long will you be staying?

M1: For two nights, please.

M2: Wait a second, Jack. The conference lasts for 4 days. We should stay here for three nights.

M1: Really? 60 *I don't buy it. No one told me about that.*

M2: 61 *There was a last-minute change of dates late last night.*

W: Okay, your reservation has been made for 3 nights for a room. Enjoy your stay.

W: 안녕하세요. Fairfield Inn and Suites에 오신 걸 환영합니다.

M1: 안녕하세요. 예약을 하고 싶어서요. 빈방 있나요?

W: 한번 확인해보겠습니다. 오, 운이 좋으시네요. 이용 가능한 방 2개가 있습니다. 얼마나 오래 머무실 건가요?

M1: 2박입니다.

M2: Jack, 잠깐만. 회의는 4일간 지속돼. 우리는 이곳에서 3일 밤을 머물러야 해.

M1: 정말? 못 믿겠어. 어느 누구도 나에게 그런 말을 한 적이 없어.

M2: 지난밤 늦게 갑작스레 날짜 변경이 있었어.

W: 그럼, 방 하나에 3일 밤 예약해드릴게요. 지내는 동안 즐겁게 보내세요.

어휘_ vacancy 빈방 be in luck 운이 좋다 last 지속되다 last-minute change 갑작스러운 변동

59. (D)

Where does the woman most likely work?
(A) At a restaurant
(B) At a ticket office
(C) At a bank
(D) At a hotel

여자는 아마도 어디서 근무하는가?
(A) 식당
(B) 매표소
(C) 은행
(D) 호텔

분석_ 대화 앞 부분에 남자가 "예약을 하고 싶다. 빈방이 있냐"고 물었기 때문에 여자는 빈방이 있는 호텔에서 근무한다고 유추할 수 있다.

60. (C)

Why does Jack say, "I don't buy it"?
(A) He has no intention to purchase the product.
(B) He is not excited about the conference.
(C) He didn't hear about the reschedule.
(D) He feels disappointed.
Jack은 왜 "못 믿겠어"라고 말하는가?
(A) 그는 제품을 구매할 의도가 없다.
(B) 그는 회의가 신나지 않는다.
(C) 그는 일정 변경에 관해 들은 바가 없다.
(D) 그는 실망했다.
분석_ M2가 지난밤 갑작스레 일정이 바뀌었다고 했고 M1인 Jack
은 이러한 일정 변경을 들은 적이 없으므로 믿을 수 없다고
말했을 거라 유추할 수 있다.

61. (A)

What do the men imply about the conference?
(A) It changes dates on short notice.
(B) It is held every year.
(C) It is exclusively for overseas buyers.
(D) There is no fee to participate in the conference.
남자들은 회의에 관해서 뭐라고 암시하는가?
(A) 갑작스레 일정이 변경되었다.
(B) 매년 개최된다.
(C) 회의는 해외 구매자들만을 위한 것이다.
(D) 회의 참석비가 없다.
분석_ 60번과 동일선상의 문제로 갑작스레 일정이 바뀌었다 언급
되었으므로 paraphrase된 (A)가 가장 적절하다.

Questions 62-64 refer to the following conversation
with three speakers.

> M1: 62 *Have you two heard about the office expansion upstairs which is scheduled to be done next week?* It looks nice!
> W: I know! 63 *It's so amazing! And we could see the entire city there.*
> M2: I am wondering which department will move up there after the construction is finished.
> W: My supervisor told me that it's the research department.
> M1: Ah, because they have the most people.
> W: Probably. I'd love to work in an office on that floor, though.
> M2: 64 *Yeah. Well, the company must have enough budget. And I think that is how they add that space!*
> M1: 64 *I think you're right, there!*

M1: 두 분 다음 주에 완성인 위층 사무실 확장에 대해서 들으셨어요? 정말 멋져요!
W: 알고 있어요. 정말 놀라워요! 그리고 거기서 도시 전체를 볼 수도 있어요.
M2: 공사가 끝나고 나면 어떤 부서가 거기로 옮길지 궁금해요.
W: 제 상사가 말하길 연구부서래요.
M1: 아, 그 부서가 직원이 가장 많아서군요.
W: 아마도요. 어쨌든 저도 그 층에 있는 사무실에서 일하면 좋겠어요.
M2: 네. 음, 회사가 예산이 충분한 게 틀림없어요. 그러니까 그런 공간을 추가했겠죠.
M1: 당신 말이 맞는 것 같아요!
어휘_ office expansion 사무실 확장 upstairs 위층 be scheduled to do ~가 예정되어 있다 entire 전체의 construction 공사 finish 끝내다 research department 연구부서 budget 예산

62. (A)

What is the conversation mainly about?
(A) Enlarging office space
(B) Moving into an international market
(C) Increasing staff numbers
(D) Changing company leadership
대화는 주로 무엇에 관한 것인가?
(A) 사무 공간 확장하기
(B) 국제 시장으로 진입하기
(C) 직원 수 늘리기
(D) 회사 지도층 바꾸기
분석_ 대화 주제를 묻고 있다. 대화 초반 위층 확장 공사에 대해 들
었는지를 언급하고 있다.

63. (D)

Why does the woman say, "It's so amazing"?
(A) She doesn't agree.
(B) She needs an explanation.
(C) She feels bored.
(D) She is happily surprised.
여자는 왜 "정말 놀라워요"라고 말하는가?
(A) 여자가 동의하지 않는다.
(B) 여자가 설명을 필요로 한다.
(C) 여자가 지루해한다.
(D) 여자가 기분 좋게 놀랐다.
분석_ 확장공사로 인해 도시 전체를 볼 수 있다는 이야기를 하고
있으므로 기뻐하고 있음을 알 수 있다.

64. (C)

What do the men imply about the company?
(A) It was recently renovated.
(B) It is planning to increase benefits.
(C) It is in a good financial condition.
(D) It has branches overseas.

남자들은 회사에 대해 무엇을 암시하는가?

(A) 회사는 최근에 개조되었다.

(B) 회사는 복지혜택을 늘릴 계획이다.

(C) 회사의 재정상태가 좋다.

(D) 회사는 해외에 지점들을 가지고 있다.

분석_ 한 남자가 예산이 충분하기에 사무실 공간을 추가했다는 이 야기를 하고 있고 다른 한 남자가 맞장구를 치고 있으므로 정답을 유추할 수 있다.

Questions 65-67 refer to the following conversation and list.

W: **65** *Mark, we have a new language instructor beginning on March and we should set her up with a desk and a chair. Can you place orders for those?*

M: Sure. **66** *You know our supplier has raised prices for their items, right?*

W: I didn't know that.

M: **66** *I just looked at the catalog on the website, and their current models are more expensive.*

W: **67** *Right. Well, our budget per work area shouldn't be over $ 500. So let's order the supplies that don't exceed budget.*

M: OK. I'll take a look at the prices again and place the order.

Desk and Chair Set	Price
Model A	$ 795
Model B	$ 695
Model C	$ 595
Model D	$ 495

W: Mark, 3월부터 우리 새로운 언어 강사를 모셔오는데 그녀를 위해 책상과 의자를 세팅해야 해요. 주문해줄 수 있어요?

M: 물론이죠. 우리 공급업체가 제품 가격 올린 거 알고 계시죠?

W: 몰랐어요.

M: 제가 방금 웹사이트에서 카탈로그를 봤는데요. 현재 모델들이 더 비싸네요.

W: 그래요. 음, 근무장소당 우리 예산이 500달러를 넘으면 안 돼요. 그러니 예산을 초과하지 않는 물건을 주문합시다.

M: 알겠어요. 가격을 다시 보고 주문을 할게요.

책걸상 세트	가격
모델 A	795달러
모델 B	695달러
모델 C	595달러
모델 D	495달러

어휘_ language instructor 언어 강사 set 세팅해주다 place an order 주문하다 supplier 공급자(업체) raise 올리다 current 현재의 expensive 비싼 exceed ~를 초과하다

65. (A)

What does the woman ask the man to do?

(A) Order some supplies

(B) Find a new supplier

(C) Repair a desk

(D) Contact a job applicant

여자는 남자에게 무엇을 요구하는가?

(A) 공급품 주문하기

(B) 새로운 공급업체 찾기

(C) 책상 수리하기

(D) 일자리 지원자에게 연락하기

분석_ 대화 초반 새로운 강사가 오기 때문에 책상과 의자를 주문해달라고 요청하고 있다.

66. (B)

What problem does the man mention?

(A) An instructor will leave the company.

(B) Prices for supplies have increased.

(C) Some desk models have been discontinued.

(D) A division budget has been decreased.

남자가 언급하는 문제점은 무엇인가?

(A) 강사가 회사를 떠날 것이다.

(B) 공급품의 가격이 올랐다.

(C) 어떤 책상 모델이 단종되었다.

(D) 부서 예산이 감소되었다.

분석_ 기존 공급업체가 가격을 올렸으며 현재 모델들이 더 비싸다고 언급하고 있다.

67. (D)

Look at the graphic. What model will the man order?

(A) Model A

(B) Model B

(C) Model C

(D) Model D

그래픽을 보자. 남자는 어떤 모델을 주문할 것인가?

(A) 모델 A

(B) 모델 B

(C) 모델 C

(D) 모델 D

분석_ 여자가 예산이 500달러라는 이야기를 하며 그 예산을 넘기지 말아야 한다고 했으므로 남자는 500달러 이하의 물건을 주문할 것임을 알 수 있다.

Questions 68-70 refer to the following conversation and schedule.

M: **68** *Hi, Serina. I was testing a new webchat system here in my office,* and browsed around our online staff forum, and...

W: Ah, what does it look like?

M: It looks great. And I notice that many employees are interested in our upcoming workshops. Do we have to set more space? We could rent a conference room on 5th floor, or...

W: 69 *We'll be OK. I'm going to make a digital video of all presentations, and post it on our staff forum.*

M: That's a good idea.

W: 70 *Oh, and we've made a change. We've switched the times for the second and third workshops. So the day's second workshop will be Market Share.* We made that switch because Mr. Kim, the presenter, has to leave before noon.

Schedule	
Workshop	Time
Sales Figures	9:30-10:30 A.M.
70 Team Project	10:40-11:40 A.M.
LUNCH	11:40 A.M.-12:40 P.M.
Market Share	12:40-1:40 P.M.
Q&A Session	1:40-2:40 P.M.

M: 안녕 Serina. 나 방금 여기 사무실에서 새로운 웹 대화 시스템을 테스트하고 온라인 직원 회의실을 둘러보고 그리고...

W: 아, 어때 보여?

M: 좋아 보여. 그리고 많은 직원들이 우리의 다가오는 워크샵에 관심이 있다는 것도 알게 됐어. 우리 더 많은 공간을 준비해야 할까? 5층에 있는 회의장도 빌릴 수 있고 혹은...

W: 우리 괜찮을 거야. 나는 모든 발표에 대한 디지털 비디오를 만들 거야, 그리고 그걸 온라인 직원 회의실에 게시할 거야.

M: 좋은 생각이야.

W: 오, 그리고 우리 변경사항이 있어. 두 번째와 세 번째 워크샵의 시간을 서로 바꿀 거야. 그래서 그날 두 번째 워크샵이 시장 점유율에 대한 것이 될 거야. 발표자인 Kim 씨가 정오 전에 떠나야 한다고 해서 그렇게 바꿨어.

일정표	
워크샵	시간
판매 수치	오전 9:30-10:30
팀 프로젝트	오전 10:40-11:40
점심식사	오전 11:40-오후 12:40
시장 점유율	오후 12:40-1:40
질의응답	오후 1:40-2:40

68. (B)

Where most likely is the conversation taking place?
(A) At a department store
(B) At a company office
(C) At a fitness center
(D) At a public library

대화는 아마도 어디에서 이루어지는가?
(A) 백화점
(B) 회사 사무실
(C) 헬스장
(D) 공공 도서관

분석_ 대화 장소를 묻는 문제이다. 대화 초반 남자가 회사 사무실에서 테스트를 하고 웹을 둘러봤다고 언급하고 있다.

69. (C)

What does the woman plan to do?
(A) Give a presentation
(B) Rent a larger meeting room
(C) Post a video on the website
(D) Look over a sales proposal

여자는 무엇을 할 것이라 계획하는가?
(A) 발표하기
(B) 더 큰 회의장 빌리기
(C) 웹사이트에 비디오 게시하기
(D) 판매 제안서 검토하기

분석_ 대화 중반 발표에 대한 비디오를 제작해서 온라인 직원 회의실에 게시하겠다고 언급하고 있다.

70. (B)

Look at the graphic. According to the speaker, which workshop will now be held third?
(A) Sales Figures
(B) Team Project
(C) Market Share
(D) Q&A Session

그래픽을 보자. 화자에 따르면 어떤 워크샵이 세 번째로 개최될 것인가?
(A) 판매 수치
(B) 팀 프로젝트
(C) 시장 점유율
(D) 질의응답

분석_ 마지막 대화에서 여자가 2번째와 3번째 워크샵의 일정을 바꾸었다고 언급하고 있으므로 원래 일정상에 두 번째 워크샵인 팀 프로젝트가 세 번째로 변경되었음을 유추할 수 있다.

Part 4 본문 p.67

Questions 71-73 refer to the following telephone message.

71 *Hello, this is Maria Hill, and I am calling at 1 o'clock on Friday afternoon. I live in apartment 2C in the San Antonio complex.* 72 *With the heavy rain we had last night, a lot of water came in around the living room window.* As you already know, this is just the beginning of the rainy season. 72 *I'd like you to fix this problem*

today. 73 Please get back to me as soon as possible and let me know when you can come. Thanks very much.

안녕하세요, 저는 Maria Hill입니다, 금요일 오후 1시에 연락드립니다. 저는 샌안토니오 아파트 단지 2C동에서 살고 있습니다. 지난밤 폭우로 인해서, 거실 창문으로 많은 물이 들어왔습니다. 아시다시피, 지금은 우기가 시작되는 시점입니다. 저는 당신이 오늘 이 문제를 해결해주셨으면 합니다. 가능한 한 빨리 회신해주세요. 그리고 언제 오실 수 있는지 알려주세요. 감사합니다.

어휘_ live in ~에 살다, 거주하다 complex 복합단지 heavy rain 폭우 living room 거실 rainy season 우기 fix 수리하다 problem 문제

71. (C)
Who most likely is the speaker?
(A) A house cleaner
(B) A patient
(C) A tenant
(D) A carpenter
화자는 아마도 누구일 것인가?
(A) 청소부
(B) 환자
(C) 세입자
(D) 목수
분석_ 처음 부분에서 화자는 자기소개를 하며 아파트 거주자임을 언급하고 있다.

72. (B)
What is the purpose of the call?
(A) To give an advice
(B) To report a problem
(C) To reschedule an appointment
(D) To settle a bill
전화의 목적은 무엇인가?
(A) 조언하기 위해
(B) 문제를 보고하기 위해
(C) 약속 일정을 조정하기 위해
(D) 정산하기 위해
분석_ 비가 많이 와서 물이 새어 들어왔다는 문제점을 제시하면서 수리를 부탁하고 있다.

73. (D)
What does the caller request?
(A) A reference letter
(B) A heavy discount
(C) A product catalogue
(D) A return call
전화를 건 사람은 무엇을 요청하는가?
(A) 추천서
(B) 대폭 할인
(C) 제품 카탈로그
(D) 회신
분석_ 마지막 부분에서 가능한 한 빨리 회신하여 언제 올지를 알려달라고 언급하고 있다.

Questions 74-76 refer to the following advertisement.

74 Now, you can subscribe to International Geographic Magazine for only 20 dollars for a year. When you buy our spectacular magazine, each month you'll receive news of the latest nature discoveries from around the world and must be inspired by them. *75 And for a limited time only, when you subscribe to International Geographic Magazine, you'll receive three complimentary coupons to the best-known local restaurant.* You will be able to have some spectacular Italian cuisine. *76 So, go to our website and type in the number 0325 to take advantage of this limited time offer.*

지금, 당신은 단돈 20달러에 International Geographic Magazine을 1년 동안 구독하실 수 있습니다. 당신이 우리의 볼거리 가득한 잡지를 구매하면, 매달 당신은 전 세계로부터의 최신 자연 발견물에 대한 소식을 받을 것이고 그것들에 의해 영감을 얻을 것입니다. 그리고 오직 한정된 시간 동안, 당신이 International Geographic Magazine를 구독한다면, 지역 유명 음식점에 대한 무료쿠폰 3장을 받을 것입니다. 당신은 몇 가지 훌륭한 이탈리아 음식을 드실 수 있습니다. 그러므로 웹사이트에 가서 0325를 입력하고 이 한정된 기회를 잡으세요.

어휘_ subscribe to ~를 구독하다 spectacular 구경거리가 많은 latest 최신의 nature 자연의 discovery 발견 inspire 영감을 주다 limited 제한된 receive ~를 받다 complimentary 무료의 take advantage of ~의 이점을 활용하다

74. (D)
What is being advertised?
(A) A musical
(B) A Italian restaurant
(C) A computer store
(D) A monthly publication
광고되고 있는 것은 무엇인가?
(A) 뮤지컬
(B) 이탈리아 음식점
(C) 컴퓨터 매장
(D) 월간 발행물
분석_ 처음 부분에서 잡지 구독에 대한 이야기를 하고 있으며 구독을 할 경우 매달 최신 정보를 받아볼 수 있다고 언급하고 있다.

75. (A)
What will a new customer receive for a limited time?
(A) Free vouchers for the restaurant
(B) Invitations to the workshop
(C) Entry tickets to a museum

(D) Souvenir mugs
신규 고객은 제한된 시간 동안 무엇을 받을 것인가?
(A) 무료 음식점 쿠폰
(B) 워크샵 초대장
(C) 박물관 입장권
(D) 기념품 컵
분석_ 제한된 시간 동안 신규 고객이 받을 수 있는 것이 무엇인지 묻고 있다. 광고 중간 부분에서 제한된 시간 동안 구독할 경우 유명 식당에 대한 무료 쿠폰을 3장 받을 수 있다고 언급하고 있다.

76. (A)

What are the listeners asked to do on the website?
(A) Use a promotional code
(B) Look at some pictures
(C) Enter a contest
(D) Join a mailing list
청자들은 웹사이트에서 무엇을 하도록 요구받는가?
(A) 홍보용 코드 이용하기
(B) 사진 보기
(C) 대회 참석하기
(D) 메일 서비스 가입하기
분석_ 광고 마지막에 웹사이트에 가서 특정 번호를 입력하고 시간이 한정된 혜택을 잡으라고 언급하고 있다.

Questions 77-79 refer to the following talk.

Hello, thank you all for attending this luncheon. **77 *We're honoring the recent graduate of the K&J Accountant Training program.*** It takes several years of persistent hard work for apprentices to complete this program and become national certified accountants. So this accomplishment must be celebrated. I'm sure that many of the friends and family who've come here are curious about what kind of training the apprentices do in the program. So, before we eat, **78 *I'll show a video about a typical day of our apprentices.* 79 *And after luncheon, you can join us for dancing in the ballroom.***

- -

안녕하세요, 오찬에 참석해주셔서 감사합니다. 우리는 최근의 K&J 회계사 훈련 프로그램의 수료자들에 경의를 표합니다. 교육생들은 이 프로그램을 수료하고 국가 공인회계사가 되기까지 수년간 꾸준히 노력해왔습니다. 그래서 이 성과는 축하를 받아야 합니다. 저는 여기 오신 많은 친구들과 가족들이 프로그램에서 교육생이 어떤 종류의 훈련을 받았는지 알고 싶어 하리라 생각합니다. 그래서 우리가 식사를 하기 전, 우리 교육생들의 일상에 대한 비디오를 보여드리겠습니다. 그리고 오찬이 끝난 후, 여러분은 무도장에서 무도에 참여하실 수 있습니다.
어휘_ attending 참석하다 luncheon 오찬 honor ~를 기념하다 graduate 졸업생, 수료자 persistent 꾸준한 hard work 근면 apprentice 견습생 complete 끝내다 certified 공인된 accountant 회계사 accomplishment 업적 celebrate 기념하다 curious 궁금해 하는 ballroom 무도장

77. (A)

What is the purpose of the event?
(A) To honor new graduates
(B) To purchase a building
(C) To celebrate a manager's retirement
(D) To raise funds for charity activities
행사의 목적은 무엇인가?
(A) 새로운 수료자들에게 경의 표하기
(B) 건물 구매하기
(C) 관리자의 은퇴 기념하기
(D) 자선 행사를 위해 모금하기
분석_ 이야기 초반 특정 프로그램의 수료자들에게 경의를 표한다고 언급하고 있다.

78. (D)

What does the video depict?
(A) A new manager
(B) The company's history
(C) The town's landmarks
(D) A training session
비디오는 무엇을 묘사하는가?
(A) 새로운 관리자
(B) 회사의 역사
(C) 도시의 특별한 건물
(D) 교육 과정
분석_ 이야기 마지막 부분에서 프로그램 내 교육생들의 일상을 담은 비디오를 보여주겠다고 언급하고 있다.

79. (B)

What will take place after the meal?
(A) A museum tour
(B) A dance party
(C) A graduate's speech
(D) A group discussion
식사 후에 무슨 일이 일어날 것인가?
(A) 박물관 투어
(B) 댄스 파티
(C) 수료자의 연설
(D) 단체 토론
분석_ 이야기 마지막에 식사 후 무도장에서 춤을 춘다고 언급하고 있다.

Questions 80-82 refer to the following excerpt from a workshop.

OK, everyone. Let's continue with the workshop. **80 *I think the discussion on business presentations went well so far.*** Another important point to consider is that some people speak faster or slower than others. **81 *I recommend that you practice your speech several times before you present. I advise presenters to monitor their speed.* 82 *And now, I'm going to play*** *some videos showing how the speed of a presenter speech impacts communication.*

좋습니다, 여러분. 워크숍을 계속 이어가겠습니다. 제 생각에 사업 발표에 대한 토론이 지금까지 잘 진행된 것 같습니다. 고민해봐야 할 또 다른 중요한 부분은 어떤 사람들은 다른 사람들보다 빠르거나 느리게 말을 한다는 것입니다. 저는 당신이 발표하기 전 몇 번 정도 연설을 연습하는 것을 권장합니다. 저는 발표자에게 자신들의 속도를 관찰할 것을 충고합니다. 그리고 지금, 저는 몇 가지 비디오를 보여드리겠습니다. 그 비디오에는 발표자의 연설 속도가 소통에 어떻게 영향을 미치는지가 담겨 있습니다.

어휘_ continue ~를 계속하다 discussion 토론 presentation 발표 go well ~가 잘 진행되다 important 중요한 consider ~를 고려하다 presenter 발표자 recommend ~를 추천하다 practice 연습하다 speech 연설 advise 조언하다 monitor ~를 관찰하다 impact ~에 영향을 미치다

80. (B)

What is the subject of the workshop?
(A) Safety procedure
(B) Business presentations
(C) Marketing strategies
(D) Career changes

워크숍의 주제는 무엇인가?
(A) 안전 절차
(B) 사업 발표
(C) 마케팅 전략
(D) 직업 변경

분석_ 이야기 초반부에서 지금까지는 비즈니스 발표가 잘 진행되고 있다고 언급하고 있다.

81. (D)

What does the speaker recommend?
(A) Getting along with other professionals
(B) Achieving goals by deadlines
(C) Looking for business trends online
(D) Practicing reading before presentation

화자는 무엇을 추천하는가?
(A) 다른 전문과들과 어울려 지내기
(B) 마감일까지 목표 달성하기
(C) 온라인상으로 사업 경향 찾아보기
(D) 발표 전에 읽기 연습하기

분석_ 이야기 중반에서 고려해볼 점에 대해 말을 하며 발표자의 연설 속도를 말하고 있다. 그러면서 동시에 발표 전 몇 번가량 연습해볼 것은 권장하고 있다.

82. (C)

What will listeners probably do next?
(A) Have a meal
(B) Work in small teams
(C) Watch videos
(D) Provide reviews

청자들은 다음에 아마도 무엇을 할 것인가?
(A) 식사하기
(B) 소규모 팀으로 일하기
(C) 비디오 시청하기
(D) 후기 제공하기

분석_ 이야기 마지막에 화자가 비디오를 보여주겠다고 언급하고 있으므로 청자들은 비디오를 보게 될 것임을 알 수 있다.

Questions 83-85 refer to the following announcement.

Attention Medical Care Center employees. Starting next month we're installing new digital locks on all doors in the building. Every employee will need to get a new digital key when entering the building. **83** *You're required to bring your ID card to the security office,* and the guard will have a new key ready for you. **84** *The new keys will be linked exclusively to your employee ID, so we will be able to check out anyone who enters and leaves the building 24 hours a day.* **85** *There's more information available about the upcoming security changes in the company magazine, so make sure to pick it up.* After reviewing it, if you have any questions, talk to your supervisor. Thanks.

의료 센터 직원들은 들어주세요. 다음 달부터 우리는 건물 내의 모든 문에 새로운 디지털 잠금 장치를 설치합니다. 모든 직원들은 건물에 들어갈 때 새로운 디지털 열쇠를 가지고 있어야 합니다. 여러분은 신분증을 보안 사무실로 가져오십시오. 보안 직원이 여러분을 위해 새로운 열쇠를 준비해둘 것입니다. 새로운 열쇠는 오직 당신의 ID에만 연동되어 있으므로 우리는 하루 24시간 누가 건물에 들어가고 나가는지를 확인할 수 있을 것입니다. 회사 잡지에 다가올 보안 변경사항에 대해 많은 정보가 있습니다, 그러므로 챙겨 가시기 바랍니다. 그걸 본 이후, 질문이 있으시면 상사에게 이야기하시면 됩니다. 감사합니다.

어휘_ starting ~부터 시작하는 install 설치하다 require ~를 요구하다 bring 가지고 오다 security office 보안 사무실 ready 준비된 link ~에 연결하다 leave 떠나다 review 검토하다

83. (D)

What are listeners asked to provide?
(A) A feedback
(B) A vacation schedule
(C) An employee contract
(D) A form of identification

청자들은 무엇을 제공하도록 요구받는가?
(A) 의견
(B) 휴가 일정
(C) 직원 계약서
(D) 신분증

분석_ 새로운 보안 방식이 도입되므로 신분증을 보안 사무실로 가져오라고 언급하고 있다.

84. (C)

What special feature is mentioned about a new digital key?
(A) It can be easily exchanged.
(B) It can be used for the new buildings.
(C) It can monitor who enters a building.
(D) It can work with a previous lock.
새로운 디지털 열쇠에 대해 어떤 특별한 특징이 언급되고 있는가?
(A) 쉽게 교환될 수 있다.
(B) 새로운 건물문에 사용될 수 있다.
(C) 건물에 누가 들어가는지 감시할 수 있다.
(D) 이전 문에도 적용이 된다.
분석_ 새로운 열쇠는 개별 직원들에게만 연결되어 있어서 누가 들어가고 나가는지를 감시할 수 있음을 언급하고 있다.

85. (C)

What does the speaker mean when she says, "Make sure to pick it up"?
(A) Employees should go on the website.
(B) Employees should find their ID.
(C) Employees should read a document.
(D) Employees should buy some cards.
화자가 "챙겨 가시기 바랍니다"라고 말한 것이 의미하는 것은 무엇인가?
(A) 직원들이 웹사이트에 들어가야 한다.
(B) 직원들이 신분증을 찾아야 한다.
(C) 직원들이 문서를 읽어야 한다.
(D) 직원들이 어떤 카드를 구매해야 한다.
분석_ 바뀌는 보안 방식에 대한 정보가 담겨 있는 회사 잡지를 가져가서 읽어보라는 의미로 유추 가능하다.

Questions 86-88 refer to the following broadcast.

Thanks for listening to today's business report. **86** **87** *This evening, Weston Apparel, a locally based company with more than 15 years of experience in manufacturing and distributing clothing, announced the highly anticipated merger with MVIA Incorporated.* MVIA Incorporated will provide an online platform for selling Weston Apparel clothing. **88** *I strongly encourage listeners to tune in at this time tomorrow, for an exclusive interview with the president of Weston Apparel.* She'll talk about more details about the impact this merger will have in the local economy.

오늘의 비즈니스 리포트를 들어주셔서 감사합니다. 오늘 저녁, 15년 이상 동안 의류를 제조하고 유통해온 지역 기업 Weston Apparel이 고대하던 MVIA사와 합병을 발표했습니다. MVIA사는 Weston Apparel의 의류를 팔 수 있는 온라인 매개체를 제공할 것입니다. 저는 청자분들이 오늘 저녁 채널 고정하셔서 Weston Apparel의 사장과의 독점 인터뷰를 들으시길 강력하게 추천합니다. 그녀는 합병이 지역 경제에 미치게 될 영향에 대해 더 자세한 내용을 이야기할 것입니다.

86. (B)

What is the purpose of the broadcast?
(A) To talk about the closure of the company
(B) To announce a business merger
(C) To discuss the latest items
(D) To report a change in policies
방송의 목적은 무엇인가?
(A) 회사의 폐쇄를 이야기하기 위해
(B) 사업 합병을 발표하기 위해
(C) 최신 제품에 대해 이야기하기 위해
(D) 정책 변화를 발표하기 위해
분석_ 방송 초반 지역 회사가 다른 회사와 합병한다고 언급하고 있다.

87. (D)

What type of business is Weston Apparel?
(A) A building company
(B) An advertising company
(C) An interior design firm
(D) A clothing company
Weston Apparel은 어떤 회사인가?
(A) 건설 회사
(B) 광고 회사
(C) 인테리어 디자인 회사
(D) 의류 회사
분석_ 회사의 이름에서도 알 수 있는 부분이며, 15년 이상 동안 의류 제조와 유통을 해왔다고 언급하고 있다.

88. (A)

What does the speaker encourage the listeners to do?
(A) Listen to an interview
(B) Visit a store
(C) Apply for a job opportunity
(D) Enter a competition
화자는 청자들이 무엇을 하기를 권장하는가?
(A) 인터뷰 내용 듣기
(B) 매장 방문하기
(C) 일자리에 지원하기
(D) 경쟁에 참여하기
분석_ 방송 마지막 부분에서 채널 고정을 하여 독점 인터뷰를 들으라고 언급하고 있다.

Questions 89-91 refer to the following excerpt from a meeting.

So I called this meeting on our contract with Seoul Advertizing Agency we should discuss. And we should decide whether we will continue to use them to develop our TV advertising materials. Yesterday, I met their people and had a discussion. **89** *Actually I feel a little concerned. They want to increase the price for advertising.* **90** *Here's the thing. If we decide to stop this business relationship, we have to pay them for anything they've already done for us.* **91** *Could you take a minute to look at this contract with me? You'll see part of the agreement.*

그래서 우리가 토론해야 할 Seoul Advertizing Agency와의 계약에 대한 회의를 소집했습니다. 그리고 우리의 텔레비전 광고 자료를 개발하기 위해 그들을 계속 이용할 것인지에 대해서 결정해야 합니다. 어제, 저는 그 회사 사람들을 만나서 토론을 했습니다. 사실, 저는 조금 우려가 됩니다. 그들은 광고비를 올리길 원하고 있습니다. 요점은 이겁니다. 만약 우리가 이 사업 관계를 그만두기로 한다면, 그들이 이미 우리를 위해 해준 것들에 대해 비용을 지불해야 합니다. 저와 함께 이 계약서를 봐주시겠습니까? 계약서의 일부분을 보시겠습니다.

어휘_ call a meeting 회의를 소집하다 contract 계약(서) discuss 토론하다 decide 결정하다 material 재료, 자료 concerned 우려하는 relationship 관계 agreement 계약서

89. (D)

What bothers the woman about Seoul Advertising Agency?
(A) Their intention to extend deadlines
(B) Their mistakes with bills
(C) Their plan to renew a contract
(D) Their focus on increasing prices
여자가 Seoul Advertising Agency에 대해 신경 쓰는 것은 무엇인가?
(A) 마감일을 연장하려는 업체의 의도
(B) 청구서에 대한 업체의 실수
(C) 계약을 갱신하려는 업체의 계획
(D) 가격을 올리려는 업체의 초점
분석_ 여자는 광고업체 사람들을 만난 이후 광고비를 올리려는 것 때문에 걱정하고 있다고 언급하고 있다.

90. (D)

What does the woman mean when she says, "Here's the thing"?
(A) She will give a demonstration of a product.
(B) She has forgotten a password.
(C) She has found the item she was seeking.
(D) She will talk about the important thing.
여자가 "요점은 이겁니다"라고 말한 것이 의미하는 것은 무엇인가?
(A) 여자가 제품을 시연할 것이다.
(B) 여자가 비밀번호를 잊어버렸다.
(C) 여자가 찾고 있던 물건을 발견했다.

(D) 여자가 중요한 것에 대해 이야기할 것이다.
분석_ 여자가 우려하고 있는 사항에 대해서 이야기한 후 이미 이루어진 작업에 대한 비용을 언급하면서 중요사항을 부연 설명하고 있다.

91. (B)

What are the listeners asked to look at?
(A) A design specification
(B) A business contract
(C) An advertising estimate
(D) A budget for the previous year
청자들은 무엇을 볼 것을 요구받는가?
(A) 디자인 세부사항
(B) 사업 계약서
(C) 광고 견적액
(D) 지난해의 예산
분석_ 이야기 마지막에 계약서의 일부분을 보여주고 있다.

Questions 92-94 refer to the following talk and program.

92 *Welcome to afternoon's workshop.* We have a lot of useful information to cover. But before the workshop, I have to tell you a few schedule details. There will be one break between second and third presentations. You can leave your laptops here when you leave the room. There will always be someone here, **93** *but don't leave small electronic devices such as phones as well as money. You're advised to keep them with you.* And please note that there's an error in the printed sheet: **94** *there will be a switch for the first two presenters. Mr. Gurida has to leave early today.*

Program	
Presenter	Time
94 *Ms. Keith*	1:00-1:40
Mr. Gurida	1:50-2:30
BREAK	2:40-3:00
Mr. Chris	3:00-3:40
Ms. Green	3:50-4:30

오후 워크숍에 오신 것을 환영합니다. 보고할 유용한 정보가 많이 있습니다. 하지만 워크숍 전에, 몇 가지 일정상 세부사항을 말씀드리겠습니다. 두 번째와 세 번째 발표 사이에 한 번의 쉬는 시간이 있을 것입니다. 여러분은 자리를 비울 때 노트북은 그대로 두셔도 됩니다. 항상 누군가가 있을 것입니다. 하지만 휴대폰과 같은 작은 전자기기나 돈은 남겨두지 마십시오. 여러분은 그것을 소지하셔야 합니다. 그리고 인쇄된 용지에 오류가 있다는 점을 명심해주십시오. Gurida 씨가 오늘 일찍 떠나야 해서 맨 위 두 명의 발표자가 서로 변경될 것입니다.

프로그램	
발표자	시간
Keith	1:00-1:40
Gurida	1:50-2:30
휴식시간	2:40-3:00
Chris	3:00-3:40
Green	3:50-4:30

어휘_ useful 유용한 information 정보 cover 보도하다, 포함하다 detail 세부사항 presentation 발표 leave 남겨두다 device 장치 advise 충고하다 sheet 양식, 종이 switch 교체

92. (D)

Where most likely is the speaker?
(A) At an electronics store
(B) At a concert hall
(C) At an opening ceremony
(D) At a training workshop

화자는 아마 어디에 있을 것인가?
(A) 전자기기 매장
(B) 콘서트 홀
(C) 개업식
(D) 교육 워크샵

분석_ 초반부에서 워크샵에 오신 걸 환영한다고 언급하고 있다.

93. (B)

What are listeners asked to do?
(A) Stay silent during the break
(B) Carry their valuables with them
(C) Return any borrowed devices
(D) Share printed sheet with others

청자들은 무엇을 하도록 요구받는가?
(A) 휴식시간에 조용히 있기
(B) 귀중품을 지니고 다니기
(C) 빌린 장치 반납하기
(D) 다른 사람들과 인쇄물 공유하기

분석_ 노트북은 두어도 괜찮지만 휴대폰과 돈은 소지하라고 언급하고 있다.

94. (A)

Look at the graphic. Who will be the second presenter?
(A) Ms. Keith
(B) Mr. Gurida
(C) Mr. Chris
(D) Ms. Green

그래픽을 보자. 누가 두 번째 발표자인가?
(A) Keith
(B) Gurida
(C) Chris
(D) Green

분석_ 마지막 부분에서 Gurida 씨가 일찍 떠나야 해서 처음 두 명의 발표자가 서로 바뀌었음을 언급하고 있다. 그러므로 원래 일정상 첫 번째 발표자였던 Keith가 두 번째 발표자가 됨을 알 수 있다.

Questions 95-97 refer to the following excerpt from a meeting and chart.

As you already know, **95 *I thought our new website would have some problems, but fortunately I was wrong.* So far we couldn't find any technical difficulties, and most of our customers are satisfied with the new services we're offering. 96 *They especially like the feature to receive e-mail notifications when new items arrive.*** But there's one thing that is surprising me. Various age groups are responding differently to the website design. The results on this graph are not what I anticipated. **97 *Chang, I want you to investigate the reason this age group is the happiest with the site.*** Hopefully we can make use of that information to increase overall satisfaction.

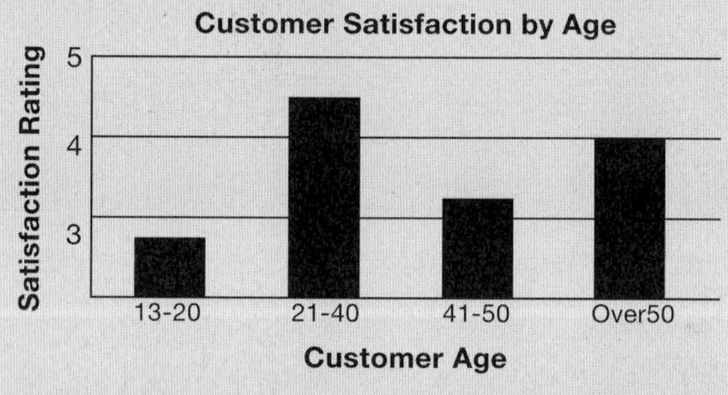

여러분이 이미 알다시피, 저는 우리 웹사이트에 문제가 있을 것이라 생각했습니다만, 다행히도 제가 틀렸습니다. 지금까지 우리는 어떤 기술상의 어려움도 찾지 못했습니다, 그리고 우리 고객들 대부분이 우리가 제공하는 새로운 서비스에 만족하고 있습니다. 그들은 특히 신제품 도착 시 이메일 통보를 받는 기능을 좋아합니다. 하지만 저를 놀라게 하는 것이 하나 있습니다. 다양한 연령대의 그룹이 웹사이트 디자인에 대해 다르게 응답하고 있습니다. 이 그래프의 결과는 제가 예상했던 것이 아닙니다. Chang 씨, 당신이 이 나이대의 그룹이 사이트에 가장 만족해하는 이유를 조사해주었으면 합니다. 전반적인 만족도를 높이기 위해 우리가 그 정보를 이용할 수 있길 바랍니다.

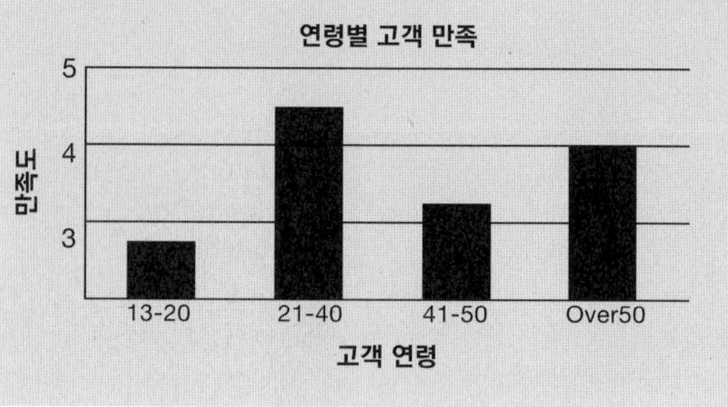

95. (B)

What does the speaker say she was wrong about?
(A) Online sales figures
(B) A website malfunctioning
(C) The availability of a product
(D) The cost of advertising
화자는 자신이 무엇에 대해 틀렸다고 말하는가?
(A) 온라인 판매 수치
(B) 웹사이트 결함
(C) 제품 이용 가능 여부
(D) 광고 비용
분석_ 이야기 초반 웹사이트에 문제가 있다고 생각했으나 자기가 잘못되었으며 고객들이 만족하고 있다고 언급하고 있다.

96. (D)

What does the speaker say is a popular website feature?
(A) Electronic billing
(B) Customer comments
(C) Free shipping
(D) E-mail notifications
화자는 어떤 웹사이트 기능이 인기 있다고 말하는가?
(A) 전자 청구
(B) 고객의 소리
(C) 무료 배송
(D) 이메일 통보
분석_ 웹사이트에서 인기 있는 기능이 무엇인지 묻고 있다. 이야기 중반에서 고객들이 만족하고 있으며 특히 신제품이 들어왔을 때 통보를 받는 기능을 좋아한다고 언급하고 있다.

97. (B)

Look at the graphic. What age group does the speaker ask Chang to look into?
(A) 13-20
(B) 21-40
(C) 41-50
(D) Over 50
그래픽을 보자. 화자가 Chang에게 조사하도록 요구하는 연령대는 어디인가?
(A) 13–20세
(B) 21–40세
(C) 41–50세
(D) 50세 이상
분석_ 표에서 Chang 씨가 조사해야 하는 그룹의 연령대를 묻고 있다. 가장 만족해하는 이유를 묻고 있으므로 만족도가 가장

높은 그룹을 조사한다는 것을 알 수 있다. 즉 가장 만족도가 높은 그룹인 21–40세가 조사 대상이 된다.

Questions 98-100 refer to the following telephone message and list.

Hi, Ross. **98** *It's Clara calling from Operations here at the head office.* I'm guessing you're on your way to Copper's Office Supply. I have a copy of your "to buy" list of things for our copy room on the second floor, and there's good news. According to the flyer I received this morning, every paper on the list is on sale except for blue paper which is still full-price. **99** *But we'll pay less for the orange paper for sure.* **100** *When you return, we'll need to put the paper away since the new copiers are coming on Tuesday,* and we should make room for them to be placed. OK. See you soon then.

To buy:	
·Blue Paper	- $ 80 full-price
·Red Paper	- $ 53 ON SALE
·Yellow Paper	- $ 45 ON SALE
99 ·*Orange Paper*	- *$ 68 full-price*

안녕하세요, Ross 씨. 여기 본사 운영부서의 Clara입니다. 제 생각에 당신이 Copper's Office Supply로 가는 중일 것 같습니다. 2층에 있는 복사실에서 사용할 구매 목록의 사본을 가지고 있는데요, 좋은 소식이 있습니다. 제가 오늘 아침 받은 전단지에 의하면, 여전히 정가에 팔리고 있는 파란 용지를 제외한 목록상의 모든 용지가 할인 중입니다. 하지만 우리는 분명 주황 용지에 대해서도 비용을 덜 지불해도 될 것입니다. 당신이 돌아오면, 화요일에 새로운 복사기가 들어오기 때문에 용지들을 치워두어야 합니다, 그리고 복사기가 놓일 공간을 만들어야 합니다. 그럼, 그때 뵙겠습니다.

구매할 것	
·파란 용지	- 80달러 정가
·빨간 용지	- 53달러 할인가
·노랑 용지	- 45달러 할인가
·주황 용지	- 68달러 정가

98. (A)

Where is the woman calling from?
(A) An office building
(B) A supply store
(C) A bike store
(D) An advertising company
여자는 어디에서 전화하는가?
(A) 사무실 건물

(B) 물품 창고
(C) 자전거 매장
(D) 광고 회사
분석_ 메시지 초반에 여자가 본사의 운영부에서 전화를 걸었다고
언급하고 있다.

99. (D)
Look at the graphic. What price is now incorrect?
(A) $ 80
(B) $ 53
(C) $ 45
(D) $ 68
그래픽을 보자. 잘못된 가격은 무엇인가?
(A) 80달러
(B) 53달러
(C) 45달러
(D) 68달러
분석_ 여자는 주황색 용지도 적은 비용이 들어갈 것이라고 이야기
하고 있지만 표에는 주황색 용지가 정가라고 표시되어 있으
므로 잘못된 가격은 주황색 용지의 가격인 68달러가 된다.

100. (B)
What most likely will happen on Tuesday?
(A) Employee training sessions will start.
(B) New equipment will be placed.
(C) A renovation will be complete.
(D) A project deadline will be extended.
화요일에는 아마도 무슨 일이 있을 것인가?
(A) 직원 교육 과정이 시작될 것이다.
(B) 새로운 장비가 설치될 것이다.
(C) 개조공사가 완료될 것이다.
(D) 프로젝트 마감일이 연장될 것이다.
분석_ 화요일에 일어날 일을 묻고 있다. 이야기 마지막 부분에서
화요일에 새로운 복사기가 들어오기 때문에 복사실의 용지
들을 치워야 한다고 언급하고 있다.

101. (D) delivery
해석_ 수화물 배송 예약을 위해 Albert 씨에게서 연락이 올 거예요.
분석_ 품사 문제이다. 수화물을 위해 약속하는 것이 아니라 수화
물 배송을 위해 약속을 정하는 것이므로 전치사 for의 실제
목적어는 빈칸이다. 따라서 명사가 필요하다. 이런 문제는
빈칸 앞 명사를 제외하고 해석해보면 정답이 명사라는 것이
더 확실해진다. for your delivery는 '배송을 위해' 예약을
한다. 해석이 매끄러우므로 가장 적절하다.

102. (A) interested
해석_ Rosemary 씨는 그녀가 인사부장 직책에 꽤 관심이 있다고 암시
했다.

분석_ 품사 문제처럼 보이는 숙어 문제이다. be interested in은 '~
에 관심 있다'이다. 빈칸 앞에 quite는 부사로 '꽤, 상당히'란
뜻을 가지고 있지만 부사로 불필수 품사이다. 따라서 빈칸
앞에 become은 2형식 동사로 빈칸에는 형용사 형태의 부
사가 필요하며 빈칸 뒤에는 목적어 명사가 없으므로 수동의
의미를 가진 과거분사가 필요하다.

103. (A) their
해석_ 부동산 전문가들은 다국적회사 고객이 최대 5000명의 근로자를 수
용하는 적절한 임대공간을 대여할 때 그들 예산 내에서 일이 처리
될 수 있게 돕는다.
분석_ 대명사 문제이다. 빈칸 뒤 명사를 수식할 수 있는 형용사
가 필요하다.

104. (B) offering
해석_ 다가오는 금요일 Vanessa's Customized Shoes는 모든 단골고
객에게 30퍼센트 할인을 제공할 것이다.
분석_ 어법 문제이다. offer는 4형식의 대표동사로 4형식으로 사
용될 경우 보통 〈offer + 사람 + 사물〉, 3형식으로 사용될
경우 보통 〈offer + 사물 + to + 사람〉 형태로 사용된다. '통
보하다'라는 의미의 notify는 〈notify + 사람 + to + V〉의
형태로 사용된다. (A) 통보하다 (C) 수행하다, 행하다 (D)
결합하다, 참가하다

105. (B) success
해석_ Ohbama 씨는 Aepple의 최신 노트북이 소매 산업에서 크게 성공
할 것이라고 예상한다.
분석_ 관사(a) 뒤 명사를 넣는 문제이다.

106. (A) and
해석_ 귀하의 가구 수리에 청구된 수수료 오류에 사죄드립니다. 그리고 새
로운 송장을 이 메모와 함께 동봉하였습니다.
분석_ 어휘 문제이다. 빈칸 앞뒤에는 주어와 동사로 이루어진 절
이 존재하므로 접속사가 필요하다. 또한 두 절의 내용이 평
이하게 이어지므로 (A)가 정답이다. (C) 그러나 (D) 또는

107. (B) expertly
해석_ Billy's Cafe의 모든 후식은 유명한 제빵사 Sophia Lucy가 전문
적으로 준비한다.
분석_ 품사 문제이다. 빈칸 앞뒤에 be p.p 수동형이 있어 수동의
동사 사이 동사를 수식하는 부사가 필요하므로 (B)가 정답
이다.

108. (B) prices
해석_ Evan 씨는 그의 재정 분석 결과에 한동안 안정되었던 가스 가격이
다음 달 오를 것 같다고 암시했다.
분석_ 어법 문제이다. 빈칸 뒤 주격관계대명사 which가 있으므로
빈칸 앞은 선행사인 명사가 필요하며 which 뒤의 동사와 수
일치가 되어야 하므로 (B)가 정답이다. 또한 가스가 오르는
것이 아니라 가스 가격이 오르는 것이 옳다.

109. (B) quietly

해석_ 공연장을 떠나고 싶은 청중들은 진행 중인 공연을 방해하지 않기 위해 조용히 떠나야 한다.

분석_ 품사 문제이다. 〈be requested to + V〉에서 V 자리의 exit 는 자동사이므로 자동사 뒤는 자동사를 수식하는 부사가 적절하다. 따라서 (B)가 정답이다.

110. (A) many

해석_ Stella Star Hotel의 많은 매력 중에는 호텔이 가진 태평양의 멋진 경치가 있다.

분석_ 어법 문제이다. 보기 중 many와 much는 형용사로 명사를 꾸밀 수 있다. many는 복수명사를 수식하고 much는 불가산명사를 수식하는데 공란 뒤에 charms라는 복수명사가 있으므로 (A)가 가장 적절하다.

111. (D) variety 　음성강의

해석_ Paris Hidden Diamond의 수석 제과사는 기존 메뉴에 훨씬 더 다양한 메뉴를 추가할 계획이다.

분석_ 선택지가 명사들로 나열된 어휘 문제이다. 메뉴에 첨가할 수 있는 대상으로 적절한 것을 골라야 한다. 기존 메뉴에 추가로 넣을 수 있는 것은 추가메뉴를 의미하는 (D) variety 이다. 메뉴에 다양성을 추가한다는 것은 보다 다양한 메뉴가 추가된 것으로 이해할 수 있다. (A) 공급물품 (B) 배분 (C) 여행

112. (C) claimed 　음성강의

해석_ 새로운 회사 정책을 준수하기 위해, 일주일 안에 주인이 찾아가지 않고 냉장고에 방치된 언 과일은 폐기될 것이다.

분석_ 품사 문제이다. 빈칸 앞에 부정을 나타내는 부사 not은 불필수 품사로 무시한다. 그러면 빈칸 앞 are라는 be동사가 있으므로 공란 자리에는 형용사 보어가 필요하다. 공란 뒤에 목적어 명사가 존재하지 않으므로 수동의 의미를 가진 과거분사 형용사 (C)가 정답이다.

113. (D) smallest 　음성강의

해석_ Adelle System은 지난 시즌 모델의 4분의 1 크기의 소형 USB 포트를 어제 공개했다. 그리고 이 모델은 시장에서 확실히 가장 작은 모델이 되었다.

분석_ 어휘 문제이다. 문장에 답이 되는 힌트가 one-quarter the size라고 언급되어 있다. 따라서 가장 작은 장비라는 표현이 가장 적절하다. (A) 가장 밝은 (B) 가장 넓은 (C) 가장 약한

114. (A) arrive 　음성강의

해석_ 45번 국도의 새로운 휴게소 개장은 초기 음식 선적이 제때 도착하지 않아서 연기되었다.

분석_ 품사 문제이다. 빈칸 앞 부정문을 만들기 위한 조동사와 부사 did not이 존재한다. 따라서 조동사 뒤에는 동사원형이 필요하므로 (A)가 가장 적절하다.

115. (D) effort 　음성강의

해석_ Helen 박사는 효과를 향상시키기 위한 노력의 일환으로 Winnie Pharmaceutical 회사의 비타민 알약 개발과정의 구조개혁을 하기 위해 뽑혔다.

분석_ 어휘 문제로 보이는 숙어 문제이다. 〈in an effort to + V〉는 'V하고자 하는 노력의 일환으로'라는 뜻으로 사용된다. (A) 물건 (B) 신문이나 잡지 호, 문제 (C) 충고

116. (C) finalized

해석_ 언어 몰입 과정에 더 많은 외국인 학생을 끌어모으자는 LA Community College의 제안은 이번 주 후반 마무리될 것이다.

분석_ 어휘 문제이다. 주어인 proposal(제안서)를 가장 잘 설명하는 것은 마무리 짓는 것이므로 (C)가 가장 적절하다. (A) 상기하다 (B) 줄이다 (D) 혼동시키다

117. (D) frequently

해석_ 고객들은 저렴한 비용과 뛰어난 고객서비스 덕분에 Perfect Wireless Broadband로 종종 되돌아온다.

분석_ 시제 문제이다. 문장의 동사는 return으로 현재시제이다. 현재시제와 가장 잘 어울리는 부사는 (D)이다. (A) 매우 (B) 적당하게 (C) 서로, 상호간에

118. (D) to discontinue

해석_ Speedy Motors의 최고 경영자는 부진한 판매가 502 Alvin 스포츠 다목적 자동차를 단종시킨 결정의 이유라고 언급했다.

분석_ 어법 문제이다. 보기를 보면 (A), (B), (C)는 동사이고 (D)는 준동사이다. 문장을 보면 이미 동사(cited)가 존재하므로 동사가 아닌 (D)가 가장 적절하다. 〈decision to + V〉를 외워두면 좋다.

119. (D) as

해석_ Catherine 씨가 싱가포르에 오기 전에, 그녀는 프랑스 예술 박물관에서 큐레이터로 일했다.

분석_ 어휘 문제이다. 자동사 work와 함께 어울리는 전치사는 work as(직책, 직책으로 근무하다)가 가장 적절하다. (A) 부사: ~ 위로 (B) 전치사: ~에게 (C) 전치사: ~로부터

120. (C) anyone

해석_ 누구든 최고 안건 항목들을 완성했으면, 인사과의 Cindy Naomi 에게 알려주세요.

분석_ 어법 문제이다. 공란은 주어 자리이며 단수동사 has completed와 함께 어울리는 단수주어가 필요하다. 명사이면서 단수형태는 (C)가 가장 적절하다. (B)는 형용사로 복수명사를 취한다.

121. (B) is being inspected 　음성강의

해석_ Edith Sports Complex의 냉방시스템은 정부의 건물안전부서에 의해 점검을 받을 것이다.

분석_ 어법 문제이다. 문장에 동사가 없고 빈칸 앞 주어는 단수주어이며 빈칸 뒤 목적어가 없으므로 수동 형태가 필요하다. 따라서 단수진행수동의 동사 (B)가 가장 적절하다.

122. (A) thoroughly 　음성강의

해석_ 새로운 인턴들은 인사과에 무슨 질문이건 묻기 전에 직원 안내 책자를 면밀히 검토하세요.

분석_ 어휘 문제이다. 보기가 모두 부사로 동사 go over를 가장 잘 수식하는 부사는 '철저히 검토하다'이므로 (A)가 가장 적절하다. (B) 부수적으로, 우연히 (C) 비교적으로, 상대적으로 (D) 이전에, 과거에

123. (D) since
해석_ Free Breeze Magazine은 올해의 사보로 지명된 이후 전국상업광고에서 가장 많이 선택되었다.
분석_ 어법 문제이다. 빈칸 앞뒤로 주어와 동사인 절이 있으므로 접속사가 필요하다. 또한 빈칸 앞절의 동사는 has been 현재완료이고 빈칸 뒤 동사는 was named 과거이다. 둘을 연결하는 가장 적절한 접속사는 (D)이다. (A) 부사: 대신에 (B) 접속사: 동안, 반면 (C) 접속부사: 그러나

124. (B) upon
해석_ Bianca Catering의 메뉴는 요리 주재료의 이용 가능성에 따라 온라인상에서 제공되는 메뉴와 매우 차이가 있다.
분석_ 어법 문제이다. 빈칸 앞 depend와 어울리는 전치사는 on 또는 보기 (B) upon이 가장 적절하다. depend on = depend upon은 '~에 의존하다, ~에 달려 있다, ~에 따라'이다. (A) 형식부사: 있다 (C) 부사: 전적으로, 완전히 (D) 전치사: ~와 함께

125. (D) after
해석_ 오후 6시 이후 받은 모든 전화는 다음 날 아침 정확히 오전 9시에 Isabel 씨에게 넘어갈 것이다.
분석_ 어휘 문제이다. 보기는 모두 전치사로 정확한 시점인 6:00 P.M과 어울리는 전치사는 (D)가 가장 적절하다. (A) 제외하고 (B) 기간, 동안 (C) 사이에

126. (C) appreciation
해석_ 우리와 계속된 거래에 대한 감사의 표현으로, 우리는 귀하와 귀하의 친인척을 Comfort First Hotel에서 열리는 비개방 만찬에 초대합니다.
분석_ 어법 문제이다. in appreciation of는 '~에 감사하여, 인정하여, 칭찬하여'라는 숙어이다. (A) 주석, 논평 (B) 반응, 대응, 응답 (D) 설명, 묘사, 기술

127. (D) as long as
해석_ 비회원들도 사전에 등록한다면 Songwriting & Producing 세미나에 참석할 수 있다.
분석_ 어휘 문제이다. 빈칸 앞뒤에 주어와 동사인 절이 있으므로 접속사가 필요하다. 비회원이 가입할 수 있는 조건을 달았으므로 조건을 나타내는 부사절 접속사 (D)가 가장 적절하다. (A) 부사: 지금까지 (B) 접속사: ~하기 위해서 (C) 접속사: 마치 ~인 것처럼

128. (B) heavy
해석_ 새로운 복사기가 굉장히 무겁기 때문에, 복사기 운반에 적어도 3명의 직원이 필요하다.
분석_ 어휘 문제이다. 복사기를 옮기는 데 적어도 3명이 필요한 이유로 가장 적절한 것은 무겁기 때문이다. (A) 조심스러운,

주의 깊은 (C) 바쁜 (D) 먼, 원격의

129. (C) over
해석_ 앞으로 5일간 모든 회사 건물에 있는 밝은 색의 창문차양은 모두 제거될 것이다.
분석_ 어휘 문제이다. 보기는 모두 전치사로 뜻이 다르다. 시간 앞에서 '시간 동안'이라고 쓰일 수 있는 가장 적절한 전치사는 (C)이다. (A) ~에 관해서 (B) ~을 따라서 (D) ~의 쪽에, ~을 향해서

130. (C) participating
해석_ 고객 만족 설문조사에 참여해주신 것에 대해서 단골고객들은 중간 크기의 커피를 마시는 데 사용할 수 있는 무료 쿠폰을 받을 것이다.
분석_ 품사 문제이다. 빈칸 앞 전치사 for 뒤에는 전치사의 목적어인 명사, 대명사, 동명사가 필요하므로 (C)가 가장 적절하다.

Part 6　　본문 p.73

Questions 131-134 refer to the following notice.

모든 조립 라인 직원들에게,
귀하도 알다시피, 우리는 자동차 문 계기판 설치에 관한 최종 계류 결정 안이 있습니다. 현재, 이 과정은 수작업으로 완료됩니다.
6월 10일부로, 이 작업은 자동화 로봇들로 대체될 것입니다. 로봇들은 측면 계기판을 자동차 문 외부에 단단히 고정시킬 것입니다.
게다가, 실내 계기판은 더 이상 단일 부품이 아닌 다양한 부품으로 구성됩니다.
조립 라인 직원들을 위한 훈련 프로그램의 일정이 곧 잡힐 겁니다. 정확한 시간과 장소는 회사 웹사이트에서 확인하세요.

131. (A) At present
분석_ 어휘 문제이다. 콤마 뒤 완벽한 문장을 수식하는 부사 역할이 필요하다. 문장 뒤를 보면 6월 10일부로 작업은 자동화로 대체되고 현재는 수작업으로 진행되므로 (A)가 가장 적절하다. (B) 설명하기 위해 (C) 그렇기는 하나 (D) 결론적으로

132. (C) They
분석_ 어법 문제이다. 앞서 문장에 나온 automatic robots를 받을 수 있는 대명사는 복수대명사 (C)이다.

133. (A) multiple
분석_ 어휘 문제이다. but 앞뒤 내용이 반대이므로 single과 반대되는 의미의 (A) multiple이 가장 적절하다.

134. (A)
(A) 정확한 시간과 장소는 회사 웹사이트에서 확인하세요.
(B) 로봇은 긴 터널을 뚫기 위해 사용됩니다.
(C) 야간교대 근무자들은 안전 규칙을 따라야 합니다.

(D) 할인된 열차 표는 25세 이하 사람들이 이용 가능합니다.

분석_ 빈칸 앞 문장이 대체되는 작업을 위해 공장 작업자를 위해 training session이 이뤄진다고 언급되었으므로 정확한 시간과 장소로 이어지는 것이 가장 매끄러우므로 (A)가 정답이다.

Questions 135-138 refer to the following memo. 음성강의

135. (A) pleased

분석_ 어법 문제이다. 감정의 의미를 지닌 동사는 사람주어와 만나는 경우에 수동태로 거의 사용된다. ⟨be pleased to + V⟩는 'V하게 되어 기쁘다'이다.

136. (B) when

분석_ 어법 문제이다. 보기는 모두 접속사이고 뜻이 다르다. 그리고 하나 더, 두 문장의 동사 시제가 다르다. 현재가 미래를 대신할 수 있는 접속사는 시간을 나타내는 부사절 접속사이므로 (B)가 가장 적절하다.

137. (C) undergo

분석_ 어휘 문제이다. 보기가 모두 동사인데 transition을 목적어로 취해서 해석이 가장 적절한 것은 변화과정을 <u>겪고 있다</u>는 의미의 (C)이다. (A) 묻다, 질문하다 (B) 재고하다 (D) 피하다

138. (C)

(A) 알록달록 무지개가 산에 걸려 있습니다.
(B) 임시 재정 보고서를 완성시키는 데 좀 더 많은 시간이 필요할 겁니다.
(C) 근무시간 동안 구내번호 4885번으로 제게 연락하실 수 있습니다.
(D) 공항을 왕복으로 운행하는 무료버스가 취소되었습니다.

분석_ 빈칸 앞에 회사에 대표직 변화가 진행되는 동안 질문이 있으면 연락을 하라고 말했으므로 연락처를 알려주는 (C)가 가장 적절하다.

Questions 139-142 refer to the following notice.

139. (B) height

분석_ 어휘 문제이다. 앞 문장에서 입구의 높이가 2.5미터라고 언급되었고 이 높이를 넘는 차량이라고 이어지는 것이 매끄러우니 (B)가 가장 적절하다. (A) 목표, 대상 (C) 목표 (D) 무게, 체중

140. (C) ahead

분석_ 어휘 문제이다. plan ahead는 '미리 계획을 세우다'라는 의미로 함께 사용되는 표현이므로 (C)가 가장 적절하다. (A) 부사, 전치사: 주변에, 대략 (B) 부사: 다시 (D) 부사, 전치사: 근처, 가깝게, 거의

141. (A) face

분석_ 어법 문제이다. 빈칸 앞에 could라는 조동사가 있으므로 조동사 뒤에는 동사원형 (A)가 가장 적절하다.

142. (C)

(A) 영업시간은 월요일부터 금요일까지입니다.
(B) 이 전시 행사는 이번 달 말까지 지속됩니다.
(C) 노점상은 대략 평균 30분 정도의 대기시간을 예상해야 합니다.
(D) 가벼운 다과가 제공됐고 복권이 배부되었습니다.

분석_ 빈칸 앞 문장에 서쪽 정문 이용 시 긴 대기시간에 직면할 수 있고 평균 대기시간이 대략 30분 정도 걸린다고 이어진다는 해석이 자연스러우므로 (C)가 가장 적절하다.

Questions 143-146 refer to the following e-mail.

당신의 제안에 감사와 축하를 드립니다.
Naomi Irene
대표
Pellcraft Chopsticks Makers

143. (D) produced

분석_ 어법 문제이다. that절의 주어 we와 동사 recycle가 있으므로 동사가 아닌 준동사가 필요하다. 또한 명사(wood shavings)를 수식하는 형용사 형태이면서 빈칸 뒤에 목적어인 명사가 없으므로 수동의 형용사 형태인 (D)가 가장 적절하다.

144. (D) practical

분석_ 어휘 문제이다. 보기가 모두 형용사로 직원의 제안이 검토되었고 실용적이라 판단되었기에 제안을 받아들일 수 있었다. 따라서 (D)가 가장 적절하다. (A) 개조된, 적합한 (B) 고분고분한, 유순한 (C) 진지한, 진심의

145. (A) This

분석_ 어휘 문제이다. 앞서 말한 이 재활용과정을 설명하고 있으므로 (A)가 가장 적절하다.

146. (D)

(A) 봉급은 당신의 이전 근무경험과 비례할 것입니다.
(B) 공장화된 농장에 다양한 가축은 훨씬 더 나은 대접을 받을 것입니다.
(C) 극 지역을 보호하기 위한 재순환은 중요합니다.
(D) 모든 근로자들은 다음 월급에서 추가 수당을 받을 것입니다.

분석_ 앞선 문장을 보면 회사의 수익이 더 좋아지고 환경도 좋아지며 근로자들에게 추가 보너스가 주어진다고 언급되었다. 그러므로 빈칸은 언제 월급을 받는지 언급된 (D)가 가장 적절하다.

Part 7   본문 p.77

Questions 147-148 refer to the following information.

귀하는 Golden Breeze Department에서 At the Corner 검은 가죽 재킷을 구입했습니다. 모든 우리 제품은 이탈리아 나폴리에서 수입되었습니다. 제품은 환경에 무해하며 가죽에 부드러운 방식으로 수작업으로 염색된 100% 짙은 가죽으로 직조되었습니다.
색상과 무늬의 차이는 염색 수작업 과정의 자연스러운 결과입니다. 이러한 차이는 각 가죽 제품을 독특한 예술작품으로 만들어줍니다. 마모를 줄이고 모양을 유지하기 위해서 드라이클리닝을 강력 추천합니다.

147. (D)

이런 정보는 어디서 발견할 수 있는가?
(A) 이탈리아 여행에 관한 안내책자
(B) 실크제품에 관한 잡지
(C) 머리 염색약 병
(D) 가죽제품 정가표

분석_ 첫 문단 가장 처음에 You have purchased a At the Corner black leather jacket from Golden Breeze Department.에서 가죽제품을 구입했다고 언급되었으므로 가죽제품 가격이 붙은 꼬리표가 가장 적절하다.

148. (C)

At the Corner 제품에 관해서 무엇이 언급되었는가?
(A) At the Corner 제품은 나폴리에서만 팔린다.
(B) At the Corner 제품은 다양한 재료로 만들어진다.
(C) At the Corner 제품은 불규칙한 색깔을 가지고 있다.
(D) At the Corner 제품은 세탁기로 쉽게 세탁이 가능하다.

분석_ 두 번째 문단 처음에 Variations in color and marking result naturally from the process of hand-dyeing.에서 색이 균등하지 못한 것은 수작업으로 염색한 결과라고 언급되었다.

Questions 149-151 refer to the following form.

Mega Sale Market은 항상 여러분의 의견을 환영합니다. 만약 비평이나 걱정, 제안사항이 있다면, 이 의견서를 작성해서 우편함에 넣어주세요. 우표는 필요하지 않습니다.
이름: Amy Dustin
제안:
귀사는 고객을 끌 수 있는 효과적인 마케팅 전략을 개발하는 데 많은 노력을 기울이는 재능 있는 팀을 갖추고 있습니다. 그러므로 저는 귀사에서의 쇼핑이 즐겁습니다. 귀사에서 온라인으로 자유롭게 쇼핑을 할 수 있게 해준다면 좋겠어요. 저는 병원에서 간호사로 일하고 있고 종종 야간근무를 합니다. 귀사의 일반적인 영업시간은 10시부터 10시까지라 제가 퇴근 후에 귀사의 상점에서 필요한 물건을 구입하기가 힘듭니다.
Star Super Store는 이미 프리미엄 온라인 쇼핑몰을 열었습니다. 만약 귀사도 온라인 쇼핑몰을 연다면, 저는 다가올 새해에 귀사의 단골이 될 것 같습니다. 감사합니다!

149. (A)

Dustin 씨에 관해 무엇을 유추할 수 있는가?
(A) Mega Sale Market의 손님이다.
(B) 병원 공석에 지원하길 원한다.
(C) 컴퓨터를 업그레이드할 계획이다.
(D) 보통 재택근무를 한다.

분석_ 제안의 하단부를 보면 And therefore I enjoy shopping in your store.에서 귀사의 상점에서 쇼핑을 즐긴다고 언급했으므로 상점의 손님이라 유추할 수 있다.

150. (B)

Dustin 씨는 Mega Sale Market이 무엇을 해야 한다고 제안했는가?
(A) 노련한 영업 사원을 고용할 것
(B) 온라인 상점을 개장할 것
(C) Star Super Store의 새 소식을 포함할 것
(D) 상점에서 신문을 팔 것

분석_ 제안의 하단부 It would be great if you could make your shop freely accessible online.에서 온라인상에서 쇼핑을 할 수 있으면 좋겠다고 언급했으므로 제안서를 작성한 Dustin이 상점에 원하는 것은 (B)가 가장 적절하다.

151. (C)

이 양식에서 언급된 것은 무엇인가?

(A) Star Super Store는 10시에 문을 닫는다.

(B) Dustin은 6개월 이내에 은퇴할 계획이지만 아직 확실하지는 않다.

(C) Amy는 야간 근무하는 동안은 퇴근 후에 Mega Sale Market에서 쇼핑할 수 없다.

(D) Mega Sale Market은 꽤 오랜 시간 온라인 쇼핑몰을 운영했다.

분석_ 제안서 하단부 I work in a hospital as a nurse and I often work a night shift. Your normal business hours are 10 to 10 so it is sometimes hard for me to buy the necessary things in your shop after work.를 보면 간호사로 재직 중이며 야간 근무 후 퇴근을 하면 상점에서 필요한 물건을 살 수 없다고 언급했으므로 (C)가 가장 적절하다.

Questions 152-153 refer to the following text message chain.

Winnie	
Rachel, 오늘 오후 바빠요?	(11:20)
Rachel	
예, 조금 바빠요. 왜요?	(11:21)
Winnie	
저는 발표 전에 Rachel이 판매 보고서에 철자오류가 있는지 확인해주면 좋겠어요.	(11:23)
Rachel	
음. 지금 해야 할 일이 있어요. 그러나 점심 식사 이후 2시쯤 시간이 있어요.	(11:24)
Rachel	
2시도 괜찮나요?	(11:25)
Winnie	
당연하죠.	(11:26)
도와주셔서 감사해요. 2시에 내 사무실로 오세요.	(11:27)

152. (B)

Winnie 씨에 관해서 제시된 것은 무엇인가?

(A) 그는 시간과 날짜를 정하기 위해 전에 Rachel을 만났다.

(B) 그는 문서를 준비하고 있다.

(C) 그는 그의 고객과 점심 약속을 취소했다.

(D) 그는 2시에 Rachel의 방에서 그녀를 만날 것이다.

분석_ 11시 23분 Winnie의 메시지 I want you to check my sales report for any spelling errors before the presentation.을 보면 Winnie는 판매보고서를 작성했으므로 (B)가 가장 적절하다.

153. (D)

11시 26분에 Winnie 씨가 "당연하죠"라고 쓴 의도는 무엇인가?

(A) 그는 Rachel과 점심을 함께 먹는 것에 동의한다.

(B) 그는 판매보고서에 그가 실수한 것을 안다.

(C) 그는 그가 판매 보고서를 완성할 수 있다고 확신한다.

(D) 그는 그녀와 언급한 시간에 만날 수 있다고 확인했다.

분석_ 11시 26분에서 "You bet"을 말했고 11시 27분에 2시에 만나자(Come and meet me at my office at 2.)고 언급했으므로 11시 24분에 Rachel이 말한 2시 약속에 응할 수 있다는 의미이다. 따라서 (D)가 가장 적절하다.

Questions 154-155 refer to the following letter.

4월 24일

Amanda Rosemary

Fantastic Parade Band

2580 Glasgow Point Blvd

Fayetteville, Arkansas 790310

Rosemary,

축하합니다. 당신의 퍼레이드 밴드는 Fayetteville Spring March의 공연자로 선정되었습니다. 퍼레이드는 5월 5일 일요일 오후 1시에 시작될 것입니다. 당신의 연주자에게 늦어도 12시에 시청으로 오라고 말해주세요. 연주자들은 시청 정문 입구 근처에서 모여서 공연을 시작하며 Fayetteville Parkway로 향해 갑니다. 국립박물관도 지나고 Memphis and Arkansas Bridge로도 갑니다. 행진은 Bluestone Park에서 끝나며 그곳에서 시청으로 돌아오는 셔틀버스를 이용할 수 있습니다.

그곳에서 뵙기를 기대합니다.

Bianca Cecil

행사 기획자

154. (A)

Rosamary 씨는 아마도 누구인가?

(A) 밴드 리더

(B) 버스 차장

(C) 시청 공무원

(D) 행사 기획자

분석_ 편지 제일 초반부 Your parade band has been chosen to perform in the Fayetteville Spring March.를 보면 당신, 즉 Rosemary의 밴드가 공연에 선출되었으므로 Rosemary는 밴드와 관련이 있는 사람이다.

155. (D)

퍼레이드는 어디서 시작되는가?

(A) 컨벤션 센터에서

(B) Memphis and Arkansas Bridge 아래에서

(C) Bluestone Park에서

(D) 시청에서

분석_ 편지 중반부를 보면 시청 정문 근처에 모여서 시작한다 (Performers will gather near the main entrance of the city hall to start.)고 언급했으므로 (D)가 가장 적절하다.

주간 영화 소식
Invisible Invader는 수상 경력이 있는 유명배우 Sam Albert를 아름다운 젊은 소녀로부터 악령을 쫓는 주인공인 신부 Dean Winchester 역으로 캐스팅한 새로운 공포영화이다. Baxter Farrell이 감독을 맡은 이 매우 오싹한 영화는 처음부터 끝까지 멈추지 않는 액션장면을 보여주고 있기에 흥행에 성공할 거라 확신한다. 1월 24일 목요일 극장에서 확인할 수 있다.

156. (C)
Sam Albert는 누구인가?
(A) 영화감독
(B) 신부
(C) 영화배우
(D) 수상 경력이 있는 작가
분석_ an award-winning cast stars Sam Albert in the leading role of Dean Winchester.에서 영화에서 신부 역을 맡은 배우라고 언급했으므로 (C)가 정답이다. 수상 경력은 있지만 작가가 아니므로 (D)는 정답이 아니다.

157. (B)
기사에 따르면, 1월 24일 어떤 일이 일어날까?
(A) 영화 대본이 마무리된다.
(B) 영화가 개봉한다.
(C) 직항 비행기를 이용할 수 있을 것이다.
(D) 상이 수여된다.
분석_ 제일 마지막 부분 Look for it in theaters on Thursday, January 24.를 보면 극장에서 영화를 보려면 1월 24일 극장으로 오라고 언급했으므로 (B)가 가장 적절하다.

Questions 158-160 refer to the following advertisement.

음성강의

언어 몰입 프로그램
수줍음 많은 사람을 위한 재미있는 수업
다가올 7월 1일 월요일이 5주년
등록비 20% 할인
다과, 경품 추첨 그리고 게임을 즐기세요
전 가족을 데려오세요
언어 몰입 프로그램에서, 우리는 여러분의 모든 필요를 충족시켜드립니다. 영어, 스페인어부터 한국어, 중국어까지 적어도 한 언어는 당신이 유창하게 구사할 수 있게 도와드립니다. 그러니 지금 바로 전국에 30개 이상인 우리 학원에 등록하세요.
쿠폰을 출력하려면 LIP.com을 방문하세요. 할인을 받으시려면 접수원에게 쿠폰을 보여주셔야 합니다. 이전에 또는 현재 등록한 수업은 할인 적용이 되지 않습니다. 쿠폰은 7월 26일까지만 유효합니다.

158. (B)
무엇이 홍보되고 있는가?
(A) 온라인 게임 할인
(B) 언어 학습 과정 할인
(C) 영국, 스페인, 또는 한국행 비행기표

(D) 상점의 개장 기념식
분석_ 광고 첫 문단 At Language Immersion Program, we meet all your needs. Help make you fluent in at least one language from English and Spanish to Korean and Chinese.를 보면 언어를 가르쳐주는 학습센터이고 5주년 기념으로 20% 할인을 해준다고 했으므로 (B)라고 유추할 수 있다.

159. (A)
언어 몰입 프로그램에 관해 무엇이 나타났는가?
(A) 다양한 지점을 가지고 있다.
(B) 스포츠 게임을 조직한다.
(C) 다양한 다과를 판매한다.
(D) 언어 교사를 구인 중이다.
분석_ 광고 첫 문단 마지막 문장 now you can enroll in more than 30 institutes across the country.에서 나라 전역에 30개 이상의 지점이 있다고 언급했으므로 (A)가 가장 적절하다.

160. (D)
고객은 어떻게 수업 20% 할인을 받을 수 있는가?
(A) 게임 대회에 참여함으로써
(B) 일찍 수업에 등록함으로써
(C) 30달러를 소비함으로써
(D) 쿠폰을 보여줌으로써
분석_ 광고 두 번째 문단 제일 첫 문장 Visit LIP.com to print out a coupon. You must present it to the receptionist to receive a discount.를 보면 쿠폰을 출력해서 보여줘야만 할인을 받을 수 있다 언급했으므로 (D)가 가장 적절하다.

Questions from 161-163 refer to the following e-mail.

발신: cards@teagarden.co.uk
수신: hdaria@cardiff-office.co.uk
주제: 귀하의 카드
날짜: 3월 10일
고객님께
Tea Garden의 실버회원권, TG Silver에 등록해주셔서 감사합니다. 귀하의 회원권은 아래의 주소로 일주일 이내에 귀하에게 보내질 것입니다.
Helen Daria
33 Ocean-view Road
Cardiff OF 10 3NP
만약 위의 주소가 정확하지 않다면, 가능한 한 빨리 www.teagarden.co.uk에 들어가 고객 프로필에 접속하셔서 필요한 변경을 해주시기 바랍니다.
만약 카드가 도착하기 전에 허브티를 구매하고 싶다면, 구매하실 때 카드 번호(TG-800109)만 말씀하셔도 됩니다.
회원권이 제공할 수 있는 모든 것을 이용하고 싶으시면 웹사이트를 방문하세요.
Tea Garden 회원들

161. (C)

이메일을 쓴 주된 목적은 무엇인가?

(A) 고객의 불만에 응답하기 위해

(B) 유기농으로 키운 약초를 수출하기 위해

(C) 회원권 등록을 확인하기 위해

(D) 회원권 소지자들에게 회사의 새로운 정책을 통보하기 위해

분석_ 주제는 보통 지문의 초반을 보면 알 수 있다. 편지 초반에 Thank you for signing up for the Tea Garden's silver membership, the TG Silver. Your membership card will be sent to you within a week at the following address.를 보면 회원 등록에 감사드리며 카드를 보낸다고 언급했으므로 (C)가 가장 적절하다.

162. (D)

Daria 씨가 웹사이트에서 할 수 있는 것으로 언급된 것은 무엇인가?

(A) 허브티를 추천하기

(B) 그녀가 가장 좋아하는 허브 티 목록 만들기

(C) 허브티에 관한 고객의 의견 검토하기

(D) 그녀의 연락 정보 최신화하기

분석_ 주소 밑에 쓰인 두 번째 문단에 If the address listed above is not correct, please access profile at www.teagarden.co.uk as soon as possible and make the necessary changes.를 보면 주소가 잘못되었을 경우 웹사이트에 가서 수정을 하라고 언급되었으므로 (D)가 가장 적절하다.

163. (D)

회원권 번호에 관해서 무엇이 언급되었는가?

(A) 영국 내에서 허브티만 유효하다.

(B) Daria의 가족이 사용할 수 있다.

(C) 유효기간이 딱 일 년이다.

(D) 지금 바로 즉시 사용할 수 있다.

분석_ 편지 하단을 보면 If you want to buy herbal teas before your card arrives, simply mention your membership number (TG-800109) when you make a purchase.에서 카드 도착 전에 물건 구입을 원하면 구입할 때 번호만 말해도 된다고 언급했으므로 카드 번호는 즉시 사용이 가능하다는 (D)가 가장 적절하다.

Questions 164-167 refer to the following letter.

Cordelia Glassware Manufacturer

7000 Fifth Street Avenue

Belgium, 82479

Adolph Corby 씨

925 Montana 주

Suite A building 3542

Corby 씨께

우리는 귀하에게 귀하가 6월 7일에 주문한 다음의 물품이 현재 재고가 없으며 더 이상 제조가 되지 않는다는 것을 알려드리게 되어 유감입니다. [1]

제품번호 201, 유리제품 (2L), 수량: 5개, 각 12.50달러 [2]

우리 제품 라인에서, 우리는 위에 언급된 물건을 아래에 나타난 비슷한 물건으로 대체했습니다.

제품번호 202, 유리제품 (2L), 각 13.00달러 [3]

새로운 유리제품과 이전 유리제품의 유일한 차이는 새로운 제품이 훨씬 더 두꺼운 유리로 만들어졌다는 것입니다. 만약 귀하가 새로운 유리제품 202를 포함하기 위해 원본 주문서를 바꾸고 싶으시다면 801-352-9256으로 연락 주세요. 귀하의 원본 주문서에 쓰인 모든 다른 주문물품은 이용 가능하며 일정대로 배송될 것입니다. [4]

구매에 감사드립니다.

Connie Dollis

고객 서비스 전문가, Cordelia Glassware Manufacturer

164. (D)

Corby 씨의 주문에 무슨 문제가 있는가?

(A) 그의 배달 정보가 잘못되었다.

(B) 요금을 완납하지 않았다.

(C) 주문품 몇 개가 배송 중 파손된 상태로 배달되었다.

(D) 그가 주문한 제품이 재고가 없다.

분석_ 편지 초반부에 We regret to notify you that the following item you ordered on June 7 is currently not in stock and moreover is no longer being manufactured.를 보면 주문한 제품 중 특정 제품이 재고가 없고 단종되었다고 언급했으므로 (D)가 가장 적절하다.

165. (B)

편지에 따르면, 왜 Corby 씨는 회사에 전화해야 하는가?

(A) 최신 제품 카탈로그를 요청하기 위해

(B) 주문의 변경을 승인하기 위해

(C) 환불을 받기 위해

(D) 유리제품 배달을 위해

분석_ 편지 하단부를 보면 전화번호 앞에 전화를 걸어야 하는 이유가 언급되어 있다. If you would like us to change your original order to include the new glassware item number 202, please contact us at 801-352-9256.를 보면 주문 변경을 위해 전화를 하는 것이므로 (B)가 가장 적절하다.

166. (A)

Cordelia Glassware Manufacturer에 대해서 제시된 것은?

(A) 회사에는 단종된 제품이 있다.

(B) Adolph Corby에게 잘못된 유리제품을 보냈다.

(C) 모든 주문품은 자동으로 처리된다.

(D) 회사의 본사가 Montana 주로 이전된다.

분석_ 지문 초반 We regret to notify you that the following item you ordered on June 7 is currently not in stock and moreover is no longer being manufactured.를 보면 더 이상 물건을 제조하지 않는다고 언급했으므로 단종된 제품이 있다고 말한 (A)가 가장 적절하다.

167. (B)

[1], [2], [3] , 그리고 [4]로 표시된 곳 중에서 다음 문장이 들어가기에 가장 적합한 곳은?

"우리 제품 라인에서, 우리는 위에 언급된 물건을 아래에 나타난 비슷한 물건으로 대체했습니다."

(A) [1]

(B) [2]

(C) [3]

(D) [4]

분석_ 위에 언급된 물건이 무엇이고 아래에 언급된 물건이 무엇인지 말할 수 있는 자리인 [2]가 정답으로 가장 적절하다.

Questions 168-171 refer to the following advertisement.

Green Clover Clothing은 개최합니다
해마다 하는 "Bag of Clothes" 세일 [1]
10월 25일 목요일 오전 9시부터 오후 9시까지
[2] 우리의 겨울 물건이 곧 입고될 것입니다. [3]
제품 선반에 공간을 만들 수 있게 도와주세요.
50유로로 쇼핑가방을 구입해서 당신에게 딱 맞는 지난 계절 물건들로 최대한 많이 가방을 채우세요. 앉아서 무료 커피도 즐겨보세요. 아니면 절반 가격에 갓 구운 과자를 구입하세요. [4]
상점은 할인기간 중 영업시간이 연장될 것입니다. 참여하기 위해 등록이 요구됩니다. 상점에 잠깐 들러 등록 서류를 작성하세요. 아니면 www.greenclothing.com에 온라인상에서 서류를 작성하세요.
상점에서 뵙기를 희망합니다!

168. (D)

할인의 주된 목적은 무엇인가?

(A) 신규고객을 유치하기 위해

(B) 새로운 옷을 홍보하기 위해

(C) 9주년 기념일을 축하하기 위해

(D) 새로운 물건에 대한 공간을 만들기 위해

분석_ 날짜와 시간 아래 부분을 보면 Our winter merchandise will be coming in soon.이라 언급되어 있어 겨울 물품이 입고되고 있다. 또한 fill the bag with as many last season items as you can fit.을 보면 지난 계절 물건으로 가방을 채우라고 언급했으므로 (D)가 가장 적절하다.

169. (C)

Green Clover Clothing에 관해서 무엇이 제시되었는가?

(A) 구운 제빵류를 무료로 고객에게 제공한다.

(B) 목요일에 보통 문을 닫는다.

(C) 상점 내에 커피 가게가 있다.

(D) 상점의 주된 옷은 각 50유로이다.

분석_ 광고 중반부 Sit down and enjoy complimentary coffee.를 보면 옷을 구매하는 이외에도 상점에 앉아서 커피를 즐길 수 있으므로 (C)가 가장 적절하다.

170. (B)

만약 고객이 행사에 참가하고 싶다면 고객은 무엇을 해야 하는가?

(A) 일찍 도착하기

(B) 서류를 작성하기

(C) 옷을 기부하기

(D) 그들 자신의 쇼핑 봉투를 가지고 오기

분석_ 광고 후반부 Registration is requested to attend. Please stop by the shop to complete a registration form or fill it out online.을 보면 등록이 필수이고 등록을 위해서는 서류를 작성하라고 언급했으므로 (B)가 가장 적절하다.

171. (C)

[1], [2], [3], 그리고 [4]로 표시된 곳 중에서 다음 문장이 들어가기에 가장 적합한 곳은?

"제품 선반에 공간을 만들 수 있게 도와주세요."

(A) [1]

(B) [2]

(C) [3]

(D) [4]

분석_ [3]의 빈칸 앞에 Our winter merchandise will be coming in soon!이라고 하여 겨울 제품이 입고 대기 중이며 빈칸 뒤에 Make a purchase of a shopping bag for € 50 and fill the bag with as many last season items as you can fit.이라고 하여 지나간 계절 옷을 구입해달라고 언급되었으므로 (C)가 가장 적절하다.

Questions 172-175 refer to the following the letter.

수신: kdorothy@gmail.com
발신: inaomi@mae.org
날짜: 4월 20일
주제: Modern Art Festival
Dorothy
우리는 귀하가 9월 9일 일요일에 현대 예술 전시장에서 열리기로 예정된 올해 Modern Art Festival에 참가해주셔서 기분이 좋습니다. 우리는 귀하의 참가비 전액을 받았고 귀하는 27번 부스로 배정됐습니다. 참가자는 정확히 오전 8시까지 도착하도록 계획해야 합니다. 도착하자마자 서쪽 입구에 있는 안내데스크에서 등록을 하세요. 그러면 자원봉사자들이 당신을 하역장소로 안내해드릴 겁니다. 이 하역장소에서 차에 있는 물건들을 부스로 옮기실 수 있습니다. 하역과 부스 설치는 오전 10시까지 마무리되어야 합니다. 하역 이후, 당신의 차량을 Jefferson Avenue에 있는 주차장에 주차시키세요. 현장에 많은 참가자가 예측되어 전시장 주차장은 축제 참가자들을 위해 예약해두었습니다.
26번에서 30번 부스로 배정받은 참가자들은 대략 300미터 거리로 물건을 옮겨야 함을 기억하세요. 소유하고 있는 카트의 수가 제한적이고 카트 대부분이 너무 작습니다. 만약 이 부스로 배정되었다면 본인 소유의 카트와 짐을 옮기는 데 도움을 줄 한 사람을 데려오세요.
일요일에 뵙기를 기대합니다.
Isabell Naomi
프로그램 기획자
Modern Art Festival

172. (A)

Dorothy 씨는 Modern Art Festival에서 무엇을 할 것인가?

(A) 예술작품을 전시하기

(B) 참가자가 물건 옮기는 것을 도와주기

(C) 자원봉사자를 훈련시키기

(D) 축제참석자들에게 주차장 알려주기

분석_ 편지 초반부에 We are excited that you will be participating in this year's Modern Art Festival.을 보면 예술축제에 참석한다고 언급되었으므로 (A)가 가장 적절하다.

173. (D)

Dorothy 씨는 도착하면 무엇을 가장 먼저 해야 하는가?

(A) 참가비를 지불하기

(B) 하역 명단을 확인하기

(C) 27번 부스로 바로 보고하기

(D) 안내데스크로 가기

분석_ 중반부 Upon arrival, please sign in at the reception desk, which is at the west entrance.를 보면 도착하자마자 안내데스크로 가라고 했으므로 (D)가 가장 적절하다.

174. (C)

편지에 따르면, 오전 10시 이후 금지된 행동은 무엇인가?

(A) 새로운 등록

(B) 부스 배정하기

(C) 차에서 하역하기

(D) 카트를 대여하기

분석_ Unloading and putting up booth must be completed by 10 A.M. sharp.를 보면 하역과 부스 설치를 10시까지 완성하라고 언급했으므로 (C)가 가장 적절하다.

175. (C)

왜 Dorothy 씨는 그녀를 도울 누군가를 데려오라고 요청받는가?

(A) 대부분의 카트가 현재 고장 났다.

(B) 그녀는 전시장에 익숙하지 않다.

(C) 그녀는 먼 거리로 물건을 운반해야 한다.

(D) 현대 예술 전시장은 일손이 부족하다.

분석_ Dorothy는 27번 부스로 배정되었다. 그리고 지문에서 Please be reminded that participants assigned to Booth 26-30 will have to transport their merchandise a distance of approximately 300 meters.를 보면 Dorothy가 배정된 27번 부스는 하역 후 물건을 옮기는 거리가 300미터로 꽤 멀기에 (C)가 가장 적절하다.

Questions 176-180 refer to the following e-mails.

발신: k_mia@redvanilla.com
수신: alyssakayla@gmail.com
날짜: 1월 9일
주제: 즐거운 소식
Kayla 씨에게
우리의 단골 고객 중 한 명으로서, 당신은 2월 한 달 동안 Red Vanilla 가 인기 있는 "3 for $ 13 Lunch Special"을 다시 시작한다는 것을

알면 기뻐할 것입니다. 이 특별 음식은 우리의 맛있는 메뉴에서 전채요리, 주요리, 그리고 후식을 포함하고 있으며 단돈 13달러에 100달러 가치의 음식을 먹을 수 있습니다.

각 항목에서 하나의 메뉴를 선택할 수 있습니다.

전채요리 선택

블루치즈를 포함한 양파 링 / 오늘의 샐러드 / 튀긴 새우

메인요리 선택

참치 샌드위치 / 치킨 & 으깬 감자 / 해산물 리조또 / 호두를 으깬 가지

후식요리 선택

당근 케이크 / 산딸기가 있는 초콜릿 무스 / 인삼 아이스크림

만약 당신이 건강한 요리를 먹기 위해 우리 상점에 오고 싶다면, 예약을 위해 우리 상점 웹사이트 www.redvanilla.com를 방문하세요. 이 제안은 월요일부터 목요일까지 11시 30분부터 2시까지만 이용 가능합니다.

곧 뵙기를 기대합니다.

Kaitlyn Mia
주인이자 최고 주방장
Red Vanilla

발신: alyssakayla@gmail.com
수신: k_mia@redvanilla.com
날짜: 2월 2일 화요일
주제: 감사
Mia
당신의 뛰어난 서비스와 맛있는 음식에 감사를 표하고 싶어요.
당신 식당에서 먹었던 전채요리는 너무 신선해서 다른 손님들에게 강력 추천하고 싶어요. 식초 드레싱 덕분에 야채를 한 접시 더 먹었어요. 메인 요리는 의심할 여지없이 완벽했습니다. 촉촉한 빵이 구운 참치의 풍미를 강화시켰습니다. 후식은 요리사가 완벽한 천재라는 것을 입증해주었죠. 요리사가 제게 후식을 추천하기 전에 나는 그 요리를 들어본 적도 없었어요. 바닐라 아이스크림 속의 인삼과 대추는 제 활력을 증진시켰어요.
어제 제가 느낀 유일한 단점은 손님을 위한 좌석이 부족하다는 것입니다. 특별음식 개장 첫날 당신의 식당을 좋아하는 사람들로 꽉 차서 앉을 자리를 찾기가 힘들었어요.

Alyssa Kayla

176. (D)

Mia는 왜 이메일을 썼는가?

(A) 다가올 요리 시연을 홍보하기 위해

(B) 최근 영업시간의 변경을 알리기 위해

(C) 새로운 수상 경력이 있는 주방장을 소개하기 위해

(D) 특별한 홍보에 관한 정보를 주기 위해

분석_ 첫 번째 지문을 보면 As one of our most loyal customers, you will be glad to know that during the month of February, Red Vanilla is bringing back the popular "3 for $ 13 Lunch Special."에서 단골고객에게 단 한 달간 저렴한 가격으로 음식을 제공하겠다고 언급했으므로 (D)가 가장 적절하다.

177. (C)

첫 번째 이메일에서 Kayla 씨에 대해 유추할 수 있는 것은 무엇인가?

(A) 그녀는 Red Vanilla의 이전 주인이다.

(B) 그녀는 Mia에게 Red Vanilla를 추천했다.

(C) 그녀는 Red Vanilla의 단골고객이다.

(D) 그녀는 Red Vanilla에 점심 예약을 했다.

분석_ 176번과 동일선상의 문제로 첫 번째 지문의 편지를 받는 수신인인 Kayla는 단골고객(As one of our most loyal customers)이라 언급했으므로 (C)가 정답이다.

178. (B)

Red Vanilla에 대해 나타난 것은 무엇인가?

(A) 목요일마다 문을 닫는다.

(B) 온라인상으로 예약을 받는다.

(C) 전국에 여러 개의 지점을 갖고 있다.

(D) 후식요리로 유명하다.

분석_ 첫 지문 후반부 If you are interested in joining us for healthy lunch, please visit our website at www. redvanilla.com to make a reservation.을 보면 식당에 오기 위해 예약을 하려면 식당 웹사이트를 방문하라고 언급했으므로 (B)가 가장 적절하다.

179. (C)

Kayla가 Lunch Special에서 먹지 않은 음식은 무엇인가?

(A) 그날의 샐러드

(B) 참치 샌드위치

(C) 해산물 리조또

(D) 인삼 아이스크림

분석_ 보기에 있는 모든 메뉴는 첫 번째 지문에 전채, 메인, 후식음식으로 모두 언급되었다. 두 번째 지문에서 Kayla가 맛있다고 언급한 음식 중 빠진 하나는 (C)이다.

180. (C)

Kayla는 그녀의 이메일에서 어떤 문제를 언급했는가?

(A) 식초 드레싱은 야채를 시들게 만들었다.

(B) 인삼 아이스크림은 약간 쓴 맛이 난다.

(C) 많은 방문객들에 비해 공간이 충분치 않았다.

(D) Lunch Special은 광고된 가격보다 더 비쌌다.

분석_ 두 번째 지문의 하단부 The only disadvantage I felt yesterday was the lack of seats for dinners.를 보면 좌석이 부족했다고 언급했으므로 (C)가 가장 적절하다.

Questions 181-185 refer to the following advertisement and e-mail.

Louisiana Skyline Residence
임대 가능

넓은 침실 한 개 / 침실 두 개 아파트

현대적인 주방과 우아한 거실을 갖춤

새로운 거주민을 위한 판촉 특별 서비스

(자격이 되려면 2년 임대에 서명해야 함)

침실 한 개 – 한 달 1500달러

침실 두 개 – 한 달 2000달러

냉방과 난방비 포함

세입자는 건물 내의 세탁실과 가구가 완비된 라운지와 휴게공간을 이용할 수 있다.

28 Louisiana Pl.

Louisiana, OFF HJW SHG

802-241-7819

www.skylineresidence.lo

수신: Vanessa Velvet

발신: Adolph Edith

주제: 최근 최신사항

날짜: 3월 10일

첨부: 아파트_612A

Velvet 씨에게

저는 Katie Kim을 위한 모든 서류작업을 준비해두었습니다. 그녀는 아파트 612A의 1년 임대 계약에 서명하기 위해 오늘 오후에 올 겁니다. 그녀는 첫 달 임대료 1500달러를 수표로 가지고 올 겁니다. 저는 완성된 서류와 수표를 오늘 저녁 당신 서랍에 넣어둘 것입니다.

이 아파트를 4월 10일까지 준비할 필요가 있다고 관리부서에 말해주겠습니까? 이 편지에 마무리해야 할 작업 목록을 첨부했습니다. Kim 씨는 거실에 무료 페인트 작업을 선택했습니다. 색깔 번호는 472이고 완전 흰색입니다.

우리는 임대 가능한 아파트가 딱 하나 더 있습니다. 저는 내일 침실 두 개인 이 방을 보여줄 약속이 있습니다. 저는 이번 주말 이전에 이 임대 계약에 서명을 할 수 있을 거라 기대합니다. 일단 이렇게만 되면, 우리는 빈방 없이 모든 방이 점유상태일 겁니다.

감사합니다.

Adolph Edith

181. (A)

아파트 임대에 관해 무엇이 언급됐는가?

(A) 아파트는 거실을 가지고 있다.

(B) 아파트는 완벽하게 개조된 욕실을 갖추고 있다.

(C) 아파트는 임대인에게 무료 그림을 제공한다.

(D) 아파트는 세대 내에 세탁기가 있다.

분석_ 첫 지문인 광고에서 Spacious one-and two-bedroom apartments with modern kitchens and elegant dining rooms를 보면 침실이 하나이건 둘이건 주방과 거실을 갖추고 있으므로 (A)가 가장 적절하다. 광고문 하단을 보면 건물 안에 세탁실이 있다(Tenants get access to an on-site laundry room.)고 언급했으므로 아파트 각 세대 내에 세탁기가 있다는 것은 유추할 수 없다.

182. (A)

Kim 씨에 관해 제시된 것은 무엇인가?

(A) 그녀는 침실 하나인 아파트를 선택했다.

(B) 그녀는 일 년 더 임대계약을 갱신했다.

(C) 그녀는 3월 10일 새로운 아파트로 이사할 것이다.

(D) 그녀는 냉방과 난방 장비를 수리해야 한다고 주장했다.

분석_ 첫 지문인 광고문에 침실이 하나인 아파트는 1500달러 (One-bedroom unit: $ 1500/month)라고 언급했고 두 번째 지문인 편지에는 첫 달 임대로 1500달러를 가지고 간다 (she will bring a check of $ 1,500 for the first month's rent.)고 언급했으므로 (A)가 가장 적절하다.

183. (B)

Velvet 씨는 무엇을 할 것을 요청받는가?

(A) 문서를 작성한다.

(B) 관리직원에게 정보를 제공한다.

(C) Edith와 약속을 한다.

(D) 세입자와 임대료를 다시 협상한다.

분석_ 두 번째 지문인 편지를 받는 사람이 Velvet으로 Could you communicate to maintenance department that this apartment needs to be ready by 10 April?을 보면 관리직원에게 알려달라는 부탁을 받았으므로 (B)가 가장 적절하다.

184. (B)

이메일의 3번째 문단 2행에 있는 "expect"와 의미가 가장 가까운 것은?

(A) 강화하다, 확고히 하다

(B) 기대하다, 예상하다

(C) 홍보하다, 승진하다

(D) 추천하다, 권고하다

분석_ 앞뒤 문맥을 보면 I have some appointments tomorrow to show the two-bedroom unit. I expect getting a lease signed before the end of this week.는 내일 고객을 만날 약속이 있고 고객이 임대 서명을 할 거라 예상하는 것이므로 (B)가 가장 적절하다.

185. (C)

Edith 씨는 Louisiana Skyline Residence 아파트에 관해 무엇을 암시했는가?

(A) 아파트의 냉방 장치가 업그레이드될 것이다.

(B) 아파트의 연간 임대료는 4월에 오를 것이다.

(C) 아파트는 곧 모두 임대될 것이다.

(D) 아파트는 완전 흰색으로 도색될 것이다.

분석_ 두 번째 지문 후반부 I expect getting a lease signed before the end of this week. Once that happens, we will be at full occupancy.를 보면 곧 아파트가 완전 임대될 것이라 언급했으므로 (C)가 가장 적절하다.

Questions 186-190 refer to the following website post, reply and e-mail.

Adagio Computers 이용자 포럼
Adagio PRO 1 Ultra가 무선 인터넷 연결이 안 돼요.
Alexander Lee가 8월 15일 오전 8시 23분에 게시
Adagio MAX 모델을 2년간 사용한 후에, 저는 새로운 Adagio PRO 1 Ultra 노트북을 이번 주 월요일에 구입했습니다. 대부분, 저는 이 새로운 컴퓨터에 만족합니다. 그러나, 이 컴퓨터 모델을 인터넷 네

트워크에 연결 상태를 유지하는 데 어려움이 있습니다. 노트북을 네트워크로 연결할 수는 있는데 일관성이 없이 끊깁니다. PRO 1 Ultra 컴퓨터를 네트워크에 다시 연결하는 등 여러 해결책을 시행해보았습니다. 어떤 해결책도 듣지 않았습니다. 누구 이런 경험 하신 분 계신가요? 이 문제가 모든 PRO 1 노트북의 문제인지 아니면 제가 구입한 것만 문제인지 확실치가 않습니다. 인터넷 그 자체는 괜찮습니다. 저희 형들도 다른 브랜드의 노트북들을 가지고 있는데 아무 문제없이 인터넷에 연결되어 있습니다.

Adagio Computers 이용자 포럼
〉〉〉〉〉 Re: Adagio PRO 1 Ultra가 무선 인터넷 연결이 안 돼요.
Tony McGuire가 8월 15일 오전 9시 34분에 게시
Alexander에게,
저는 처음으로 Adagio에서 PRO 1 Ultra 노트북을 구입했어요. 불행히도 저와 직장 동료 몇 명도 당신과 똑같은 문제를 겪고 있었어요. 저는 인터넷 설정을 조절했고 전선을 검사하고 다시 연결했고 컴퓨터를 다시 시작했지만 소용없었어요.
그 후 저는 Adagio 컴퓨터 서비스 센터로 전화를 했어요. Steven이라는 이름의 기술자가 바로 도움을 주었죠. 제가 Steven의 설명이 포함된 그가 저에게 보낸 편지를 첨부했어요. 이 편지가 당신의 문제를 해결하길 희망해요.

발신: Steven Buck 〈steven@adagio.com〉
수신: Tony McGuire 〈tony@gmail.com〉
귀하와 귀하의 동료들이 겪고 있는 불편함에 사죄드립니다. 저는 Adagio의 고객 만족 부서의 총 매니저로 지금 바로 지체 없이 당신의 문제를 해결할 수 있습니다.
우선, 우리 회사 웹사이트로 가세요. "update"를 다운받아 설치하시기만 하면 됩니다. (즉, 파일을 귀하의 노트북에 저장해서, 파일을 열고, 그 후 일련의 메시지를 따라 하시기 바랍니다.) 귀하는 무료로 Adagio 회사의 웹사이트 소프트웨어 업데이트페이지에서 다운받을 수 있습니다. 일단 귀하가 "update"를 설치하면, 인터넷 연결 유지에 전혀 문제가 없을 겁니다.
다시 한번 불편을 드려 죄송합니다.
Steven Buck
Head manager of customer satisfaction department

186. (D)

답장의 2번째 문단 1행에 있는 "called"와 의미가 가장 가까운 것은?

(A) 호명하다

(B) 지명하다

(C) 증명하다

(D) 연락하다

분석_ 두 번째 지문을 보면 컴퓨터의 오작동으로 인해 컴퓨터 회사로 연락했다(I then called the Adagio Computers Service desk.)가 가장 적절하므로 (D)가 정답이다.

187. (D)

Alexander는 그의 웹사이트 게시물에서 어떤 문제를 언급했는가?

(A) 그는 잘못된 컴퓨터를 받았다.

(B) 그는 잘못된 요금을 청구받았다.
(C) 배달 시간이 약속한 것보다 더 오래 걸렸다.
(D) 그는 인터넷 연결에 문제를 겪었다.

분석_ Alexander가 언급한 문제는 Alexander가 쓴 첫 지문을 보면 알 수 있다. 첫 지문에 However, I am having difficulty keeping the model connected to my Internet network.를 보면 인터넷 연결이 지속되지 않는다고 언급했으므로 (D)가 가장 적절하다.

188. (C)

Tony에 대한 내용 중 아마도 올바른 것은?
(A) 인터넷 연결 문제가 그의 동료에 의해 해결되었다.
(B) 그는 처음으로 Steven에게 편지를 보냈다.
(C) Adagio에서 컴퓨터를 처음으로 구입했다.
(D) 그는 컴퓨터 오작동으로 환불을 요청했다.

분석_ Tony에 관한 정답은 Tony가 작성한 두 번째 지문을 보면 알 수 있다. I just purchased PRO 1 Ultra laptop from Adagio for the first time.에서 처음으로 Adagio의 컴퓨터를 구입했다고 언급했으므로 (C)가 가장 적절하다.

189. (B)

Alexander와 Tony의 공통점은 무엇인가?
(A) 둘은 Adagio Computer의 직장동료이다.
(B) 둘은 모두 PRO 1 Ultra 노트북을 소유하고 있다.
(C) 둘은 과거 2년간 Adagio MAX 모델을 가지고 있었다.
(D) 둘은 Adagio의 고객만족부서 총 매니저인 Steven에게 편지를 받았다.

분석_ 첫 지문과 두 번째 지문을 보면 둘 모두 PRO 1 Ultra 노트북을 가지고 있고 같은 문제를 겪었으므로 (B)가 가장 적절하다.

190. (C)

Steven은 Tony에게 무엇을 하라고 했는가?
(A) Adagio의 기술자에게 연락하기
(B) 컴퓨터를 그가 있는 근처 지역 상점으로 가져가기
(C) 웹사이트에 가서 "update"를 다운받기
(D) 인터넷 서비스 제공업체를 바꾸기

분석_ Steven이 요구한 것은 Steven이 쓴 세 번째 지문을 보면 알 수 있다. First of all, go to our website. All you have to do is to download and install the "update."에서 보면 웹사이트에 가서 다운받으라고 언급했으므로 (C)가 정답이다.

Questions 191-195 refer to the following article and two e-mails. 음성강의

9월 1일 – 잘 사는 비결은 무엇인가?
Elizabeth Lucy가 작성
Follow the One Institution의 설립자 Nicholas Hunter는 5년 전 자신에게 질문을 했다. 그는 말했다. "나는 유명한 예술가 Agatha Della의 전기를 읽는 데 집중하고 있는 여인과 기차에서 대화를 했어요. 그 이야기는 그녀를 그녀 자신의 어린 시절로 되돌려놓았어요. 나는 그때 유명한 인물의 인생이 어떻게 우리 자신의 경험과 서로 연관이 되는지 깨닫게 되었어요."

여행에서 돌아온 이후, Hunter는 3백만이 넘는 구독자를 가진 수상 경력이 있는 Followtheone.com을 시작했다. 이 웹사이트는 다양한 유명인들의 수천 가지 이야기를 특색 있게 다루며 새로운 이야기가 매일 추가된다. "성공은 이러한 이야기의 힘 덕분입니다"라고 Hunter가 말했다. "사람들은 사회의 유명 인물들의 개인적인 경험에 관해서 읽은 후 자기 자신의 삶을 더 잘 이해합니다."
더 많이 알고 싶다면 www.Followtheone.com/notablepeople을 방문하면 된다.

발신: wdvaunt@followtheone.co.ca
수신: elucy@mostmagazine.com
주제: 오류
날짜: 9월 5일
Lucy 씨
9월 1일 당신의 기사에 관해 감사드립니다. 그러나 저는 당신이 지역 신문에 기사를 쓴 이후에도 왜 구독자의 수가 변하지 않는지 궁금했습니다.
당신 기사에서 오류를 발견했습니다. 우리 웹사이트 주소는 Followtheone.com이 아니라 followtheone.co.ca입니다. 이 문제를 정정해주시겠습니까?
그리고 우리는 Enlightening People이라 불리는 종이 잡지를 출간할 것입니다. 이 새로운 잡지는 훌륭한 일반인들뿐 아니라 유명인에 관한 감동적인 이야기를 특색 있게 다룰 것입니다.
Winnie De Vaunt
Nicholas Hunter의 비서

발신: elucy@mostmagazine.com
수신: wdvaunt@followtheone.co.ca
주제: 답장 – 오류
날짜: 9월 6일
당신의 편지를 받고 기사를 확인 후, 저는 바로 실수를 정정했습니다. 제가 한 실수에 관해 사과드립니다. 수정된 기사를 웹사이트 www.mostmagazine.com/article24.business에서 확인할 수 있습니다.
저는 당신이 최근 편지에서 언급한 당신의 새로운 잡지 Enlightening에 관심이 있습니다. 저는 당신과 인터뷰 약속을 잡고 싶습니다. 이번 주 금요일 12시에 인터뷰 시간 되십니까? 원하시면 다른 시간으로 정하셔도 됩니다. 언제 시간이 가능하신지 제 비서 Sarah에게 알려주세요.
감사합니다.
Elizabeth Kucy

191. (B)

기사의 주된 목적은 무엇인가?
(A) 숨겨진 관광 명소를 추천하기 위해
(B) Hunter의 일을 묘사하기 위해
(C) 작가들을 위한 조언을 제공하기 위해
(D) 새로운 잡지를 구독하기 위해

분석_ 기사문의 목적은 기사문이 쓰여진 첫 지문을 보면 알 수 있다. 첫 지문 전반에 걸쳐서 Hunter가 어떻게 성공적인 웹사이트 'followtheone'을 시작하고 성공했는지에 관해 기술하고 있으므로 (B)가 가장 적절하다.

192. (A)

Hunter 씨에 따르면, 왜 이야기가 흥미로운가?
(A) 이야기는 독자들이 자신들의 삶을 더 잘 이해하게 도와준다.
(B) 이야기는 유명한 사람들에 의해 쓰여졌다.
(C) 이야기는 읽고 이해하기 쉽다.
(D) 이야기는 독자들이 다양한 블로그 스타일에 익숙하게 해준다.

분석_ 첫 지문의 후반부를 보면 "Success has come because of the power of these stories," Mr. Hunter says. "People understand their own lives better after reading about the personal experiences of notable members of society." 에서 사람들은 유명인들의 경험을 읽은 후 자신의 삶을 더 잘 이해한다고 말하고 있으므로 (A)가 가장 적절하다.

193. (A)

Enlightening People에 관해 유추할 수 있는 것은 무엇인가?
(A) 잡지는 곧 출간될 것이다.
(B) 잡지는 유명인의 감동적인 이야기만 다룬다.
(C) 독자들은 웹사이트상에서 잡지를 볼 수 있다.
(D) 구독료는 모든 잡지 편집자에게 무료이다.

분석_ 두 번째 지문인 편지에 we will be launching a print magazine called Enlightening People.이라고 언급했으므로 (A)가 가장 적절하다.

194. (C)

첫 이메일에서, Winnie 씨는 기사에 관해 뭐라고 말했는가?
(A) 유명인이 기사를 추천한다.
(B) 기사는 책으로 재출간될 것이다.
(C) 기사는 구독자 수에 영향을 미치는 치명적인 문제가 있다.
(D) 곧 전국 신문에 등장할 것이다.

분석_ 두 번째 지문인 첫 편지에서 I have found some errors in your story. Our website address is followtheone.co.ca but not Followtheone.com.을 보면 구독자 수에 변화가 없어 기사를 확인했더니 인터넷 주소가 잘못되었으므로 (C)가 가장 적절하다.

195. (A)

Elizabeth가 Winnie에게 요구하는 것은 무엇인가?
(A) 새로운 잡지에 관해 인터뷰할 시간을 내는 것
(B) 기사에 오류를 수정하는 것
(C) 잠재적인 취업 후보생을 인터뷰하는 것
(D) Nicholas Hunter에게 전화하는 것

분석_ Elizabeth가 Winnie에게 요구하는 것은 Elizabeth가 쓴 세 번째 지문을 보면 알 수 있다. 마지막 지문 후반부를 보면 Can you make time for this interview this Friday at noon? You can make it in a different time if you like. Please let my assistant, Sarah when you are available. 이라고 인터뷰 시간을 요구했고, 비서인 Sarah에게 연락 달라고 부탁했으므로 (A)가 가장 적절하다.

Questions 196-200 refer to following letter, attachment and e-mail.

Excellent Partner와 계약해주셔서 감사합니다. 우리는 귀하의 공장에 회사 환경 기준 증명서를 위해 선택되어 기쁘고 귀사와 함께 일하길 기대합니다.

전에 얘기했듯이, 감사는 귀사가 깨끗한 공기와 물, 쓰레기 처리를 관장하는 정부 규제를 준수하는지 아닌지를 검토할 겁니다. 이 편지에 다뤄질 네 개의 주된 분야가 첨부되었습니다.

모든 분야의 등급이 귀사의 전체등급과 더불어 보고서에 포함될 것입니다. 우리는 귀사의 제조 공장과 창고, 선적 장소 각각을 감사하고 등급을 매길 것입니다.

이미 아시다시피, 감사 기간은 적어도 2주간 지속되고 모든 운영이 원활하고 정상적으로 진행될 때 시작됩니다. 등록서류에서, 귀사는 감사가 7월 마지막 2주간 진행되기를 요청하셨습니다. 이 시간은 우리도 좋습니다. 만약 귀사로부터 달리 들은 바가 없다면 저는 이 날짜를 귀사 공장의 환경평가 일정으로 잡을 최적의 시간이라 간주하겠습니다. 감사를 어떻게 준비할지 세부사항을 검토할 수 있게 가능하면 빨리 연락 주세요.

Evan
Excellent Partner

Excellent Partner
항상 당신과 함께합니다
Green Technology의 환경 규격 증명서

제조 공장 / 창고 / 선적 장소	등급 A	등급 B	등급 C
일반적 관행			
방출공기의 질			
방출폐수의 질			
폐기물 처리와 재활용			
전체			

수신: Farrel_Lautner@greentechnology.com
발신: Max_Wahlberg@greentechnology.com
주제: 3분기 일정
날짜: 7월 1일
첨부: 3qschedule.pdf

Lautner 씨에게

저는 7, 8, 그리고 9월에 잡힌 회사 일정의 현재 초안을 동봉했습니다. 우리 창고직원은 중국에서 발주한 플라스틱 주문에 따라 이 기간 동안 야근을 해야 할 수도 있다는 것을 기억해두시길 바랍니다. 우리 회사는 늦어도 이번 주말까지 이 주문이 발주될 거라 예상합니다. 이번 주말에 우리는 일정을 마무리 지을 수 있을 겁니다. 다른 모든 기존 주문은 마무리되고 일정에 포함되어야 합니다.

지난 회의에서, 당신은 우리가 일정을 추가해야 할 수도 있다고 말했습니다. 저는 이미 7월 안전 훈련 과정을 추가했는데 다른 무엇을 더 추가할지 알려주시겠습니까? 저는 다음 주말까지 지역 담당자에게 일정을 전달하고 싶습니다.

Dwayne Douglas

196. (C)

왜 Evan 씨는 편지를 썼는가?

(A) 잠재 고객을 끌기 위해

(B) 고객의 정보 요청에 응답하기 위해

(C) 제안된 일정을 확인하기 위해

(D) 업무 절차의 변경을 상기시키기 위해

분석_ Evan이 편지를 쓴 이유는 Evan이 쓴 첫 지문을 보면 알 수 있다. 편지 후반부에 you requested that the audit happen during the last two weeks of July. This time frame works well for us를 보면 고객이 요청한 시간이 7월 마지막 2주인데 이 시간으로 검사시간을 잡겠다고 언급했으므로 (C)가 가장 적절하다.

197. (D)

Excellent Partner는 어떤 서비스를 제공하는가?

(A) 제조공장과 창고의 직원을 찾아주기

(B) 기술 학회의 재정 보고서를 준비하기

(C) 조립 라인 직원들을 훈련시키기

(D) 회사가 정부기준을 얼마나 잘 준수하는지 평가하기

분석_ 첫 지문을 보면 We are happy to be your choice for corporate environmental standards certification.이라고 언급되었고 두 번째 평가서류를 보면 "environmental standards certification of 특정회사"라고 특정회사의 환경 기준 증명서를 발급하고 아래에 등급을 매겼으므로 (D)가 가장 적절하다.

198. (A)

이메일에 따르면, 다음 달 창고에서 아마도 어떤 일이 발생할 것인가?

(A) 몇몇 근로자들은 더 긴 시간 근무를 할 것이다.

(B) 몇몇 자동화 장비가 설치될 것이다.

(C) 폐기물이 재활용되기 위해 적절히 취급되고 보호될 것이다.

(D) 회사 일정 복사본이 모든 직원에게 보내질 것이다.

분석_ 질문이 답과 연관된 힌트가 많으므로 잘 읽어보아야 한다. 질문에서 창고에서 다음 달 일어날 일을 물었는데 세 번째 지문인 이메일을 보면 Please be reminded that staff in our repository will need to work overtime.에서 창고직원은 야근을 해야 한다고 했으므로 (A)가 가장 적절하다.

199. (C)

감사에서 다뤄지지 않는 분야는 무엇인가?

(A) 일반적 관행

(B) 방출 공기의 질

(C) 폐기물 용기

(D) 깨끗한 물

분석_ 두 번째 지문의 표를 보아도 답이 있으며 첫 번째 지문의 in observance of government regulations governing clean air, clean water, and waste disposal을 보면 폐기물 처리와 재활용에 관한 언급은 있었으나 폐기물을 담는 용기에 관한 언급은 없으므로 (C)가 정답이다.

200. (B)

Lautner 씨는 이메일에 대한 답장에서 아마도 무엇을 얘기할 것인가?

(A) 제조 시설은 증가된 사업기회에 준비해야 한다.

(B) 회사의 감사가 회사 일정에 포함되어야 한다.

(C) 8월 안전 훈련이 준비되어야 한다.

(D) 중국의 플라스틱 주문을 완전히 이행해야 한다.

분석_ 첫 번째 지문에서 7월 마지막 2주간 감사가 이행된다(the audit happen during the last two weeks of July)고 언급되었다. 세 번째 지문에서 7월, 8월, 9월에 회사에서 일어나는 회사일정을 언급하고 있는데 I have added the July security training sessions on it already, but could you let me know what else I should add?를 보면 안전 훈련 과정은 추가했으나, 감사에 관한 내용이 빠져 있으므로 감사 내용을 추가하라고 언급하는 (B)가 가장 적절하다.

Actual Test 03

Part 1
본문 p.101

1. (B)
(A) They are fixing the guitars.
(B) They are playing musical instruments.
(C) They are wearing long sleeve shirts.
(D) They are lying on the grass.
(A) 그들은 기타를 수리 중이다.
(B) 그들은 악기를 연주 중이다.
(C) 그들은 긴소매 셔츠를 입고 있다.
(D) 그들은 잔디 위에 누워 있다.

어휘_ fix 수리하다 instrument 악기 도구 lie 누워 있다

분석_ 두 사람 이상 있는 사진은 그들의 공통된 동작을 유심히 관찰해볼 필요가 있다. 사진 속 등장인물들은 악기를 연주 중이다. (B) 사진에 등장한 사람들의 동작과 일치하므로 정답이다. 오답분석 (A) 사진에 기타가 나오지만 수리하는 모습은 아니다. (C) 사진 속의 등장인물들은 긴소매가 아닌 민소매와 짧은 소매 셔츠를 입고 있다. (D) 잔디 위에 앉아 있으므로 오답이다.

2. (B)
(A) She's turning on the light.
(B) She's using a photocopier.
(C) She's speaking over the phone.
(D) She's putting on her red jacket.
(A) 여자가 불을 켜는 중이다.
(B) 여자가 복사기를 이용 중이다.
(C) 여자가 전화상으로 말하는 중이다.
(D) 여자가 빨간색 외투를 입는 중이다.

어휘_ turn on ~를 켜다 photocopier 복사기 put on 입다

분석_ 사진 속에 한 명의 사람이 있는 사진은 의류 및 장신구 착용상태를 표현하거나 동작을 나타낸다. (B) 여자가 복사기를 만지고 있으므로 정답이다. 오답분석 (A) 불을 켜는 동작이 아니므로 동작 불일치 오답이다. (C) 사진 속에 전화기가 없으므로 오답이다. (D) put on은 입고 있는 동작을 의미하며, 현재 착용한 상태를 표현하는 경우에는 wear가 올바른 표현이다.

3. (D)
(A) Potatoes are grown in the yard.
(B) Vegetable is being moved into the box.
(C) Some fruits are cooked.
(D) Items are arranged for sale.
(A) 감자가 마당에서 재배되고 있다.
(B) 야채가 상자 안으로 옮겨지고 있다.
(C) 몇몇 과일이 조리된다.
(D) 상품들이 판매를 위해 준비되어 있다.

어휘_ yard 마당 cook 요리하다 arrange 준비하다 배열하다

분석_ 사람 없는 사진으로 배경과 사물의 위치 파악을 해두어야 한다. (D) 농산물이 판매대에서 판매를 위해 전시되어 있는 사진이므로 정답이다. 오답분석 (A) 마당이 사진 속에 없으므로 오답이다. (B) 사람이 없는 사진에서는 물품이 동작을 취할 수 없으므로 동작의 의미를 지닌 being이 나오는 경우 대부분 오답이다. (C) 농산물이 조리되지 않은 원재료 상태이다.

4. (C)
(A) The monitor is being checked for repair.
(B) They are attending the presentation.
(C) The man is pointing at the monitor.
(D) The man is writing on the notebook.
(A) 모니터가 수리를 위해 점검받는 중이다.
(B) 그들은 발표에 참석 중이다.
(C) 남자가 모니터를 가리키고 있다.
(D) 남자가 공책에 적고 있다.

어휘_ repair 수리 presentation 발표 point at 가리키다

분석_ 여러 명의 사람이 사진 속에 등장하는 경우에는 그들의 공통된 동작을 보거나, 혹은 부각된 한 명의 동작이나 착용상태를 유심히 관찰해야 한다. (C) 남자가 모니터 화면을 손으로 가리키는 사진이므로 정답이다. 오답분석 (A) 수리하는 장면으로 보기에는 무리가 따른다. (B) 발표자와 청중이 없으므로 오답이다. (D) 사진 속에 공책이 없으므로 오답이다.

5. (D)
(A) Pedestrians are moving in the same direction.
(B) The people are working on the pavement.
(C) Taxis are parked along the sidewalk.
(D) Vehicles are stopped in front of the crosswalk.
(A) 보행자들이 같은 방향으로 이동 중이다.
(B) 사람들이 포장도로 위에서 근무 중이다.
(C) 택시들이 길가를 따라서 주차되어 있다.
(D) 차량들이 횡단보도 앞에 정차되어 있다.

어휘_ pedestrian 보행자 direction 방향 pavement 포장도로(아스팔트 도로) sidewalk 인도 crosswalk 횡단보도

분석_ 교통 관련 문제는 토익시험에서 출제빈도가 높다. 차량 상태 및 보행자의 동작을 관찰한다. (D) 차량들이 주차가 아닌 잠시 정차가 된 모습이기 때문에 정답이다. 오답분석 (A) 보행자는 있지만 서로 반대방향으로 걸어가고 있으므로 오답이다. (B) '걷다'의 walk와 '일하다'의 work의 발음을 유의해야 한다. (C) 차량이 완전히 주차되는 경우에 park을 사용한다.

6. (A)
(A) Most of the seats are occupied.
(B) The slide show is about to be over.
(C) Some chairs are lying on the floor.
(D) The speaker is reaching for the projector on the ceiling.
(A) 대부분의 좌석이 채워져 있다.

(B) 슬라이드 발표가 곧 끝난다.
(C) 몇몇 의자들이 바닥에 눕혀져 있다.
(D) 발표자가 천장의 프로젝터기에 손을 뻗는 중이다.

어휘_ occupy (자리를) 점유하다 be about to 막 ~하려 하다 reach for ~로 손을 뻗다 ceiling 천장

분석_ 다수의 사람들이 나오는 사진이다. 공통된 동작을 정답으로 골라준다. 식당이나 버스 안의 좌석이 사진에 있는 경우에는 채워져 있는지 여부를 유심히 관찰한다. (A) 비어 있는 좌석이 거의 없으므로 정답이다. **오답분석** (B) 슬라이드 발표가 이루어지고 있지만 곧 끝나는지 여부는 사진상으로 판단이 어렵다. (C) 바닥에 누워 있는 의지가 없으므로 오답이다. (D) 발표자가 천장을 향해 손을 뻗는 장면은 아니므로 오답이다.

Part 2   본문 p.104

7. (A)

Aren't you attending the annual sales meeting?
(A) No, it was canceled.
(B) The sales director arrives at nine.
(C) I can't meet the requirement.

연례판매모임에 참석할 거예요?
(A) 아니요, 연례판매모임은 취소됐어요.
(B) 판매부장은 9시에 도착해요.
(C) 저는 요구조건을 충족할 수 없어요.

어휘_ attend 참석하다 cancel 취소하다 requirement 요구조건

분석_ 부정의문문은 부정어를 빼고 긍정으로 해석하면 쉽게 해결된다. 일반의문문은 기본적으로 yes or no가 정답이 된다. 모임의 참석 여부를 물었고 모임이 취소되어 가지 않는다는 (A)가 적절하다.

8. (B)

Have you still got the error message logging in our website?
(A) On our website.
(B) Yes, do you know why?
(C) Put them back during logout.

아직도 우리 웹사이트에 로그인할 때 오류메시지를 받나요?
(A) 우리 웹사이트에요.
(B) 예, 왜 그런지 이유를 아시나요?
(C) 로그아웃 동안 그것들을 되돌려주세요.

어휘_ error message 오류 메시지 still 여전히

분석_ 질문에 있는 특정 단어가 보기 속에서 반복되면 오답일 확률이 높다. 메시지를 받는지 그 여부를 물었고 아직도 받고 있고 왜 그런지 이유를 묻는 (B)가 정답이다. **오답분석** (A) website 반복은 오답이다.

9. (B)

Where is the nearest pharmacy store?
(A) Store food the fridge.
(B) Right next to the library.
(C) It takes nearly two hours.

가장 가까운 약국은 어디에요?
(A) 냉장고에 음식을 보관하세요.
(B) 도서관 바로 옆이요.
(C) 거의 2시간이 걸립니다.

어휘_ pharmacy 약국 fridge 냉장고 store 저장하다, 보관하다

분석_ 질문에 있는 특정 단어가 보기 속에서 반복되며 또한 그 뜻이 다른 경우는 오답일 확률이 높다. 질문에 store는 상점이고 (A)의 store는 '저장하다, 보관하다'라는 뜻이다. 장소(where)를 묻고 있고 장소를 설명하는 (B) next to가 있으므로 가장 적절한 정답은 (B)이다.

10. (A)

Isn't the museum closed on weekends?
(A) No, it's open everyday.
(B) He lives close by.
(C) There are more weekday classes.

박물관은 주말에 문을 닫나요?
(A) 아니요, 박물관은 매일 문을 열어요.
(B) 그는 근처에 살아요.
(C) 평일 강좌는 더 많이 있어요.

어휘_ close 문을 닫다 weekends 주말 close 가까운

분석_ paraphrase된 표현들은 정답으로 자주 등장한다. 질문에 있는 museum이 보기에 it으로 paraphrase되었다. 또한 질문의 close는 '문을 닫다'라는 의미이고 보기 (B)의 close는 '가까이'란 뜻이므로 중복음이며 다의어라 오답일 확률이 높다. 박물관 운영 여부를 물었고 영업을 계속한다는 (A)가 정답이다.

11. (C)

Why are the workers working overtime?
(A) Five hour shifts.
(B) Near the facility entrance.
(C) To fill a special order.

왜 근로자들이 야근을 해야 하나요?
(A) 5시간 교대근무입니다.
(B) 공장 입구 근처에요.
(C) 특별 주문에 응하기 위해서요.

어휘_ work over time 야근하다 shift 근무 교대 fill 주문을 이행하다

분석_ 이유를 묻는 why의문문에 대한 대답은 보통 접속사, 전치사, to부정사, ⟨for + 명사⟩ 등이 있다. 야근의 이유를 물었고 이유를 대답하는 (C)가 정답이다.

12. (B)

When will hospital renovation project on the east wing be completed?
(A) Yes, the nurse has a health certificate.
(B) Probably in late November.
(C) Host a party.

병원의 동쪽 별관 재건 프로젝트는 언제 끝나나요?
(A) 예, 간호사는 건강증명서를 가지고 있어요.

(B) 아마 11월 후반에요.

(C) 파티를 개최합시다.

어휘_ renovation 재건, 수리 wing 별관 certificate 증명서

분석_ 질문에 hospital과 연상되는 단어 nurse가 있는 (A)는 오답이다. 언제(when)인지 시간을 물었고 시점(in November)를 말한 (B)가 가장 적절하다.

13. (C)

Which marketing proposal did the client prefer?

(A) They prefer to speak in person.

(B) Because it was new to them.

(C) She liked the last one.

고객은 어느 마케팅 제안을 선호했나요?

(A) 그들은 직접 말하는 것을 선호해요.

(B) 왜냐면 그것은 그들에게 새로운 것이라서요.

(C) 그녀는 마지막 제안을 좋아했어요.

어휘_ prefer 선호하다 in person 직접 last 마지막

분석_ 질문의 proposal이 (C)에서 one으로 paraphrase되었다. 선호하는 제안을 물었고 마지막 제안이라고 답한 (C)가 가장 적절하다. 오답분석 (A)질문의 prefer가 반복된 오답이다.

14. (B)

You already signed the contract to a new car lease, didn't you?

(A) A thousand at least.

(B) Yes, last week.

(C) I didn't contact Leeds.

귀하는 새로운 자동차 임대 계약에 이미 서명했죠, 그렇죠?

(A) 최소 천 명입니다.

(B) 예, 지난주에 서명했습니다.

(C) Leeds와 연락하지 않았습니다.

어휘_ contract 계약서 lease 임대 at least 적어도 contact 연락하다

분석_ 정답으로 나오는 표현 중에는 질문에 있는 단어를 반복하기 싫어서 생략하는 경우가 많다. (B)는 Yes, I already signed the contract to a new car lease last week.를 의미하지만 반복되는 단어를 다 생략한 형태이다. 계약 여부를 물었고 지난주에 계약을 했다고 대답하는 (B)가 정답이다.

15. (A)

How did Sarah decide where to stay on summer vacation?

(A) She searched for places on the Internet.

(B) Sometimes by air.

(C) No, I am driving there.

Sarah는 여름 휴가기간에 어디서 머물지 어떻게 결정했죠?

(A) 그녀는 인터넷으로 장소를 물색했어요.

(B) 가끔은 비행기를 타고 가요.

(C) 아니요, 나는 그곳에 운전해서 가요.

어휘_ decide 결심하다 stay 머물다 search for 찾다 by air 비행기로

분석_ 질문의 Sarah가 정답 보기 (A)에서 She로, where to stay는 place로 paraphrase되었다. 질문에서 어떻게(how)라는 수단을 물었고 방법을 얘기하는 (A)가 정답이다. 오답분석

(B) by는 여름 휴가 장소로 가는 방법을 얘기하므로 혼동되는 오답이다.

16. (C)

Don't you want to bring a digital recorder to the conference?

(A) Through a teleconference.

(B) Between December 3rd and December 5th.

(C) Yes, it's in my bag.

회의에 디지털녹음기를 가지고 갈 건가요?

(A) 원격회의를 통해서요.

(B) 12월 3일과 12월 5일 사이에요.

(C) 예, 디지털녹음기는 내 가방 안에 있어요.

어휘_ bring 가져오다 recorder 기록장비 through 통해서

분석_ 질문의 a digital recorder가 정답 보기 (C)에서 it으로 paraphrase되었다. 녹음기를 가져갈 것인지 물었고 가방에 가지고 있다고 말하는 (C)가 정답이다.

17. (B)

What about looking at some colors to paint the building exterior?

(A) Paint in oil and watercolor.

(B) Sure, I'm free after lunch.

(C) The reception desk.

건물 외벽에 칠을 하기 위해 색을 살펴보는 게 어때요?

(A) 유성과 수성물감으로 색을 칠해요.

(B) 그래요, 점심 이후에 시간 돼요.

(C) 안내 데스크요.

어휘_ exterior 외부 free 한가한, 시간이 있는 reception desk 안내 데스크

분석_ 질문의 paint가 보기 (A)에 반복되며 이런 경우 오답일 확률이 높다. 질문에서 what about으로 시작되는 제안을 하였고 제안을 수락하는 (B)가 정답이다.

18. (A)

When will Professor Hubert be available?

(A) He's busy all day long I'm afraid.

(B) Just down the street.

(C) Because he got stuck in traffic.

Hubert 교수님은 언제 시간이 가능한가요?

(A) 유감스럽게도 교수님은 하루 종일 바빠요.

(B) 그냥 길 아래로요.

(C) 왜냐면 교수님은 교통체증에 시달려서요.

어휘_ busy 바쁜 stuck in traffic 옴짝달싹 못하다, 교통이 막히다

분석_ 질문의 Professor Hubert가 (A)에서 He로 paraphrase되었다. 교수님 시간이 언제 가능한지를 물었고 하루 종일 바쁘다고 말한 (A)가 정답이다. 오답분석 (C) when이 아닌 why라고 질문했을 경우 정답이 된다.

19. (A)

Why is the museum so crowded today?

(A) There comes a renowned speaker later.

(B) The closest parking lot.
(C) No, not cloudy but windy.
왜 오늘 박물관이 이렇게 붐비죠?
(A) 조금 있다 유명한 연설자가 온대요.
(B) 가장 가까운 주차장이요.
(C) 아니요, 구름 낀 게 아니라 바람이 불어요.
어휘_ crowd 복잡한, 혼잡한 renowned 유명한 cloudy 구름 낀 windy 바람 부는
분석_ Why라고 이유를 물었을 때 (A)처럼 because를 생략하고 바로 문장이 나오는 정답이 자주 등장한다. 박물관이 붐비는 이유를 물었고 유명 연설자가 박물관에 오기 때문이라 대답하는 (A)가 정답이다. [오답분석] (C)질문의 crowded와 보기 cloudy는 발음 혼동 함정이다.

20. (B)
Don't forget to put up a notice on the bulletin board.
(A) Put up with inconvenience.
(B) Don't worry, I won't.
(C) I didn't notice the difference.
게시판에 공지문 공고하는 것을 잊지 마세요.
(A) 불편함을 참으세요.
(B) 걱정 마세요. 잊지 않을게요.
(C) 차이를 인식하지 못하겠어요.
어휘_ put up 게시하다 bulletin board 게시판 put up with 참다, 견디다, 인내하다
분석_ (B)는 I won't forget to put up a notice on the bulletin board.에서 질문과 중복이 되는 단어들은 모두 생략되었다. 생략된 것이 정답으로 자주 등장한다. 공지문을 꼭 공지하라는 말에 잊지 않겠다고 대답하는 (B)가 가장 적절하다.

21. (C)
There were more participants at the trader's workshop this month, weren't there?
(A) During spring training.
(B) No, he won't be able to attend.
(C) Yes, it was a big success.
이번 달 무역업자들의 워크샵에 훨씬 더 많은 참가자가 있었죠, 그렇죠?
(A) 봄 훈련기간 동안이요.
(B) 아니요, 그는 참석할 수 없을 것입니다.
(C) 예, 그것은 크게 성공했어요.
어휘_ participant 참가자 during ~하는 동안 trader 무역업자
분석_ 질문의 the trader's workshop이 정답 보기 (C)으로 it으로 paraphrase되었다. 참가자가 많았는지 여부를 묻고 있고, 참가자가 많아 성공했다는 (C)가 정답이다.

22. (B)
How can we have the copy machine repaired?
(A) A local appliance store.
(B) Check with the technical assistant.
(C) When are we leaving?
복사기를 어떻게 수리하죠?
(A) 지역 전자 제품 상점이요.

(B) 기술 보조에게 확인해보세요.
(C) 언제 떠나죠?
어휘_ repair 수리하다 appliance store 가전제품 상점 technical 기술적인
분석_ 복사기 수리 방법을 물었고 다른 사람에게 방법을 확인해보라는 (B)가 정답이다. [오답분석] (A) 전자 제품 상점은 how가 아니라 where의 정답이 될 수 있다.

23. (C)
We still need to place price labels on the new bottles.
(A) On the bottom of the drawer.
(B) The desk costs $ 60.
(C) Let me go get them.
우리는 아직 새로운 병에 가격표를 붙여야 합니다.
(A) 서랍장 하단에요.
(B) 식탁은 60달러입니다.
(C) 제가 가서 가져올게요.
어휘_ price label 가격표 bottle 병 place 놓다, 두다, 하다 (c.f place an order 주문하다)
분석_ 질문의 price labels가 정답 보기 (C)에서는 them으로 paraphrase되었다. 병에 가격표를 붙여야 한다고 언급했고 가격표를 가지고 오겠다는 (C)가 정답이다.

24. (C)
Is the new luxury sedan going to be recalled soon?
(A) We just use the elevator.
(B) The performance results from the experiment are in.
(C) Actually, the work has already begun.
새로운 중형차량이 곧 회수 조치되나요?
(A) 우리는 엘리베이터를 이용합니다.
(B) 실험의 성능결과가 들어왔어요.
(C) 사실, 회수 조치는 이미 시작되었어요.
어휘_ recall 회수하다 performance result 성능 결과 actually 사실 sedan 중형차
분석_ 질문의 recall이 정답 보기 (C)에서 work로 paraphrase되었다. 차량의 회수 조치 여부를 물었고 이미 회수 조치가 시작되었다는 (C)가 정답이다.

25. (B)
You should present financial data at the next executive meeting.
(A) No, I didn't receive a present.
(B) I'd be happy to.
(C) In online data bank.
당신은 다음 이사회모임에서 재정자료를 발표해야 해요.
(A) 아니요, 나는 선물을 받지 않았어요.
(B) 기꺼이 발표를 할게요.
(C) 온라인 자료 은행에서요.
어휘_ present 발표하다, 선물 be happy to 기꺼이 하다
분석_ 정답 보기 (B)는 I'd be happy to present financial data at the next executive meeting.에서 질문과 중복되는 단어들이 모두 생략된 것이다. 질문의 단어가 생략되어 등장하는

보기는 거의가 정답이다. 재정자료 발표를 해야 한다고 언급했고 기꺼이 발표를 하겠다는 (B)가 정답이다.

26. (A)

Do you want the latest report to be mailed to you or sent electronically?
(A) Please send me a hard copy.
(B) Sure, let me deliver the mail.
(C) Yes, I already sent them.

최신 보고서를 우편으로 보내드릴까요, 이메일로 보내드릴까요?
(A) 인쇄물 출력 자료로 보내주세요.
(B) 물론이죠, 제가 우편을 배달할게요.
(C) 예, 제가 이미 보냈습니다.

어휘_ latest 최신의 mail 우편으로 보내다 hard copy 출력본 deliver 배달하다

분석_ 질문의 mail을 정답 보기 (A)에서 hard copy로 paraphrase 했다. 질문은 선택의문문이다. 우편 또는 이메일 둘 중 선호하는 방식을 물었고 출력자료, 즉 우편으로 보내달라고 선택한 (A)가 정답이다.

27. (A)

I don't seem to be able to find my documents anywhere.
(A) Have you looked in your file?
(B) You can pick up your prescription in a moment.
(C) We haven't seen the most recent version.

내 문서를 어디서도 찾을 수가 없네요.
(A) 당신 파일 안은 확인했어요?
(B) 곧 처방전을 받아갈 수 있어요.
(C) 우리는 가장 최신판을 볼 수 없었어요.

어휘_ document 문서 prescription 처방전 in a moment 바로, 당장, 곧

분석_ 문서를 찾을 수 없다고 말했고 파일 안에서 문서를 찾아봤냐고 물어보는 (A)가 가장 적절하다.

28. (A)

You can help me download this coupon on my phone, can't you?
(A) I'm not sure I know how.
(B) Yes, they can carry heavy loads.
(C) It has been very helpful.

휴대전화로 이 쿠폰을 다운받는 방법을 도와줄 수 있죠, 그렇죠?
(A) 방법을 잘 모르겠어요.
(B) 예, 그것들은 큰 짐도 운반할 수 있어요.
(C) 매우 도움이 되었어요.

어휘_ coupon 쿠폰 carry 옮기다 heavy 무거운 helpful 도움이 되는

분석_ 정답 (A) I'm not sure I know how to download this coupon on your phone.에서 질문과 중복이 되는 단어들은 생략되었다. 보통 생략된 단어들이 있는 보기는 정답이다. 쿠폰 다운방법을 물었고 본인도 방법을 모른다고 말한 (A)가 정답이다.

29. (C)

Would you like a table with drawers or one without them?
(A) It's just around the desk.
(B) I prefer the floor plan.
(C) Either one is fine with me.

서랍장이 있는 탁자를 원하시나요, 아니면 서랍장이 없는 탁자를 원하시나요?
(A) 책상 주변에 있어요.
(B) 평면도를 선호해요.
(C) 어느 것이든 좋아요.

어휘_ drawer 서랍장 floor plan 평면도 either 어느 것이든

분석_ 선택의문문에서 either = anything = anyone이 자주 정답으로 출제된다. 질문은 선택의문문이다. 서랍장이 있는 탁자와 없는 탁자 중 선호하는 것을 물었고 뭐든 좋다고 대답한 (C)가 정답이다.

30. (B)

I think the longer dress would be more suitable for the function.
(A) The women's section is downstairs.
(B) Then that's the one I'll buy.
(C) No, we can't wait any longer.

내 생각에는 좀 긴 드레스가 그 연회에 더 적합하다 생각해요.
(A) 여성복은 아래층입니다.
(B) 그렇다면 긴 드레스를 살게요.
(C) 아니요, 우리는 더 이상 기다릴 수 없어요.

어휘_ suitable 적합한, 적절한 function 연회 not any longer 더 이상 ~않다

분석_ 질문의 longer dress가 (B)에서 the one으로 paraphrase되었다. 긴 드레스가 더 적합하다는 말에 긴 드레스를 구입하겠다는 (B)가 정답이다.

31. (A)

Do you want me to bring you a sandwich from the cafeteria?
(A) I just had, but thanks.
(B) How was your business trip?
(C) Yes, we will bring interns to the picnic.

식당에서 샌드위치 하나 가져다드릴까요?
(A) 이미 먹었어요, 고마워요.
(B) 출장은 어땠나요?
(C) 예, 우리는 신입 인턴들을 야유회로 데려갈 겁니다.

어휘_ business trip 출장 intern 신입사원

분석_ 정답 보기 (A) I just had a sandwich에서 질문이랑 중복된 단어들은 생략되었다. 생략된 것은 보통 정답으로 출제된다. 샌드위치를 사다 주겠다고 제안했고 이미 밥을 먹어서 괜찮다고 거절한 (A)가 가장 적절하다. **오답분석** (C) 질문의 bring이 보기에도 반복된 오답이다.

Questions 32-34 refer to the following conversation.

W: Hi, what can I do for you?
M: **32** *Yes, I'm looking for the A-phone9. It's a wide screen cell phone with a touch pen.*
W: The A-phone9... let's see. This wall here has all of the latest phone from around the world.
M: Hmm. I don't think A-phone9 is on display here. I'm an insurance agent and need a cell phone that has a wide screen for my business.
W: Wait. I can show you another one in a display case. **33** *This is Utopia5 and it's similar in design to A-phone9.*
M: **33** *Oh, that's great. Do you take credit cards?*
W: Sure, I'll ring it right up. It'll come to 60 dollars with tax. **34** *And please feel free to take our shop's weekly newsletter, Into the Cellular. It has lots of useful tips.*
M: OK. Thanks.

W: 안녕하세요, 무엇을 도와드릴까요?
M: 네, 저는 A-phone9를 찾고 있는데요. 터치펜이 있는 대화면 휴대폰이에요.
W: A-phone9이라면... 봅시다. 이 벽에 진열된 것들이 전 세계의 모든 최신 휴대폰입니다.
M: 흠, 제 생각에 A-phone9는 여기 진열되어 있지 않은 것 같네요. 저는 보험 설계사인데 업무 때문에 넓은 화면이 있는 휴대폰이 필요해요.
W: 잠시만요. 진열함에 있는 다른 휴대폰을 보여드릴게요. 이것은 Utopia5인데 디자인 면에서 A-phone9과 유사합니다.
M: 오, 좋아요. 신용카드 결제 가능한가요?
W: 물론이죠, 계산해드릴게요. 세금 포함해서 60달러입니다. 그리고 저희 매장의 주간 신문인 '휴대폰 속으로'를 가져가서 보세요. 유용한 팁이 많이 있습니다.
M: 네. 감사합니다.

어휘_ latest 최신의 on display 진열되어 있는 similar 유사한 credit card 신용카드 ring up 결제하다 feel free to do 얼마든지 ~하다 useful 유용한

32. (D)
What is the man inquiring about?
(A) A cell phone case
(B) A wide screen TV
(C) A insurance policy
(D) A cellular phone
남자는 무엇에 대해 문의하고 있는가?
(A) 휴대폰 케이스
(B) 넓은 화면 텔레비전
(C) 보험 증권
(D) 휴대폰

분석_ 남자가 문의하는 것이 무엇인지 묻고 있다. 대화 초반 특정 모델을 이야기하면서 휴대폰을 찾고 있다는 언급을 하고 있다.

33. (C)
What does the man mean when he says, "Oh, that's great"?
(A) He is aware of cellular's feature.
(B) He receives a discount.
(C) He is satisfied with an item selection.
(D) He wants shop's newsletter.
남자가 "오, 좋아요"라고 말한 것의 의미는 무엇인가?
(A) 남자는 핸드폰의 기능을 깨달았다.
(B) 남자는 할인을 받는다.
(C) 남자는 제품 선택에 만족한다.
(D) 남자는 매장 신문을 원한다.

분석_ 대화 중반 점원이 유사한 다른 모델을 보여주고 남자가 곧장 결제를 하는 걸로 보아 제품에 만족했음을 유추할 수 있다.

34. (D)
What does the woman encourage the man to take?
(A) An employment contract
(B) A discount coupon
(C) A product manual
(D) A store newsletter
여자는 남자에게 무엇을 가져갈 것을 권장하는가?
(A) 고용 계약서
(B) 할인 쿠폰
(C) 제품 설명서
(D) 매장 신문

분석_ 대화 마지막에 많은 팁이 있다면서 매장의 신문을 가져가라고 언급하고 있다.

Questions 35-37 refer to the following conversation and price list.

M: Hi this is James Alvin, I just made an online reservation at your hotel, but when I saw the confirmation page, **35** *I found that I'd made a mistake in the dates. What should I do?*
W: I'll be glad to make a change in your reservation, only if we have a room available. Could you please give me your confirmation number?
M: Of course. It's SA415. I want the reservation for the next weekend, from May 5th to May 7th. Will the price be the same?
W: Let me see. **37** *James Alvin, on the 4th floor, room number 15. Yes, we do have a room available for those two days at the same rate.* So, I've changed your reservation with us. **36** *You can expect an updated confirmation in your e-mail shortly.*

<table>
<tr><th colspan="2">Room No.</th><th>Room Price</th></tr>
<tr><td colspan="2">3rd floor(301-315)</td><td>$ 399</td></tr>
<tr><td>37</td><td>4th floor(401-415)</td><td>$ 499</td></tr>
<tr><td colspan="2">5th floor(501-515)</td><td>$ 599</td></tr>
<tr><td colspan="2">6th floor(601-615)</td><td>$ 699</td></tr>
</table>

M: 안녕하세요. James Alvin입니다. 귀하의 호텔에 방금 온라인상으로 예약을 했습니다. 그런데 예약확정 페이지를 봤는데 제가 날짜에 실수를 했네요. 어떻게 해야 할까요?

W: 만약 이용 가능한 방이 있다면 제가 귀하의 예약을 기꺼이 바꿔드릴게요. 예약확인번호를 말씀해주시겠어요?

M: 물론이죠. SA415입니다. 저는 그 예약을 다음 주말인 5월 5일부터 5월 7일로 변경하기를 원합니다. 가격은 동일한가요?

W: 확인해볼게요. James Alvin, 4층 15호실. 예. 우리 호텔에 귀하가 원하시는 이틀간 동일가격으로 이용 가능한 방이 있습니다. 그래서 제가 바로 예약을 변경했습니다. 곧 귀하의 전자우편으로 바뀐 예약정보를 받을 수 있을 겁니다.

객실번호	객실가
3층 (301-315)	399달러
4층 (401-415)	499달러
5층 (501-515)	599달러
6층 (601-615)	699달러

어휘_ reservation 예약 make a mistake 실수하다 make a change 바꾸다 confirmation number 확인번호 rate 요금

35. (C)

Why is the man calling?
(A) To get directions to the hotel
(B) To ask for a refund
(C) To change a reservation
(D) To check a confirmation number
남자는 왜 전화를 했는가?
(A) 호텔로 가는 약도를 얻기 위해
(B) 환불을 요청하기 위해
(C) 예약 변경을 하기 위해
(D) 예약확정번호를 확인하기 위해
분석_ 남자가 말한 첫 문장에서 I'd made a mistake in the dates. What should I do?라고 언급했다. 따라서 잘못한 예약을 바꾸기 위해서라는 (C)가 가장 적절하다.

36. (A)

What will the woman e-mail the man?
(A) A confirmation information
(B) A discounted coupon
(C) An application form
(D) A complete list of menu options
여자는 남자에게 무엇을 이메일로 보낼것인가?
(A) 확정정보

(B) 할인 쿠폰
(C) 지원 서류
(D) 완전한 메뉴 선택 목록
분석_ 여자는 마지막에 You can expect an updated confirmation in your e-mail shortly.라 언급했다. 따라서 여자가 바꿔준 남자의 새로운 예약확정정보를 보낼 것이므로 (A)가 가장 적절하다.

37. (B)

Look at the graphic. Which floor will the man stay?
(A) 3rd floor
(B) 4th floor
(C) 5th floor
(D) 6th floor
그래프를 보자. 남자는 몇 층에서 머물 것인가?
(A) 3층
(B) 4층
(C) 5층
(D) 6층
분석_ 마지막 여자의 말에 James Alvin, on the 4th floor, room number 15. Yes, we do have a room available for those two days at the same rate.라고 언급되었다. 같은 요금으로 이용 가능한 방이 있는 것이므로 그래프에서 같은 가격은 4층이다. 따라서 (B)가 가장 적절하다.

Questions 38-40 refer to the following conversation.

W: Good afternoon, Mr. Edith. **38 We have a package for you to pick up here at the West Virginia Post Office.** You should have received a missed delivery card when we tried to deliver it two days ago.

M: **39 I'm looking through my mail now, and I can't find any notice about a missed package.** I just got back from my vacation. What should I bring to pick it up?

W: Oh, I see. Well, that shouldn't be a problem. **40 Please make sure to bring along valid photo identification when you come to pick yours up.**

W: Edith 씨 안녕하세요. West Post Office에 오셔서 소포 찾아가세요. 이틀 전 우리가 배송하려 했을 때 남긴 배달 누락 카드를 받으셨어야 했는데요.

M: 지금 우편물을 확인하고 있어요. 빠진 소포에 관한 공지를 찾을 수 없어요. 저는 방금 휴가에서 돌아왔어요. 물건을 찾아가려면 뭘 가지고 가야 하죠?

W: 아. 알겠어요. 문제 될 것 없어요. 빠진 소포를 찾으러 오실 때 유효한 사진 신분증을 꼭 가지고 오세요.

어휘_ package 소포 should have p.p ~했어야 했다 get back from ~서 돌아오다 valid 유효한 make sure 확실히 하다

38. (D)

Who most likely is the woman?
(A) An award-winning florist
(B) A card designer
(C) A photographer
(D) A postal worker
여자는 아마도 직업이 무엇인가?
(A) 수상 경력이 있는 화초 재배가
(B) 카드 디자이너
(C) 사진작가
(D) 우체국 직원
분석_ 첫 번째 여자의 말을 보면 We have a package for you to pick up here at the West Virginia Post Office.라고 언급했다. 여기가 바로 우체국이므로 여자는 우체국 직원으로 유추할 수 있다.

39. (B)

What can't the man find?
(A) A valid credit card
(B) A delivery notice
(C) A trip itinerary
(D) A mailing list
남자가 찾을 수 없는 것은?
(A) 유효한 신용카드
(B) 배달 공지
(C) 여행 일정표
(D) 우편 목록
분석_ 남자가 한 말을 보면 I'm looking through my mail now, and I can't find any notice about a missed package.라고 언급했다. 우편물을 찾았지만 빠진 소포에 관한 공지가 없다고 말했으므로 (B)가 적절하다.

40. (C)

What does the woman request the man to bring with him?
(A) Proof of receipt
(B) An account number
(C) Photo identification
(D) Some office supplies
여자가 남자에게 가지고 오라고 요청한 것은?
(A) 수령 증명서
(B) 계좌 번호
(C) 사진 신분증
(D) 사무용품들
분석_ 여자의 대화 가장 마지막 부분을 보면 Please make sure to bring along valid photo identification when you come to pick yours up.이라고 말하고 있다. 소포를 찾으러 올 때 신분증을 가지고 오라고 말했으므로 (C)가 가장 적절하다.

Questions 41-43 refer to the following conversation and table.

W: Excuse me. I saw the leaflet posted in the window of your store, advertising cooking classes. I wondered **41** *if I could enroll in the chocolate cake making class on Friday morning.*

M: I am sorry, **42** *but the kitchen is too small to accommodate more than ten people, and that class is already full.*

W: Oh, what a pity. **43** *Is there any chance you'll offer another chocolate cake making class?*

M: Yes, we're thinking about holding several baking classes next week. Here is class schedule for next week. Which class would you sign up for?

Date	Class description
Monday Morning	vanilla macaroon
43 *Tuesday Afternoon*	*dark chocolate cake*
Friday Morning	strawberry cup cake
Saturday Afternoon	snowman cookie

W: 실례합니다. 당신 상점 창문에 붙여진 요리 수업 광고지를 봤습니다. 금요일 아침에 있는 초콜릿 케이크 만들기 수업에 등록 가능한지 궁금합니다.

M: 죄송하지만 주방이 협소해 10명 이상의 수강생을 수용할 수 없습니다. 그리고 그 수업은 이미 정원이 다 찼습니다.

W: 아, 아쉽네요. 혹시 다른 초콜릿 케이크 만들기 강좌도 제공하시나요?

M: 예, 다음 주에 여러 개의 제빵 수업을 개최할 생각입니다. 여기 다음 주 수업 일정이 있습니다. 어느 수업에 등록하실 건가요?

날짜	수업 설명
월요일 오전	바닐라 마카롱
화요일 오후	다크 초콜릿 케이크
금요일 오전	딸기 컵케이크
토요일 오후	눈사람 과자

어휘_ leaflet 전단지, 광고 wonder 궁금하다 enroll in 등록하다 accommodate 수용하다 hold 개최하다 sing up for 등록하다, 신청하다

41. (D)

What does the woman want to do at the store?
(A) Display her signature dishes
(B) Interview an advertising expert
(C) Apply for a cooking job
(D) Register for a class
여자는 상점에서 무엇을 하고 싶어 하는가?
(A) 그녀만의 요리를 선보이기
(B) 광고 전문가를 인터뷰하기
(C) 주방 일자리 지원하기
(D) 요리 수업 등록하기

분석_ 처음 여자가 한 말을 보면 I wondered if I could enroll in the chocolate cake making class on Friday morning.이라고 하여 초콜릿 케이크 수업에 관심이 있다고 말했으므로 (D)가 가장 적절하다.

42. (A)

What problem does the man mention?
(A) A room is not big enough.
(B) An instructor is not available right now.
(C) A kitchen utensil is missing.
(D) A cup of chocolate is out of stock.
남자는 어떤 문제를 언급했는가?
(A) 공간이 충분히 크지 않다.
(B) 강사가 지금 시간이 없다.
(C) 주방용품이 사라졌다.
(D) 초콜릿 한 컵이 재고가 없다.
분석_ 남자가 처음 한 대답에서 the kitchen is too small to accommodate more than ten people.을 보면 주방이 작아서 특정 인원 이상의 수강생을 수용할 수 없다고 언급했으므로 (A)가 가장 적절하다.

43. (B)

Look at the graphic. Which day will the woman register for?
(A) Monday Morning
(B) Tuesday Afternoon
(C) Friday Morning
(D) Saturday Afternoon
그래프를 보자. 여자는 어느 요일에 등록을 할 것인가?
(A) 월요일 오전
(B) 화요일 오후
(C) 금요일 오전
(D) 토요일 오후
분석_ 여자의 마지막 말을 보면 Is there any chance you'll offer another chocolate cake making class?에서 초콜릿 케이크에 관심이 있음을 알 수 있으므로 초콜릿과 관련된 수업을 그래프에서 찾으면 (B)가 가장 적절하다.

Questions 44-46 refer to the following conversation.

M: Hi, Ms. Agnes. **44 This is Charles Matthew calling from Diana Realtors.** A private house has just been listed that I believe you might be interested in. It's a two bedroom house that's available right now, **45 but best of all, it's near Mountain Park.**
W: Near Mountain Park? Oh, that's great news. **45 The park is very close to my college.** That's exactly what I hoped for.
M: Would you like to look at the house? **46 We can get in to see it sometime next week,** if you're free.
W: I'm busy on Monday, **46 but Tuesday would be fine.** Let me jot down where it is and I can meet you there.

M: Agnes 씨 안녕하세요. 저는 Diana Realtors에서 근무하는 Charles Matthew입니다. 당신이 관심 있어 할 개인 주택이 등재되었습니다. 지금 바로 입주 가능한 침실 두 개짜리 집입니다. 더욱 좋은 건, 주택이 Mountain Park 근처에 있다는 것입니다.
W: Mountain Park 근처요? 좋네요. 그 공원은 제가 다니는 대학과 매우 가까워요. 바로 제가 원했던 것입니다.
M: 집을 직접 보시겠어요? 다음 주에 언제든 집을 볼 수 있습니다. 당신 시간만 괜찮다면요.
W: 월요일에는 바쁘지만 화요일은 괜찮아요. 집이 어딘지 알려주세요. 그럼 거기서 만나요.
어휘_ realtor 부동산 사무소 close 가까운 jot down 쓰다, 받아 적다

44. (C)

Where does the man work for?
(A) An architecture firm in Mountain Park
(B) A construction company
(C) A real estate agency
(D) A multinational bank
남자는 어디서 근무하는가?
(A) Mountain Park에 있는 건축회사
(B) 건설 회사
(C) 부동산 중개 사무실
(D) 다국적 은행
분석_ 남자가 제일 처음 본인 소개로 This is Charles Matthew calling from Diana Realtors.라고 하여 직접 부동산 사무실에서 근무한다고 언급했으므로 (C)가 정답이다.

45. (A)

What is the woman satisfied with?
(A) A house is conveniently located.
(B) A job position is opening shortly.
(C) Housing funding has been finally approved.
(D) Some renovations have been done as scheduled.
여자가 만족하는 것은 무엇인가?
(A) 집이 편리한 곳에 위치해 있다.
(B) 취업 공석이 곧 생긴다.
(C) 주택 대출이 마침내 승인되었다.
(D) 재건작업이 일정대로 끝났다.
분석_ 중반부 여자의 대화를 보면 The park is very close to my college. That's exactly what I hoped for.에서 대학과 가까워서 좋다고 언급했으므로 장소가 가장 마음에 든다고 유추할 수 있다.

46. (B)

What is the woman planning to do next week?
(A) Fill out some documents
(B) View a property
(C) Attend a housing fair
(D) Make a reservation in advance
여자는 다음 주 무엇을 계획하고 있는가?

(A) 문서 작성하기
(B) 주택 보기
(C) 주택 박람회 참석하기
(D) 미리 예약하기

분석_ 마지막 대화에서 남자가 다음 주에 집을 보러 가자고 권했고 여자는 그렇게 하자(Let me jot down where it is and I can meet you there)고 대답했으므로 (B)가 가장 적절하다.

Questions 47-49 refer to the following conversation with three speakers.

W1: Mr. Park, I just finished cleaning the floor, so it looks like we're all ready to open the restaurant at 11 o'clock. Is there anything else you'd like me to do?

M: Yes. Someone from the city maintenance department called late last night and told me that 47 *the crew will be repairing the pavement right outside the restaurant today.* I'm concerned that our customers won't know we're open.

W2: 48 *It's a piece of cake. I can put out a sign in front of the door that shows we're open.*

W1: That sounds perfect. 49 *I will take out the sign from the storage and give it to you right away.*

M: That's even more of a relief.

W1: Park 씨, 방금 바닥 청소를 끝냈어요. 11시에 식당을 오픈할 모든 준비가 된 것 같아요. 제가 다른 뭔가 해야 할 일이 있나요?

M: 예. 시 관리부서의 직원이 어제 저녁 늦게 전화를 해서 오늘 식당 밖 도로 수리 작업을 한다고 말해줬어요. 우리 고객들이 우리가 영업한다는 것을 모를까 봐 걱정되네요.

W2: 그건 식은 죽 먹기죠. 영업 중이라는 것을 보여주는 간판을 문 앞에 세울게요.

W1: 완벽한 계획이네요. 창고에서 간판을 가지고 나올게요, 그리고 바로 당신에게 전해줄게요.

M: 그럼 안심이 되네요.

어휘_ clean 청소하다 maintenance 관리, 유지 pavement 도로 포장 a piece of cake 쉬운 일, 누워서 떡 먹기 storage 창고 relief 안심

47. (B)

What does the man say will happen today?
(A) A thorough inspection will take place.
(B) Repair work will begin.
(C) A maintenance department will stop by.
(D) Some equipment will be installed.

남자는 오늘 어떤 일이 일어날 거라 말했는가?
(A) 철저한 검사가 이뤄질 것이다.
(B) 수리 작업이 시작될 것이다.
(C) 관리 부서가 잠깐 들를 것이다.
(D) 기계가 설치될 것이다.

분석_ 남자의 대화 중간을 들어보면 that the crew will be repairing the pavement right outside the restaurant

today.라고 언급했으므로 수리 작업이 시작된다는 (B)가 가장 적절하다.

48. (D)

Why does the woman say, "It's a piece of cake"?
(A) It is hard to believe, but it is actually a cake.
(B) She is eating a piece of cake.
(C) It is not a whole cake but a piece of cake.
(D) The work is easy to accomplish.

왜 여자는 "그건 식은 죽 먹기죠"라고 말하는가?
(A) 믿을 수 없지만, 그것은 진짜 케이크다.
(B) 그녀는 케이크 한 조각을 먹고 있다.
(C) 케이크 전체가 아니라 한 조각이다.
(D) 그 일이 해결하기 쉽다.

분석_ 남자가 걱정하고 있는 일에 여자는 "식은 죽 먹기"라고 대답하고 해결책을 제시했다. 따라서 남자의 걱정은 해결하기 쉬운 문제라는 것을 유추할 수 있다.

49. (A)

What will the woman do after the talk?
(A) Put out a sign
(B) Make a piece of cake
(C) Extend business hours
(D) Open the door

대화가 끝난 후 여자는 무엇을 할까?
(A) 간판을 세우기
(B) 케이크 한 조각을 만들기
(C) 영업시간을 연장하기
(D) 문을 열기

분석_ 대화 속 여자는 2명이고 한 여자는 간판을 설치하겠다(I can put out a sign in front of the door.)고 말했고 다른 여자는 간판을 가지러 창고로 가겠다(I will take out the sign from the storage.)고 말했으므로 (A)가 가장 적절하다.

Questions 50-52 refer to the following conversation.

W: I don't know 50 *how I'm going to look over all the résumés that were submitted for the sales positions we'd advertised.* We received thousands of applications for these ten openings.

M: There are too many applications. 51 *I can help you review those resumes. Why don't I take some of them?*

W: That would be nice. I don't have hard copies of them though. The applications are all saved on my portable USB drive.

M: Okay, I prefer to look over them on paper. 52 *Would you print them out for me? So I can go over the hard copy applications thoroughly.*

50. (B)

What are the speakers scheduled to do?
(A) Arrange a filing system
(B) Review some resume
(C) Schedule a training seminar
(D) Brainstorm a budget in sales
화자들이 계획하고 있는 것은 무엇인가?
(A) 파일 시스템을 준비하기
(B) 이력서를 검토하기
(C) 훈련 세미나 일정잡기
(D) 영업부 예산 토의하기
분석_ 대화 중 여자가 말한 가장 첫 번째 대사에서 I don't know
how I'm going to look over all the résumés that were
submitted for the sales positions we'd advertise.를 보면
여자가 이력서를 검토해야 한다고 언급했고 뒤에 남자가 그
일을 도와주겠다고 언급했으므로 (B)가 적절하다.

51. (A)

What does the man imply?
(A) Dividing some work
(B) Signing a complete procedure
(C) Extending a deadline
(D) Putting an advertisement on a web
남자가 암시하는 것은 무엇인가?
(A) 일을 나누기
(B) 완성된 절차에 서명하기
(C) 마감일을 연장하기
(D) 인터넷에 광고 게재하기
분석_ 남자의 대화를 보면 Why don't I take some of them?에서
이력서 검토를 도와준다고 말한 후, 이력서 중 몇몇을 가져
가겠다고 말했으므로 (A)가 가장 적절하다.

52. (D)

What does the man expect the woman to do?
(A) Go over a journal article
(B) Develop an application design
(C) Hand in a resume
(D) Print out some documents
남자가 여자가 무엇을 해줄 거라 기대하는가?
(A) 잡지 기사를 검토하기
(B) 지원서 디자인 개발하기
(C) 이력서 제출하기
(D) 문서를 출력하기
분석_ 남자의 대화 마지막에 Would you print them out for me?
라고 언급했다. 따라서 남자가 여자에게 원한 건 이력서를
출력하는 것이므로 (D)가 적절하다.

**Questions 53-55 refer to the following conversation
with three speakers.**

W: Excuse me. 53 *I'm a junior reporter for the Hong
Kong Times. I'm here to interview people* at the
music festival. Have you seen many performances?
M1: Yes, I've been three music concerts and I'm
planning to see some more. They've been excellent.
W: How about you? Have you enjoyed performances?
M2: The musical performance itself is good but I feel
bad about the venue. There are so many people
at the concert hall. And there are long lines for
everything including the food booths.
W: Well, the festival has always attracted people from
across the country. And more tickets have been
sold this year than in any other year so that might
account for the overcrowding.
M1: There are so many different kinds of music this
year. 55 *I love seeing this festival become a great
success.*
M2: 55 *I oppose his idea.* 54 *Overcrowded spaces
stop people enjoying the music.*

W: 실례합니다. 저는 Hong Kong Times의 수습기자입니다. 저는
여기 음악 축제에 사람들을 인터뷰하러 왔습니다. 공연을 많이
관람하셨나요?
M1: 예, 저는 3개의 콘서트 장에 갔었어요. 그리고 앞으로도 좀 더 많
은 콘서트를 볼 계획이에요. 공연이 멋졌어요.
W: 당신은 어떠세요? 공연을 즐기셨나요?
M2: 축제 자체는 좋아요. 근데 장소가 약간 불편해요. 공연장에 사람
이 너무 많아요. 그리고 음식점을 포함해서 모든 곳이 대기 줄이
너무 길어요.
W: 축제가 항상 나라 전역의 사람들을 끌어모으네요. 그리고 올해는
다른 해보다 더 많은 표가 팔렸대요. 그래서 혼잡한 것 같아요.
M1: 올해는 정말 많은 다른 종류의 음악이 있어요. 저는 이 축제가 크
게 성공한 것을 봐서 좋아요.
M2: 저는 반대예요. 사람들로 가득 찬 공간은 사람들이 음악을 즐기
는 걸 어렵게 만들어요.
어휘_ reporter 기자 performance 공연 venue 장소 attract 끌다, 유
치하다 oppose 반대하다

53. (C)

What is the woman's occupation?

(A) A festival organizer

(B) An event planner

(C) A reporter

(D) An accountant

여자의 직업은 무엇인가?

(A) 축제 조직자

(B) 이벤트 기획자

(C) 기자

(D) 회계사

분석_ 여자가 제일 처음에 잡지사 기자(I'm a junior reporter for the Hong Kong Times.)라고 언급했으므로 (C)가 가장 적절하다.

54. (A)

What problem is described in the festival?

(A) A venue is very crowded.

(B) A trip has been called off.

(C) Passes are much too expensive.

(D) Musical performances do not begin on time.

축제에 대해 묘사된 문제는 무엇인가?

(A) 장소가 매우 혼잡하다.

(B) 여행이 취소되었다.

(C) 입장료가 너무 많이 비싸다.

(D) 음악 공연이 제시간에 시작되지 않았다.

분석_ 남자 둘 중 한 명이 사람이 너무 많아서 힘들다(There are so many people at the concert hall. And there are long lines for everything including the food booths.)고 언급했으므로 (A)가 가장 적절하다.

55. (D)

According to the conversation, what do the men think about the festival?

(A) They both think it is better than previous one.

(B) The performers all live nearby.

(C) There are many food selections.

(D) The men have voiced different opinions.

대화에 따르면, 남자는 축제에 관해 어떻게 생각하는가?

(A) 그들 모두 이번 축제가 이전보다 더 낫다고 생각한다.

(B) 연주자 모두 근처에 산다.

(C) 음식 선택권이 많다.

(D) 남자들은 다른 의견을 가지고 있다.

분석_ 대화를 보면 한 남자는 I love seeing this festival become a great success.라고 해서 이번 공연에 사람이 많은 게 좋다는 의견을 피력했고 다른 남자는 I oppose his idea.라고 해서 반대 의견을 가지고 있으므로 (D)가 가장 적절하다.

Questions 56-58 refer to the following conversation.

M: Hi, I'm calling from Happy Memories Tours. **56** *We're interested in having bath towels made for our customers and I saw your advertisement in the magazine.* Could you give me some details on your quantities and prices?

W: Sure, bath towels are 10 dollars each, but **57** *if you place an order for more than 100 towels, you'll get a twenty percent discount off of the total cost.*

M: That price seems affordable. So we'd like to have our company title printed on the bath towels. Is that hard to do?

W: No, it's actually easy. **58** *Just go to our website and upload the image of your title and then place your order.*

M: 안녕하세요. Happy Memories Tours에서 연락드립니다. 우리는 우리의 고객을 위해 목욕타월을 주문하고 싶은데 잡지에서 귀사의 광고를 봤어요. 귀사의 제품 수량과 가격에 대한 세부사항을 주실 수 있나요?

W: 물론이죠. 목욕타월은 하나당 10달러입니다. 하지만 만약 100개 이상의 타월을 주문하신다면 전체 금액에서 20프로로 할인을 받을 수 있어요.

M: 가격이 적당하네요. 그리고 우리는 우리 회사 이름을 목욕타월에 출력하고 싶어요. 이름 출력이 힘들까요?

W: 아니요. 사실 그 작업은 쉬워요. 우리 회사 웹사이트로 가세요. 그리고 귀사의 이름 이미지를 올려주시고 주문해주세요.

어휘_ advertisement 광고 quantity 양 place an order 주문하다 total cost 합계비용 affordable 가격이 적절한 company title 회사 이름

56. (C)

What is the man interested in making a purchase?

(A) Office stationery

(B) Advertising space in a newspaper

(C) Promotional products

(D) Bathroom tiles

남자가 구매하고 싶어 하는 것은?

(A) 사무 용품

(B) 신문에 광고 게재하기

(C) 홍보용 용품

(D) 화장실 타일

분석_ 남자의 대화를 보면 We're interested in having bath towels made for our customers.에서 고객을 위한 목욕타월을 구매하고 싶어 함을 알 수 있으므로 (C)가 가장 적절하다.

57. (D)

How can the man receive a discount?

(A) By donating used products

(B) By uploading a company image

(C) By paying the bill well in advance

(D) By placing a large order

남자는 어떻게 할인을 받을 수 있는가?

(A) 중고제품을 기부함으로써

(B) 회사 이미지를 업로드함으로써

(C) 지불을 사전에 함으로써

(D) 대량 주문을 함으로써

분석_ 여자의 대화 중간 부분 but if you place an order for more than 100 towels, you'll get a twenty percent discount off of the total cost.를 보면 원래 가격은 10달러지만 100개 이상이면 20프로 할인을 받을 수 있으므로 (D)가 가장 적절하다.

58. (B)

What does the woman ask the man to do?

(A) Speak with an advertising manager

(B) Visit a company website

(C) Make a payment early

(D) Request a sample

여자가 남자에게 요구한 것은 무엇인가?

(A) 광고 매니저와 얘기하기

(B) 회사 웹사이트에 방문하기

(C) 조기에 납부하기

(D) 견본을 요청하기

분석_ 대화 마지막 여자의 말 Just go to our website and upload the image of your title and then place your order.를 보면 여자 회사의 웹사이트에 방문하라고 언급되었으므로 (A)가 가장 적절하다.

Questions 59-61 refer to the following conversation.

M: Hi, Judy. Thanks for taking a look at my car to see if it needs repair work. I'd like to list my car for sale by the end of this month **59** *because I need to buy a larger car.*

W: Well… **60** *I think buyers will like it since the exterior of the car has been well maintained.* However, I can see daily wear and tear on the front leather seat. I strongly recommend having that repaired.

M: Okay, do you know how much it will cost to have new leather put on the seat?

W: I have a friend who does that kind of work and the prices are fairly reasonable. **61** *I'll look for his business card so you can reach him anytime for an estimate.*

- -

M: Judy, 안녕하세요. 제 차가 수리가 필요한지 확인하기 위해 제 차를 확인해주셔서 감사해요. 더 큰 차량을 구매하기 위해 이번 달 말까지 제 차를 판매 명부에 올리고 싶어요.

W: 음. 제 생각에 차량의 외관이 잘 유지가 되어서 구매자들이 당신 차량을 좋아할 것 같아요. 그러나 앞좌석 가죽 시트가 닳고 찢어진 게 눈에 띄어요. 좌석 수리를 강력히 추천드립니다.

M: 네, 새로운 가죽을 좌석에 설치하는 데 비용이 얼마나 들지 아시나요?

W: 그런 일을 하는 친구를 알고 있어요. 가격도 꽤 합리적입니다. 그 친구 명함을 찾아볼게요. 그러면 견적을 위해서 언제든 당신이 그 친구에게 전화할 수 있어요.

어휘_ take a look at 살펴보다 exterior 외부 wear and tear 닳아 없어짐 leather 가죽 estimate 추정가

59. (C)

Why does the man want to sell his car?

(A) He has had car accidents several times.

(B) He plans to take public transportation.

(C) He needs a bigger vehicle.

(D) He is transferred to an overseas branch.

남자는 왜 그의 차량을 팔고 싶어 하는가?

(A) 그는 여러 번 사고를 당했다.

(B) 그는 대중교통을 이용할 계획이다.

(C) 그는 더 큰 차량을 필요로 한다.

(D) 그는 해외지사로 전근 간다.

분석_ 남자의 대화 중 I'd like to list my car for sale by the end of this month because I need to buy a larger car.를 보면 차를 판매 명부에 올리고 싶은 이유가 큰 차가 필요해서라고 언급되어 있으므로 (C)가 가장 적절하다.

60. (D)

According to the woman, why will buyers like the car?

(A) It is a fuel efficient sedan.

(B) It has brand new leather seats.

(C) The model is very popular with customers now.

(D) The outside is in good condition.

여자에 따르면, 왜 구매자들이 남자의 차량을 좋아할 것인가?

(A) 연료 효율적인 중형차이다.

(B) 새로운 가죽 시트를 가지고 있다.

(C) 현재 남자의 차량 모델이 소비자들에게 인기가 있다.

(D) 차량 외부가 관리가 잘되어 있다.

분석_ 여자의 대화 중 I think buyers will like it since the exterior of the car has been well maintained.를 보면 차량 외부가 유지가 잘되었다고 언급했으므로 (D)가 가장 적절하다.

61. (B)

What will the woman most likely do next?

(A) Repair the front seat

(B) Find contact information

(C) Check a catalog online

(D) Take a measure of some fabric

여자는 아마도 다음에 무엇을 할 것인가?

(A) 앞좌석을 수리하기

(B) 연락 정보를 찾기

(C) 온라인상 카탈로그를 확인하기

(D) 천의 길이를 측정하기

분석_ 여자의 마지막 말을 보면 I'll look for his business card.라
고 하여 차량 시트를 복원할 친구 명함을 찾아보겠다고 언
급했으므로 (B)가 가장 적절하다.

Questions 62-64 refer to the following conversation.

W: Hi, Rick. Did you go over my draft report about the
company's new employee manual? My manager
wants me to finalize the manual by the end of today.
**62 She needs me to send the final version before
she leaves today around 7.**

M: I finished reviewing it this morning and **63 I found
a typo on the second page.** Could we go over the
error during our brief meeting at 2?

W: Actually I can't make it to the meeting. I have a prior
engagement with my clients. **64 Can we meet later
instead around 4? Is it okay with you?**

M: No problem at all. See you then.

W: Rick, 안녕하세요. 회사의 새로운 직원 매뉴얼에 관한 제 초안 보
고서를 검토하셨나요? 제 매니저는 제가 오늘 퇴근까지 매뉴얼을
마무리 짓기를 원해요. 그녀는 제가 대략 7시 그녀가 퇴근하기 전
에 최종안을 보내길 원합니다.

M: 오늘 아침 검토를 끝냈어요. 그리고 2페이지에서 철자오류를 찾았
어요. 2시에 잠깐 만나서 오류를 검토할까요?

W: 사실 약속을 지킬 수 없어요. 고객과 사전 약속이 있어요. 대신 4
시에 만날까요? 괜찮나요?

M: 전혀 문제 될 것 없죠. 그럼 그때 만나요.

어휘_ draft 초안 employee manual 직원 매뉴얼 typo 철자오류
engagement 약속

62. (C)

What does the woman say she must do by the end of
today?

(A) Speak in a meeting
(B) Finalize agenda items
(C) Submit a report
(D) Check the manual for some errors

여자는 오늘 퇴근 전까지 무엇을 해야 한다고 말하는가?

(A) 모임에서 발표하기
(B) 안건 목록을 마무리하기
(C) 보고서를 제출하기
(D) 매뉴얼의 오류를 확인하기

분석_ 여자의 대화 제일 처음 부분 My manager wants me to
finalize the manual by the end of today. She needs
me to send the final version before she leaves today
around 7.을 보면 여자의 매니저가 여자가 보고서를 마무리
짓고 제출하기를 원하므로 (C)가 가장 적절하다.

63. (A)

What problem does the man mention?
(A) Some misspellings are found.

(B) An engagement with clients is coming.
(C) The wrong equipment was used.
(D) A deadline has passed.

남자는 어떤 문제를 언급하는가?
(A) 철자 오류가 발견되었다.
(B) 고객과의 약속이 다가온다.
(C) 잘못된 장비를 사용했다.
(D) 마감일이 지났다.

분석_ 남자의 대화를 보면 보고서 2페이지에서 typo, 다시 말해 철
자 오류를 발견했다(I finished reviewing it this morning
and I found a typo on the second page.)고 언급했으므
로 (A)가 정답이다.

64. (B)

What solution does the woman offer?
(A) Looking for a different venue
(B) Meeting at a later time
(C) Dividing the work with other colleagues
(D) Asking for an extension

여자가 제안한 해결책은 무엇인가?
(A) 다른 장소 찾기
(B) 나중에 만나기
(C) 다른 동료와 업무를 분담하기
(D) 연장을 요구하기

분석_ 여자의 마지막 말을 보면 I have a prior engagement with
my clients. Can we meet later instead around 4?라고 해
서 남자가 제안한 2시에는 이미 고객 약속이 있어 4시에 만
나기를 제안했으므로 (B)가 가장 적절하다.

**Questions 65-67 refer to the following conversation
with three speakers.**

M1: Have you two checked out the sales results we've
made during the first quarter?

W: I saw them this morning. **66 They didn't seem real.
65 We broke the best record of the company.**

M2: I haven't had a chance yet. Where can I find the
documents?

M1: Here you are. These are our sales results. We made
it. We finally did it.

M2: Oh. I can't believe my eyes. **66 We set a brilliant
record in our company.**

W: I am so proud of our sales team. And we couldn't
do that without them, including you two guys. **67
Let's celebrate our success at the luncheon this
evening.**

M1: 두 사람 우리가 이번 첫 분기 동안 만든 판매 결과를 확인했어요?

W: 오늘 아침에 확인했어요. 그게 현실처럼 보이지 않아요. 우리는
회사의 최고 판매 기록을 깼어요.

M2: 저는 아직 확인하지 못했어요. 판매 결과를 어디서 찾을 수 있나요?

M1: 여기 있어요. 이것이 우리의 판매 결과예요. 우리가 해냈어요. 마침내 우리가 해냈다고요.

M2: 오, 내 눈을 믿을 수 없어요. 우리는 회사에서 빛나는 기록을 세웠어요.

W: 저는 우리 영업 팀이 자랑스러워요. 그리고 여러분 둘을 포함한 우리 팀이 없었다면 우리는 해낼 수 없을 거예요. 오늘 저녁 만찬에서 우리의 성공을 기념합시다.

어휘_ break the record 기록을 깨다 chance 기회 made it 해내다 proud 자랑스러운 celebrate 기념하다

65. (B)

What is the conversation mainly about?
(A) An enlargement of manufacturing facility
(B) A dramatic increase in sales
(C) A change in company newsletter
(D) A move into the athletic apparel

대화는 주로 무엇에 대한 것인가?
(A) 제조 시설의 확대
(B) 엄청난 판매 증가
(C) 회사 사보의 변화
(D) 운동복으로의 이전

분석_ 대화 속 여자의 말에서 We broke the best record of the company.를 보면 판매 기록을 깼다고 언급했으므로 (B)가 가장 적절하다.

66. (C)

Why does the woman say, "They didn't seem real"?
(A) She strongly disagrees.
(B) She would like an explanation.
(C) She is happily surprised.
(D) She feels unsatisfied with the reports.

여자가 "그게 현실처럼 보이지 않아요"라고 말한 이유는?
(A) 그녀는 강하게 부인한다.
(B) 그녀는 설명을 원한다.
(C) 그녀는 기분 좋게 깜짝 놀랐다.
(D) 그녀는 보고서에 불만을 느꼈다.

분석_ 65번과 비슷한 문제로 "보고서가 실제 같지 않다. 그 이유는 판매 기록을 깼으므로(We broke the best record of the company.)"라고 언급되었으므로 판매액에 관해 기분 좋게 놀람을 나타낸다.

67. (A)

What will the sales team do after work?
(A) Commemorate their achievement
(B) Update their sales reports
(C) Hire new addition to their team
(D) Postpone their presentation

퇴근 후 영업 팀은 무엇을 할 것인가?
(A) 그들의 성취를 기념하기
(B) 그들의 판매보고서를 최신화하기
(C) 팀에 신입사원 고용하기
(D) 그들 발표를 미루기

분석_ 여자의 마지막 말을 보면 Let's celebrate our success at the luncheon this evening.이라고 하여 저녁 오찬에서 성공을 기념하자고 언급했으므로 (A)가 가장 적절하다.

Questions 68-70 refer to the following conversation and list.

W: Zack, **69** *we ordered 100 desktop computers last week and we will receive the shipment next Tuesday.*

M: That's great! Should we replace our current computers with the new ones by ourselves?

W: No, we don't need to. Since our budget permits, we can hire temporary workers by the hour. **68** *Can you help me choose the right employment agency?*

M: It's my pleasure. What should I do?

W: **70** *Our budget is $ 500 maximum. And we should complete the replacement of the old computers by 11. How many workers should we hire?*

M: I just found the perfect agency that fits your requirements. Look at this list.

Green Bee Agency	
Hourly wage $ 20 per person	50 workers complete the work by 9
Central Place	
Hourly wage $ 15 per person	20 workers complete the work by 12
Mountain High	
Hourly wage $ 30 per person	30 workers complete the work by 11
Rainbow Ocean	
Hourly wage $ 9 per person	50 workers complete the work by 10

W: Zack, 우리는 지난주 100대의 컴퓨터를 주문했고 다음 주 화요일에 선적을 받을 거예요.

M: 잘됐네요. 새로운 컴퓨터는 우리가 직접 교체해야 하나요?

W: 아니요, 그럴 필요가 없어요. 예산이 충분하기 때문에 우리는 시간제 임시직원을 고용할 수 있어요. 적절한 인력사무소를 선택할 수 있게 저를 도와줄 수 있나요?

M: 물론이죠. 뭘 할까요?

W: 우리 예산은 최대 500달러예요. 그리고 우리는 11시까지 낡은 컴퓨터의 교체를 마쳐야 해요. 몇 명을 고용해야 할까요?

M: 조건에 딱 맞는 완벽한 인력사무소를 발견했어요. 이 목록을 보세요.

Green Bee Agency	
한 명당 시급 20달러	50명의 직원이 9시까지 일을 완수
Central Place	
한 명당 시급 15달러	20명의 직원이 12시까지 일을 완수
Mountain High	
한 명당 시급 30달러	30명의 직원이 11시까지 일을 완수
Rainbow Ocean	
한 명당 시급 9달러	50명의 직원이 10시까지 일을 완수

어휘_ shipment 선적 temporary worker 임시 근로자 budget 예산 permit 허락하다 pleasure 기쁨 fit 잘 맞다 hourly wage 시급

68. (B)

What does the woman ask the man to do?
(A) Order some merchandise
(B) Help her select the agency
(C) Repair the old computers
(D) Contact job candidates
여자가 남자에게 요구한 것은 무엇인가?
(A) 물건을 주문하기
(B) 여자가 인력사무소 선택하는 것을 도와주기
(C) 낡은 컴퓨터를 수리하기
(D) 취업 후보자와 연락하기
분석_ 여자의 대화 중간을 보면 Can you help me choose the right employment agency?에서 인력사무소 선택을 도와달라고 부탁했으므로 (B)가 가장 적절하다.

69. (B)

What will happen next Tuesday?
(A) Place an order of the new computers
(B) Receive the shipment of new computers
(C) Choose the good employment agency
(D) Hire more office workers
다음 주 화요일 무슨 일이 발생할 것인가?
(A) 새로운 컴퓨터를 주문하기
(B) 새로운 컴퓨터 선적받기
(C) 좋은 인력사무소 고르기
(D) 더 많은 사무실 근로자 고용하기
분석_ 여자의 대화 중 처음을 보면 주문한 컴퓨터가 다음 주 화요일에 도착한다(we will receive the shipment next Tuesday.)고 말했으므로 (B)가 가장 적절하다.

70. (D)

Look at the graphic. Which agency will they choose?
(A) Green Bee Agency
(B) Central Place
(C) Mountain High
(D) Rainbow Ocean
그래프를 보자. 그들은 어떤 인력사무소를 선택할 것인가?
(A) Green Bee Agency

(B) Central Place
(C) Mountain High
(D) Rainbow Ocean
분석_ 여자의 대화 중 마지막 부분 Our budget is $ 500 maximum. And we should complete the replacement of the old computers by 11.을 보면 최대 예산이 500달러고 일이 11시에 끝나야 한다. 그래프와 비교해봤을 때 가장 적절한 곳은 (D)이다.

Questions 71-73 refer to the following announcement.

71 *I hope you are enjoying this month's marketing workshop.* Before I introduce our next keynote speaker, 72 *I have a short announcement to make. A brown leather bag has been found in the restroom.* So please take a moment to see if you are missing your item. If you are, make you way to 73 *the reception desk* at the main entrance of the workshop center. 73 *Mr. Dustin is the one on duty and he has your lost one.*

여러분이 이번 달 마케팅 워크샵에서 즐거운 시간을 보내고 계시길 희망합니다. 다음 기조연설자를 소개하기 전에 짧게 공지드리겠습니다. 화장실에서 갈색 가죽 가방이 발견되었습니다. 그러니 시간을 내서 혹시 가방을 잃어버리셨는지 확인해주시기 바랍니다. 만약 가방을 잃어버리셨다면, 워크샵 센터 현관에 있는 안내데스크로 와주세요. Dustin 씨가 근무 중이며 잃어버린 가방을 가지고 있습니다.
어휘_ keynote speaker 기조연설자 make an announcement 발표하다 take a moment 시간을 가지다 reception desk 안내데스크 make one's way to ~로 가다

71. (B)

Where is the announcement being heard?
(A) At an appliance store
(B) At a workshop meeting
(C) At an international sporting event
(D) At a brunch cafe
이 안내방송은 어디서 들을 수 있는가?
(A) 가전제품 상점
(B) 워크샵 모임
(C) 국제 스포츠 행사
(D) 브런치 카페
분석_ 안내방송 초반에 I hope you are enjoying this month's marketing workshop.라고 말했으므로 (B)가 가장 적절하다.

72. (C)

What is the announcement mainly discussing?
(A) Keeping the restroom clean
(B) Correcting contact information

(C) Reclaiming a lost item
(D) Taking on a duty
안내방송에서 주로 논의되는 것은 무엇인가?
(A) 화장실을 깨끗이 유지하는 것
(B) 연락정보를 수정하는 것
(C) 분실된 물건을 되찾는 것
(D) 직무를 떠맡는 것
분석_ 안내 방송에서 기조연설자 소개에 앞서서 할 말이 있다고 했고 이어서 A brown leather bag has been found in the restroom.이라고 하며 화장실에서 발견된 분실물에 관해 언급했으므로 (C)가 가장 적절하다.

73. (D)
Who most likely is Mr. Dustin?
(A) An announcer
(B) A store manager
(C) A handcraft man
(D) A receptionist
Dustin 씨는 누구일 것인가?
(A) 아나운서
(B) 상점 관리자
(C) 수공예가
(D) 접수원
분석_ 고유명사가 문제에 있으면 고유명사 앞뒤로 정답과 관련된 힌트가 존재한다. 안내방송에서 잃어버린 물건을 찾고 싶으면 안내데스크로 오라(make you way to the reception desk)고 언급했고 이어서 Dustin이 오늘 근무 중이며 물건을 가지고 있다(Mr. Dustin is the one on duty and he has your lost one)고 언급했으므로 (D)가 가장 적절하다.

Questions 74-76 refer to the following telephone message.

Hello Mr. Winnie, **74 I am calling from Alvin's Floral shop** about the bouquet you ordered. I am really sorry **75 but we've made a mistake. We used the wrong flowers for the bouquet. Instead of roses, we put lilies in it. You have two choices.** If you don't mind the different floral arrangement, we'll give you this bouquet for free. Or, if you still want the one with roses, we'll offer you a 40% discount and send you a new bouquet by Thursday. **76 Please let us know what you decide.**

안녕하세요. Winnie 씨. Alvin's Floral Shop에서 귀하가 당신이 주문한 꽃다발 때문에 연락드려요. 죄송하지만 저희 상점에서 실수를 했습니다. 우리는 꽃다발에 잘못된 꽃을 사용했어요. 장미 대신에, 꽃다발에 백합을 넣었어요. 당신은 두 가지 중에 선택하실 수 있습니다. 다른 꽃을 쓴 꽃다발을 개의치 않으시면 무료로 꽃다발을 드릴게요. 아니면, 여전히 장미로 만든 꽃다발을 원하시면 40% 할인을 제공해드리고 새로운 꽃다발은 목요일까지 보내드리겠습니다. 어떻게 결정하실지 알려주세요.

어휘_ bouquet 꽃다발 make a mistake 실수하다 rose 장미 lily 백합 floral arrangement 꽃다발 for free 공짜, 무료

74. (D)
Where does the caller work?
(A) At an organic farm
(B) At a boutique shop
(C) At a vegetarian restaurant
(D) At a flower shop
화자는 어디서 근무하는가?
(A) 유기농 농장
(B) 여성복 상점
(C) 채식주의 식당
(D) 꽃가게
분석_ 전화 메시지에서 메시지를 남기는 화자는 제일 처음 본인 소개를 하므로 근무지를 알고 싶으면 메시지 제일 처음에 집중한다. I am calling from Alvin's Floral shop.이라고 하여 꽃가게에서 근무한다고 언급했으므로 (D)가 가장 적절하다.

75. (A)
What problem does the caller mention?
(A) An order was filled incorrectly.
(B) An appliance is not working properly.
(C) A bulk discount has not been applied.
(D) Billing statement has been sent to the wrong address.
화자는 어떤 문제를 언급했는가?
(A) 주문을 잘못 이행했다.
(B) 가전제품이 제대로 작동하지 않는다.
(C) 대량주문 할인이 적용되지 않았다.
(D) 요금 청구서가 잘못된 주소로 보내졌다.
분석_ 전화를 건 사람이 언급한 문제는 바로 전화를 건 이유와 일맥상통한다. 전화를 건 이유는 본인 소개 이후에 주로 정답이 나온다. We used the wrong flowers for the bouquet.을 보면 꽃다발에 잘못된 꽃을 썼다고 언급했으므로 (A)가 가장 적절하다.

76. (B)
What is Mr. Winnie requested to do?
(A) Make an arrangement
(B) Indicate his preference
(C) Contact the delivery person
(D) Make an overdue payment
Winnie 씨는 무엇을 할 것을 요청받는가?
(A) 계약하기
(B) 선호하는 것을 나타내기
(C) 배달사원에게 연락하기
(D) 연체대금을 납부하기
분석_ 전화를 받는 Winnie에게 부탁하는 것을 찾는 문제이다. 상대에게 원하는 것은 녹음메시지 하단에 주로 정답이 나온다. Please let us know what you decide.에서 두 가지 선택사항을 알려준 후 고객에게 선호하는 것을 말해달라고 언급했으므로 (B)가 가장 적절하다.

Questions 77-79 refer to the following talk.

Good evening. My name is Vanessa and **77 *I'll be your tour guide*** for the next couple of days in Hong Kong city. During this time, **78 *you'll get to see many local night markets*** including several late night festivals. This evening, we'll be visiting a famous dim sum factory in Hong Kong. It's very fun and exciting and you'll get free samples. When you **79 *return to the hotel at eleven o'clock, you will be receiving a foot massage in your room.*** We'll have some tea available and I'll give you information regarding tomorrow's plan.

안녕하세요. 제 이름은 Vanessa이고 제가 앞으로 며칠간 홍콩에서 여러분을 안내할 여행 가이드입니다. 이 기간 동안 여러분은 여러 개의 야간 축제를 포함한 많은 지역의 야시장을 관광할 것입니다. 오늘 저녁 우리는 홍콩의 유명한 딤섬 공장을 관람할 것입니다. 매우 재미있고 흥미로울 겁니다. 또한 무료 시식도 할 수 있습니다. 11시에 호텔에 도착하면 방에서 발 마사지를 받을 것입니다. 이용 가능한 차도 있으며 내일 계획에 관한 정보도 제공해드리겠습니다.

어휘_ night market 야시장 exciting 흥미로운 sample 시식 janitor 수위

77. (D)

What most likely is the speaker's job?
(A) A marketing manager
(B) A hotel janitor
(C) A renowned cook
(D) A tour guide

화자의 직업은 아마도 무엇일 것인가?
(A) 마케팅 매니저
(B) 호텔 수위
(C) 유명한 요리사
(D) 여행 가이드

분석_ 본인 소개를 할 때는 보통 본인 이름 뒤에 직업을 말한다. 지문의 처음에 My name is Vanessa and I'll be your tour guide.를 보면 화자는 Vanessa이며 여행 가이드이므로 (D)가 가장 적절하다.

78. (A)

What will the listeners plan to do this evening?
(A) Visit a local night fair
(B) Move to a different hotel
(C) Change a room
(D) Attend a tea class

오늘 저녁 청자들은 무엇을 할 계획인가?
(A) 지역 야시장 방문하기
(B) 다른 호텔로 옮기기
(C) 방을 바꾸기
(D) 차 수업에 참석하기

분석_ 질문에 '오늘 저녁'이 정답의 힌트가 될 수 있다. 여행 가이드는 여행 일정에 대해 언제 무엇을 할 것인지 설명하므로 순서대로 기억하는 것이 중요하다. 밤마다 야시장을 구경

간다고 언급했고 이어지는 지문 속 This evening, we'll be visiting a famous dim sum factory in Hong Kong.에서 딤섬 공장으로 방문한다고 언급했으므로 지역 야시장에 방문하는 (A)가 가장 적절하다.

79. (A)

What does the speaker say is scheduled to do at eleven o'clock?
(A) A massage
(B) An outdoor concert
(C) An exciting flight
(D) A museum tour

화자는 11시에 일정 잡힌 행사가 무엇이라 말하는가?
(A) 마사지
(B) 야외 콘서트
(C) 흥미로운 비행
(D) 박물관 관람

분석_ 질문의 '11시'에 집중해서 듣기를 하면 지문 후반부 When you return to the hotel at eleven o'clock, you will be receiving a foot massage in your room.에서 11시는 호텔로 돌아오는 것 그리고 발 마사지를 받는 것이므로 (A)가 가장 적절하다.

Questions 80-82 refer to the following announcement.

Good afternoon ladies and gentlemen and welcome to this afternoon's performance of Daria Della. **80 *I'm Bianca Cecil, the coordinator of this art and theater group.*** I am very excited to tell you that our show has once again sold out, **81 *which means we've sold every ticket to every show since opening day this year.*** During a short intermission, please feel free to buy refreshments out in the hallway or visit our theater souvenir shop on the second floor. **82 *All proceeds from this afternoon's ticket sales will go to financial support of local arts program at our community middle school so thank you all in advance.*** Now, please enjoy the Daria Della's recital.

안녕하세요, 신사 숙녀 여러분. 오늘 오후 Daria Della의 공연에 오심을 환영합니다. 저는 이 예술공연 그룹의 책임자 Bianca Cecil입니다. 여러분에게 우리 행사가 다시 한 번 매진되었음을 알리게 되어 기쁩니다. 이것은 우리가 오픈 첫날 이후 모든 쇼의 모든 표를 다 팔았음을 의미합니다. 짧은 휴식기간 동안 복도에서 마음껏 다과를 구입하시거나 2층에 있는 극장 기념품점을 방문하세요. 오늘 오후 티켓 판매로 인한 모든 수익은 우리 지역사회 중학교의 지역 예술 프로그램의 재정적인 후원으로 쓰일 것입니다. 미리 여러분 모두에게 감사드립니다. 이제 Daria Dell의 독주회를 감상하시죠.

어휘_ performance 공연 coordinator 책임자 sold out 매진된 intermission 중간 휴식 feel free to V 마음껏 V해라 proceeds 수익금 in advance 미리, 먼저, 앞서서

80. (A)

Who is the speaker?
(A) A theater coordinator
(B) A tour guide
(C) A middle school art teacher
(D) A financial supporter

화자는 누구인가?
(A) 극장 책임자
(B) 여행 가이드
(C) 중학교 미술 교사
(D) 재정 후원자

분석_ 직업을 묻는 표현은 대부분 앞 부분에 정답이 등장한다. I'm Bianca Cecil, the coordinator of this art and theater group.을 보면 화자의 이름은 Bianca Cecil이며 극장의 책임자라고 언급했으므로 (A)가 가장 적절하다.

81. (D)

What does the speaker say is special about performance during this season?
(A) It has won many awards.
(B) It was written by a middle school student.
(C) Free souvenir has been given to all performers.
(D) All shows have sold out.

화자는 이번 시즌 공연에서 무엇이 특별하다고 말하는가?
(A) 많은 상을 받았다.
(B) 중학교 학생에 의해 쓰였다.
(C) 모든 연주자에게 무료 기념품을 제공한다.
(D) 모든 공연이 매진되었다.

분석_ 화자는 I am very excited to tell you that our show has once again sold out, which means we've sold every ticket to every show since opening day this year.에서 올해 오픈 이후 계속 매진되었다고 언급했으므로 (D)가 가장 적절하다.

82. (C)

How will proceeds from the afternoon's sales be used?
(A) To replace computers with new ones
(B) To fund restoration of the theater
(C) To support programs in local school
(D) To repair the musical instrument

오늘 오후 공연 판매로 인한 수익금은 어떻게 쓰일 것인가?
(A) 기존 컴퓨터를 새 컴퓨터로 교체하기 위해
(B) 극장의 재건작업에 자금을 대기 위해
(C) 지역 학교 프로그램을 후원하기 위해
(D) 악기를 수리하기 위해

분석_ 후반부를 들어보면 All proceeds from this afternoon's ticket sales will go to financial support of local arts program at our community middle school에서 수익금 전액을 지역학교 프로그램 후원에 사용한다고 언급했으므로 (C)가 가장 적절하다.

Questions 83-85 refer to the telephone message.

Irene, this is Alex. **83** *Thank you for sending me an invitation* to the training on the new interoffice messenger software. **83** *Unfortunately, I won't be able to attend.* **84** *I'll be interviewing some of the job applicants at that time, next Friday.* And I think I don't need the training. I tried the software on my own and I thought it was really convenient and easy to use. It has many features that record conversations and share them online. So I think it'll help our regional managers a lot. **85** *Please give me a call after the training though, I'd really want to know if the rest of the managers liked the software as much as I did.*

Irene. 저는 Alex입니다. 제게 새로운 회사 내 메신저 소프트웨어 훈련과정에 초대장을 보내주셔서 감사합니다. 불행히도, 저는 참가할 수 없습니다. 저는 다음 주 금요일 그 시간에 취업 후보자들의 면접을 진행 중일 것입니다. 그리고 저는 훈련이 필요하지 않을 것 같습니다. 그 소프트웨어를 혼자 힘으로 시도해봤고 저는 그 프로그램이 사용하기 정말 편리하고 쉽다고 생각합니다. 그 프로그램은 온라인상으로 대화를 녹음하고 녹음자료를 공유하는 많은 기능을 가지고 있습니다. 그래서 저는 그것이 우리 지역 매니저를 많이 도울 수 있을 거라 생각합니다. 하지만 훈련 이후에 연락 주세요. 제가 좋아한 만큼 나머지 매니저들도 소프트웨어를 좋아하는지 아닌지 꼭 알고 싶습니다.

어휘_ send 보내다 invitation 초대장 interoffice 사무실 안, 사무실 내 convenient 편리한 give me a call 전화 달라 rest 나머지 regional 지역의 decline 거절하다

83. (B)

What is the main purpose of the call?
(A) To announce a job opening
(B) To decline an invitation
(C) To interview job applicants
(D) To sign up for a training

전화의 주 목적은 무엇인가?
(A) 취업 공석을 발표하기 위해
(B) 초대를 거절하기 위해
(C) 취업 후보자를 인터뷰하기 위해
(D) 훈련에 등록하기 위해

분석_ 대화 초반 초대장을 보내줘서 감사하다는 말 이후 초대한 훈련과정에 참석할 수 없다(Unfortunately, I won't be able to attend.)고 언급했으므로 (B)가 가장 적절하다.

84. (D)

What does the speaker plan to do next Friday?
(A) Meet with the new clients
(B) Take a rest
(C) Record a conversation
(D) Conduct some interview

다음 주 금요일에 화자는 무엇을 계획하고 있는가?
(A) 새로운 고객과 만나기

(B) 휴식을 취하기
(C) 대화를 녹음하기
(D) 면접을 시행하기

분석_ '금요일'이란 명사에 집중해서 듣는다. 훈련과정에 참석할 수 없음을 밝힌 후, I'll be interviewing some of the job applicants at that time, next Friday.라고 언급했으므로 다음 주 금요일은 (D)가 가장 적절하다.

85. (A)

What does the speaker request the listener to offer?
(A) Feedback about some training
(B) Details of job interview
(C) A complete list of participants
(D) Photos of regional managers

화자는 청자에게 무엇을 제공해달라고 요청했는가?
(A) 훈련에 관한 의견
(B) 취업 인터뷰 세부사항
(C) 모든 참가자의 목록
(D) 지역 매니저들의 사진

분석_ 녹음 메시지에서 화자가 청자에게 요구하는 것은 보통 후반부에 등장한다. Please give me a call after the training though, I'd really want to know if the rest of the managers liked the software as much as I did.를 보면 훈련이 끝난 후 연락을 달라고 요구했고 나머지 매니저들의 반응을 알고 싶다고 언급했으므로 (A)가 가장 적절하다.

Questions 86-88 refer to the following talk.

86 *As the head director of the city's Recreation Department,* I'd like to thank each of you for volunteering to paint the walls today here in Florence Playground. I'd like to point out that **87** *the green colors you'll be painting were selected specifically because they are known to help reduce stress.* **88** *The Recreation Department has provided enough paints and brushes for everyone, so please grab one and let's get started.*

시의 휴양부 수석 관리자로서, 오늘 이곳 Florence Playground에 벽 도색작업에 자원해주신 여러분께 감사드립니다. 여러분이 칠할 녹색은 스트레스를 줄이는 것으로 알려졌기에 특별히 선택되었다는 점을 알려드리고 싶습니다. 휴양부는 모두에게 충분한 페인트와 붓을 제공할 것입니다. 그러니 붓을 잡고 이제 일을 시작해봅시다.

어휘_ recreation 오락 paint 칠하다 volunteer 자원봉사 reduce 줄이다 grab 잡다

86. (B)

Who most likely is the speaker?
(A) A flower shop manager
(B) A city official
(C) A landscape painter
(D) A mechanical specialist

화자는 아마도 누구일 것인가?

(A) 꽃 가게 매니저
(B) 시 공무원
(C) 풍경 화가
(D) 기계 전문가

분석_ 자기소개는 보통 가장 먼저 등장하므로 지문의 초반부에 집중한다. As the head director of the city's Recreation Department라고 언급했으므로 (B)가 가장 적절하다.

87. (D)

What does the speaker say about the color?
(A) It has increased in numbers recently.
(B) It can be viewed in an outdoor exhibit.
(C) It is recommended by a painter.
(D) It will ease one's mind

화자는 색깔에 대해 무엇이라 말하는가?
(A) 최근에 수적으로 증가했다.
(B) 야외 전시장에서 볼 수 있다.
(C) 화가에 의해 추천되었다.
(D) 사람의 마음을 편안하게 해줄 것이다.

분석_ 질문의 '색깔'에 집중하며 듣는다. 대화 중반부 I'd like to point out that the green colors you'll be painting were selected specifically because they are known to help reduce stress.에서 녹색이라고 언급한 이후에 스트레스를 줄인다고 언급했으므로 (D)가 가장 적절하다.

88. (A)

What has been offered for the listeners?
(A) Some drawing tools
(B) A crab sandwich
(C) A complimentary lunch
(D) A map of the park

청자들에게 제공된 것은 무엇인가?
(A) 몇 가지 그림 재료
(B) 게살 샌드위치
(C) 무료 점심식사
(D) 공원 지도

분석_ 마지막 문제는 보통 후반부에 답이 등장한다. 지문 후반 The Recreation Department has provided enough paints and brushes for everyone.에서 페인트와 붓을 제공한다고 언급했으므로 (A)가 가장 적절하다.

Questions 89-91 refer to the following broadcast.

In business news, **89** *one of the world's biggest producers of vehicle tires,* Pro Tire has been contracted to supply passenger vehicle tires for the new DM-3 car. In order to be able to manufacture the large number of tires required by the contract, **90** *Pro Tire is scheduled to open another manufacturing plant at the beginning of November.* The new facility will be located in the city of Detroit. In a press conference earlier this morning,

경제 뉴스입니다. 자동차 타이어를 만드는 세계적 제조업체 중 하나인 Pro Tire는 새로운 DM-3자동차의 승객용 차량 타이어를 공급하기로 계약을 맺었습니다. 계약에 의해 요구되는 많은 수의 타이어를 제조하기 위해서 Pro Tire는 11월 초에 또 다른 제조 공장을 개장하겠다고 밝혔습니다. 새로운 공장은 Detroit 시에 위치할 것입니다. 오늘 아침 일찍 기자 회견장에서 Detroit 시 공무원은 공장 개장이 지역사회에 추정컨대 400개의 추가 일자리를 가져올 것이라 언급하며 공장의 개장에 대한 그의 열망을 표현했습니다.

어휘_ contract 계약서, 계약을 맺다 manufacture 제조하다 be scheduled to 일정 잡다 facility 시설 aspiration 열망 express 표하다 estimated 추정된

89. (C)

What does the business mainly focus on?
(A) Passenger buses
(B) Portable MP3 player
(C) Automobile tires
(D) Plant engines

회사가 집중하는 것은 무엇인가?
(A) 승객용 버스
(B) 휴대용 MP3 플레이어
(C) 자동차 타이어
(D) 공장 엔진

분석_ 대화 초반부 In business news, one of the world's biggest producers of vehicle tires.에서 세계적인 자동차 타이어 제조업체 중 한 곳이라 언급했으므로 회사가 집중하는 것은 (C)가 가장 적절하다.

90. (C)

According to the speaker, what will Pro Tire do in November?
(A) Hold a press conference
(B) Launch an online advertising campaign
(C) Open a new manufacturing plant
(D) Raise the public awareness in environment

화자에 따르면, Pro Tire는 11월에 무엇을 할 것인가?
(A) 기자회견 개최하기
(B) 온라인 광고 캠페인 시작하기
(C) 새로운 제조 공장 개장하기
(D) 환경에 대한 시민의식 고취하기

분석_ 질문에 있는 '11월'이라는 명사에 집중해서 듣는다. Pro Tire is scheduled to open another manufacturing plant at the beginning of November.를 보면 11월에 또 다른 제조 공장을 개장할 예정이므로 (C)가 가장 적절하다.

91. (B)

What does the mayor hope to take place in Detroit?
(A) More traffic regulations will be passed.
(B) Employment opportunities will increase
(C) Net profits of the plant will drop shortly.
(D) Public transportation will be added.

시장은 Detroit에 어떤 일이 일어날 것이라 희망하는가?
(A) 더 많은 교통 규제가 통과할 것이다.
(B) 고용 기회가 증가할 것이다.
(C) 공장의 순 이익이 곧 떨어질 것이다.
(D) 대중교통이 추가될 것이다.

분석_ 문제 중 '시장'이라는 명사에 집중하고, 마지막 문제에 맞게 지문 후반부에 집중한다. the city official of Detroit expressed his aspiration for the opening of the plant, saying that it will bring an estimated 400 additional jobs to the community.를 보면 시 공무원이 열망을 표현한다고 언급한 이후 400개의 추가 일자리를 말했으므로 (B)가 가장 적절하다.

Questions 92-94 refer to the following talk and table.

Welcome to the seminar	
Presenter	**Subject**
Mr. Baek	Efficient sales skills
Ms. Oha	Marketing strategy
Break	Lunch
92 David S.	**Business portfolio**
Caren Van De	How to avoid typo

사업 포트폴리오 제작에 관한 세미나에 오신 걸 환영합니다. 포트폴리오가 무엇인지 간단한 설명으로 시작하겠습니다. 사업 포트폴리오는 일련의 창조적인 작업들을 설명하고 어떻게 이러한 작업을 성취할지 계획하는 진술서입니다. 잘 쓰여진 사업 포트폴리오는 오래 지속되는 인상을 남길 수 있고 이것은 귀하 회사에 투자하고자 하는 사람들로부터 재정적인 후원을 얻는 데 필수입니다. 이제 창의적인 사업 포트폴리오의 몇몇 예를 보기에 앞서 저는 세미나실을 돌아다니며 여러분 모두가 그룹 멤버와 여러분의 이전 근무 경험을 공유하길 원합니다. 누가 먼저 시작해볼까요?

<table>
<tr><td colspan="2">세미나에 오신 것을 환영합니다</td></tr>
<tr><td>발표자</td><td>주제</td></tr>
<tr><td>Baek 씨</td><td>효과적인 판매 기술</td></tr>
<tr><td>Oha 씨</td><td>마케팅 전략</td></tr>
<tr><td>휴식</td><td>점심</td></tr>
<tr><td>David S.</td><td>사업 포트폴리오</td></tr>
<tr><td>Caren Van De</td><td>철자오류를 피하는 방법</td></tr>
</table>

어휘_ explanation 설명 creative 창의적인 describe 묘사하다 long lasting 오래 지속하는 impression 인상 support 후원, 지지 essential 필수적인 invest 투자하다 share 공유하다

92. (C)

Look at the graphic. Who most likely is the speaker?
(A) Mr. Baek
(B) Ms. Oha
(C) David S.
(D) Caren Van De
그래픽을 보자. 화자는 아마도 누구일 것인가?
(A) Baek 씨
(B) Oha 씨
(C) David S.
(D) Caren Van De

분석_ 화자의 말을 들어보면 Welcome to this seminar on developing a business portfolio.에서 사업 포트폴리오 작성에 관한 세미나라고 언급했다. 도표에 사업 포트폴리오를 작성하는 사람은 (C)이다.

93. (D)

According to the speaker, why is it essential to make a good first impression?
(A) To attract new clients
(B) To take advantage of sales skills
(C) To share work experience
(D) To get investor's support
화자에 따르면, 좋은 첫인상을 만드는 것이 왜 중요한가?
(A) 새로운 고객을 끌기 위해
(B) 판매 기술을 이용하기 위해
(C) 근무 경험을 공유하기 위해
(D) 투자가의 후원을 받기 위해

분석_ 질문의 '첫인상'에 집중하며 듣다 보면 A well-written business portfolio makes a long lasting impression and this is essential for getting financial support from people willing to invest in your company.에서 오래 지속되는 첫인상을 만들고, 이것이 필수인 이유는 투자가로부터 자금을 받기 때문이라고 언급되었으므로 (D)가 가장 적절하다.

94. (B)

What does the speaker advise members of the group to do?
(A) Review a business portfolio
(B) Describe past work experience
(C) Give a demonstration
(D) Make some examples
화자는 그룹 멤버들에게 무엇을 하라고 조언하는가?
(A) 사업 포트폴리오를 검토하기
(B) 과거 근무 경험을 묘사하기
(C) 시연하기
(D) 몇몇 예시를 만들기

분석_ 요구하는 것은 보통 지문 후반부에 답이 등장하므로 후반부를 집중해서 듣는다. I want to go around and have all of you share your prior work experience with the group members.에서 화자가 돌아다닐 것이니 이전 근무 경험을 공유하라고 언급했으므로 (B)가 가장 적절하다.

Questions 95-97 refer to the following announcement and screen.

95 *Attention BlueSky Airlines passengers!* 96 *We have recently introduced a new automated ticketing system.* The ticketing machines are situated near the main entrance on the first floor. The touchscreens are quick and easy to use when purchasing your plane tickets and for your convenience, 97 *detailed instructions about how to use the system are available in a majority of languages. Passengers whose language is not serviced are advised to go to the BlueSky Airlines air ticket booth for ticketing.* If you need help with the ticketing machines, a BlueSky Airlines customer service representative can assist you.

English	German	Korean	Japanese
Attention!			
New System			
1. Where - Main entrance			
2. How - Touch screen			
3. Benefit - Quick and Easy to use			

BlueSky Airlines 승객 여러분 집중해주세요. 우리는 최근에 새로운 자동 발권 시스템을 도입했습니다. 발권기계는 일층 주 출입구 근처에 위치해 있습니다. 터치스크린은 승객들이 비행기 표를 구매할 대 사용하기 빠르고 쉽습니다. 또한 승객의 편의를 위해 어떻게 발권시스템을 이용하는지에 관한 자세한 설명이 다양한 언어로 이용 가능합니다. 서비스되지 않는 언어를 사용하는 승객들은 발권을 위해 BlueSky Airlines 발권창구로 가시기 바랍니다. 만약 터치스크린 기계 사용에 도움이 필요하시면 BlueSky Airlines 고객 서비스 직원이 승객 여러분을 도울 것입니다.

영어	독일어	한국어	일본어
집중! 새로운 시스템 1. 장소 – 주 출입구 2. 방법 – 터치 스크린 3. 이점 – 사용하기 빠르고 편리함			

어휘_ introduce 도입하다 automated 자동화된 ticketing system 발권시스템 situate 위치하다 detailed 자세한, 상세한 instruction 지시사항 a majority of 다양한

95. (A)

Where most likely is this announcement being heard?
(A) At an airport
(B) At a train station
(C) At a department store
(D) At a ticket booth
이런 안내방송은 아마도 어디서 들을 수 있는가?
(A) 공항
(B) 기차역
(C) 백화점
(D) 매표소
분석_ 장소에 관한 정답은 지문 초반부를 듣고 유추할 수 있다. Attention BlueSky Airlines passengers.를 보면 항공사 승객을 상대로 하는 안내방송이므로 (A)가 가장 적절하다.

96. (D)

What does the speaker mention is now available?
(A) A renovated cafeteria
(B) An expanded airline seat
(C) Free Internet access
(D) Automated ticketing machines
화자는 무엇이 현재 이용 가능하다고 언급하는가?
(A) 개조한 구내식당
(B) 확장된 비행기 좌석 공간
(C) 무료 인터넷 접속
(D) 자동화된 발권 기계
분석_ 지문 초반부 We have recently introduced a new automated ticketing system.을 보면 최근에 자동화된 발권 시스템을 도입했다 언급했으므로 (D)가 가장 적절하다.

97. (B)

Look at the graphic. What are Chinese passengers instructed to do for ticketing?
(A) They can get an air ticket exclusively on the website.
(B) They can use ticketing service at the air ticket booth.
(C) They can receive detailed instructions from the airport managerial office.
(D) They can use the new automated ticketing system.
그래픽을 보자. 중국인 탑승객들은 발권을 위해 무엇을 하라는 지침을 받는가?

(A) 웹사이트에서만 항공원을 얻을 수 있다.
(B) 항공권 발권 창구에서 발권 서비스를 이용할 수 있다.
(C) 공항 관리사무소로부터 상세한 지침을 얻을 수 있다.
(D) 새로운 자동 발권시스템을 이용할 수 있다.
분석_ 서비스되지 않는 언어를 사용하는 승객들은 발권 창구로 가라고 이야기하고 있으며, 스크린 화면에는 영어, 독일어, 한국어, 일본어만 서비스되고 있음을 알 수 있으므로 중국인은 창구로 가서 발권해야 한다.

Questions 98-100 refer to the following telephone message and list.

Hi Ms. Stella, I'm calling from Natural Energy Solutions. **98** *I would like to let you know about the services we provide to help small businesses like yours conserve on significant water usage.* We do a considerable study of the company's operations and identify areas for feasible cost savings. For instance, we've helped many companies decide whether switching to **100** *rainwater for their water usage is worth the initial cost.* If you're interested in our services, **99** *I'd be glad to send you references from other customers.* I can be reached at 777-9870.

Natural Energy Solutions	
Expert area	Initial cost
Rainwater usage	$ 1,000
Steam powered electricity	$ 1,500
Waste recycling	$ 1,200

안녕하세요, Stella. Natural Energy Solutions에서 연락드립니다. 귀하와 같은 소규모 사업체가 엄청난 수도 사용을 절약하는 것을 돕기 위해 우리가 제공하는 서비스에 관해 알려주고 싶습니다. 우리는 회사의 운영에 관해 상당한 연구를 했고 실행 가능한 비용 절약을 위한 분야를 확인했습니다. 예를 들어, 우리는 많은 회사가 수도 사용을 빗물로 바꾸는 것이 초기 비용만큼의 값어치가 있는지 없는지 결정하는 데 도움을 주었습니다. 만약 우리 서비스에 관심 있으시면 다른 고객들로부터 받은 추천서를 귀하에게 기꺼이 보내겠습니다. 저는 777-9870으로 연락 가능합니다.
Natural Solutions

Natural Energy Solutions	
전문 분야	초기 비용
빗물 이용	1,000달러
증기 동력 전기	1,500달러
폐기물 재활용	1,200달러

어휘_ small business 소규모 사업체 significant 엄청난 usage 사용 conserve 절약하다 considerable 상당한 feasible 실행 가능한 switch 바꾸다 rainwater 빗물 reference 추천

98. (D)

What is the main purpose of the recorded message?
(A) To change a delivery schedule
(B) To clarify some procedures
(C) To make payment arrangements
(D) To promote a service
녹음 메시지의 주된 목적은 무엇인가?
(A) 배달 일정을 바꾸기 위해
(B) 몇몇 절차를 명확히 하기 위해
(C) 지불 약속을 정하기 위해
(D) 서비스를 홍보하기 위해
분석_ 녹음 메시지에서 본인 소개 이후 I would like to let you know about the services we provide라고 하여 우리 회사에서 제공하는 서비스를 알려주고 싶다고 언급했으므로 (D)가 가장 적절하다.

99. (C)

What does the speaker plan to send?
(A) A feasible solution
(B) A product sample
(C) Customer recommendations
(D) A detailed refund process
화자가 보내고자 계획하는 것은 무엇인가?
(A) 실행 가능한 해결책
(B) 제품 견본
(C) 고객 추천서
(D) 상세한 환불 과정
분석_ 계획하고 있다는 말은 아직 행하지 않은 미래행동이고 미래행동은 보통 지문의 후반부에 등장한다. 지문 후반에 다른 고객에게 받은 추천서를 보내주겠다(I'd be glad to send you references from other customers.)고 언급했으므로 (C)가 가장 적절하다.

100. (A)

Look at the graphic. How much will Ms. Stella pay for the service that the speaker mentions?
(A) $ 1,000
(B) $ 1,500
(C) $ 1,200
(D) $ 3,700
화자가 언급한 서비스에 대해 Stella 씨는 얼마를 지불할 것인가?
(A) 1,000달러
(B) 1,500달러
(C) 1,200달러
(D) 3,700달러
분석_ 화자가 언급한 서비스는 rainwater for their water usage에서 알 수 있으며 표에서 1,000달러로 표시되어 있으므로, 정답은 (A)이다.

101. (A) publication

해석_ Super Economics 잡지는 전문가들을 위한 최신 무역출판물이다.
분석_ 관사 the 뒤에 명사를 넣는 문제이다. 주어 Super Economic과 동격이 되는 명사는 출판물인 (A)이다.

102. (D) by

해석_ 그룹의 최고 경영진은 지난해의 판매 문서가 이번 주말까지 제출되어야 한다고 명했다.
분석_ 빈칸 뒤 시점까지 제출을 완료해야 하므로 전치사 by와 어울린다. (C) 〈throughout + 시간〉은 '시간 내내'라는 뜻으로 완료의 의미가 아니다.

103. (C) into

해석_ 세계적 SPA 브랜드인 '7 Hours'는 공식기자회견에서 중국으로의 확장계획을 언급했다.
분석_ 보기가 모두 전치사이다. 빈칸 앞 동사 '확장하다'와 빈칸 뒤 장소를 연결하는 가장 적절한 전치사는 (C) into이다.

104. (A) their

해석_ 부사장 Marie De Charlotte은 그의 직원에게 국내 판매를 20% 증대시킨 그들의 헌신에 감사했다.
분석_ 명사 앞 소유격 대명사를 넣는 문제이다. 전치사와 명사 사이 명사를 수식하는 소유격 their가 적절하다.

105. (B) attended

해석_ Dean Winchester는 지난주 그가 런던에서 참석했던 개인정보보호에 관한 회의를 논할 것이다.
분석_ 동사 어휘 문제로 보이는 능동, 수동 구분 문제이다. 보기의 동사 중 (A), (C), (D)는 모두 자동사로 빈칸 뒤에 전치사가 필요하다. (B)는 타동사로 빈칸 앞 주어인 he와 함께 목적격관계대명사절을 이루어 앞의 명사를 수식한다. he participated in in London 혹은 he enrolled in in London, he registered for in London 등이 올바른 표현이다.

106. (C) After　음성강의

해석_ 첫 영화의 성공 이후, Jeremy Lucas는 치밀한 구성의 차기작을 개발하기 위해 훨씬 더 많은 예산을 제공받았다.
분석_ 빈칸 뒤 명사를 취할 수 있는 전치사가 들어갈 자리이다. After는 전치사와 접속사 모두 가능하지만 이 문장에서는 명사를 취하는 전치사로 사용되었다.

107. (B) before　음성강의

해석_ Laster Rink 병원의 최고 재무 책임자는 그의 은퇴파티 전 간단한 인사를 할 것이다.
분석_ 보기가 전치사로 어휘 문제이다. 은퇴 전 인사를 하는 것이 적절하므로 (B) before가 정답이다.

108. (C) totally　음성강의

해석_ 저작권 침해에 관한 유서 깊은 웹사이트가 완전 새로워진 모습으로

내달 초 다시 온라인상으로 돌아올 것이다.

분석_ 〈관 + 부 + 형 + 명〉의 형태이다. 관사와 분사형용사 upgraded 사이에 '완전히'라는 뜻의 부사가 필요하다.

109. (B) expanded　　음성강의

해석_ Quebec 시의 가장 오래된 이발소는 많은 고객에게 서비스하기 위해 세계 전역에 사업장을 확장했다.

분석_ 현재완료동사를 만들기 위해 has 다음 빈칸에는 과거분사 형태인 (B) expanded가 필요하다.

110. (A) firm　　음성강의

해석_ 소규모 병원기업, Big Mama Dermatology는 여드름 흉터를 없애는 것을 전문으로 한다.

분석_ 빈칸 뒤 콤마는 동격을 의미한다. Big Mama Dermatology는 프로그램, 조각, 차트가 아닌 기업이므로 (A) firm이 정답이다.

111. (D) local

해석_ 각 메뉴의 신선함을 보장하기 위해, Jamba Jumbo Juice는 지역 농장에서 온 다양한 과일만을 활용한다.

분석_ 형용사 어휘 문제이다. 농장과 가장 적절히 어울리며 과일의 신선함을 보장하는 것은 지역 농장에서 길러진 것이므로 (D) local이 정답이다.

112. (B) its

해석_ 기술자들은 Tech Pro의 세탁기 모델 부품이 단종되었기 때문에 수리를 할 수 없다.

분석_ 보기가 모두 대명사의 소유격이다. 빈칸 뒤에 부품이란 뜻의 parts를 수식할 수 있는 것은 Tech Pro washing machine의 부품이므로 이를 받을 수 있는 대명사 소유격은 its이다.

113. (B) reduced

해석_ Michael Consulting Group은 휴대전화로 화상회의를 함으로써 비용은 줄이고 업무능력은 개선시켰다.

분석_ 등위접속사 and 앞뒤로 적절한 뜻의 동사가 필요한 어휘 문제이다. 업무는 개선하고 비용은 줄여야 하므로 (B) reduced가 정답이다.

114. (D) buyers

해석_ Marvel Fragrance Franchise는 첫 구매고객에게 약 30% 할인을 제공한다.

분석_ 전치사 to 뒤에 할인을 받을 수 있는 사람명사가 필요하다. 단수를 나타내는 a/an이 없으므로 복수사람명사 (D) buyers가 정답이다.

115. (C) nearly

해석_ 우리는 100대의 새 컴퓨터를 주문한 이후로 거의 한 달이 지났기 때문에 환불과 서면사과문을 요구할 것이다.

분석_ 보기가 모두 부사로 어휘 문제이다. 숫자 형용사 앞에서 '대략'이란 뜻으로 쓰이는 부사는 (C) nearly이다. (A) 부분적으로 (B) 즉시 (C) 철저히 모두 해석이 부자연스럽다.

116. (B) who　　음성강의

해석_ Miami에 있는 Space One Theater는 음식을 주제로 영화를 만드는 아시아 최고 영화감독의 작품을 특색 있게 다룬다.

분석_ 빈칸의 명사를 선행사로 꾸며주며 빈칸 뒤에 동사 make를 취할 수 있는 것은 주격관계대명사 (B) who이다.

117. (B) whatever　　음성강의

해석_ Standstill Science College 교직원은 새로운 이력으로의 전환을 가능한 한 원활하게 하기 위해 그들이 할 수 있는 무엇이든 할 것이다.

분석_ 동사 do의 목적어 역할을 하는 명사형태가 필요하다. 빈칸 뒤에 불완전한 문장이 있으며 명사절 접속사 역할을 하는 의문대명사 (B) whatever가 필요하다.

118. (B) following　　음성강의

해석_ 사무용품 대량주문은 다음 영업일에야 행해질 것이다.

분석_ 형용사 어휘 문제이다. 영업일을 가장 잘 수식하는 형용사는 (B) following이 적절하다. (A) 대강의, 가까운 (C) 최근의 (D) 선도적인, 대표적인 모두 문맥에 적절히 어울리지 않는다.

119. (C) completely　　음성강의

해석_ 적절한 사용 지침을 위한 사용자 설명서는 잠재고객들에게 특정 색깔의 유리는 다른 것들과 완전히 융화되지 않는다고 경고했다.

분석_ 품사 문제이다. fuse는 자동사로 '융합하다'란 뜻을 가지고 있다. 자동사이므로 전치사 with를 취하고 목적어 명사 other를 취했다. 그러므로 자동사와 전치사 사이에 필요한 품사는 부사이다.

120. (D) arrange　　음성강의

해석_ Wentworth Brown은 다가오는 토요일 그의 직속상관이 해외 투자가들과 만날 수 있게 준비할 것이다.

분석_ arrange는 to부정사를 취하여 '~하는 것을 준비하다'라는 뜻을 가지고 있으며 to부정사 앞에 부정사가 취하는 행위의 의미상 주어로 〈for + 명사〉 형태를 취하기도 한다. 즉, 〈arrange + for + 명사 + to부정사〉 형태로 '명사가 to V하도록 준비해두다'라는 뜻을 가진다.

121. (C) collections

해석_ Eaton Rosemead 도서관은 만 권이 넘는 매우 다양한 어린이용 종이책과 전자책을 보유하고 있다.

분석_ 품사 문제이다. a variety of는 숙어로 '다양한'이란 뜻이다. a variety of는 복수명사를 취하므로 (C) collections가 정답이다.

122. (C) change

해석_ 우리가 해외 배송 회사를 바꿨기 때문에 이번 주 금요일 주문 처리 과정에서 약간의 변화가 있을 것으로 예상된다.

분석_ 어휘 문제로 보이는 어법 문제이다. 〈change in + 분야〉는 '분야에서의 변화'라는 숙어로 자주 사용된다. (A) 소포 (B) 반납 (D) 우편 요금

123. (D) experienced

해석_ 유명한 영화 제작 회사, Casablanca는 이번 주 금요일 Cat Walk Theater에서 경력 배우를 뽑기 위한 오디션을 개최할 것이다.

분석_ 품사 문제이다. 전치사 for와 명사 actors 사이에 명사를 수식할 수 있는 형용사가 필요하다.

124. (B) official

해석_ 단골 고객들은 5월 10일 공식 발표 전, 새로운 고급 세단을 미리 사용하고 미리 소유할 수 있다.

분석_ 어휘 문제이다. 보기가 모두 형용사로 명사 release를 수식할 수 있다. 공식 출시가 가장 어울리므로 (B) official이 정답이다.

125. (C) selection

해석_ Comfort Two는 거의 모든 종류의 가죽으로 모든 나이 대를 위한 매우 다양한 고객 맞춤 신발을 자랑스럽게 내세운다.

분석_ 어휘 문제로 보이는 숙어 문제이다. 보기가 모두 명사이고 해석으로 풀려고 하기 쉬우나 a selection of 숙어를 찾는 문제이다.

126. (B) specifically

해석_ 특히나 관련된 양측이 그들의 기대치를 넘어설 수 있게 서로 이득이 되는 관계가 성립되었다.

분석_ 품사 문제이다. 수동태 be p.p 뒤에는 동사를 수식할 수 있는 부사가 필요하다.

127. (B) whom

해석_ Edmond Hair Salon은 10명의 미용사를 고용했는데, 그 미용사 중 대부분은 Patrick Anderson School에서 미용 학위를 획득했다.

분석_ 관계대명사 문제이다. 선행사인 명사가 사람 hairdressers 이고 전치사 of 뒤에 빈칸이 있으므로 목적격관계대명사 (B) whom이 정답이다.

128. (A) effective

해석_ 제5회 연례 Kansas 세미나는 참석자들에게 새로운 기술에 익숙해질 수 있는 가장 효과적인 방법을 제공한다.

분석_ 어휘 문제이다. 보기가 모두 형용사로 명사 way를 가장 적절하게 수식하는 것은 '효과적인'이라는 의미의 (A)이다. (B) 주저하는 (C) 걱정하는 (D) 포함된 모두 적절하지 않다.

129. (C) pick up

해석_ The Cherry Popped Ice Cream Factory에 방문하는 모든 방문객은 안내데스크에서 신분증을 받아야 한다.

분석_ 어휘 문제이다. 신분증을 목적어로 취할 수 있는 가장 적절한 동사는 (C) pick up(받아가다, 찾아가다)이다. (A) 따라잡다 (B) 닮다, 흉내 내다 (C) 방문하다, 부탁하다 모두 어울리지 않는다.

130. (D) Lately

해석_ Anderson Darcy는 최근 출품작 제출의 마감일을 맞추기 위해 늦게까지 일했다.

분석_ 품사 문제이다. 빈칸 뒤 완벽한 문장을 수식하면서 현재완료 동사 has been working과 어울리는 부사는 (D) lately 또는 recently가 있다.

Questions 131-134 refer to the following press release.

분기별 Stanford Marathon Competition이 9월 1일 개최되었다. 이 유명한 국내 마라톤 경기는 1972년 첫 시작 이후 여태껏 Stanford World Stadium에서 개최되었지만, 올해 조직위원회는 더 넓은 장소로 옮길 것을 결심했다.
유례없는 많은 참가자가 이번 대회에 참석했기 때문에 훨씬 더 큰 장소로의 이전은 옳은 결정이라고 판명되었다.
위원회 의장인 Lim Charles은 이 대회의 성공을 정기적인 운동을 통해 얻는 많은 건강상의 이점에 대한 전 세계적인 의식 덕이라 돌렸다. *그는 또한 이러한 좋은 결과에 대해 조직위원회 모두에게 감사를 표했다.*

131. (B) happened

분석_ 동사 시제 문제이다. 문맥을 보면 이번 대회가 9월 1일 이미 개최되었기 때문에 과거 시제가 정답이다.

132. (C) larger

분석_ 어휘 문제이다. 보기가 모두 형용사로 빈칸 뒤 명사 location을 수식한다. 빈칸 아래 문단을 보면 much bigger venue라고 다시 한 번 paraphrase된 것을 확인할 수 있다. 따라서 bigger와 같은 의미의 (C) larger가 정답이다.

133. (A) to

분석_ 어휘 문제로 보이는 숙어 문제이다. 보기는 모두 전치사이다. 문장의 동사 attribute는 숙어의 형태로 쓰인다. attribute A to B는 'A를 B 덕이라 여기다'라는 뜻이다.

134. (A)

(A) 그는 또한 이러한 좋은 결과에 대해 조직위원회 모두에게 감사를 표했다.

(B) 매우 많은 판매자들이 그 경매에 참가할 것이다.

(C) 당신이 세미나에 참석할 수 없는 이유를 알려주세요.

(D) 가수, 무용가, 곡예사는 미리 등록을 해야 한다.

분석_ 앞에서 언급된 내용을 보면, 조직위원장이 마라톤 대회의 성공에 관해서 얘기하고 있다. 뒤에 따라올 문장도 마라톤 대회의 성공에 관해서 공로를 치하하는 문장이 오는 것이 가장 적절하다.

Questions 135-138 refer to the following e-mail.

발신: sanders@hcs.com
수신: madeline@ecs.com
날짜: 11월 11일

135. (A) loyalty

분석_ 품사 문제이다. 빈칸 앞 소유격 your의 수식을 받을 수 있는 품사는 명사이다. 또한 불가산명사이기 때문에 복수형으로 사용할 수 없다.

136. (D) savings

분석_ 어휘 문제이다. 보기가 모두 명사이다. 뒤에 문장을 보면 특정 금액 이상의 물건을 사면 가격 할인을 받을 수 있으므로 savings program, 즉 절약프로그램이 가장 적절하다.

137. (C)

(A) 우리는 당신의 메시지를 받았음을 인정합니다.
(B) 그러나, 과도한 인용의 사용은 그 문제를 애매하게 만들 수 있습니다.
(C) 만약 당신이 가격을 더 많이 할인받고 싶다면, 대량주문을 함으로써 훨씬 더 저렴한 가격으로 구입할 수 있습니다.
(D) 학생들은 수업에 대해서 그룹할인을 받을 수 있습니다.

분석_ 빈칸 앞 내용이 할인을 말하고 있으므로 뒤에도 할인에 관한 내용이 추가되어 나오는 것이 문맥에 맞다.

138. (C) your

분석_ 보기가 모두 대명사의 소유격이다. 앞서 편지의 내용들이 편지의 수령인인 Adeline에게 보내는 내용이고 빈칸 앞에 you are a frequent shopper가 있으므로 (C) your가 가장 적절하다.

Questions 139-142 refer to the following e-mail. 음성강의

139. (B) in

분석_ 어휘 문제이다. 보기 중 (D) away가 부사이고 나머지는 모두 전치사이다. 장소 branch 앞에 쓰이며 '체류'라는 명사 sojourn와 가장 어울리는 전치사는 (B) in이다.

140. (D) This

분석_ 어휘 문제이다. 앞서 얘기한 내용을 가리키며 이런 일에 이만큼의 시간이 걸린다는 것을 설명하므로 대명사 (D) This가 가장 적절하다.

141. (B) improve

분석_ 어휘 문제이다. 고객에게 받은 질문지는 고객을 응대하는 방식을 더 좋게 개선시켜주므로 (B) improve가 가장 적절하다. (A) 보고하다 (C) 평가하다, 존중하다 (D) 제공하다

142. (C)

(A) 특별무료버스가 시카고 공항을 왕복 운행했습니다.
(B) 고객들은 언제든 모닝콜을 요청할 수 있습니다.
(C) 감사의 표현으로, 우리는 모든 응답자들의 다음 방문 때 무료 샴페인을 제공할 것입니다.
(D) 기념품가게와 이발소는 우리 호텔 정문 근처에 있습니다.

분석_ 앞서 나온 내용이 호텔에 머문 고객에게 고객만족질문지 작성을 요구하는 것이므로 그 이후 내용은 질문지를 작성했을 때 호텔에서 제공할 수 있는 것이 이어지는 것이 가장 적절하다.

Questions 143-146 refer to the following notice.

143. (D) will expand

분석_ 동사와 준동사 구분 + 시제 문제이다. 우선 문장에 동사가 없으므로 동사 형태가 필요하다. 또한 상점 재건작업이 계획 단계이므로 아직 시작 전이기 때문에 미래시제 (D) will expand가 정답이다.

144. (B) Nevertheless

분석_ 어휘 문제이다. 보기가 모두 부사이므로 적절하게 문장이 이어지는 부사가 필요하다. 문맥상 앞뒤 문장이 반대이므로 (B) Nevertheless가 적절하다. (A) 다소, 상당히 (C) 비슷하게 (D) 이전에

145. (D) inaccessible

분석_ 어휘 문제이다. 문장 앞에 '이용이 불가능하다'라는 의미의 unavailable과 비슷한 의미의 형용사가 필요하므로 (D) inaccessible이 적절하다. Part 6은 앞뒤 문장을 잘 살펴보면 비슷한 뜻의 단어가 존재한다.

146. (C)

(A) 회사는 5월에 새로운 소형차량을 공개할 계획입니다.
(B) 적절한 환기에 관한 일련의 강연이 제공될 것입니다.
(C) 상점 매니저는 토요일을 제외하고 아침부터 저녁까지 상점에 있습니다.
(D) 10억 대가 넘는 자전거가 Los Angeles에 있습니다.

분석_ 앞서 문장에서 특정 자동차가 없을 수 있으니 웹사이트에서 명단을 확인하거나 상점 매니저와 연락을 취하라고 말했다. 따라서 상점 매니저와 언제 연락이 가능한지를 의미하는 문장이 뒤에 오는 것이 가장 적절하다.

Part 7   본문 p.119

Questions 147-148 refer to the following letter.

> 4월 24일
> Angela Sheen
> 568 Blue Bird Boulevard
> Boston, MT 147050
> 답장: 계좌번호 790310-486
> Sheen 씨께
> 우리에게 귀하의 새로운 연락정보를 알리는 편지를 보내주셔서 감사드립니다. 우리는 귀하의 계좌에 연락정보를 최신화했고, 모든 그 이후의 은행 명세서와 왕래서신은 귀하의 새로운 주소로 보내질 겁니다. 우리가 귀하의 편지를 오늘 받았다는 것을 기억해주세요. 귀하의 가장 최근 명세서는 이미 귀하의 옛 주소로 보내졌습니다. 그러나, 귀하는 우리 웹사이트에 있는 귀하의 계정에 접속함으로써 언제든 귀하의 계좌정보(계좌 잔액, 최근 청구액, 받은 금액)를 자세히 볼 수 있습니다. 소중한 고객이 되어주셔서 감사합니다.
> Felicia Bocelli
> 고객 관리 부서

147. (C)

편지는 주로 무엇에 관한 것인가?
(A) 체납
(B) 새롭게 개설한 저축 계좌
(C) 주소 변경 요청
(D) 잘못된 은행명세서

분석_ 편지 내용 전반에 걸쳐 고객의 연락정보가 바뀌어서 연락정보를 최신화시킨 것을 말하고 있다.

148. (A)

Bocelli 씨는 Sheen 씨가 무엇을 해야 한다고 제시했는가?
(A) 웹사이트를 방문하기
(B) 고객관리부서에 전화하기
(C) 기한이 지난 금액을 보내기
(D) 새로운 연락정보를 최신화하기

분석_ 편지 하단에 명세서를 상세히 보고 싶을 경우 웹사이트에 있는 본인의 계정으로 접속하라고 명시했다.

Questions 149-151 refer to the following e-mail.

> 발신: jstweart@marionvilledialnet.com
> 수신: admin@marionvillemedical.com
> 날짜: 10월 10일
> 주제: 다시 알림
> Stewart 씨에게,
> 이것은 다음 주 Big Smile Medical Group에서 당신의 치과진료약속을 확인을 다시금 상기시켜주는 메일입니다. 잠시 시간을 내서 당신 예약의 세부사항을 검토해주세요.
> 치과의사: Amanda Corby
> 날짜: 10월 17일 목요일
> 시간: 10시 30분
> 목적: 치아 스케일링과 치아 광택
> 만약 이 정보가 잘못된 것 같다면, 우리 안내데스크로 연락 주세요. 전화번호는 (802) 333-0128입니다. 또한, 만약 이 약속을 지킬 수 없다면, 우리가 당신의 예약 일정을 바꿀 수 있게 가능한 한 빨리 우리 접수원에게 연락해주세요. 사전공지 하루 전에 취소된 예약은 100달러의 취소수수료를 물게 됩니다.
> Big Smile Medical Group

149. (A)

이메일은 주로 무엇에 관한 것인가?
(A) 다가올 예약
(B) 건강 검진 결과
(C) 건강 검진 과정의 변화
(D) 취소수수료에 관한 공지

분석_ 치과 예약을 한 고객에게 다시 한번 치과 예약날짜와 내용을 공지하는 글이다.

150. (A)

이메일에 따르면, Stewart 씨가 사무실에 연락해야 하는 이유는 무엇인가?
(A) 정확하지 않은 정보를 알리기 위해

(B) 치과 예약을 확인하기 위해
(C) Corby 박사와 이야기하기 위해
(D) 청구 명세서를 요청하기 위해
분석_ 치과 예약 정보를 날짜, 시간, 목적까지 상세하게 고객에게
　　　설명해주고 있다. 이 정보가 잘못 작성된 경우 연락을 취하
　　　라고 되어 있으므로 (A)가 정답이다.

151. (D)
이메일에 따르면 왜 추가 요금이 청구되는가?
(A) 접수원으로부터 사전 공지를 받았기 때문에
(B) 의료기록을 다른 병원으로 전송했기 때문에
(C) 당일 의료 진단 결과를 받기 위해
(D) 진료 예약을 늦게 취소해서
분석_ 편지의 하단부에 사전공지 하루 전에 예약 취소를 하면 취소
　　　수수료를 납부해야 한다고 명시되어 있다.

Questions 152-153 refer to the following text message chain.

Jeffery Benet	(10:13)

갑작스레 집안에 급한 일이 생겨서, Seattle에서 기차를 놓쳤어요.

Jeffery Benet (10:15)
어쩔 수 없이 10시 40분에 떠나는 다음 기차를 타야 해요.

Norah Jones (10:45)
방금 메시지를 확인했어요. 늦게 답해서 미안해요.

Norah Jones (10:46)
기차에 탑승하셨나요?

Jeffery Benet (10:47)
당연하죠.

Norah Jones (10:47)
당신은 모임에 제시간에 도착할 수 있나요?

Jeffery Benet (10:48)
물론이에요. 이 기차는 급행열차라서 모임시간 훨씬 전에 도착할 수 있어요. 그럼 그때 봐요.

152. (D)
Benet 씨에 대해 무엇이 제시되는가?
(A) 그는 Seattle에 2번 이상 가본 적이 있다.
(B) 그는 현재 Seattle 공항에 있다.
(C) 그는 10시 15분에 기차를 탑승했다.
(D) 그는 모임 시간을 지킬 수 있다.
분석_ 10시 48분 마지막 메시지에서 급행열차를 타서 모임시간 훨
　　　씬 전에 도착할 수 있다고 언급됐다.

153. (C)
10시 47분 Jeffery 씨가 "당연하죠"라고 말한 의도는 무엇인가?
(A) 그는 기차 도착 시간을 확인했다.
(B) 그는 집안에 급한 일을 처리할 수 있다고 확신한다.
(C) 그는 Jones에게 그가 그 기차에 탑승했다고 확신시켜준다.
(D) 그는 Jones가 역에서 그를 데리러 올 것을 안다.
분석_ 기차에 탑승했는지를 물었고 그에 대한 응답으로 한 대답
　　　이다.

Questions 154-155 refer to the following online form.

http://www.pinkdiamond.com
PINK DIAMOND
품질을 가장 먼저 생각합니다
고객 관리 부서와 연락을 취하기 위해 아래의 정보를 작성하세요. 우리는 매일 24시간 이내에 당신의 질문에 빠르게 응대해드릴 겁니다.
이름: Henry
성: Donavan
이메일: bianca@officepro.com
주제: 흔들의자 번호 325
메시지
나는 나무로 만든 흔들의자(스타일번호 325) 구매에 관심 있습니다. 귀사 웹사이트는 물건의 무게와 직경에 따라 선적요금이 계산된다고 적혀 있네요. 이 선적요금을 물지 않고 제가 직접 의자를 가져가도 되나요? 나는 귀사의 창고에서 대략 한 시간 거리에 살고 있고 큰 의자를 쉽게 실을 수 있는 트럭도 가지고 있습니다. 감사합니다.

154. (A)
Donavan 씨는 왜 서류를 작성했는가?
(A) 배송정책에 관해 문의하기 위해서
(B) 그가 구입한 의자에 관해 불평하기 위해서
(C) 흔들의자 할인을 요청하기 위해
(D) 공장으로 가는 길을 알아보기 위해
분석_ 메시지의 내용을 보면 선적요금이 물건의 무게와 직경에 따
　　　라 부과되는데 이것을 피하고자 직접 트럭으로 싣고 가는
　　　것이 가능한지를 물어보고 있다.

155. (B)
Pink Diamond는 무엇을 약속하는가?
(A) 대량주문에 대해 선적요금을 줄이기
(B) 24시간 이내에 메시지에 응답하기
(C) 트럭대여점을 추천하기
(D) 배송 중 파손된 의자를 수리하기
분석_ 서류 앞부분을 보면 고객이 질문을 하면 less than a day에
　　　답변해준다는 표현이 있다

Questions 156-157 refer to the following notice.

전면광고 마감일
World Sports Weekly는 금요일 출간이므로 전면광고를 게재하기 위한 마감일은 늦어도 목요일 오전 10시입니다. 첫 내용을 받은 후, 변경은 받아들여지지 않을 겁니다. 우리는 내용을 바꿀 권리를 보유하고 있습니다.
모든 광고비는 미리 선납되어야 합니다. 일주일 넘게 게재되기로 약속된 광고라도 앞으로의 광고 명성을 위해 일주일 후 취소될 수 있습니다. 귀하의 광고 내용을 메일로 보내주세요. 메일주소는 ads@worldsportsweekly.com입니다. 다수의 광고는 할인도 가능합니다. 가격을 알고 싶으면 346-0989로 연락 주세요.

156. (A)

광고주가 금요일 오전에 광고를 제출하면 어떤 일이 발생할까?
(A) 광고는 다음 주 금요일에 게재될 것이다.
(B) 광고는 그날 늦게 출력될 것이다.
(C) 광고는 신문사에 의해 거절될 것이다.
(D) 광고는 훨씬 더 많은 돈을 광고주에게 지불할 것이다.
분석_ 첫 문단을 보면 광고 출력이 금요일이므로 늦어도 목요일
까지 광고를 제출하라고 했다. 따라서 금요일에 제출한다면
다음 주 금요일에 출력이 가능해진다.

157. (A)

공지에 따르면, 광고를 게재하기 위해 광고주는 무엇을 해야 하는가?
(A) 마감일까지 첫 광고내용을 제출하기
(B) World Sports Weekly 편집자와 연락하기
(C) 저작권 소유주로부터 서면 허락을 받기
(D) 목요일 10시에 최고 편집장을 만나기
분석_ 광고주는 마감일인 목요일까지 광고내용을 제출하고 비용
을 선납해야 한다고 명시되어 있다.

Questions 158-160 refer to the following article.

Welcome Bags Available
AVWA는 새로운 거주민을 위한 놀랍고도 독특한 선물을 준비했다.
American Village에 관한 도움이 되는 정보로 가득한 재사용 가능한
쇼핑가방이다. 앞 부분에 Welcome American Village라고 인쇄되
어 있는 이 면 가방은 지역 최신소식과 할인 쿠폰 그리고 단체 회원들
이 제공한 직접 구운 수제 쿠키로 가득 차 있다.
이 프로젝트를 돕는 데 관심 있는 지역 사업체는 가방 뒷면에 그들 회
사 로고를 인쇄하는 대가로 돈을 지불하면 된다. American Village
거주민들은 개인적으로 이 가방을 새로운 전입자에게 직접 건네줌으
로써 이웃을 맞이할 수 있다.
참가하기 위해, 온라인상 최신화된 지역 웹사이트로 방문해보세요.

158. (D)

어떤 종류의 신문에서 이런 기사를 볼 수 있는가?
(A) 주거 디자인 잡지
(B) 여행 잡지
(C) 연예 신문
(D) 지역사회 회보
분석_ American Village에 살고 있는 거주민들에게 새로운 거주
민을 환영하는 방법을 설명하고 있으므로 지역사회 회보가
가장 적절하다.

159. (C)

지역 사업체는 어떻게 이 프로젝트를 후원할 수 있는가?
(A) 무료 견본품을 배포함으로써
(B) 재사용 가능한 상품을 사용함으로써
(C) 광고 공간을 구매함으로써
(D) 지역사회봉사에 자원함으로써
분석_ 두 번째 문단 첫 문장에 가방 뒷면에 회사로고를 프린트하기
위해 돈을 지불하면 된다고 작성되어 있으므로 가방 뒷면
= 광고 공간을 구매하라는 표현으로 바꾼 (C)가 정답이다.

160. (A)

기사에 따르면 American Village 거주민은 무엇을 해야 하는가?
(A) 인사용 물건을 나눠주기
(B) 새로운 지역사회 로고를 고안하기
(C) 지역 상점에서 쇼핑하기
(D) 그들이 좋아하는 요리법을 공유하기
분석_ 요구하는 것을 찾는 문제는 보통 지문 내용 하단에 위치한
다. 지문 하단을 보면 personally handing these bags to
each newcomer라고 나와 있으므로 이 내용을 다른 말로
표현한 (A)가 정답이다.

Questions 161-164 refer to the following article.

Vert et Blanc Group에서 야심 찬 계획을 발표하다
3월 2일 – Vert et Blanc Group은 Brunch in Paris라는 패스트푸
드 체인점을 개발할 계획을 발표했다. 새로운 체인점은 Vert et Blanc
Group의 한국 본사가 관리할 것이다. 이 다국적 기업은 궁극적으로
아시아와 남아메리카 전역에 100여 개의 Brunch in Paris 지점을 도
입할 수 있기를 기대하고 있다.
"지난 십여 년간 인스턴트 식품 분야는 전 세계적인 성장을 보여왔습
니다."라고 treadhunter.com의 산업 분석가인 Sandra Brienne
가 말했다. Vert et Blanc은 이러한 흐름을 현명하게 이용하려 한다.
Vert et Blanc이 지난 한 해 시행한 시장조사는 소비자들이 외식을 할
때 좀 더 몸에 좋고 건강에 좋은 음식을 선호한다고 나타냈다.
Vert et Blanc의 최고경영자 Edward Lee는 사업체가 일반적으로
튀긴 음식은 덜 중시하며 신선한 재료와 영양적인 가치에 좀 더 집중한
다고 언급했다. "우리는 고객에게 점심으로 평균 5.20달러, 저녁으로
는 8.20달러에 유쾌하고 만족스러운 경험을 제공합니다. 또한 아침식
사와 간식으로는 더 저렴한 음식들도 제공합니다." 이것은 동종 식당
들보다 훨씬 더 저렴한 것이다.
"게다가, 우리는 주로 빠른 속도의 생활양식을 가진 도시 거주민에게
서비스할 것입니다. 그래서 우리는 그들이 우리 메뉴가 제공하는 편리
함에 만족할 것이라 생각합니다." Vert et Blanc Group은 새로운 자
회사인 Brunch in Paris가 운영 2번째 해에 수익이 나기 시작할 것
이라 낙관한다. 그룹은 현재 사업을 시작하기 위해 빌린 장기대출금을
여전히 보유하고 있다.

161. (D)

Brienne 씨는 아마도 누구일 것인가?
(A) Vert et Blanc Group의 법률 컨설턴트
(B) 한국은행 직원
(C) 건강 전문가
(D) 식품 분야 연구원
분석_ 독해 문제에 고유명사, 예를 들어 사람 이름이 나와 있으면
그 이름 앞 또는 뒤에 정답이 되는 힌트가 있다. 두 번째 문
단 Sandra Brienne 뒤 industry analyst라고 작성되어 있
으므로 (D)가 정답이다.

162. (C)

Vert et Blanc Group에 대해서 무엇이 발표되었는가?
(A) 그룹은 새로운 경영자를 고용했다.
(B) 그룹은 더딘 판매 증가로 영향을 받았다.

(C) 그룹은 사람들의 식사 선호도를 조사했다.
(D) 그룹은 남아메리카로 본사를 이전할 계획이다.
분석_ 네 번째 문단에서 그룹이 조사한 결과를 발표한 내용이 있
으므로 (C)가 정답이다.

163. (A)
Lee 씨는 Brunch in Paris의 장점을 무엇이라 나타내는가?
(A) Brunch in Paris는 비슷한 식당의 음식보다 훨씬 더 저렴하다.
(B) Brunch in Paris는 24시간 내내 이용 가능하다.
(C) Brunch in Paris는 지역에서 자란 재료를 포함한다.
(D) Brunch in Paris는 바로 음식이 제공된다.
분석_ 네 번째 문단 마지막에 at an average price라고 가격을 언
급한 내용이 있고 뒤에는 가격이 저렴하다고 언급되었다.

164. (C)
Brunch in Paris에 대해 제시된 것은?
(A) 성공하지 못한 Vert et Blanc Group을 대체했다.
(B) 단골 고객들에게 주된 요리법을 제공할 것이다.
(C) 바로 수익이 나지는 않을 것이다.
(D) 튀긴 음식에 주로 집중한다.
분석_ 마지막 문단을 보면 turn profits by its second year of
operations.라고 나와 있다. 운영 2년차가 되면 수익이 나
므로 바로 수익이 나지 않는다는 (C)가 정답이다.

Questions 165-168 refer to the following information.

Scottish Village Musical Festival

최고의 음악 천재들의 이야기를 즐기면서 여유시간을 기부하는 데 관
심 있나요? 제14회 연례 Scottish Village Music Festival에서의
자원봉사! 올해 축제는 8월 17일부터 23일까지 Scottish Village 지
역 전람회장에서 진행됩니다. 지역의 유명인을 포함해 재즈 아티스트
Norah Brightman, 발라드 가수 Sarah Jones 그리고 전문 현악 4
중주 Danny Cho Brothers까지 약 24명의 재능 있는 예술가들의
음악이 펼쳐질 것입니다.
자원봉사자들이 해야 할 일은
- 홍보 돕기 – 모든 소책자를 고안하고 붙이기, 공식 발표 배포하기
  – 8월 1일부터
- 음악가를 환영하고 그들의 주거지로 안내하는 것을 돕기
  – 8월 15일부터 24일
  모든 타 지역 예술가들은 지역가족들이 접대할 것입니다.
- 전람회장 정문에서 매표소를 운영하기, 축제기간 동안 손님을 주차
  장에 안내하기, 일반적인 정보 제공하기
도움에 대한 감사의 의미로, 모든 자원봉사자들은 Scottish Village
Musical Festival의 한정판 티셔츠와 2장의 무료 표를 받을 수 있
을 것입니다.
자원 봉사에 관심이 있으시면 7월 17일까지 Cordelia Benny에게
cbenny@scottishvillagemusical.org로 메일 주세요.

165. (B)
축제에 대해서 유추할 수 있는 내용은 무엇인가?
(A) 8월 1일에 축제가 개최될 것이다.
(B) 다양한 종류의 음악을 특색 있게 다룬다.

(C) 연주자들에게 무료 오찬을 제공한다.
(D) 악천후로 인해 축제가 재조정될 것이다.
분석_ 첫 번째 문단 하단을 보면 재즈, 발라드, 현악 4중주 등 다양
한 음악을 들을 수 있으므로 (B)가 정답이다.

166. (C)
몇몇 연주자에 관해서 제시된 것은?
(A) 그들은 그들의 악기를 기부할 것이다.
(B) 그들은 축제를 위한 포스터를 고안할 것이다.
(C) 그들은 Scottish Village의 가정집에 머물 것이다.
(D) 그들은 자원봉사자들에게 무료 표를 제공할 것이다.
분석_ 자원봉사자가 해야 할 일 두 번째를 보면 All out-of-town
artists will be hosted by area families.란 단서가 나와
있다.

167. (B)
자원봉사자들이 하는 업무가 아닌 것은 무엇인가?
(A) 축제 공연을 위한 표 팔기
(B) 전람회장으로 장비를 옮기기
(C) 방문객에게 주차 장소 알리기
(D) 홍보자료 배포하기
분석_ 자원봉사자가 해야 할 일들을 살펴보면 장비 옮기는 것은 없
으므로 (B)가 정답이다.

168. (A)
자원봉사자들은 무료로 무엇을 받게 되는가?
(A) 의류
(B) 공연장 뒤로 접근 가능한 통행권
(C) 모든 공연의 비디오 녹화
(D) 축제 기간 동안 간식과 식사
분석_ 세 번째 문단 In appreciation of ~로 시작되는 문장을 살
펴보면 자원봉사자들은 옷과 2장의 무료 표를 받을 수 있으
므로 (A)가 정답이다.

Questions 169-172 refer to the following web page.

http://www.mysterystory.org.uk
The Mystery Story in the World
기록 / MSW에 관해 / 표 / 홈
The Mystery Story in the World는 전 세계의 유명한 추리소설가
와 수천 명의 참가자를 런던으로 끌어모으는 가장 거대한 소설대회 중
하나입니다. 위에 있는 "기록" 탭을 누르시면 지난 대회의 독해 비디
오를 볼 수 있습니다. 또한 특색 있게 다뤄진 작가들의 짧은 약력 또
한 볼 수 있습니다.
올해, 이 대회는 런던의 Harrods Park에서 9월 12일-13일에 개
최될 것입니다. 표는 성인은 20파운드, 13세 그리고 그 이하의 어린
이들은 15파운드입니다. 사전 표 구입은 6월 18일부터 온라인상에
서 가능합니다. 사이트 주소는 http://www.mysterystory.org.uk/
tickets입니다. (위의 "표" 탭)

누구든 이 대회에 공식발표를 위한 자신의 작품을 제출할 수 있는 자격이 있습니다. 제출작품은 700에서 1000줄 사이를 포함한 작품 견본을 포함해야 합니다. 또한 견본은 한 페이지 요약본으로 구성되어야 합니다. [1]

출판된 책, 출판되지 않은 책 모두 제출 가능합니다. 작품을 읽는 지원자의 비디오는 선호하지만 반드시 요구되지는 않습니다. [2]

제출작품은 늦어도 5월 24일까지 제출되어야 합니다. 제출작품의 상태에 관해 질문하는 것을 삼가주십시오. [3] *모든 후보자들은 우편으로 수령 확인 편지를 받을 것입니다. 그리고 뽑힌 후보자들은 4월 25일까지 전화 연락이 갈 것입니다.*

제출물의 양이 상당하기 때문에, 선출과정 마지막에 우리는 참석이 허락된 지원자들에게만 통보를 할 것입니다. [4]

평가받을 당신의 작품을 다음의 주소로 보내주세요.

169. (D)

대회 웹페이지에서 할 수 있는 것으로 언급되지 않은 것은 무엇인가?

(A) 지난 작품 영상 보기

(B) 유명한 작가의 삶에 대하여 읽기

(C) 축제에 참석하기 위해 표를 구입하기

(D) 글쓰기 수업에 참석하기 위해 등록하기

분석_ 글쓰기 수업을 제외한 나머지 모든 보기들이 지문에 언급되었기 때문에 (D)가 정답이다.

170. (C)

지원자가 제출한 소설의 요구조건은 무엇인가?

(A) 소설은 전에 출간된 적이 없어야 한다.

(B) 소설은 비디오로 녹화되어야 한다.

(C) 소설은 특정 길이 이내로 쓰여져야 한다.

(D) 소설은 특정 언어로 쓰여져야 한다.

분석_ 세 번째 문단에 제출작품이 700~1000줄 사이로 작성되어야 한다고 언급되어 있으므로 (C)가 정답이다.

171. (B)

7번째 문단 1행에 있는 "consideration"과 의미가 가장 가까운 것은?

(A) 사려 깊음

(B) 평가

(C) 준수

(D) 안내

분석_ 가장 근접한 뜻을 찾는 문제이다. 작품에 대한 '고려, 평가'가 가장 적절하다.

172. (C)

[1], [2], [3], 그리고 [4]로 표시된 곳 중에서 다음 문장이 들어가기에 가장 적합한 곳은?

"모든 후보자들은 우편으로 수령 확인 편지를 받을 것입니다. 그리고 뽑힌 후보자들은 4월 25일까지 전화 연락이 갈 것입니다."

(A) [1]

(B) [2]

(C) [3]

(D) [4]

분석_ 제출작품을 받았는지 전화 문의를 하지 마세요. 우편으로 알려드릴 겁니다.라고 이어지는 것이 문맥상 가장 적절하다.

Questions 173-175 refer to the following article. 음성강의

12월 11일
Rachel Bessie

시카고 중심부의 혼잡을 억제하기 위한 시도의 일환으로, 시의회는 길거리 주차 규칙에 대한 변화사항을 발표했다. [1]

"우리 길거리는 저녁 시간대에 가장 혼잡합니다." 시카고 시의회 대변인인 Sophia Cara가 말했다. "거주민들과 비 거주민 모두 식당, 극장, 공연장을 가기 위해 오락지구로 옵니다. [2] *사람들은 상당한 요금을 부과하는 주차장을 피하는 경향이 있습니다. 그들은 무료 주차 공간을 찾기 위해 주변을 계속 주행하고 이것이 교통 혼잡을 증대시킵니다.*"

현재, 주차에 대한 요금은 오전 8시부터 오후 6시까지이고 6시 이후로는 주차요금을 부과하지 않는다. [3] "이러한 규정을 수정할 필요가 있습니다."라고 Cara가 말했다. "우리는 다른 도시의 사례를 따르고 싶습니다. 그 도시는 하루 24시간 내내 요금을 부과합니다."

만약 제안된 변화가 효력을 발휘한다면, 최근 들어서 2번째 변화가 될 것이다. 9월에 특별한 시카고 주차 카드뿐만 아니라 동전과 신용카드를 받는 새로운 주차요금 징수기가 설치되었다. [4] 새로운 시카고 주차 카드는 10월부터 이용이 가능하다. 그리고 시카고 시장 또는 쇼핑몰 어디서건 구매가 가능하다.

173. (C)

시카고에 관해서 제시된 것은?

(A) 시카고의 도로는 수리가 필요하다.

(B) 도로 건설에 관한 시민의 인지도를 높여야 한다.

(C) 시카고는 교통혼잡을 겪고 있다.

(D) 시카고 주민들은 시의 주차장에 그들의 차량을 무료로 주차 가능하다.

분석_ 두 번째 문단 하단을 보면 무료주차를 위해 주변을 계속 주행하고 이로 인해 교통혼잡이 늘고 있다는 표현이 언급되었으므로 (C)가 정답이다.

174. (D)

시의회는 무엇을 고려 중인가?

(A) 기존 주차장을 확대하기

(B) 새로운 주차 공간을 찾기

(C) 주차 시간당 요금 인상하기

(D) 저녁 주차 요금을 도입하기

분석_ 세 번째 문단 하단을 보면 24시간 내내 주차요금을 부과하는 다른 도시들을 선례로 삼아 그 도시를 따르고 싶다는 표현이 언급되었으므로 (D)가 정답이다. 시카고는 오전 8시부터 6시까지만 요금을 부과하므로 저녁 요금을 부과하지 않는다는 언급도 있었다.

175. (B)

[1], [2], [3], 그리고 [4]로 표시된 곳 중에서 다음 문장이 들어가기에 가장 적합한 곳은?

"사람들은 상당한 요금을 부과하는 주차장을 피하는 경향이 있습니다."

(A) [1]
(B) [2]
(C) [3]
(D) [4]

분석_ 두 번째 문단을 보면 하단에 많은 사람들이 유흥을 즐기기 위해 시내로 모여들고 요금을 지불하기 싫어서 무료 주차공간을 찾느라 헤매고 이로 인해 교통 혼잡이 이어진다는 결론으로 귀결된다. 지문에서는 [2]번 앞에 왜 사람들이 무료 주차를 찾는지 이유가 빠져 있으므로 [2]가 가장 적절하다.

Questions 176-180 refer to the following web page and e-mail.

http://www.luxurylifeinvermont.com/advertising
홈 / 연락방안 / 주문하기 / 고객 리뷰
Luxurylifeinvermont에 광고: Luxurylifeinvermont는 Vermont 지역에서 음식을 쇼핑하고 외식할 믿을 수 있고 유익한 정보를 찾는 수백 명의 구독자를 가진 수상경력이 있는 온라인 잡지입니다.
우리 웹 페이지에 아래 4가지 디자인으로 광고를 게재할 수 있습니다.

디자인 1	디자인 2
이 가로형 배너는 웹 페이지 상단부에 나타날 것이고 독자의 눈을 사로잡을 첫 번째 광고가 될 것입니다. 음성과 사진은 제외됩니다.	이 작은 형태 광고는 특집기사 중간 중심부에 등장할 것입니다. 사진 한 장과 음성이 원본과 함께 포함될 수 있습니다.
디자인 3	디자인 4
이 세로형 배너는 특집기사 측면을 따라 게재될 것입니다. 음성과 사진은 포함될 수 없습니다.	가장 큰 형태의 광고로, 페이지 절반 분량의 광고는 원본과 더불어 다수의 사진과 음성을 포함할 수 있습니다.

광고를 구매하고 싶으시면, Sandra Jill에게 연락하세요. (jill@luxurylifeinvestmont.com)

발신: Nathaniel Travis (travis@bighotdog.com)
수신: Sandra Jill (jill@luxurylifeinvermont.com)
주제: Big Hot Dog 광고
날짜: 11월 11일
Jill 씨
Luxury Life in Vermont에 추가광고를 게재할 수 있는지 궁금합니다. 다시 한번 큰 형태의 광고를 게재하고 싶습니다. 전에 제공해드린 같은 원본과 음성을 사용해주세요. 최근에 개조한 4장의 새로운 상점 사진을 보내겠습니다. 사진은 신중한 방식으로 사진을 어디에 배치할지 결정하는 책임을 지는 배치 담당자에게 보내겠습니다. 어떤 사이즈와 모양으로 사진을 제출해야 하는지 자세히 말해주세요.
Nathaniel Travis, Big Hot Dog 최고 요리사이자 상점 주인

176. (D)

Jill 씨는 어디서 근무하는가?
(A) 식품 제조 회사
(B) 마케팅 연구 단체
(C) 채식주의자 식당
(D) 음식 관련 출판회사

분석_ 첫 번째 web page를 보면 award-winning online magazine with hundreds of subscribers who look to us for dependable and beneficial information on shopping for food and eating out in the Vermont area.라는 표현이 있다. 음식 쇼핑과 외식에 관한 정보를 가진 온라인 잡지이며, 이 회사에 광고를 하기 위해 Sandra Jill과 연락을 해야 하므로 Sandra는 음식 관련 출판회사에 근무 중이다.

177. (B)

Design 1에 대해서 무엇이 언급되었는가?
(A) 가격이 적당하다.
(B) 매우 쉽게 눈에 띈다.
(C) 가장 많은 원본과 사진을 포함한다.
(D) 빠르게 준비가 가능하다.

분석_ 네모 상자로 된 디자인 설명을 보면 This horizontal banner will appear on the top of a page and is the first thing that attracts the reader's eye.라고 하여 가장 상단에 있으며 처음으로 고객의 눈을 끌어모은다는 표현이 있으므로 (B)가 가장 적절하다.

178. (D)

광고에서 Travis 씨가 가장 관심 있어 할 디자인은 무엇인가?
(A) 디자인 1
(B) 디자인 2
(C) 디자인 3
(D) 디자인 4

분석_ 두 번째 지문을 보면 Nathaniel Travis는 원본과 더불어 4장의 사진과 음성을 함께 게재하고자 한다. 따라서 첫 번째 지문의 디자인 4가지 유형을 살펴보면 여러 장의 사진과 음성을 모두 게재 할 수 있는 광고는 디자인 4이다.

179. (C)

Big Hot Dog에 대해 제시된 것은?
(A) 지역 예술가에 의해 외관을 고치는 중이다.
(B) 꾸준히 상을 받고 있다.
(C) Luxury Life in Vermont에 광고를 게재한 경험이 있다.
(D) 재건하는 동안 상점 문을 닫을 것이다.

분석_ 메일 속 내용을 보면 I am eager to place large-format advertisement once again. I want you to use the same text and audio as supplied before.에서 다시 한 번 광고를 게재하고 싶고 원문과 음성은 전에 게재한 것을 그대로 사용해달라고 언급했으므로 (C)가 정답이다.

180. (A)

Travis 씨는 사진에 대해 무엇을 문의하는가?
(A) 사진 크기가 어떻게 되는지
(B) 언제 사진을 보내야 하는지
(C) 몇 장의 사진을 사용하는지
(D) 사진을 출판하기 위해 추가 금액이 얼마인지

분석_ 두 번째 지문인 편지 하단을 보면 Could you tell me in detail what size and shape is requested to hand in the photographs?이라고 묻고 있다. 따라서 (A)가 정답이다.

Questions 181-185 refer to the following notice and e-mail.

중요한 공지

지난주 깡통 옥수수를 구입하셨나요? San Diego의 Aveda Energy 는 그들의 야채 통조림 중 몇몇이 잘못된 라벨이 붙여진 채 지난주 지역 의 쇼핑센터로 배송되었다고 발표했습니다. Aveda Energy의 스위트 콘과 연유 옥수수의 라벨이 컴퓨터의 오작동으로 인해 바뀌었습니다. 이 잘못된 통조림은 제품번호 C4885 또는 C4886으로 각인되었습니 다. 전액 환불을 요청하시려면, 상품을 구입한 쇼핑센터로 5월 10일 또는 그 이전에 제품을 반납하세요. 제조정책을 준수하기 위해, 원본 영수증이 반납물품과 함께 제출되어야 합니다.

이 문제에 관한 더 많은 정보는 www.avedaenergy.com에서 찾아 볼 수 있습니다.

발신: Charlie Dion ⟨cdion@goldsuperstore.com⟩

수신: Ally Lee ⟨alee@lemaison.com⟩

날짜: 2월 15일

주제: 환불 요청

Lee 씨

우리는 귀하의 상점으로부터 옥수수 통조림 선적을 받았습니다. 대략 3~4영업일 후, 귀하는 42.80달러 금액의 수표를 우편으로 받을 것입 니다. 이 금액은 귀하의 실제 고객이 잘못된 라벨의 통조림을 반품할 때 귀하께서 환불해주신 돈을 충당할 것입니다. 우리가 약속한 대로, 이 금액은 원본 영수증을 가지고 있지 않는 고객에게 환불해주신 5.20 달러까지 포함하고 있습니다.

우리는 이러한 일이 귀하와 귀하의 단골고객에게 끼친 불편에 관해 사 과드립니다. 우리는 Le Maison Shopping Store와 꾸준히 영업을 이어가기를 희망합니다.

Charlie Dion

고객관리부서

Aveda Energy, Inc.

181. (A)

이 공지는 누구를 위한 것인가?

(A) 포장 제품을 구매한 고객

(B) Aveda Energy Inc. 직원

(C) 알루미늄 캔 제조회사

(D) San Diego와 그 주변 지역 슈퍼마켓 매니저

분석_ 공지문의 첫 문단을 보면 Did you buy canned corn last week?이란 표현이 언급되었다. 지난주 통조림 물건을 구매 한 고객에게 보내는 안내장이므로 (A)가 정답이다.

182. (C)

통조림에 관해서 무엇이 나타나 있는가?

(A) 통조림은 운송 중 파손되었다.

(B) 통조림은 잘못된 가격이 각인되었다.

(C) 통조림은 제품 코드로 식별 가능하다.

(D) 통조림은 잘못된 쇼핑센터로 배송되었다.

분석_ 공지문의 첫 문단 하단을 보면 The mislabeled cans are stamped with product codes C4885 or C4886.라고 언 급되어 있다. 따라서 문제가 되고 있는 잘못된 라벨이 붙은 통조림은 제품번호로 식별이 가능하므로 (C)가 정답이다.

183. (D)

공지에 따르면, 이 문제에 관해 더 자세한 정보를 포함한 인터넷 사이트 는 어디인가?

(A) 신문의 웹사이트

(B) 슈퍼마켓의 웹사이트

(C) 쇼핑센터의 웹사이트

(D) 통조림 제품 제조회사의 웹사이트

분석_ 첫 지문 마지막 문단을 보면 More information in regard to this matter can be found at www.avedaenergy.com. 이라 언급되어 있다. 통조림 제품에 관한 더 자세한 내용은 통조림을 만든 제조회사인 Aveda Energy, Inc. 홈페이지 에서 확인 가능하다.

184. (D)

이메일의 1번째 문단 4행에 있는 "cover"와 의미가 가장 가까운 것은?

(A) 떼다

(B) 다재다능한

(C) 숨기다

(D) 제공하다

분석_ cover는 '덮다'라는 뜻 말고도 '충당하다'라는 뜻도 가지고 있다. 여기서는 '고객에게 환불해준 돈을 충당한다'라는 의 미이다.

185. (C)

Lee 씨에 대해 암시된 것은 무엇인가?

(A) 그녀는 추가 통조림 제품을 받을 것이다.

(B) 그녀는 처음 약속했던 수표를 보낼 것이다.

(C) 그녀는 회사 정책에 예외를 두었다.

(D) 그녀는 Dion 씨를 만날 것이다.

분석_ 첫 지문인 공지를 보면 In observance of manufacturer policy, the original receipt must be submitted along with the returned merchandise.에서 제조회사 정책에 따라 영수증을 제품과 함께 제출해야 한다고 언급되었 다. 두 번째 지문인 메일을 보면 this includes the $ 5.20 that you refunded a customer who did not have the original receipt.에서 영수증이 없는 고객에게 환불해준 돈 5.20달러도 포함했다는 언급이 있다. 따라서 Le Maison Shopping Store 사장인 Lee 씨는 정책에 예외를 두었다.

Questions 186-190 refer to the following form, evaluation result and memo.

Singapore International Laboratory Inspection

회사 이름: General Laboratory

위치: 19 South Parkway

검사일: 12월 10일

S=만족

걱정거리가 발견되지 않았음

추가 검사가 필요 없음

U=불만족

위반사항이 확인되었음

후속 검사가 한 달 이내 개선사항을 확인해야 함

R=위반
이전 조사에서 언급된 것들이 다시 확인됨
금전상의 벌금은 위반의 정도에 따라 달라질 것임
후속 검사가 한 달 이내 개선사항을 확인해야 함
만약 후속 검사가 필요하다면, 이 양식과 후속 방문 양식 모두를 제출
해야 합니다. 두 양식 모두를 제출하는 데 실패하면 추가 벌금이 발생
될 것입니다.
출력 이름: Vanessa De Van Haney
서명 이름: Vanessa De Van Haney
실험 평가 관리 검시관

16번 평가서와 점수
1. 출구표식이 문 위에 배치되었다. (S)
2. 실험실 직원은 항상 신분카드를 소지하고 있다. (R)
3. 문 잠금 장치가 완벽히 작동을 한다. (S)
4. 근무장소에 과도한 물건이 없다. (U)
5. 창문은 쉽게 개방이 가능하다. (U)
6. 응급 알림은 완벽히 작동을 한다. (S)
7. 바닥은 깨끗하고 건조되어 있다. (U)
언급: 벌금 250달러 / 후속 검사는 1월 10일로 일정 잡힘
평가자: Vanessa De van Haney
실험 평가 관리 검시관

수신: 모든 직원에게
발신: S. Florence 시험실 관리자
주제: 새로운 회사 정책
날짜: 12월 12일
경영진은 지금 현재 우리 최근 검사에서 관리 감독자에 의해 명시된 이
러한 문제를 해결하기 위해 엄청난 조치를 취하고자 합니다.
우선, 모든 직원들은 항상 착용해야 하는, 사진이 부착된 신분배지를
제공받을 겁니다. 내일 직원들이 그들의 사진을 찍을 시간을 등록하기
위한 목록이 공지될 것입니다. 사진사는 12월 17일부터 12월 19일까
지 현장에 있을 것입니다. 만약 직원들이 이 날짜에 시간이 되지 않는
다면, 제게 연락하세요. 우리는 또한 방문객을 위해 만든 수많은 배지
를 가지고 있습니다. 우리는 안내데스크에 있을 것입니다.
다음, 앞으로 5일간 코트와 핸드백, 서류가방 같은 개인 소지품을 보
관하기 위한 추가적인 벽장과 가구가 추가될 것입니다. 이러한 물건
들은 근무장소가 깔끔하고 단정하게 유지될 수 있게 적절히 보관되어
야 합니다.
경영진은 근무환경이 깨끗하고 바닥이 깔끔하게 주기적인 검사를 행
해야 할 것입니다. 액체가 흐른 자국은 경영진에게 바로 보고해주세요.
이러한 새로운 정책은 1월 3일 공식적으로 발효될 것입니다.

186. (A)
16번 평가서는 어떤 종류의 검사를 위한 것으로 예상되는가?
(A) 일반적 안전
(B) 실험실 장비 점검
(C) 전기 수리
(D) 화학제품 저장

분석_ 두 번째 지문을 보면 '비상구 사인, 문과 창문의 개폐, 바닥
의 건조' 여부는 일하는 근무 공간의 전반적인 안전에 관한
내용이므로 (A)가 적절하다.

187. (C)
왜 General Laboratory에 벌금이 부과되었는가?
(A) 필요한 훈련이 이행되지 않았기 때문에
(B) 검사가 원래 일정보다 늦게 행해졌기 때문에
(C) 이전 위반이 정정되지 않았기 때문에
(D) 필요한 서류가 제출되지 않았기 때문에

분석_ 첫 지문을 보면 Those noted at a previous inspection
were identified again. Monetary fine will vary based
on the severity of the violation.이란 언급이 있다. 두 번
째 지문을 보면 벌금 250달러가 부과되었으므로 이전 위
반이 정정되지 않았기에 벌금이 부과되었다고 유추할 수
있다.

188. (D)
Florence 씨는 직원에게 무엇을 요구했는가?
(A) 실험실에서 보호용 의료 장비를 입을 것
(B) 지정된 장소에 음식을 보관할 것
(C) 직원 모임에 참석할 것
(D) 사진을 찍을 것

분석_ 세 번째 지문 Tomorrow, a list will be posted for workers
to sign up for a time to have their photographs taken.에
직원들의 사진을 촬영하겠다는 언급이 있으므로 (D)가 적
절하다.

189. (A)
신청명단을 언제 공지할 것인가?
(A) 12월 13일
(B) 12월 17일
(C) 1월 3일
(D) 1월 10일

분석_ 세 번째 지문에 편지를 발송한 날짜가 12월 12일이라 언급
되었다. 또한 편지 중간을 보면 Tomorrow, a list will be
posted for workers to sign up for a time to have their
photographs taken.에서 내일 사진 촬영이 진행된다고 언
급되었으므로 12월 13일이 정답이다.

190. (C)
메모에서 다루지 않은 위반은 무엇인가?
(A) 2번 항목
(B) 4번 항목
(C) 5번 항목
(D) 7번 항목

분석_ 세 번째 지문에 all employees will be offered photo
identification badges that must be worn at all times.이
있으므로 2번 항목은 언급되었다. 또한 These items
should be properly stowed in order that work spaces
are neat and tidy.이 언급되었으므로 4번 항목도 위반으
로 언급되었다. 지문 마지막에 make sure that work areas

are clear and floors are clean.도 있으므로 7번 항목도 언급되었다.

Questions 191-195 refer to the following form and two e-mails.

Trustworthy 소포 배달 서비스
고객 질문과 걱정
귀하의 문제를 가장 잘 설명하는 문장에 표시하세요.
(V) 편지를 받지 못함
( ) 취급 중 내용물이 파손됨
( ) 우편을 받고 난 후
( ) 내용물이 빠진 채 소포 도착
(V) 비이성적인 지연
발송인 정보: Adrian Randolph
연락 정보: 314 Hong Kong District
소속: Fresh Milk 207 Hainan Avenue
우편 유형: 작은 소포
메일발송일: 5월 18일
문제 설명
창고에서 소포가 발송된 이후 거의 14일이 되었습니다. 내용물에는 저장 수명이 대략 30일인 상하기 쉬운 음식물이 포함되어 있습니다. 빠른 관심과 이 문의에 관한 대답을 주신다면 감사하겠습니다.
이름: Adrian Randolph
서명: Adrian Randolph

발신: scordelia@tpds.com
수신: arandolph@freshmilk.com
날짜: 5월 28일
주제: 메일 참조 #FM518-1
Randolph 씨께,
우리는 귀하의 소포에 관해 문의를 받았습니다. 2주간의 지체는 용인될 수 없으며 우리 사무실은 소포를 찾기 위해 최선을 다할 것입니다. 그 사이에, 이 소포가 목적지에 도달할 수 있으니, 귀하는 수취 대상에게 계속 확인 부탁드립니다.
사과의 의미로, 우리는 이 편지에 귀하에게 드릴 쿠폰을 첨부했습니다. 귀하는 이 쿠폰으로 추가 비용 없이 6개월 더 VIP 배달 서비스에 가입할 수 있습니다.
이 문제에 관해 앞으로 서신을 주고받을 때, 이 메시지 제목에 기재된 사건번호를 언급하세요.
Stella Cordelia
Trustworthy 소포 배송 서비스

발신: arandolph@freshmilk.com
수신: scordelia@tpds.com
날짜: 5월 31일
주제: #FM518-1
Cordelia 씨
제 문의에 빠르게 응답해주셔서 감사합니다. 우리는 5월 30일 소포를 받았습니다. 소포 안 음식은 신선했고 원래 상태 그대로 유지되었습니다.

귀사에서 저에게 준 쿠폰에 관해 질문이 있습니다. 지금 귀사의 서비스 프로그램에 등록을 해야 합니까 아니면 내년에 서비스에 등록할 수도 있습니까?
이 질문에 관해 빠른 답변 주시면 감사하겠습니다.
감사합니다.
Adrian Randolph

191. (B)
Randolph 씨에 따르면, 소포는 어떻게 되었는가?
(A) 잘못된 내용물을 포함된 소포가 발송되었다.
(B) 목적지에 소포가 도착하지 않았다.
(C) 잘못된 주소로 보내졌다.
(D) 물품이 파손된 상태로 소포가 도착했다.
분석_ 첫 번째 지문을 보면 It has been nearly 14 days since the parcel were sent from the warehouse라고 언급되어 있다. 창고에서 발송된 이후 14일이 되었으나 소포가 도착하지 않았으므로 (B)가 정답이다.

192. (C)
Randolph 씨는 무엇을 받았는가?
(A) 공급품을 추가 비용 없이 선적
(B) 소포 가치만큼의 보상
(C) 프리미엄 서비스 계획
(D) 무료 이메일 계정
분석_ 두 번째 지문인 회사가 고객을 상대로 보낸 사과 편지를 보면 By way of apology, we would like to give you a coupon which is attached this letter. You can enroll in our VIP Delivery Service for another 6 months at no additional charge with this voucher.에서 사과의 뜻으로 VIP Delivery Service를 6개월 더 제공한다고 나와 있으므로 (C)가 정답이다.

193. (A)
첫 번째 이메일의 3번째 문단 1행에 있는 "matter"와 의미가 가장 가까운 것은?
(A) 상황
(B) 이유
(C) 해결책
(D) 잡일
분석_ 문맥상 저자가 처한 상황, 다시 말해 소포가 목적지에 도착하지 못한 상황을 언급하므로 (A)가 가장 적절하다.

194. (A)
Randolph 씨는 다음에 연락을 할 때 무엇을 해야 하는가?
(A) 구체적인 식별 변호를 포함하기
(B) Cordelia 씨의 비서와 연락하기
(C) 서비스 부서로 바로 전화하기
(D) 연락 정보를 최신화하기
분석_ 두 번째 지문인 편지 가장 하단부를 보면 In future correspondence concerning this matter, please refer to the case number listed in the subject line of this message.에서 앞으로 이 문제에 관해 말하고 싶을 때는

case number를 말하라고 언급되어 있으므로 (A)가 가장 적절하다.

195. (D)

두 번째 이메일에서 나타난 것은 무엇인가?
(A) 주된 목적은 늦은 배송에 관해 불평하는 것이다.
(B) Randolph는 5월 31일 소포를 받았다.
(C) Cordelia는 사과의 의미로 무료 쿠폰을 제공했다.
(D) 이 메일의 목적은 쿠폰의 사용에 관해 문의하는 것이다.

분석_ 세 번째 지문인 마지막 편지 두 번째 문단을 보면 I have another question concerning the coupon you gave me. Should we register for your service program right now or can we enroll in that service next year?이라고 질문하고 있다. 따라서 선물로 받은 쿠폰의 사용 여부를 묻고 있으므로 (D)가 가장 적절하다.

Questions 196-200 refer to the following e-mails and table.

발신: Catherine Dorothy 〈cdorothy@waterindeepwell.com〉
수신: Stanley Cube 〈scube@marinecomputer.com〉
날짜: 4월 20일
주제: 물 배송
Cube 씨

귀하가 우리 회사에 보여준 관심에 감사드립니다.
우리 Water in Deep Well은 Quebec 지역에 가장 맛 좋은 물을 제공합니다. 우리는 귀하의 필요를 가장 잘 채울 수 있는 정수기를 선택함에 있어 함께할 수 있어 기쁩니다.
귀하가 옵션과 가격을 비교할 수 있게 아래에 표를 첨부했습니다. 12리터 물병은 보통 가정용입니다. 사무용으로는 우리가 20리터 사이즈의 물병을 추천합니다. 만약 귀하가 귀하의 회사에 몇 명의 직원이 있는지 그리고 직원 중 몇 퍼센트가 정수시스템을 사용할지 알려주신다면, 저희는 귀하께 일주일에 몇 병의 물병이 필요한지 견적을 드릴 겁니다.
리필비용과 더불어, 처음 주문을 하실 때 환불이 가능한 보증금 45,000동이 요구됩니다. 배달 운전자가 2주마다 귀하의 빈 물병을 수거하고 물이 가득 찬 물병을 차에서 내릴 것입니다.
배달비는 우리 회사 운전자가 얼마나 쉽게 수거 장소에 도달할 수 있는지와 주문된 물병의 수에 비례할 것입니다. 수거 장소는 간단한 현장 방문으로 결정이 될 겁니다.
우리 회사 서비스에 관한 자세한 토론을 위해 귀하의 회사에 우리 회사 영업 직원을 기꺼이 급파할 수 있습니다. 시간을 정하시려면 (315) 425-0975번으로 저에게 연락 주세요.
Catherine Dorothy
Water in Deep Well

Water in Deep Well

시스템	정수기 기능	병 사이즈	리필 비용	매월 자판기 비용
화이트	온수, 냉수, 얼음 정수기	12L	45,000동	60,000동
골드	냉수 정수기	12L	45,000동	40,000동
실버	얼음과 냉수 정수기	20L	65,000동	65,000동
핑크	온수, 냉수 정수기	20L	65,000동	50,000동

발신: Stanley Cube 〈scube@marinecomputer.com〉
수신: Catherine Dorothy 〈cdorothy@waterindeepwell.com〉
날짜: 4월 21일
주제: re: 물 배송
우리 소프트웨어 회사는 최근 캐나다 Vancouver 7120으로 이전했습니다. 그리고 우리는 정기적인 식수 배달에 관심이 있습니다. 우리는 또한 냉온수 기능이 내장된 리필 가능한 정수기를 임대할 계획도 있습니다. 우리는 몇몇 다른 회사와 연락을 취했습니다. 그러나 Water in Deep Well에 대한 긍정적인 후기를 읽은 후, 귀사에 먼저 이 메일을 보내기로 결심했습니다. 그리고 우리는 이 결정이 옳았다고 생각합니다.
우리 회사에는 대략 200명의 직원이 있고 직원 모두가 정수기를 이용할 것입니다. 우리는 냉온수가 모두 나오는 정수기를 원합니다. 우리는 또한 주거용이 아닌 사무용 물병크기를 사용하길 원합니다.
우리는 귀사의 서비스를 더 논의하기 위해 월요일부터 금요일, 9시부터 1시까지 시간이 가능합니다.
Stanley Cube
Marine Computer

196. (D)

첫 이메일을 쓴 목적은 무엇인가?
(A) 청구서 오류에 관해 문의하기 위해
(B) 주소 변경을 통보하기 위해
(C) 회사에 관해 문의하기 위해
(D) 정수기 서비스를 소개하기 위해

분석_ 첫 번째 지문은 편지 초반부에 We are happy to work with you to select which dispenser system best meets your needs.라고 언급되어 있다. 따라서 정수기 서비스를 소개하는 (D)가 가장 적절하다.

197. (D)

Cube 씨의 필요에 가장 충족되는 시스템은 아마도 무엇일 것인가?
(A) 화이트
(B) 골드
(C) 실버
(D) 핑크

분석_ 세 번째 지문의 편지 후반부 We need to use a bottle size for business use but not for residential one.을 보면 Marine Computer 회사는 사무용 냉온수 정수기를 원하고 있다. 두 번째 지문의 표를 보면 냉온수 모두 나오고 용량이 큰 물병을 제공하는 서비스는 (D)이다.

198. (A)

지불에 관해서 무엇이 언급되었는가?

(A) 초기 주문은 추가 비용이 포함되어 있다.

(B) 고객들은 격주로 청구서를 받을 것이다.

(C) 대량주문에 할인이 제공된다.

(D) 첫 달은 배송이 무료이다.

분석_ 첫 번째 지문의 두 번째 문단을 보면 In addition to the refill costs, a one-time refundable deposit of 45,000 VND is requested when you place your initial order.라고 언급되어 있다. 따라서 첫 주문에 보증금이 포함되므로 (A)가 가장 적절하다.

199. (A)

배송비를 추정할 때 고려되는 정보는 무엇인가?

(A) 배달 거리

(B) 사용자 수

(C) 고객의 장소

(D) 선호하는 정수기

분석_ 첫 지문인 편지를 보면 Delivery fees commensurate with the number of bottles ordered as well as with how easy it is for our delivery driver to access the drop-off and pickup area.에서 배달비가 주문되는 물병의 수와 배송장소의 접근 용이성으로 결정된다는 것을 알 수 있으므로 (A)가 가장 적절하다.

200. (B)

두 번째 이메일에 따르면, 왜 Cube 씨는 Dorothy 씨에게 연락해야 하는가?

(A) 배송 날짜를 확정하기 위해

(B) 요구에 응하기 위해

(C) 현금 보증금을 납부하기 위해

(D) 주문을 취소하기 위해

분석_ 첫 지문인 편지에서 I would be glad to dispatch a sales representative to your venue to discuss our service in detail.을 보면 더 자세한 논의를 위해 직원을 보내고 싶다고 언급했다. 그리고 세 번째 지문인 편지에서 We are available from 9 to 1, Monday through Friday to discuss your service.라고 응답했으므로 (B) 정수기 회사가 고객의 회사로 방문하고 싶은 요구에 응하는 것이 가장 적절하다.

LC Script

Actual Test 01

Part 1

1. (A) The man is repairing the car door.
(B) The man is looking under the hood of the car.
(C) The man is parking the vehicle on the road.
(D) The man is taking the engine out of the car.

2. (A) She's turning on the light.
(B) She's holding up a book.
(C) She's speaking to the audience.
(D) She's rearranging the bookshelf.

3. (A) The couple is standing next to each other.
(B) The road is closed to traffic.
(C) A tree has fallen onto the road.
(D) Some cars are parked along the road.

4. (A) The waves are hitting the shore.
(B) A boat has been pulled onto the beach.
(C) The boats are floating on the water.
(D) The ducks are flying over the sea.

5. (A) Dishes have been set on the table.
(B) The people have finished their meals.
(C) They are waiting for their food to arrive.
(D) All of the seats are unoccupied.

6. (A) The people are strolling on the sidewalk.
(B) The people are crossing the street.
(C) Commuters are waiting for the bus.
(D) They are waiting for the traffic light to change.

Part 2

7. Where's the supply room?
(A) On the lower level.
(B) No, it wasn't supplied yet.
(C) Some mushrooms, please.

8. When will today's computer training end?
(A) At the Washington Station.
(B) Mr. Bonds trained us.
(C) Around 12 P.M.

9. What kind of hotel did Mike choose for the annual banquet?
(A) Yes, it was near the bank.
(B) I made a choice.
(C) The same one we used last year.

10. Who's in charge of the next year's advertising budget?
(A) In the newspaper advertisement.
(B) The final changes.
(C) I heard Julia is.

11. Is the workshop for new employees in this room or in the room C?
(A) Beginning on Tuesday.
(B) Ask Marcel.
(C) For the new employees.

12. Have you talked with the project organizer yet?
(A) We're meeting tomorrow.
(B) 40 organizations.
(C) That's a nice project.

13. Aren't you going to see that horror movie with Jennifer this weekend?
(A) I've moved a few of them.
(B) A recently renovated theater.
(C) Actually, we just saw it.

14. This new refrigerator is going to be on sale until the end of the month, won't it?
(A) It holds more than seven liters.
(B) It's a specialty store.
(C) Yes, until 30th.

15. Where can I leave these additional charts?
(A) Right there on the desk is fine.
(B) You must do it by Monday.
(C) Ms. Green lives there.

16. Can you please turn off the copier when you're done with the job?
(A) Yes, I can get you some coffee.
(B) It's already off.
(C) Please turn down the volume.

17. Would you rather work here or in the accounting department?
(A) I prefer to stay here.
(B) I will count them down.
(C) Yes, for ten years.

18. Which of the candidates did the committee select?
(A) I think we'll find out today.
(B) The selection committee.
(C) I'm going out with him.

19. The ferry to Fukuoka departs every thirty minutes, doesn't it?
(A) 30 dollars round trip.
(B) Please turn left at the dock.
(C) No, it's every 40 minutes.

20. Who should I talk to about changing my e-mail address?
(A) At the mall on Bell Street.
(B) That's my password.
(C) Contact the Human Resources.

21. Shouldn't we order some more sandwiches for the presentation?
(A) No, they're not.
(B) Yes, we need more.
(C) Present them to me.

22. The facility will be closed for the month of May.
(A) Close it carefully.
(B) The latest shipment.
(C) Can you tell me why?

23. Why was the routine inspection for the quality control delayed?
(A) I'll take the route.
(B) The inspector was out of town.
(C) The controller's office is upstairs.

24. How will Lois get to Seoul?
(A) She's flying there from New Mexico.
(B) Sure, I'll return the key.
(C) It'll only last for a few weeks.

25. We have to finish painting the second floor by the end of the week.
(A) The door on the right.
(B) On Armenian Street.
(C) Why don't we find more workers?

26. Was Jenny at the orientation on Friday?
(A) It was extremely informative.
(B) I'll check the attendance list.
(C) Open Tuesday to Sunday.

27. Is it cheaper to buy a sedan, or to lease one?
(A) Around 5000 euros.
(B) A one-year warranty.
(C) I think lease is more competitive.

28. Why wasn't Ms. Geller's package delivered on Thursday?
(A) From that electronics store in Eastern district.
(B) She wasn't home to sign for it.
(C) Sometime this afternoon.

29. Can't I just pick that up at the event supply store?
(A) I don't think he's been there before.
(B) Yes, it must be in stock now.
(C) We all had a great time.

30. How many volunteers are working on the Asian Travel Project?
(A) Let me call the manager right away.
(B) There's a heavy workload.
(C) A variety of products.

31. I'd like your comments on our new production line.
(A) Go through the front door.
(B) I can review it later today.
(C) Let's order some products.

Part 3

Questions 32-34 refer to the following conversation.

W: I am wondering if you have any apple sandwiches available. I can't see any in the display case.

M: I'm sorry, but all the apple sandwiches we had today were sold out. We still have a nice selection of other sandwiches, though.

W: Hmm... It's for a mother's birthday party tomorrow and she really likes apple.

M: If you don't need the sandwiches until tomorrow, I can place an order for it right now. Why don't you specify exactly what you want and we can have it ready for you first thing tomorrow in the morning.

Questions 35-37 refer to the following conversation.

M: Excuse me, I'm here to repair the computer in your lab. It should only take me about 30 minutes.

W: Right now? But I didn't get any notice informing me that you would be coming. I don't think this is a good time. I'm very busy now. Why don't you come back later today?

M: Actually, I have several other work orders today, so I am not sure I'll have the time. I'll send another technician to help you today at 4 o'clock.

Questions 38-40 refer to the following conversation.

M: Hi, I'm staying here at the hotel on business, but I've decided to extend my trip to do some shopping. Is it possible for me to keep my room another day?

W: Of course. We're not fully booked this week. I can extend the reservation for you. And if you'd like, I can book a city shopping tour for you.

M: Oh, thanks, but that won't be necessary. Actually, a brother of mine lives in the area, so I'm going for shopping together with him tomorrow.

Questions 41-43 refer to the following conversation.

M: I'm here to locate an article that was published in the local newspaper about four or five years ago. Is there a copy in the library? I don't know how far back you keep newspapers.

W: We only keep issues of the local paper for the last 3 months. But articles from the last 5 years are kept on our website. So, I can help you find an electronic copy of the article.

M: Great! How much will it cost to print?

W: It's 5 cents a page. But unfortunately, our printer is out of order right now. A technician will come in any minute, and it should be fixed by noon, so you can come back anytime this afternoon.

Questions 44-46 refer to the following conversation.

M: Hello, I'm calling because I'd like to register for the economics workshop. I have a group of 20 people who would like to participate in the event.

W: Unfortunately, we don't process group registrations over the phone. You should complete a form online.

M: You know, I just tried filling out that form several times, but whenever I pressed the submit button, I got an error message. Is there any other way to register?

W: Oh, I'm so sorry to hear that. Could you please give me your name, e-mail address and phone number? I'll have our technical support team contact you right away.

Questions 47-49 refer to the following conversation.

W: Hi, Jacob. It's Melissa. I just arrived at the sales department office in corporation headquarters to meet with their sales team. But I can't find my files in client folder. I think I left it on my desk. Can you check and see if it is there? It's red.

M: OK, Melissa. Let me have a look. Yes, it's here on your desk. Do you want me to scan any of the files for you?

W: No, that won't be necessary. I just need some data. If you look on the last page, you'll see the figures for item sales for this year. Can you read those numbers to me?

Questions 50-52 refer to the following conversation.

W: Hello, and welcome to the monthly resume-building workshop. Today, you'll have the opportunity to learn what makes your resume more competitive than others. Are there any Questions before we begin?

M: Yes, are we also going to discuss job interviews? That part of the application process has always been the most challenging to me.

W: I'm sorry, but today's workshop doesn't have that part. But we'll be offering a separate workshop for those who want to know about interviews next week. You might want to attend that session as well.

Questions 53-55 refer to the following conversation with three speakers.

M1: That laser show was just the best way to end this party.

W: Yes, I think so!

M2: It is amazing that the company's been in business for 30 years. I've worked here since it opened its first store. And I've grown with this firm since then.

W: I'm happy to hear that, Tony. Haven't you been here for a long time too, Kross?

M1: Certainly. It's a fulfilling job, and the company is generous to employees.

W: According to my supervisor, the company is offering heavy discounts on furniture in celebration of its anniversary.

M2: I heard that, too. The catalog released last week included the list of furniture.

Questions 56-58 refer to the following conversation.

W: Hi, Paul. You're an organizer for the museum's charity event this year, right? I have a suggestion for the event. A friend of mine is a member of the community musical band, and I think they'd be great for this event.

M: Oh, Monica, that's a great idea! Unfortunately, our budget is not enough to pay them for an event.

W: No problem. My friend told me they'd be happy to volunteer their services. The exposure would be good for them. And it might bring future jobs to them.

M: OK, I'll ask my supervisor about it first, and let you know.

Questions 59-61 refer to the following conversation.

M: Hello, it's James Turker. I'd like to ask about the delivery of some materials for construction. I've been waiting for it since Thursday.

W: Hello, Mr. Turker. I'll check it. Oh... This is embarrassing. Our records indicate your order hasn't been processed yet. It seems like our warehouse didn't receive it.

M: Seriously? I didn't get any notice about it.

W: I apologize, Mr. Turker. There must have been some mistakes among our staff members.

M: I need the supplies the day after tomorrow. My client is waiting for them. (61) Can you deliver them tomorrow?

W: Definitely, Mr. Turker. I promise. I will have your order delivered right now and contact you again.

M: Okay. I'll look forward to your call.

Questions 62-64 refer to the following conversation with three speakers.

W: I'm pleased to tell you that both of you accepted my offer to lead our new sales teams.

M1: It's our pleasure, Ms. Geller.

M2: Thank you for the opportunity to work here. It means a lot.

M1: So, when do we start hiring new employees?

W: Personnel Department told me that some applicants are scheduled for interviews next week.

M1: Great! We need additional salespeople for the launch of our latest cars in March.

M2: That's two months from now. I hope we'll finish hiring by the end of the month, so we can train new people.

W: Of course. Also, the two of you will interview applicants with me. Personnel Department will send you the resume they received.

Questions 65-67 refer to the following conversation and schedule.

W: Excuse me, Mr. Evans. I have to tell you something about your schedule tomorrow.

M: Do we need to change it?

W: I think so. Mr. Hill of Simmons Furniture called this morning. He would like to discuss our office desks.

His company needs them for its next furniture convention.

M: Simmons Furniture is our main account, so we can't say no. Do I have an appointment I can reschedule?

W: There are two meetings you can cancel now.

M: Hmm. I must meet the budget committee. I'll just skip the second one. Please call Mr. Hill and say that I'll meet him then.

Questions 68-70 refer to the following conversation and schedule.

M: It's been a long day! Are there any other client meetings we should attend this week?

W: The last one is on Thursday at 1:00 P.M. It's a brief meeting, so it'll probably be over by 2 P.M. Afterwards, we will visit one of our branches in London.

M: Oh, you're right. What railway are we using?

W: Newtown Railways. It takes about two hours to get there by train.

M: The branch manager told me that someone will pick us up at London Train Station at 7:00 P.M. We should arrive before then.

W: I see. I'll reserve two ticket right away.

Part 4

Questions 71-73 refer to the following introduction.
You're watching our local history on Fellows television. Today we're fortunate to have a special guest, John Smith who recently wrote a book 'A Great Starting.' John's book talks about a detailed and interesting description of when our community was established. In honor of John's appearance on today's show, we will arrange for a special game where callers will be encouraged to answer Questions about the community's past. Give the right answers, and you'll win a free coupon for two at Roll's Restaurant. And now, please welcome John Smith.

Questions 74-76 refer to the following broadcast.
Now, Radio KTDT is pleased to announce that a special event is going to be held in town this weekend. As most of you already know, the local youth gym has recently been renovated. And it is expected to open this Thursday. At the event, staff will be ready to show the new yoga facility, basketball courts and fitness rooms to every community member. Parents will also have the opportunity to sign their children up for fitness classes at the center. And those who pay for class registration at the event will get a free gym suit.

Questions 77-79 refer to the following announcement.
Attention all Merriam Tang Shoes factory workers. This is your senior manager, Johnny Peterson. Because mechanical problem with a leather-cutting machine occurs again, production will be shut down tomorrow so that maintenance work can be done. Tomorrow is pay day, but your paychecks are available today. Please pick them up at the payroll department before leaving this evening.

Questions 80-82 refer to the following excerpt from a meeting.
I'd like to start today's meeting by welcoming our hospital's new chief financial officer Tony Chang. Mr. Chang has more than 20-year experience as a chief financial officer. With abilities to speak both English and German, his first official duty here at Coastal Hospital will be to help negotiate a business contract with one of our Germany-based medical suppliers. Tomorrow, there will be a welcoming reception for Mr. Chang beginning at 1 P.M. in conference room on the fourth floor. I hope you will all join us for that.

Questions 83-85 refer to the following telephone message.
I'm calling to ask about your advertisement for an apartment with a short-term lease in Seoul city center. I'm moving to Seoul because I was offered a teaching job at a local school. And I'd be interested in renting your apartment starting March 25. The ad mentioned that the lease is only for nine months. I'm really glad about that. Because I'd like to get familiar with the area for a few months before committing to a longer lease, I think the apartment is perfectly suitable for me. But I'm wondering if your building is pet-friendly or if pets are not allowed.

Questions 86-88 refer to the following announcement.
Good afternoon, Myungseong Gym members. I'm sorry to announce that we need to temporarily close the health club because a water pipe in the locker room is now broken. So, please gather your belongings and exit the building. Plumbers are coming in to fix the pipe soon, but it may take three or four days for the repairs to be completed. Please visit our website at msgym. com for updated information on the status of the repair job and when we will open again. We are sorry for this inconvenience. Thank you for your cooperation.

Questions 89-91 refer to the following news.
In business news, World Smith, Inc., has grown over the last three years. And now it has been trying to expand its capacity abroad. To do so, it attempted to merge with newspaper provider Neo International. This would have helped sales, especially in Europe. However, Jimmy Carter, a spokesperson for World Smith, Inc., announced the status of the firm's business arrangement with Neo International, and it won't happen. Instead of pursuing the merger, Neo International accepted an investment from another company. World Smith, Inc., is starting over, looking for solutions to be competitive.

Questions 92-94 refer to the following event advertisement and list.
Spring is around the corner. Are you looking for something exciting? You can join the community celebration on Sunday, March 25, at Dalseong Park. This special event will begin at 1 P.M. and will feature dance performances, craft workshops, and live music. Besides, celebration attendees can register for the prize drawing to be held at 6 P.M. This will include prizes sponsored by some local companies: Hunde Motors, Toyoda Electronics, and Hummel Fashions. There will be one grand prize, three gold prizes, ten silver prizes, and twenty bronze prizes. So, there are lots of chances to be a winner!

Questions 95-97 refer to the following telephone message and list.
Hello, Ms. Yang. Thanks for your interest in Pears Electronics. Our records indicate that one of our representatives visited your store on March 25. I heard she demonstrated our desktop products. I just wanted to see if you decided to stock our products. You may also want to know that since that visit, we have expanded our product line to include mobile phones, tablet computers, and laptops. These are perfectly compatible with our popular desktop products. I'm going to ask one of our representatives to tell you more about the new tablet line. If you have any Questions, please contact me at 231-4723.

Questions 98-100 refer to the following broadcast and schedule.
I hope you all enjoyed that cooking demonstration by Grace Kent, the head chef for Willa Hotel. The next guest at the show will be Selina Blond. I'm sure many of you are familiar with Ms. Blond's dishes, as she is the leading chef and the host on a popular TV cooking show. Today she'll be sharing her method for easily making healthy food in today's busy life. Using these tips, you can keep your body healthy. And after Ms. Blond finishes her demonstration, we will have our scheduled break. Let's give her big applause.

Actual Test 02

1. (A) She is wearing a hat.
(B) She is trying on clothes.
(C) She is examining an article of clothing.
(D) She is standing in front of a store.

2. (A) She is plugging in the cord.
(B) She is facing some equipment.
(C) She is looking at a clock.
(D) The test tubes are being labeled.

3. (A) The audience is standing up to applaud.
(B) Some musicians are leaving the stage.
(C) All of the seats at the concert hall are being cleaned.
(D) Some people are attending a concert.

4. (A) The women are standing by a wall.
(B) One woman is stacking shelves with items.
(C) One woman is paying for her purchase.
(D) The women are filling up a bag.

5. (A) There are blankets lying on the table.
(B) The mirror is next to a television.
(C) The beds are on opposite sides of the room.
(D) A picture has been placed over the beds.

6. (A) A ladder is lying on the floor.
(B) The windows are being opened.
(C) Stools have been placed beside the table.
(D) Tables have been arranged under the lights.

Part 2

7. How much is the whole package including an air fare?
(A) Three miles from here.
(B) Yes, it includes all of them.
(C) It comes to 95 dollars.

8. Where could I find some really interesting souvenirs?
(A) Oh, did you buy any interesting ones?
(B) Are you sure you checked out your room?
(C) Have you tried the craft stalls in the market?

9. When is the board meeting in Chicago?
(A) At the end of the month, but not for sure.
(B) I lost my boarding pass.
(C) To select the new director.

10. Which building is the library?
(A) It's the one next door.
(B) I came from the library.
(C) Thanks, but I'll do it by myself.

11. Who's responsible for purchasing office supplies?
(A) They're very reliable suppliers.
(B) We've just bought an office.
(C) That would be the manager.

12. When should I call back tomorrow?
(A) No, it's on the front.
(B) Between the hours of 10 A.M and 5 P.M.
(C) You must return it in three days.

13. Has your vehicle been repaired or is still being worked on?
(A) Please go ahead.
(B) It was fixed today.
(C) I'd like to walk, thanks.

14. Who was the guest of honor at the banquet?
(A) It was held in honor of the retiring president.
(B) It was Jeff Edwards.
(C) Yes, guest lectures were cancelled.

15. Excuse me, does anyone have an extra pen?
(A) She needs an extra charge.
(B) No, it closes early on Sunday.
(C) You can borrow mine.

16. Have you already turned in your application form?
(A) No, make a left turn.
(B) It's on the form.
(C) Yes, I have.

17. How would you feel about going to the lake this weekend?
(A) That sounds like a good plan.
(B) I felt the price was better than last weekend.
(C) Mostly, I work in the garden.

18. Why don't we review this case next?
(A) My suitcase is located right next to yours.
(B) If you insist, that's O.K.
(C) The view isn't so important.

19. What's the charge for dry-cleaning a tie?
(A) It depends on the condition of a tie.
(B) No, it supposed to rain.
(C) There's one at the post office.

20. Mr. Petal will be in charge of the Sales and Marketing.
(A) No, he didn't sell much.
(B) I don't think he is the best qualified.
(C) I believe it costs 5 dollars.

21. When will the performance start?
(A) All players will come soon.
(B) As soon as all audience is seated.
(C) It started five years ago.

22. Would you prefer to meet over lunch, or another time?
(A) I prefer fish.
(B) Today's not good for me.
(C) It was delicious, thank you.

23. Where do you plan to stay while you're in Seoul?
(A) Our company has an arrangement with the Holiday Inn.
(B) I have a conference there next week.
(C) I'll be in Korea for four days.

24. How long have you been supervising this project?
(A) For almost 5 years.
(B) Overhead projectors seem too expensive.
(C) Yes, my supervisor has.

25. What time are we going to the theater?
(A) In the entrance of the theater.
(B) Yes, you always have to go to the theater.
(C) We will leave right after dinner.

26. John was supposed to have finished that market review by last Wednesday, wasn't he?
(A) No, it's not due yet.
(B) I review the contract.
(C) Yes, he will.

27. Is this year's trade conference going to be in Canada?
(A) I don't know anyone in our office.
(B) They have a good trade relationship.
(C) Why don't you ask Matilda, staff member in human resources?

28. Is the agenda prepared?
(A) No, it's still out of order.
(B) Yes, they compared very well.
(C) Not yet, the vice president needs to review it.

29. I heard the parking garage is near the conference center.
(A) Yes, it's across the street.
(B) The park is gorgeous.
(C) No, move it to the left.

30. Did you hear that the product trial was just cancelled?
(A) I planned to visit the castle in Rome.
(B) Everyone has been talking about it.
(C) Try on the shoes.

31. You're not going to be in the office this Thursday, are you?
(A) Yes, the new offices are very nice.
(B) Yes, that would be fine.
(C) No, I'm leaving on vacation that day.

Part 3

Questions 32-34 refer to the following conversation.

W: I'm going to be away on holiday starting Friday, March 25 and I'd like you to put a hold on my mail.

M: Certainly. We can keep your mail here at the post office until you get back. Ms. Taylor, did you hear that you could have your mail delivered to another address instead?

W: Yes, I know about that. But I'm actually going to be traveling overseas. So, I don't think I could use that service. I'd like you to keep everything at the post office while I am out of town.

M: OK. So when do you want the delivery to restart?

Questions 35-37 refer to the following conversation.

W: Hi, I've never been here before, but your watch repair shop was strongly recommended. Can you fix these watches? The hour hand is broken and I'd like to have it replaced with new one.

M: We have a large selection of parts for watches. Unfortunately, I don't think I have the exact same item. But if you want, I can replace both the hour and minute hand so they match. Here, take a look in the display case.

W: Oh, I really like red ones up there. I will go with those ones. Are they very expensive?

M: Well, it's one of our most expensive styles. But since I'm not able to fulfill your original request, I'll give 20% off the price.

Questions 38-40 refer to the following conversation.

M: Hi, Laurence. My senior manager on the technical support team just told me again about Mr. Steve's orientation next week. I'm still leading the job training, right?

W: That's correct.

M: And all of my sessions meet in the morning...

W: Right. Here's the full schedule for the orientation. You need to check it out.

M: Sure thing.

W: Great. There is one more thing. You can coordinate your job training with Ms. Lee's afternoon training session. It may be helpful to meet her briefly to get information about the training material.

M: Thanks a lot. I'll do that today.

Questions 41-43 refer to the following conversation.

M: I'm calling to know about a new furniture for the waiting room of my law firm. I've found the four piece set from a copy of your spring catalog and I'm interested in purchasing it.

W: Great! Have you had a chance to visit our website yet? We have an online tool that will enable you to upload your photo of your waiting room and to see what the furniture will look like in your office.

M: Oh, I'll do that right away. But before I do, I'd like to make sure it'll fit in the room. I don't see any measurements listed for the furniture in your catalog.

W: Oh, please check the page 28 in the back of the catalog. You can see all the dimensions of items.

Questions 44-46 refer to the following conversation.

W: Brian, I'm having a problem using our restaurant's new coffee maker. I noticed that the red light on the side of the machine came on after I poured ingredients into it. Do you know what that means?

M: Oh, that light warns you that you need to put more ingredients into it. This new machine has a larger capacity and makes a bigger batch than the previous one.

W: I was just following the recipe for the old device that we used. Do you have a new recipe with an amount just for this machine? If you can get that for me, I'll finish making coffee right now.

Questions 47-49 refer to the following conversation.

M: Hi, my name is Raymond Wang. I'm calling about the advertisement I saw online for the job opening in your graphic design division. Are you still accepting applications?

W: Yes, we are. There's been a lot of positions you may be interested in. If applicants want to be considered for the positions, they have experience using several different kinds of design software.

M: Well, I know how to use all the major design software programs. So, that's not a problem. I also worked as a freelance artist. So, I have a lot of experience of drawing and painting.

W: Then, you sound like a qualified candidate. Can you submit your resume right now? The interviews are scheduled for next week.

Questions 50-52 refer to the following conversation.

W: David, I'm looking for a new fitness center for jogging. I really like the one I currently go to, but I heard yesterday that it's closing down in March.

M: Why don't you join mine? The monthly fee is affordable and the gym is equipped with some new exercise machines. Actually, I go there to run, too. I usually go there first in the morning because the track is almost empty then.

W: Oh, that sounds good. I prefer going to the gym when it's less crowded too. Can I try out the equipment before applying for membership?

M: Yes, it offers one-day trials. And now it has promotion for new members. When you sign up, mention my name, and you'll get a discount on the first month.

Questions 53-55 refer to the following conversation.

W: Hi, I saw on a television commercial that your shop gives guitar lessons, and I'd like to sign up.

M: Great. Do you have any previous experience playing the guitar?

W: Well, I played a little in my university band.

M: I think you'll probably fit into our intermediate class, then. Those classes start next week.

W: Excellent.

M: And there are instructional videos on our website. You can watch them if you sign up for our monthly e-mails. Would you like to join?

W: Oh, that would be helpful. My e-mail address is tony25@hatmail.net.

M: All right, you're signed up, and the first lesson will be next Thursday at 6 P.M. See you then!

Questions 56-58 refer to the following conversation.

M: Hi Lisa, can we talk about the budget presentation you're giving at next week's executive meeting? How's the preparation going? Has the accounting department sent their expense report to you?

W: Yes, they did. But there are some calculation errors in the report. It's taking longer than I expected to check the figures and make corrections.

M: Oh, I'm sorry to hear that. Well, the meeting is on Tuesday. I think we need someone to help finish the presentation on time. I'll assign colleagues to assist you.

W: Thank you. I'm sure this will go quickly if there is someone to help me.

Questions 59-61 refer to the following conversation.
W: Hi, what can I do for you?
M: Yes, I'm looking for the A-phone9. It's a wide screen cell phone with a touch pen.
W: The A-phone9... let's see. This wall here has all of the latest phone from around the world.
M: Hmm. I don't think A-phone9 is on display here. I'm an insurance agent and need a cell phone that has a wide screen for my business.
W: Wait. I can show you another one in a display case. This is Utopia5 and it's similar in design to A-phone9.
M: Oh, that's great. Do you take credit cards?
W: Sure, I'll ring it right up. It'll come to 60 dollars with tax. And please feel free to take our shop's weekly newsletter, Into the Cellular. It has lots of useful tips.
M: OK. Thanks.

Questions 62-64 refer to the following conversation with three speakers.
M1: Have you two heard about the office expansion upstairs which is scheduled to be done next week? It looks nice!
W: I know! It's so amazing! And we could see the entire city there.
M2: I am wondering which department will move up there after the construction is finished.
W: My supervisor told me that it's the research department.
M1: Ah, because they have the most people.
W: Probably. I'd love to work in an office on that floor, though.
M2: Yeah. Well, the company must have enough budget. And I think that is how they add that space!
M1: I think you're right, there!

Questions 65-67 refer to the following conversation and list.
W: Mark, we have a new language instructor beginning on March and we should set her up with a desk and a chair. Can you place orders for those?
M: Sure. You know our supplier has raised prices for their items, right?
W: I didn't know that.
M: I just looked at the catalog on the website, and their current models are more expensive.
W: Right. Well, our budget per work area shouldn't be over $ 500. So let's order the supplies that don't exceed budget.
M: OK. I'll take a look at the prices again and place the order.

Questions 68-70 refer to the following conversation and schedule.
M: Hi, Serina. I was testing a new web chat system here in my office, and browsed around our online staff forum, and...
W: Ah, what does it look like?
M: It looks great. And I notice that many employees are interested in our upcoming workshops. Do we have to set more space? We could rent a conference room on 5th floor, or...
W: We'll be OK. I'm going to make a digital video of all presentations, and post it on our staff forum.
M: That's a good idea.
W: Oh, and we've made a change. We've switched the times for the second and third workshops. So the day's second workshop will be Market Share. We made that switch because Mr. Kim, the presenter, has to leave before noon.

Part 4

Questions 71-73 refer to the following telephone message.
Hello, this is Maria Hill, and I am calling at 1 o'clock on Friday afternoon. I live in apartment 2C in the San Antonio complex. With the heavy rain we had last night, a lot of water came in around the living room window. As you already know, this is just the beginning of the rainy season. I'd like you to fix this problem today. Please get back to me as soon as possible and let me know when you can come. Thanks very much.

Questions 74-76 refer to the following advertisement.
Now, you can subscribe to International Geographic Magazine for only 20 dollars for a year. When you buy our spectacular magazine, each month you'll receive news of the latest nature discoveries from around the world and must be inspired by them. And for a limited time only, when you subscribe to International Geographic Magazine, you'll receive three complimentary coupons to the best-known local restaurant. You will be able to have some spectacular Italian cuisine. So, go to our website and type in the number 0325 to take advantage of this limited time offer.

Questions 77-79 refer to the following talk.
Hello, thank you all for attending this luncheon. We're honoring the recent graduate of the K&J Accountant Training program. It takes several years of persistent hard work for apprentices to complete this program and become national certified accountants. So this

accomplishment must be celebrated. I'm sure that many of the friends and family who've come here are curious about what kind of training the apprentices do in the program. So, before we eat, I'll show a video about a typical day of our apprentices. And after luncheon, you can join us for dancing in the ballroom.

Questions 80-82 refer to the following excerpt from a workshop.
OK, everyone. Let's continue with the workshop. I think the discussion on business presentations went well so far. Another important point to consider is that some people speak faster or slower than others. I recommend that you practice your speech several times before you present. I advise presenters to monitor their speed. And now, I'm going to play some videos showing how the speed of a presenter speech impacts communication.

Questions 83-85 refer to the following announcement.
Attention Medical Care Center employees. Starting next month we're installing new digital locks on all doors in the building. Every employee will need to get a new digital key when entering the building. You're required to bring your ID card to the security office, and the guard will have a new key ready for you. The new keys will be linked exclusively to your employee ID, so we will be able to check out anyone who enters and leaves the building 24 hours a day. There's more information available about the upcoming security changes in the company magazine, so make sure to pick it up. After reviewing it, if you have any Questions, talk to your supervisor. Thanks.

Questions 86-88 refer to the following broadcast.
Thanks for listening to today's business report. This evening, Weston Apparel, a locally based company with more than 15 years of experience in manufacturing and distributing clothing, announced the highly anticipated merger with MVIA Incorporated. MVIA Incorporated will provide an online platform for selling Weston Apparel clothing. I strongly encourage listeners to tune in at this time tomorrow, for an exclusive interview with the president of Weston Apparel. She'll talk about more details about the impact this merger will have in the local economy.

Questions 89-91 refer to the following excerpt from a meeting.
So I called this meeting on our contract with Seoul Advertizing Agency we should discuss. And we should decide whether we will continue to use them to develop our TV advertising materials. Yesterday, I met their people and had a discussion. Actually I feel a little concerned. They want to increase the price for advertising. Here's the thing. If we decide to stop this business relationship, we have to pay them for anything they've already done for us. Could you take a minute to look at this contract with me? You'll see part of the agreement.

Questions 92-94 refer to the following talk and program.
Welcome to afternoon's workshop. We have a lot of useful information to cover. But before the workshop, I have to tell you a few schedule details. There will be one break between second and third presentations. You can leave your laptops here when you leave the room. There will always be someone here, but don't leave small electronic devices such as phones as well as money. You're advised to keep them with you. And please note that there's an error in the printed sheet: there will be a switch for the first two presenters. Mr. Gurida has to leave early today.

Questions 95-97 refer to the following excerpt from a meeting and chart.
As you already know, I thought our new website would have some problems, but fortunately I was wrong. So far we couldn't find any technical difficulties, and most of our customers are satisfied with the new services we're offering. They especially like the feature to receive e-mail notifications when new items arrive. But there's one thing that is surprising me. Various age groups are responding differently to the website design. The results on this graph are not what I anticipated. Chang, I want you to investigate the reason this age group is the happiest with the site. Hopefully we can make use of that information to increase overall satisfaction.

Questions 98-100 refer to the following telephone message and list.
Hi, Ross. It's Clara calling from Operations here at the head office. I'm guessing you're on your way to Copper's Office Supply. I have a copy of your "to buy" list of things for our copy room on the second floor, and there's good news. According to the flyer I received this morning, every paper on the list is on sale except for blue paper which is still full-price. But we'll pay less for the orange paper for sure. When you return, we'll need to put the paper away since the new copiers are coming on Tuesday, and we should make room for them to be placed. OK. See you soon then.

Part 1

1. (A) They are fixing the guitars.
(B) They are playing musical instruments.
(C) They are wearing long sleeve shirts.
(D) They are lying on the grass.

2. (A) She's turning on the light.
(B) She's using a photocopier.
(C) She's speaking over the phone.
(D) She's putting on her red jacket.

3. (A) Potatoes are grown in the yard.
(B) Vegetable is being moved into the box.
(C) Some fruits are cooked.
(D) Items are arranged for sale.

4. (A) The monitor is being checked for repair.
(B) They are attending the presentation.
(C) The man is pointing at the monitor.
(D) The man is writing on the notebook.

5. (A) Pedestrians are moving in the same direction.
(B) The people are working on the pavement.
(C) Taxis are parked along the sidewalk.
(D) Vehicles are stopped in front of the crosswalk.

6. (A) Most of the seats are occupied.
(B) The slide show is about to be over.
(C) Some chairs are lying on the floor.
(D) The speaker is reaching for the projector on the ceiling.

Part 2

7. Aren't you attending the annual sales meeting?
(A) No, it was canceled.
(B) The sales director arrives at nine.
(C) I can't meet the requirement.

8. Have you still got the error message logging in our website?
(A) On our website.
(B) Yes, do you know why?
(C) Put them back during logout.

9. Where is the nearest pharmacy store?
(A) Store food the fridge.
(B) Right next to the library.
(C) It takes nearly two hours.

10. Isn't the museum closed on weekends?
(A) No, it's open everyday.
(B) He lives close by.
(C) There are more weekday classes.

11. Why are the workers working overtime?
(A) Five hour shifts.
(B) Near the facility entrance.
(C) To fill a special order.

12. When will hospital renovation project on the east wing be completed?
(A) Yes, the nurse has a health certificate.
(B) Probably in late November.
(C) Host a party.

13. Which marketing proposal did the client prefer?
(A) They prefer to speak in person.
(B) Because it was new to them.
(C) She liked the last one.

14. You already signed the contract to a new car lease, didn't you?
(A) A thousand at least.
(B) Yes, last week.
(C) I didn't contact Leeds.

15. How did Sarah decide where to stay on summer vacation?
(A) She searched for places on the Internet.
(B) Sometimes by air.
(C) No, I am driving there.

16. Don't you want to bring a digital recorder to the conference?
(A) Through a teleconference.
(B) Between December 3rd and December 5th.
(C) Yes, it's in my bag.

17. What about looking at some colors to paint the building exterior?
(A) Paint in oil and watercolor.
(B) Sure, I'm free after lunch.
(C) The reception desk.

18. When will Professor Hubert be available?
(A) He's busy all day long I'm afraid.
(B) Just down the street.
(C) Because he got stuck in traffic.

19. Why is the museum so crowded today?
(A) There comes a renowned speaker later.
(B) The closest parking lot.
(C) No, not cloudy but windy.

20. Don't forget to put up a notice on the bulletin board.
(A) Put up with inconvenience.
(B) Don't worry, I won't.
(C) I didn't notice the difference.

21. There were more participants at the trader's workshop this month, weren't there?
(A) During spring training.
(B) No, he won't be able to attend.
(C) Yes, it was a big success.

22. How can we have the copy machine repaired?
(A) A local appliance store.
(B) Check with the technical assistant.
(C) When are we leaving?

23. We still need to place price labels on the new bottles.
(A) On the bottom of the drawer.
(B) The desk costs $ 60.
(C) Let me go get them.

24. Is the new luxury sedan going to be recalled soon?
(A) We just use the elevator.
(B) The performance results from the experiment are in.
(C) Actually, the work has already begun.

25. You should present financial data at the next executive meeting.
(A) No, I didn't receive a present.
(B) I'd be happy to.
(C) In online data bank.

26. Do you want the latest report to be mailed to you or sent electronically?
(A) Please send me a hard copy.
(B) Sure, let me deliver the mail.
(C) Yes, I already sent them.

27. I don't seem to be able to find my documents anywhere.
(A) Have you looked in your file?
(B) You can pick up your prescription in a moment.
(C) We haven't seen the most recent version.

28. You can help me download this coupon on my phone, can't you?
(A) I'm not sure I know how.
(B) Yes, they can carry heavy loads.
(C) It has been very helpful.

29. Would you like a table with drawers or one without them?
(A) It's just around the desk.
(B) I prefer the floor plan.
(C) Either one is fine with me.

30. I think the longer dress would be more suitable for the function.
(A) The women's section is downstairs.
(B) Then that's the one I'll buy.
(C) No, we can't wait any longer.

31. Do you want me to bring you a sandwich from the cafeteria?
(A) I just had, but thanks.
(B) How was your business trip?
(C) Yes, we will bring interns to the picnic.

Questions 32-34 refer to the following conversation with three speakers.
W: Good evening. Welcome to the Fairfield Inn and Suites.
M1: Hi, good evening. I'd like to make a reservation. Do you have any vacancies?
W: Let me see what I can do for you. Oh, you are in luck. We do have two rooms available. How long will you be staying?
M1: For two nights, please.
M2: Wait a second, Jack. The conference lasts for 4 days. We should stay here for three nights.
M1: Really? I don't buy it. No one told me about that.
M2: There was a last-minute change of dates late last night.
W: Okay, your reservation has been made for 3 nights for a room. Enjoy your stay.

Questions 35-37 refer to the following conversation and price list.
M: Hi this is James Alvin, I just made an online reservation at your hotel, but when I saw the confirmation page, I found that I'd made a mistake in the dates. What should I do?

W: I'll be glad to make a change in your reservation, only if we have a room available. Could you please give me your confirmation number?

M: Of course. It's SA415. I want the reservation for the next weekend, from May 5th to May 7th. Will the price be the same?

W: Let me see. James Alvin, on the 4th floor, room number 15. Yes, we do have a room available for those two days at the same rate. So, I've changed your reservation with us. You can expect an updated confirmation in your e-mail shortly.

Questions 38-40 refer to the following conversation.

W: Good afternoon, Mr. Edith. We have a package for you to pick up here at the West Virginia Post Office. You should have received a missed delivery card when we tried to deliver it two days ago.

M: I'm looking through my mail now, and I can't find any notice about a missed package. I just got back from my vacation. What should I bring to pick it up?

W: Oh, I see. Well, that shouldn't be a problem. Please make sure to bring along valid photo identification when you come to pick yours up.

Questions 41-43 refer to the following conversation and table.

W: Excuse me. I saw the leaflet posted in the window of your store, advertising cooking classes. I wondered if I could enroll in the chocolate cake making class on Friday morning.

M: I am sorry, but the kitchen is too small to accommodate more than ten people, and that class is already full.

W: Oh, what a pity. Is there any chance you'll offer another chocolate cake making class?

M: Yes, we're thinking about holding several baking classes next week. Here is class schedule for next week. Which class would you sign up for?

Questions 44-46 refer to the following conversation.

M: Hi, Ms. Agnes. This is Charles Matthew calling from Diana Realtors. A private house has just been listed that I believe you might be interested in. It's a two bedroom house that's available right now, but best of all, it's near Mountain Park.

W: Near Mountain Park? Oh, that's great news. The park is very close to my college. That's exactly what I hoped for.

M: Would you like to look at the house? We can get in to see it sometime next week, if you're free.

W: I'm busy on Monday, but Tuesday would be fine. Let me jot down where it is and I can meet you there.

Questions 47-49 refer to the following conversation with three speakers.

W1: Mr. Park, I just finished cleaning the floor, so it looks like we're all ready to open the restaurant at 11 o'clock. Is there anything else you'd like me to do?

M: Yes. Someone from the city maintenance department called late last night and told me that the crew will be repairing the pavement right outside the restaurant today. I'm concerned that our customers won't know we're open.

W2: It's a piece of cake. I can put out a sign in front of the door that shows we're open.

W1: That sounds perfect. I will take out the sign from the storage and give it to you right away.

M: That's even more of a relief.

Questions 50-52 refer to the following conversation.

W: I don't know how I'm going to look over all the résumés that were submitted for the sales positions we'd advertised. We received thousands of applications for these ten openings.

M: There are too many applications. I can help you review those resumes. Why don't I take some of them?

W: That would be nice. I don't have hard copies of them though. The applications are all saved on my portable USB drive.

M: Okay, I prefer to look over them on paper. Would you print them out for me? So I can go over the hard copy applications thoroughly.

Questions 53-55 refer to the following conversation with three speakers.

W: Excuse me. I'm a junior reporter for the Hong Kong Times. I'm here to interview people at the music festival. Have you seen many performances?

M1: Yes, I've been three music concerts and I'm planning to see some more. They've been excellent.

W: How about you? Have you enjoyed performances?

M2: The musical performance itself is good but I feel bad about the venue. There are so many people at the concert hall. And there are long lines for everything including the food booths.

W: Well, the festival has always attracted people from across the country. And more tickets have been sold this year than in any other year so that might account for the overcrowding.

M1: There are so many different kinds of music this year. I love seeing this festival become a great success.

M2: I oppose his idea. Overcrowded spaces stop people enjoying the music.

Questions 56-58 refer to the following conversation.

M: Hi, I'm calling from Happy Memories Tours. We're interested in having bath towels made for our customers and I saw your advertisement in the magazine. Could you give me some details on your quantities and prices?

W: Sure, bath towels are 10 dollars each, but if you place an order for more than 100 towels, you'll get a twenty percent discount off of the total cost.

M: That price seems affordable. So we'd like to have our company title printed on the bath towels. Is that hard to do?

W: No, it's actually easy. Just go to our website and upload the image of your title and then place your order.

Questions 59-61 refer to the following conversation.

M: Hi, Judy. Thanks for taking a look at my car to see if it needs repair work. I'd like to list my car for sale by the end of this month because I need to buy a larger car.

W: Well… I think buyers will like it since the exterior of the car has been well maintained. However, I can see daily wear and tear on the front leather seat. I strongly recommend having that repaired.

M: Okay, do you know how much it will cost to have new leather put on the seat?

W: I have a friend who does that kind of work and the prices are fairly reasonable. I'll look for his business card so you can reach him anytime for an estimate.

Questions 62-64 refer to the following conversation.

W: Hi, Rick. Did you go over my draft report about the company's new employee manual? My manager wants me to finalize the manual by the end of today. She needs me to send the final version before she leaves today around 7.

M: I finished reviewing it this morning and I found a typo on the second page. Could we go over the error during our brief meeting at 2?

W: Actually I can't make it to the meeting. I have a prior engagement with my clients. Can we meet later instead around 4? Is it okay with you?

M: No problem at all. See you then.

Questions 65-67 refer to the following conversation with three speakers.

M1: Have you two checked out the sales results we've made during the first quarter?

W: I saw them this morning. They didn't seem real. We broke the best record of the company.

M2: I haven't had a chance yet. Where can I find the documents?

M1: Here you are. These are our sales results. We made it. We finally did it.

M2: Oh. I can't believe my eyes. We set a brilliant record in our company.

W: I am so proud of our sales team. And we couldn't do that without them, including you two guys. Let's celebrate our success at the luncheon this evening.

Questions 68-70 refer to the following conversation and list.

W: Zack, we ordered 100 desktop computers last week and we will receive the shipment next Tuesday.

M: That's great! Should we replace our current computers with the new ones by ourselves?

W: No, we don't need to. Since our budget permits, we can hire temporary workers by the hour. Can you help me choose the right employment agency?

M: It's my pleasure. What should I do?

W: Our budget is $ 500 maximum. And we should complete the replacement of the old computers by 11. How many workers should we hire?

M: I just found the perfect agency that fits your requirements. Look at this list.

Part 4

Questions 71-73 refer to the following announcement.
I hope you are enjoying this month's marketing workshop. Before I introduce our next keynote speaker, I have a short announcement to make. A brown leather bag has been found in the restroom. So please take a moment to see if you are missing your item. If you are, make you way to the reception desk at the main entrance of the workshop center. Mr. Dustin is the one on duty and he has your lost one.

Questions 74-76 refer to the following telephone message.
Hello Mr. Winnie, I am calling from Alvin's Floral shop about the bouquet you ordered. I am really sorry but we've made a mistake. We used the wrong flowers for the bouquet. Instead of roses, we put lilies in it. You have two choices. If you don't mind the different floral arrangement, we'll give you this bouquet for free. Or, if you still want the one with roses, we'll offer you a 40% discount and send you a new bouquet by Thursday. Please let us know what you decide.

Questions 77-79 refer to the following talk.

Good evening. My name is Vanessa and I'll be your tour guide for the next couple of days in Hong Kong city. During this time, you'll get to see many local night markets including several late night festivals. This evening, we'll be visiting a famous dim sum factory in Hong Kong. It's very fun and exciting and you'll get free samples. When you return to the hotel at eleven o'clock, you will be receiving a foot massage in your room. We'll have some tea available and I'll give you information regarding tomorrow's plan.

Questions 80-82 refer to the following announcement.

Good afternoon ladies and gentlemen and welcome to this afternoon's performance of Daria Della. I'm Bianca Cecil, the coordinator of this art and theater group. I am very excited to tell you that our show has once again sold out, which means we've sold every ticket to every show since opening day this year. During a short intermission, please feel free to buy refreshments out in the hallway or visit our theater souvenir shop on the second floor. All proceeds from this afternoon's ticket sales will go to financial support of local arts program at our community middle school so thank you all in advance. Now, please enjoy the Daria Della's recital.

Questions 83-85 refer to the telephone message.

Irene, this is Alex. Thank you for sending me an invitation to the training on the new interoffice messenger software. Unfortunately, I won't be able to attend. I'll be interviewing some of the job applicants at that time, next Friday. And I think I don't need the training. I tried the software on my own and I thought it was really convenient and easy to use. It has many features that record conversations and share them online. So I think it'll help our regional managers a lot. Please give me a call after the training though, I'd really want to know if the rest of the managers liked the software as much as I did.

Questions 86-88 refer to the following talk.

As the head director of the city's Recreation Department, I'd like to thank each of you for volunteering to paint the walls today here in Florence Playground. I'd like to point out that the green colors you'll be painting were selected specifically because they are known to help reduce stress. The Recreation Department has provided enough paints and brushes for everyone, so please grab one and let's get started.

Questions 89-91 refer to the following broadcast.

In business news, one of the world's biggest producers of vehicle tires, Pro Tire has been contracted to supply passenger vehicle tires for the new DM-3 car. In order to be able to manufacture the large number of tires required by the contract, Pro Tire is scheduled to open another manufacturing plant at the beginning of November. The new facility will be located in the city of Detroit. In a press conference earlier this morning, the city official of Detroit expressed his aspiration for the opening of the plant, saying that it will bring estimated 400 additional jobs to the community.

Questions 92-94 refer to the following talk and table.

Welcome to this seminar on developing a business portfolio. Let's start with a simple explanation of what that is. A business portfolio is a statement that describes a set of pieces of creative work and how you plan to achieve them. A well-written business portfolio makes a long lasting impression and this is essential for getting financial support from people willing to invest in your company. Now before we review some examples of creative business portfolio, I want to go around and have all of you share your prior work experience with the group members. Now who would like to start?

Questions 95-97 refer to the following announcement and screen.

Attention BlueSky Airlines passengers! We have recently introduced a new automated ticketing system. The ticketing machines are situated near the main entrance on the first floor. The touchscreens are quick and easy to use when purchasing your plane tickets and for your convenience, detailed instructions about how to use the system are available in a majority of languages. Passengers whose language is not serviced are advised to go to the BlueSky Airlines air ticket booth for ticketing. If you need help with the ticketing machines, a BlueSky Airlines customer service representative can assist you.

Questions 98-100 refer to the following telephone message and list.

Hi Ms. Stella, I'm calling from Natural Energy Solutions. I would like to let you know about the services we provide to help small businesses like yours conserve on significant water usage. We do a considerable study of the company's operations and identify areas for feasible cost savings. For instance, we've helped many companies decide whether switching to rainwater for their water usage is worth the initial cost. If you're interested in our services, I'd be glad to send you references from other customers. I can be reached at 777-9870.

新 이지투 토익 급상승 퍼펙트 600제 제❷라운드
박영수 저 | 188*258mm | 12,800원(mp3 CD 포함)

新 이지투 토익 급상승 퍼펙트 600제 제❸라운드
임현진 저 | 188*258mm | 12,800원(mp3 CD 포함)

미국 명연설문 베스트 50

김정우 저 | 170*220mm

448쪽 | 15,000원(mp3 CD 포함)

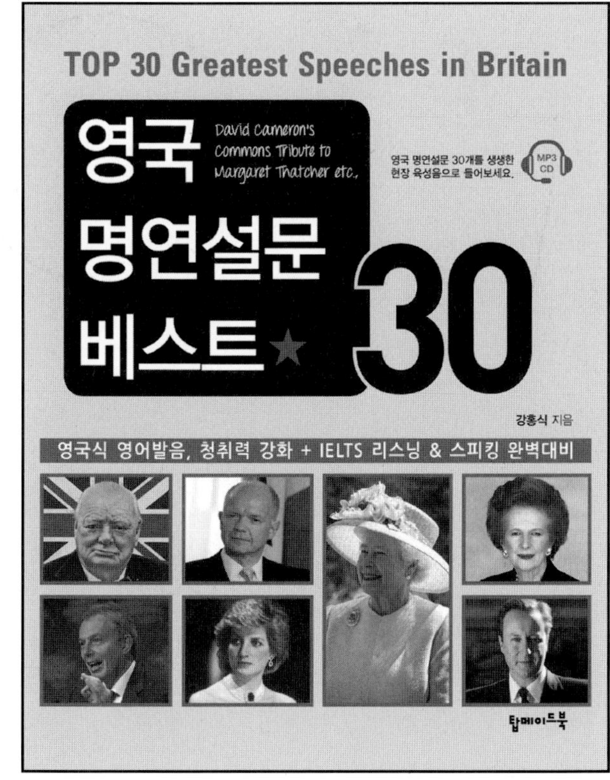

영국 명연설문 베스트 30

강홍식 저 | 170*220mm

336쪽 | 15,000원(mp3 CD 포함)

리더들의 명연설문 베스트 30

강홍식 저 | 170*220mm

328쪽 | 15,000원(mp3 CD 포함)

**세계유명 여성리더들의
명연설문 베스트 30**

박예든 저 | 170*220mm

264쪽 | 15,000원(mp3 CD 포함)